23-

SOCIALIST REGISTER 2 0 0 0

THE SOCIALIST REGISTER
Founded in 1964

EDITORS:
LEO PANITCH
COLIN LEYS

Visit our website at:

http://www.yorku.ca/org/socreg/
for a detailed list of all our issues, order forms and an online selection of
past prefaces and essays,

...and join our listserv by contacting
socreg@yorku.ca
for a discussion of the essays from this volume and issues relevant to socialists.

NECESSARY AND UNNECESSARY UTOPIAS

SOCIALIST REGISTER 2000

Edited by LEO PANITCH and COLIN LEYS

MERLIN PRESS
FERNWOOD PRESS
MONTHLY REVIEW PRESS

First published in 1999
by the Merlin Press Ltd.
2 Rendlesham Mews, Rendlesham,
Near Woodbridge, Suffolk,
IP12 2SZ

British Library in Cataloguing in Publication Data
1. The Socialist Register. —2000
I. Panitch, Leo, and Leys, Colin
355'. 005

ISBN:
0 85036 487 6 Paperback
0 85036 488 4 Hardback

Except for paperback edition published for the USA by Monthly Review Press
1 58367 021 1

Typset by Jon Carpenter
Printed in Finland by WSOY

Contents

Martin Eve, socialist publisher
1924–1998

PREFACE

THE THEME OF THIS VOLUME of the *Socialist Register* was first conceived in 1995 with the following general question in mind: as we approach the end of the millennium, what is to succeed the first great socialist project that was conceived in Western Europe in the nineteenth century, and variously implemented and frustrated by communism and social democracy in the twentieth? We had no illusions that an answer to this question would be found by cudgelling the brains of however large a number of left-wing intellectuals. But we did think that the time had come to renew the left's vision and spirit and that the *Register* could hope to contribute something useful for this purpose. We wanted to break with the legacy of a certain orthodox kind of Marxist thinking which rejected utopian thought as 'unscientific' just because it was utopian, ignoring the fact that sustained political struggle is impossible without the hope of a better society that we can, in principle and in outline, imagine. And we particularly felt that in face of the collapse of communism, as well as the rejection by 'third way' social democracy of any identification with the socialist project, there was now, especially in the context of the growing crisis of the neo-liberal restoration, an opening as well as a need for imaginative thought.

Our goals were relatively modest. We wanted to sample some of the elements of new socialist utopias that are already emerging from the rethinking and regrouping that has been taking place among progressives of many kinds – trade unionists, feminists, ecologists, scientists, philosophers, political economists, etc – since the 1980s. And we wanted to challenge our contributors – and our readers – to reflect on how these elements might be combined to inform and inspire a new socialist project for the new millennium. The elements of this project are *necessary* in that the ideas and models they provide – or something like them – are essential to any new socialist project worth fighting for; some of them may even be necessary for the survival of the species. We also wanted to contrast these ideas and models with others that are being canvassed today and which are *unnecessary*, in the sense that on closer inspection they prove not to be utopias at all, but blind alleys. And re-imagining a humane socialist future is all the more required in light of the positively dystopian 'brave new worlds' that the organic intellectuals of capitalism are promoting for the twenty-first century, such as those touted by the spin-doctors of the bio-engineering industry, on the one hand, and NATO on the other.

Obviously we could not hope to be at all comprehensive, or even 'balanced' in our coverage (what exactly should be balanced with what?), but we could hope to help put the question of renewing the socialist goal back on the agenda. Above all, we hope this volume will contribute to loosening the grip that the narrow, alienated conception of 'reality' peddled by the neoliberals has had on too much left thinking in the past decade, and encourage people to refocus their imaginations and their political ambitions on the fundamental ideals that have inspired socialism throughout its history. It is time to refuse definitively the etiolated, increasingly hypocritical conception of 'democracy' which even social-democratic parties have come to accept and to insist on a far fuller and richer democracy than anything now available. It is time to reject the prevailing disparagement of everything collective as 'unrealistic' and to insist on the moral and practical rightness, as well as the necessity, of egalitarian social and economic relations. It is time to assert the attractions, as well as the necessity, of a society unhooked from subordination to 'growth' based on production for profit, consumerism, sexism, militarism and the rest; and to spell out some of the conditions under which socialist goals can be realised – above all the development of popular democratic capacities and the structures that nurture rather than stifle or trivialise them. And, taking even a slightly longer view, what could be more *realistic* than this?

It is sad that this volume, the thirty-sixth since the *Register* was launched in 1964, is the first one not to have been seen through every stage of its production by Martin Eve, the founder and publisher of Merlin Press, since its theme was very close to his heart. Martin died in October 1998 at the age of 74, after a twelve-year fight against cancer which gradually robbed him of his physical mobility, but never of his keen intellect, his wry sense of humour or his phenomenal personal courage.

A fascinating and moving book of memoirs of Martin and his work (*Martin Eve Remembered*, edited by Walter Kemsley) has now been published by Merlin, but his special relationship with the *Register* makes it more than just appropriate to commemorate him briefly here too. Having read volume I of Marx's *Capital* at the age of sixteen and in his own words, having 'got the general idea', Martin never subsequently departed from it; whether he was in the Communist Party or later, after 1956, in the Labour Party, for him 'it was always one line,' as he told his friend and Merlin author Istvan Meszaros, and the *Socialist Register* was very much its flagship. He founded Merlin Press in 1956 with virtually no capital and built it into one of the most distinguished small left-wing publishing houses in Britain by sheer hard work – doing everything himself, from editing and proofreading to marketing and shipping – and extraordinarily shrewd judgement. His close friendship with Edward Thompson led to his publishing many of Thompson's famous works and his wide culture enabled him to bring out successful English translations of much important work originally published in foreign languages, including books by Lukacs, Levi-Strauss, Bohm-Bawerk, Mandel and others, in addition to many other leading British authors.

Martin was always willing, as well, to put his money (what little he had) where his mouth was: when the British civil servant Sarah Tisdall was jailed in 1984 under the Official Secrets Act (for, as Martin put it, 'revealing a political secret, not a military one – i.e. one that has to be kept not from foreign governments but from the British people'), he wrote to congratulate her and offered her a job as his assistant, which she duly took up following her release. In politics as in sailing – his other great passion was a wooden gaff-rigged smack, almost as old as himself – he was never tempted to compromise but kept steadfastly to his course, always steering, as he would say, 'in the general direction of' socialism because there was no worthwhile alternative, and getting the utmost out of the voyage.

The relationship between the *Socialist Register* and its publisher was an unusually close one. It was Martin who in 1963 suggested the name to its founding editors, Ralph Miliband and John Saville (brought to mind by Thompson's account of Cobbett's *Political Register* in *The Making of the English Working Class*). The thanks expressed to him in every preface since 1964 were never pro-forma: they spoke to – indeed they may have understated – what they often called his 'indispensable' help. The Editors sought his advice on the topics to be covered and took very seriously his comments on the essays submitted by our contributors. And Martin was the very rare case of a publisher who also took his turn as editor and author: he edited (with David Musson who was then working with him at Merlin Press) the 1982 volume while Miliband and Saville took a well-deserved 'sabbatical'; and he contributed his own essay on 'Anti-Communism and the American Intervention in Greece' to the 1984 volume.

Despite the fact that for most of the *Register*'s existence the manuscript for each annual volume would arrive at Merlin bit by bit, 'with each contributor having written their piece on different types of paper and in different formats' (as Sarah Tisdall gingerly put it), Martin and his staff would greet each essay with enthusiasm and interest – and in remarkably short order would produce a high-quality book with very few errors. Our belated conversion in recent years to computer and internet modernized the process, but what remained unchanged was that our publisher still never saw what we were publishing as a commodity. This is not to say that Martin was unconcerned with the marketing of the *Register*, but it is to say, as Diane Elson does in her essay in this volume, that the *Socialist Register*'s production was not market-determined. Not profit, but commitment to a common 'socialist humanist project', as he put it, was what motivated Martin as publisher of the *Register*, and nothing pleased him more in recent years, as socialist politics and theory went into decline in

Britain, than to see the growing international enthusiasm for the *Register*. It was typical of him that he gave away the rights to publish editions of the *Register* in India and Greece. And it was no less typical that even in the last weeks of his life, he continued to work enthusiastically in preparing for publication the essays for the 1999 volume. That volume was dedicated to him without our knowing how near death he was. He knew – and was moved by the dedication.

Martin Eve will be sadly missed, but before he died he had identified a successor, Tony Zurbrugg; and we are very glad indeed that Tony has accepted the challenge, and extremely grateful for the energy and skill he, with the help of Bruce Brine, has immediately brought to bear in the copy-editing and production of this volume, several signs of which are already evident in its design. Both he and we have been helped enormously in the transition by Pat Eve, for which we are greatly indebted. We also once again owe considerable thanks, especially for his help in the editing and proofreading of each essay, to the *Register*'s graduate assistant at York University Alan Zuege. He has been joined this year by Marsha Niemeijer, who has been responsible for preparing the *Register*'s website, which can be reached at http://www.yorku.ca/org/socreg/. For his help on this, we want to express our thanks to David d'Andrea, as we do also to Dave Timms in London, Carlos Torres in Toronto and all the staff of Monthly Review in New York for their ongoing contribution to 'socialist marketing' the *Register*. Finally, we want to express our appreciation to Eric Canepa and Amy Holmes for helping with the translation of Frigga Haug's essay for this volume.

Among our contributors, Sam Gindin is Assistant to the President of the Canadian Autoworkers Union. Norman Geras is Chair of the Department of Government at the University of Manchester; and Terry Eagleton is Warton Professor of English at Oxford University. Frigga Haug teaches sociology and social psychology at the Hochschule für Wirtschaft und Politik in Hamburg; and Diane Elson teaches development studies at the University of Manchester. Alan Zuege is a doctoral candidate in political science at York University, Toronto. Kate Soper teaches philosophy at the University of North London; and Johanna Brenner coordinates and teaches women's studies at Portland State University in Portland, Oregon. Ricardo Blaug teaches politics at the University of Leeds; and Judith Adler Hellman teaches in the social science and political science departments at York University, Toronto. Colin Duncan teaches history at McGill University in Montréal. Julian Tudor Hart is a general practitioner in Wales who is President of the Socialist Health Association in Britain; and Varda Burstyn is an independent writer and consultant who is Vice-Chair of Greenpeace Canada. Carl Boggs is Professor of Social Sciences at the National University in Los Angeles; and Peter Gowan teaches politics at the University of North London. While reminding our readers of the *Register*'s traditional disclaimer that neither the contributors nor editors necessarily agree with everything in the volume, we want to express our gratitude to our contributors for all the effort they have put into the *Socialist Register 2000*.

Readers may have noted as they opened this volume that we are initiating another change this year. It concerns the *Register*'s contributing editors which have until now been grouped in two editorial collectives in Manchester and Toronto. These collectives were established to assist Leo Panitch following the death of the *Register*'s founding editor Ralph Miliband, and fulfilled this role brilliantly at a critical time. The subsequent appointment of Colin Leys as co-editor, however, and the movement of several people away from Manchester and Toronto, have changed the situation again. Instead of two 'collectives' we will now just have contributing editors in the UK and North America, and corresponding editors elsewhere, and we will perhaps shift the balance further towards the latter over time. Meantime this year sees the retirement of two contributing editors, Anthony Arblaster and John Saul, to whom we extend our very grateful thanks.

One of the most important functions of our contributing editors has been to help us map out the themes of all the volumes of the *Register* since 1996, when we set out what may well have been the last 'five year plan' of the century. We will complete that plan with next year's volume, which will follow up on this year's theme of rethinking socialist vision by reexamining socialist agency. Growing inequality and the spread of capitalist social relations that accompanies globalization makes class as central to understanding the dynamics of contemporary capitalism as it ever has been; yet class as a political relation – in the sense of workers 'consciously forming a class insofar as they engage in a common battle against another class' – remains deep in crisis. To begin the new century, therefore, we thought it would be appropriate for socialist thinkers to undertake a detailed register of the state of the global proletariat, the changing experiences of work and 'ways of living', the transformations entailed by migration and feminization, the new patterns of working class organisation, identity formation and politics that are emerging in various zones of the world. We plan to publish the 2001 *Register* in the fall of 2000. We invite our readers to send us their ideas for subsequent volumes and to partake in discussion on *Register* essays and themes by visiting the website at http://www.yorku.ca/org/socreg/ or by contacting the Socialist Register at socreg@yorku.ca.

July 1999   L.P.   C.L.

TRANSCENDING PESSIMISM: REKINDLING SOCIALIST IMAGINATION

LEO PANITCH AND SAM GINDIN

'WE'RE FREE... WE'RE FREE.' The last words of Arthur Miller's master-piece, *Death of a Salesman*, are uttered, sobbing, by Linda Loman over her husband Willy's grave. Weary and penniless after a life of selling 'a smile and a shoeshine', overwhelmed by feelings of emptiness and failure, yet mesmerized by the thought that his life insurance will provide his estranged son with the stake that might induce him to compete and 'succeed', Willy Loman's suicide famously symbolises the tragic dimension of the relentless competi-tiveness at the heart of the American capitalist dream. 'He had the wrong dreams. All, all, wrong', this son laments at the grave side, even as his other son dedicates himself to 'beat this racket' so that 'Willy Loman didn't die in vain.... It's the only dream you can have – to come out number-one man.' At the end Linda stands over the grave alone. Telling Willy that she had just made the last payment on their mortgage, a sob rises in her throat: 'We're free and clear.... We're free.... We're free...'[1]

When first uttered on stage in 1949, at the start of the Cold War, these words spoke to the ambiguity of the freedom represented by the 'free world'. Fifty years later, when Linda sobs 'we're free' at the end of *Death of a Salesman*'s 1999 revival on Broadway, she seems to embody the angst of an entire world enveloped by the American dream at the end of the twentieth century. One can everywhere sense the anxiety – an anxiety as omnipresent as 'globalization' itself – that has emerged with accumulating awareness of the enormous odds against actually 'beating this racket' and escalating doubts about the worth of a life defined by the freedom to compete.

At the same time, however, we still live in an era of foreclosed hope in the possibility of a better world. What makes the tragedy of Willie Loman so universal now is that even people who wonder whether the capitalist dream isn't the wrong dream see no way of realizing a life beyond capitalism, or fear that any attempt to do so can only result in another nightmare. Overcoming this debilitating political pessimism is the most important question anyone seriously interested in social change must confront.

CONCRETE UTOPIAS

As socialists search for what direction to take under these conditions, it helps to know that others before have faced the same problem. How to make 'the defeated man ... try the outside world again' was precisely the question that impelled Ernst Bloch in the 1930s to write his magnum opus, *The Principle of Hope*.[2] Pessimism – 'paralysis per se' – was the first obstacle to be confronted:

> …people who do not believe at all in a happy end impede changing the world almost as much as the sweet swindlers, the marriage-swindlers, the charlatans of apotheosis. Unconditional pessimism therefore promotes the business of reaction not much less than artificially conditioned optimism; the latter is nevertheless not so stupid that it does not believe in anything at all. It does not immortalize the trudging of the little life, does not give humanity the face of a chloroformed gravestone. It does not give the world the deathly sad background in front of which it is not worth doing anything at all. In contrast to a pessimism which itself belongs to rottenness and may serve it, a tested optimism, when the scales fall from the eyes, does not deny the goal-belief in general; on the contrary, what matters now is to find the right one and to prove it…. That is why the most dogged enemy of socialism is not only… great capital, but equally the load of indifference, hopelessness; otherwise great capital would stand alone.[3]

Bloch's response was to try to revive the idea of utopia. He insisted that even in a world where socialist politics are marginalised, we can still discover, if only in daydreams, the indestructible human desire for happiness and harmony, a yearning which consistently runs up against economic competition, private property and the bureaucratic state. The 'utopian intention', which is, for Bloch, the real 'motor force of history', may be found in architecture, painting, literature, music, ethics and religion: 'every work of art, every central philosophy had and has a utopian window in which there lies a landscape which is still developing.' Bending the stick against orthodox Marxism's traditional dismissal of 'utopian socialism', Bloch's project was in good part to rehabilitate what Marx himself once called 'the dream of the matter' which the world had long possessed. 'The power of the great old utopian books', Bloch demonstrated, was that 'they almost always named the same thing: Omnia sint communia, let everything be in common. It is a credit to pre-Marxist political literature to possess these isolated and rebellious enthusiasms among its many ideological insights. Even if they did not seem to contain a shred of possibility... the society projected within them managed without self-interest at the expense of others and was to keep going without the spur of the bourgeois drive for acquisition.' It was this literature which first established that one of the main prerequisites to realize 'the leap of humanity out of the realm of necessity into the realm of freedom... is the abolition of private property and the classes this has produced. Another prerequisite is the consistent will towards the negation of the state in so far as it rules individuals and is an instrument of oppression in the hands of the privileged.'[4] What made More's *Utopia* 'with all its dross, the first modern portrait of democratic communist wishful dreams' was that

> For the first time democracy was linked here in a humane sense, the sense of public freedom and tolerance, with a collective economy (always easily threatened by bureaucracy, and indeed clericalism) ... [T]he end of the first part of the 'Utopia' states openly: 'Where private ownership still exists, where all people measure all values by the yardstick of money, it will hardly ever be possible to pursue a just and happy policy... Thus possessions certainly cannot be distributed in any just and fair way... unless property is done away with beforehand. As long as it continues to exist, poverty, toil and care will hang instead an inescapable burden on by far the biggest and by far the best part of humanity. The burden may be lightened a little but to remove it entirely (without abolishing property) is impossible.'[5]

It was the abstractness of such utopian thinking, of course, that led Marx to insist on the crucial importance of analysing 'objective conditions'. Bloch had no doubt about how necessary this was for 'cooling down... totally extravagant abstractly utopian fanaticism' and for the development of the kind of practical consciousness that would allow the carrying through of the dream to reality through the transformation of social relations. But the unmasking of ideologies and illusions by what he called the 'cold stream' of Marxism's 'historical and current practical conditional analysis' had always to be mixed with the kind of appreciation of 'subjective conditions' present in the 'warm stream' of the Marxist tradition. '[F]ermenting in the process of the real itself', Bloch insisted, '[is] the concrete forward dream: anticipating elements are a component of reality itself. Thus the will towards utopia is entirely compatible with object-based tendency, in fact is confirmed and at home within it.' The best kind of Marxism demonstrates that 'enthusiasm and sobriety, awareness of the goal and analysis of the given facts go hand in hand. When the young Marx called on people to think at last, to act "like a disillusioned man who has come to his senses", it was not to dampen the enthusiasm of the goal, but to sharpen it.'[6]

In recent years we have seen all too many disillusioned people on the left 'coming to their senses' by abandoning the goal of socialism. Some have succumbed to a post-modernist pessimism, which has indeed proved to be 'paralysis per se'. Even more seem to have jumped from what Bloch called the 'evils of putschist activism' all the way to social democracy's 'third way', whose presumption that neo-liberal prescriptions of efficiency are compatible with social justice is the contemporary expression of what Bloch designated as one of the key hallmarks of ideology – 'the premature harmonization of social contradictions' within the confines of existing social relations. Frustrated by their inability to change the world overnight through sheer activism, they have not so much abandoned the idea of change but, like the Greek God Procrustes who adjusted the size of his guests to fit the size of his bed, they have shrunk the meaning of change to fit what capital and the state will accommodate.

Yet it is increasingly apparent from the extreme limitations of the 'third way' in practice that reviving the goal of socialism is necessary even to make small improvements in the current state of the world. As Bloch put it: 'If the will-content of the goal is missing, then even the good probable is left undone; if the goal remains, however, then even the improbable can be done, or at least made more probable for later.' Moreover, as against the kind of 'third way' thinking that embraces the novelty, inevitability and progressive character of globaliza-tion, 'even a dash of pessimism' does not go amiss, for, as Bloch suggested, 'at least pessimism with a realistic perspective is not so helplessly surprised by mistakes and catastrophes, by the horrifying possibilities which have been concealed and will continue to be concealed precisely in capitalist progress.'[7]

But if such a healthy pessimism about capitalist progress is indeed growing as we end the century, what persists alongside it, even through repeated and deepening capitalist crises, is a profound pessimism about the possibility of real-izing any better world. This debilitating pessimism derives not only from the feeling that nothing can be done, or even that nothing other than capitalism is possible, but also from a fear, well-honed by twentieth century experience as well as ruling class propaganda, of the perverse consequences of the attempt to put utopian visions into practice. This is not surprising in light of the experi-ence with Communist regimes in this century, where there occurred, as *The Principle of Hope* already suggested, 'an undernourishment of revolutionary imagination' and 'a schematic pragmatic reduction of totality' through an over-emphasis on science and technology 'such that the pillar of fire in utopias, the thing which was powerfully leading the way, could be liquidated.'[8] 'All the worse', as Bloch later wrote after his self-exile from East Germany, was that once it became clear that the 'revolutionary capacity is not there to execute ideals which have been represented abstractly', the Communist regimes acted so as 'to discredit or even destroy with catastrophic means ideals which have not appeared in the concrete.' This stifled 'transitional tendencies' within them which would have been able to move towards 'active freedom only if the utopian goal is clearly visible, unadulterated and unrenounced.'[9]

It must be said, of course, that Bloch's remarks only implicitly identify the weakest aspect of the classical Marxian legacy in this respect: the theorization of the role of the political in the transition to socialism. Marx's central concepts of the 'dictatorship of the proletariat', 'smashing the bourgeois state' and 'the withering away of the state' all obscured rather than clarified the fundamental issues; and Marxists in the twentieth century did not go nearly far enough in overcoming the limits of this legacy.[10] Yet it is at the level of the political that transitions from one socio-economic order to another are effected – or come to grief in the attempt.

But whether the socialist utopian goal can be revived must obviously depend on much more than a clarification and enrichment of socialist political theory. It will above all depend on agency, that is, on what human beings can still discover about their potential. For all the valuable insights, promising signposts and rich hints even the 'warm stream' of Marxism bequeaths, it must be said that the historical optimism in Marx that inspired generations of socialists came with an underestimation of the chasm between the scale and scope of the utopian dream and the capitalism-created agency honoured – or saddled – with carrying it out: the working class. Between Marx's broad historically-inspired vision of revolution/transformation and his detailed critique of political economy, there was an analytical and strategic gap – unbridgeable without addressing the problematic of working class capacities – which later Marxists sometimes addressed, but never overcame.[11] Nor has the problem been overcome by recent social movement theory. For the rethinking that is required must be more profound than just imagining that the problem can be resolved by substituting a plurality of new social movements for the old workers' movements. The compensatory stifling of ideals we saw in the institutions of the labour movement has also appeared in the new social movements. Every progressive social movement must, sooner or later, confront the inescapable fact that capitalism cripples our capacities, stunts our dreams, and incorporates our politics.

Where then can socialism, as a movement linking the present with the possible, once again find the air to breathe and space to grow? To answer this we need both to clarify the socialist 'utopian goal' today and to develop a clearer sense of where our potential capacities to create that better world will come from. The rest of this essay concerns itself with these questions, but a few preliminary guidelines will be useful before moving on.

The socialist 'utopian goal' is built around realizing our potential to be full human beings. What separates this ideal from its liberal roots is not only socialism's commitment to extending this principle to all members of society, but also its insistence that the flowering of human capacities isn't a liberation of the individual from the social, but is only achievable through the social. Ideals are always linked to some notion of justice and freedom. Notions of justice revolve around the egalitarianism of certain outcomes (like distribution of income or wealth) or the legitimacy of a process for reaching goals even if the ultimate results are unequal (equal access to opportunities). Notions of freedom generally divide into freedom from an external arbitrary authority (the state) or the freedom to participate in setting the broad parameters that frame the context of our lives (as in current liberal democracies). The socialist ideal does not exclude these other moral spaces, but locates them on the specific terrain of capacities: capitalism is unjust and undemocratic not because of this or that imperfection in relation to equality or freedom, but because at its core it involves the control by some of the use and development of the potential of others, and because the competition it fosters frustrates humanity's capacity for liberation through the social.

And what is especially important is that conceiving freedom and justice on the terrain of capacities leads beyond mere dreaming: it links the ideal to the possibility of change and so to what is politically achievable. This is what Bloch meant by 'concrete utopias' which, always operating on the level of 'possibility as capacity', incorporate the objective contradictions that create an opening for socialist goals ('capability-of-being-done'), the subjective element of agency ('capability-of-doing-other'), and therefore the possibility of changing ourselves and the world ('capability-of-becoming-other').[12]

These concrete utopias are not blueprints for a new order entirely external to this one. Socialism, as Marx noted, is not '*a state of affairs* which is to be established, an ideal to which reality will have to adjust itself... [but] the *real* movement which abolishes the present state of things.'[13] That 'real movement' will live or die based on whether the necessary capacities and possibilities can first show themselves, in some substantive way, inside everyday capitalism. Terry Eagleton argues in another essay in this volume that 'the only authentic image of the future is, in the end, the failure of the present.' This is indeed true. And the best measure of the failure of the present is its inability to redeem the glimpses of our potential afforded by our own experiences. In Barbara Kingsolver's novel *Animal Dreams*, a woman asks her lover: 'Didn't you ever dream you could fly?' He answers: 'Not when I was sorting pecans all day.' When she persists and demands: 'Really though, didn't you ever fly in your dreams?', he replies: 'Only when I was close to flying in real life... Your dreams, what you hope for and all that, its not separate from your life. It grows right out of it.'[14]

Unreal Utopias

Despite what is sometimes alleged about the lack of attention paid to 'alternatives' on the left today, there has actually been no shortage of attempts by progressive intellectuals in recent years to rethink and reformulate the utopian goal. While the institutional content of such alternatives extends beyond social democracy, many of those who advance these new utopias for our time do so in ways that, like today's social democracy, reflect a defeatism and thus an over-cautious pragmatism. In the name of 'getting real', these utopias limit democratic expectations of the state and/or the scale of the economic transformations they consider. The result is what Bloch has referred to as 'abstract utopias': a world too small to deliver on the large promises it holds out and a telling neglect of the politics of getting there. An examination of three important books by prominent authors published in the last year, each influenced by a different current of contemporary thought, provides a rather clear perspective on the demoralized nature of much utopian thinking today and on why the real challenge before us is not to contract, but to expand, utopia's inspirational and visionary function.

The main concern of James C. Scott, in *Seeing Like a State: How Certain Schemes to Improve the Human Condition Have Failed*,[15] is the 'great state-sponsored calamities of the twentieth century' epitomized by Soviet collectivization and Tanzanian Ujamaa villagization of agriculture. Reflecting postmodernism's influence, Scott characterizes the utopian ideal not in terms of emancipation and liberation but rather in terms of 'high modernist aspirations to a finely tuned social control' implemented by 'progressive, often revolutionary elites... who have come to power with a comprehensive critique of existing society and a popular mandate to transform it.' In taking up the 'utilitarian simplifications' which states employ to 'map' societies, these elites repressed the complex, varied and practical local knowledge which is the fount of human creativity.' Borrowing from Kropotkin's famous declaration that 'it is impossible to legislate for the future', Scott concludes that strategies for change must now be founded on 'taking small steps', with preference, moreover, for the kind of interventions that 'can be easily undone.'[16]

This approach sensibly begins from the premise of incomplete knowledge in relation to 'the necessary contingency and uncertainty of the future', and from 'confidence in the skills, intelligence and experience of ordinary people.' His rejection of detailed super-rationalist blueprints is equally valid. But this only takes us back to Marx's own critique of abstract utopias for ignoring what Marx also saw as 'the radical contingency of the future' – hence his refusal to write blueprints that might minimize the potential for humanity's creativity and inventiveness which could be unleashed in the process of transcending capitalist social relations. Scott allows, in passing, that 'utopian aspirations per se are not dangerous' (he approvingly quotes Oscar Wilde's remark: 'A map of the world which does not include Utopia is not even worth glancing at, for it leaves out the one country at which Humanity is always arriving.'). Yet it is clear that he has a very limited awareness and appreciation of the 'warm stream' of utopian (including Marxist) thought. And although he counterposes Luxemburg and Kollontai to Lenin, and acknowledges his debt to classic anarchists writers like Kropotkin and Bakunin, his own conception of social change is far removed from their revolutionary spirit.

The trouble with this all-too-common response to the socialist failures of the past century is not only its strategic but also its visionary inadequacy in relation to a global capitalism that Scott himself identifies as 'the most powerful force for homogenization' today. Such passing comments hardly take the measure of global capitalism's ruthless remaking of societies in the name of efficiency, productivity, comparative advantage, and the rest. While Scott recognises that the capitalist market, far from being 'free' is 'an instituted, formal system of coordination' which rests on that 'larger system of social relations', his reversion to 'the science of muddling through' and 'disjointed incrementalism' provides no larger vision or strategy for transcending that system of social relations.[17] He appears to see 'the private sector' as some sort of genial brake on the excesses of political leaders with utopian dreams, rather than as the alienated and socially destructive monster it is.

No progress can be made in this respect unless we can go beyond conceiving the future of the state only in terms of Foucauldian surveillance and Weberian bureaucratic rationality. Scott recognizes the positive role of certain institutions – especially ones that are 'multifunctional, plastic, diverse, and adaptable' but he can't conceive of any beyond those local institutions ('the family, the small community, the small farm, the family firm in certain businesses') which have survived and adapted through history – and which he considerably romanticizes. His conception of the good state is entirely in terms of 'negative freedom' – that liberal democratic state which allows space for activity outside of, and for resistance to, itself, and which 'may in some instances be the defender of local difference and variety' against global capitalism. Although his argument against social engineering and in favour of local practical knowledges replicates Hilary Wainwright's important book *Arguments for a New Left*[18] (which he does not, however, cite), he shows, unlike her, little sense of the feminist, environmentalist, labour, and socialist consciousness and institutional practices in our time which have valued and fostered practical local knowledges, impelled by a vision of changing broader social relations, and sought to connect them to political parties, unions and the local and national state. Not to romanticize these is one thing. To ignore them is to cut one's intellectual contribution off from those broader forces 'fermenting in the process of the real' that might realize a better world.

An apparently more positive approach to reviving utopian aspirations has inspired the books published in Verso's Real Utopia Project, under the editorship of Eric Olin Wright, whose goals are to nurture 'clear-sighted understandings of what it would take to create social institutions free of oppression [as] part of creating a political will for radical social changes to reduce oppression… utopian designs of institutions that can inform our practical tasks of muddling through in a world of imperfect conditions for social change.'[19] In the most recent volume in that series, *Recasting Egalitarianism: New Rules for Communities, States and Markets*, Sam Bowles and Herb Gintis, set out to bridge the democratization of the economy, expressed through a radical redistribution of capital assets, with what they view as the real-world need for raising productivity. This is utopia under the influence of supply-side economics.

Bowles and Gintis are, like Scott, sure that states can never be substantively democratized. While they readily assume that managers of firms will be subject to democratic accountability, they emphatically stress 'the many unavoidable obstacles to citizen accountability over government actions' and they reject 'the presumption that state managers and functionaries will faithfully carry out what an egalitarian citizenry would have them do.'[20] On the other hand, they claim, again like Scott, that at the level of communities – families, residential neighbourhoods and the workplace – people can readily monitor each others' activities so as to guarantee reciprocity and trust (even if not altruism and affection) within the context of 'structurally determined individual incentives and sanctions' to maximize economic efficiency. It is the reciprocity of fair trade in the market governed by individual material self-interest, rather than the substance of local democracy, that is determining, and this is why they also advocate school vouchers and private home ownership alongside the redistribution of capital assets to workers in enterprises.

Bowles and Gintis accept the doctrine that market competition is necessary for economic efficiency, but they claim that the unequal distribution of capital impedes productivity by imposing costs on the private sector in terms of work supervision and security in the face of labour indiscipline and lack of effort. If workers owned the capital assets of the firm they worked in, while 'the beneficial disciplining effects of market competition' between firms were maintained, then all the 'behaviours critical to high levels of productivity – hard work, maintenance of productive equipment, risk-taking and the like' – would be forthcoming. Since conventional redistributive policies are *passé* in a global world where all policies have to be 'sensitive to the competitive position of each economy', then what is needed is a 'productivity enhancing' redistribution of property rights in order to 'strengthen the economy's competitive position.' It is never made clear how Bowles and Gintis imagine the redistribution of capital assets would come about – except that it would not be mandated universally by 'government fiat'. It seems likely that the authors have some kind of notion of pension fund socialism in mind or that they expect that the banks would be induced to lend workers the money to buy their firms at non-prohibitive rates of interest. Whether banks are also to be worker-owned is not addressed, but there is in any case to be 'ample room for innovative private entrepreneurship', including that based on 'venture capital.'[21]

The main effect of this schema would be to ensure that competition rather than solidarity was the goal – indeed the primary structural characteristic – of the working class itself. For the discipline of competition to be effective, considerable inequalities in wealth and income among workers would necessarily have to be sustained, and it would be rooted in an original arbitrary endowment based on which workers happen to 'own' General Motors as opposed to a small asset-poor company – not to mention those who would suffer the effects of the bankruptcies and lay-offs that go with risk taking and competition.[22] Although Bowles and Gintis do not situate their model in the 1980s debate about market socialism, the attempt to 'get real' involves incorporating so much capitalist rationality that the result, while perhaps 'feasible', seems anything but utopian.[23] A number of the critical contributions to that debate were very creative in imagining what the institutions of a democratic economy, in which market relations were subordinated and marginalised, might look like; this was especially true of those that stressed the importance of mechanisms within each firm to attenuate the division of labour.[24] But

Bowles and Gintis seem to feel they don't have to delve too deeply into the actual requisites of substantive democracy in worker-owned firms,[25] because what really concerns them is to demonstrate that the external coercion of competitive markets, and the internal compulsion that will come from worker-owners pressuring each other to work hard, will yield the main goal: greater productivity and efficiency, greater even, they suggest, than what current advanced capitalist structures might achieve.

Bowles and Gintis have no patience with a vision in which people are primarily inspired by collective rather than individualist concerns. Egalitarian projects, they claim, founder on a presumption of 'oversocialized decision makers'; they fail to take account of the 'incentive structures of the relevant actors.' As for why egalitarians should accommodate to an acquisitive morality rather than attempt to change it, their answer is a familiar – reactionary – one: 'we have no choice', they say, because this morality, founded in 'some combination of genes and culture', has an 'inertial character'.[26] For this, they wrongly appeal to Barrington Moore's explanation of revolution and revolt in terms of peoples outrage at the flouting of long-rooted conceptions of social justice and reciprocity.[27] But Bowles and Gintis are not inviting people to revolt against the capitalist value system: they are inviting them to buy into it.[28]

Roberto Unger's 'anti-necessitarian' social theory – most recently advanced in programmatic form in *Democracy Realized: The Progressive Alternative* – seems to provide an antidote to Bowles and Gintis' dictum that we are 'trapped by the present in designing the future.' Reiterating a challenge he has put forth over the past two decades, Unger asserts:

> There is always more in us than there is in our contexts. They are finite. We relative to them, are not. We can hope to diminish this disproportion between circumstance and personality by building institutional and cultural worlds that become more supportive of our context transcending powers. Such contexts may fortify our resources and powers of resistance, even as they invite their own revision.[29]

What has been so important about Unger's work has been his thinking about the kind of reconfiguration of the state that would best facilitate the radical democracy of the socialist utopian vision. As he put it in *False Necessity* in 1987: 'To understand the leftist as the person who values equality over freedom and fraternity is to miss the main point of the leftist undertaking.' This has meant, for him, stressing the need to go beyond the redistributive programmes of the social democratic welfare state, and to embrace a 'vision of solidarity that simultaneously contributes to the enabling conditions for the [generalized] development of practical capabilities.' The greatest problem with social democracy throughout the past century was not its gradualism, Unger has understood, but a reformism limited to policy outputs while leaving the institutional design of the state itself untouched. A different kind of state could only be brought about through the 'militant organization of the oppressed, the poor, and the angry... [but] it is not enough for these sectors to mobilize, they must remain mobilized. They and their leaders must use the favoring circumstances of crisis, revolution and radical enthusiasm to establish economic and governmental institutions that help perpetuate in the midst of humdrum social routine something of the transitory experience of mass mobilization.'[30] A transformative state needs to see itself as engaged in a constant process of democratic experimentalism, developing new branches of government 'friendly to the rise of popular engagement', endowed with the political legitimacy and practical capacity to facilitate the organization of the unorganized and disadvantaged, and operating under a system of public law which allows for state interventions to maintain these organizations as inclusive and internally democratic while at the same time leaving them 'free from any taint of government control or tutelage.'[31]

The manifesto for change now presented in *Democracy Realized* still gives priority to strategies for institutional reform over redistributive reform. It seeks to deepen democracy and accelerate political change by removing the constitutional checks and balances, parliamentarist rules and electoralist practices that maintain society at a low level of political mobilization and introducing constitutional reforms that expand direct democracy, encourage popular political engagement in the state and 'promote democratic experimentalism in all fields of social life.'[32] Unfortunately, Unger's contribution to trying to conceptualize a different kind of state appropriate to a transformative democratic strategy is considerably weakened by its attachment to an economic program that is astonishingly conventional – and, by now, rather dated – in its advancement of a strategy for economic growth founded on the notion of 'flexible specialization'. Unger's utopian vision is determinedly post-fordist, and his particular *bête noire*, therefore, is the defensive response of unionized workers in capital intensive industries to the employment of temporary workers and subcontractors. Rather than use solidarity as a means of protecting themselves against this trend, he urges them to make 'common cause' with subcontractors in support of schemes for decentralized access to venture capital so as to finance 'the small and the new' firms which he takes to be the 'vanguard' of economic growth. In face of the difficulty of giving practical institutional content to the notion of securing social control over investment decisions while preserving 'the decentralized vitality of a market economy', Unger now calls for an 'easier' option than any attempt to expropriate or redirect capital, and arrives at nothing more radical than the public mobilisation of pension funds to finance these vanguard firms.

Even in his earlier work, his notion of skilled process workers, managers, technicians and small-scale entrepreneurs making common cause as a 'productive vanguard' by joining together to reap the advantages of flexible, high-tech production was problematic, but the general abstractness of that work, together with the assumption of the socialization of finance, made this less obvious. His more recent proposal, in which the 'established system' of finance and corporate power is largely left alone, clearly exemplifies what Bloch meant by the premature harmonization of contradictions. Unger assumes that a legal reform which 'automatically unionizes all workers, job seekers and smallscale business owners' will itself lay the foundations for a 'growth-friendly' moderation of conflict between workers and managers so that they work together according to a 'partnership principle' governed by 'cooperation and innovation.'[33] His earlier vision of solidarity that stressed the militant organization of the oppressed, the poor, and the angry to the end of developing their practical capabilities is little in evidence.

Indeed, Unger scarcely seems to notice that social democracy, far from being mainly concerned 'to defend at all costs the historical constituency of organized labor', has long since taken up the Blairite 'third way' which, except for its continuing institutional conservatism in terms of representative and administrative (if not electoral) procedures, looks suspiciously similar to his own proposals for transcending the sterile debate between state and market at the economic level through the strategy of 'progressive' competitiveness. Unger shows he is aware (albeit only in a brief passing paragraph) that the 'language of flexible specialization and worker engagement in the planning of production…is ready to be captured by the managerial program.'[34] But his own proposals, far from exploring the contradictions between the call for cooperation and workers' resistance to flexibility in a world where 'capital has the right to move where it pleases', smother the contradictions in the verbiage of partnership, innovation and cooperation.

What a let-down. It may be said in Unger's defence that his concern to secure growth via competitiveness for a third world economy like Brazil is rather less obscene than is the concern of Bowles and Gintis to further enhance the competitiveness of the already rich American economy. But his full embrace of post-fordism's commitment to 'progressive competitiveness' and the unstated but consequent logic of subordinating the economy and society into an export-oriented strategy within international capitalism (structured by imperial relations, which Unger scarcely seems to notice), demonstrates how difficult it is for even someone as self-conscious of the problem as Unger to escape being trapped by the present in designing the future. Competition is a constraint that any project for structural reforms has to take into account; but the whole point of addressing alternatives is to liberate ourselves from the notion that it is only through competitiveness that we can address the development of our productive capacities. To accept competition as the goal – even for a poor country and even qualified as progressive competitiveness – is to give up on the project before you begin.

That so much of the contemporary literature seems 'incapable of imagining any world definitively different than their own' (as Terry Eagleton puts it), and of even going so far as some pre-Marxist utopias in projecting a social order capable of keeping going 'without the spur of the bourgeois drive for acquisition' (as Bloch put it), stands as a sorry comment on the limits of the utopian imagination today. This is intimately related to the failure to come to grips with the question of agency. To Scott, the question of agency is reduced to getting the state out of the way. Bowles and Gintis don't even bother to dwell on why workers would commit to a struggle for control over capital assets if the economic decisions ultimately made will still be determined by competitive markets. And in Unger, the folding of an independent working class project into cross-class partnerships with export-oriented 'vanguard' firms, erodes the very possibility of the militant organization of the 'oppressed, the poor, and the angry.' There seems little point in worrying a great deal about agency if the transformation being considered is not really a transformation at all.

UTOPIAS AND CAPACITIES: WORK AND 'NON-WORK'

In contrast to the above, and much more fruitful in coming to grips with what really needs to be thought through in rekindling the socialist imagination, stands the work of André Gorz – starting with his primary principle of the strategy of 'non-reformist reforms' enunciated over three decades ago: i.e., 'one which does not base its validity and its right to exist on capitalist needs, criteria and rationales.'[35] His eco-socialist critique of productivism in face of the ecological contradictions of capitalist development is obviously of great importance, as is the contribution he has made to prioritizing the redistribution of working time in an egalitarian project. But what is especially significant about his approach is his claim that workers define themselves in terms of productivism and therefore that the problem for any strategy for transformation lies in the way workers are blocked from developing their full human potential, not only by the context of ideology, politics, the consumer culture, but by the very fact of being workers. It is notable that Gorz's critique of Marx came to rest less on the inability of Marxist thought to transcend the productivism inherent in 'economic reason'[36] rather than on Marx's investment of the working class with potential transformative capacities – what we designated earlier as the underestimation by Marx and later Marxists of the chasm that needed to be overcome between the scale and scope of the utopian dream and the sheer extent of the stunting by capitalism of working class capacities.

Why has socialist politics given such a special status to 'work' and 'workers'? Ontologically work is a stand-in for the specifically human capacity to conceive of that which does not exist and then to effect its realization. Conceived in historical terms, the use of that capacity to create our material reality through work is intimately linked to the dynamics of social change. And in the specific context of capitalism, the organization of work provides a defining contradiction of the social system and a foundation for working class politics. It is on the basis of these ontological, historical and sociological dimensions of work that so many socialists have concluded that the working class, in spite of surrendering its labour power, is strategically positioned to lead the struggle for universal liberation.

It is in the workplace that capitalism brings diverse people into direct physical contact, and it is here – or at least in the communities that surround these workplaces – that they first build sustainable organisations, backed to some degree by independent ideologies and resources, to overcome their fragmentation. Workers develop potential leverage on the stability of production and profits, and therefore a base for a degree of countervailing power, by regularly testing their collective strength in the workplace. But what socialists must directly address is the question of whether workers can in fact develop, on the basis of this foundation, a vision of a new society and the 'all-round development' which Marx insisted was the condition for the abolition of capitalism. For the workplace is also where workers' potentials and collective hopes may be crushed.

The worker seems condemned by the very 'circumstances in which the individual lives … [to] achieve only a one-sided crippled development.'[37] And although the logic of capitalism leads workers into direct conflict with employers and the state, and even though such struggles lead to the creation of new needs, it is not clear that these needs eventuate in a vision of an alternative society rather than in a pragmatic reformism.[38] It is not just a matter of a political emphasis on the need for alliances outside the workplace and the need to address the larger question of the state – as important as these issues are. The deeper problem lies in the barriers imposed by the nature of work – and also non-work – under capitalism.

The problem becomes clearer if we consider the limits to developing capacities in the context of workers' dependency on capitalists' active role within the economy: in production, the application of science, the introduction of innovations, the economic coordination across regions and the widest and most diverse workplaces. Capitalists are not only privileged, but *needed*; their authority as economic leaders is set against workers' uncertain ability to do without them. As long as the paradigm is the workplace, there is at least some plausibility to the idea of it being run by workers who are already familiar with its daily operations. But once we begin to address the role of competition in linking workplaces, coordinating inputs and outputs, and enforcing dynamic change, we have to confront the imposing challenge of developing an entirely new order – including an entirely new workplace.

It would, of course, be somewhat easier if our goal was simply to catch up to capitalist capacities – if we failed to question the nature of capitalist economic growth and only sought to mimic it. But the socialist project goes beyond 'catching up and taking over' because the particular capacities and institutions that we face in capitalism were developed historically within particular social relations. While some may be adapted, it is not enough to simply 'democratize' them to fit a new set of relations and goals. Going beyond capital requires transforming existing capacities and developing new ones, transforming existing institutions and inventing historically unique ones.

It is important to emphasize that competition doesn't just complicate the question of implementing workers' control some day, but it especially affects the political capacities needed to get to that point. The competitive process of eroding barriers to accumulation and disciplining any resistance to its logic involves a constant restructuring of all aspects of economic and social life. For capital, this can happen without disturbing their class unity: capital remains united around the accumulation project; it has the resources to continuously introduce necessary institutional innovations; the state adds its support for maintaining capital's coherence; and capital has the technological and administrative capacity to combine a sweeping degree of capital mobility with a continuity, for the elites involved, in their local and national networks. But for workers, who draw on social, geographic and generational continuities to develop their collective capacities, capitalist competition and restructuring often undermines class unity and identity.[39] We should not therefore count very heavily on the dynamics of capitalism to do much for maintaining or building a truly independent working class identity and culture; it can only happen *in spite of* capitalism's logic.

If the work-time realities and confusions of power, dependency, and economic complexity make it hard for the working class to develop a post-capitalist vision, can this then happen – as Gorz suggests – in the realm of leisure, in private, family, and community spaces?

If only. Gorz's inspiring utopia at the end of *Farewell to the Working Class* nevertheless still fell short of Marx's integrated and radical democratic vision. This is not only because Gorz's utopia is confined to one rich country (France), but also because Gorz accepts, in a Habermasian fashion, the inevitability of an alienated, albeit much reduced, sphere of production and another of bureaucratic planning and administration. And in spite of his valid criticism of an orthodox forces of production determined socialism, Gorz's own argument is dependent on the assumption that the productive forces of a rich economy will sustain the liberation from work – i.e. that there is no serious on-going economic problem to worry about in his utopia. But while work and non-work occupy different compartments in terms of time and space, the problem lies in how those compartments are integrated within the whole. Capitalism's world of necessity doesn't just lay the material base for less wage-work; it limits, shapes and creates specific necessities even in the realm of non-work. Work time and the location of work determine how much leisure we have, when we have it, and how much of it is absorbed by the need for some minimum of physical and mental recovery time. In capitalism 'recreation' means just what it says: re-creating our ability to work. And leisure, when it is not heavily committed to necessary and compensatory consumption, tends, as Henri Lefebvre has remarked, to be reduced to a respite from work.[40] Like a school recess or a coffee break, it is devalued by the fact that our relief is short-lived. Free time, it turns out, is not all that free. If non-work time is to play a liberating role, this can only happen if it is part of a broader individual and social project that transcends the barrier between non-work and work, fundamentally changing them both rather than just reducing working time.

Of the variety of physical spaces non-work time inhabits, the household is especially important. The gendered and patriarchal division of labour within the household pre-dates capitalism, but the nature of the household's new link to the outside world imposed a distinctive dimension to the relationships between men and women, work and family life, work and leisure, and consequently on both women and their potentials and men and their sense of what being a 'whole' person entailed. Housework continued, under capitalism, to directly produce use values necessary for the household's survival and reproduction; for this it needed no external approval or market incentives. But once wages were required for buying necessities, the importance of getting and keeping a job gave wage-work and the wage-earner a special importance and status within the household. The household's activities, schedules, moods, and even its (re)location were subordinated, by way of the its dependence on wage-work, to the needs of the wage-earner. The corollary was a supportive and secondary role for women. A woman might make the bread, but it was the man who was considered the 'breadwinner' because his wages paid for the ingredients.

The negative impact on women's options, capacities and potentials needs no elaboration. But the issue extends beyond that of gender equality. The fact that men are generally not expected to actively deal with household and community responsibilities – such as the caring of children, daily coordination with school routines, dealing with sudden needs for emergency medical care as well as routine ones, coping with the impact of pollution to family health as well as with neighbourhood crime and the absence of community recreational space – this cannot avoid also limiting men's sense of themselves. Without the broader everyday engagements and frustrations that situate working class men as more than just workers, it is difficult to imagine them developing the expectations of themselves and of society that are at the center of socialist consciousness: the belief in their own potential as *full* human beings and their demand for social structures to support that dream.

The women's movement has added something crucial to traditional socialist approaches to developing confidence, capacities, and consciousness. Out of necessity, as well as in reaction to male-dominated politics, it has shown a special sensitivity to the need to help people assert their rights and participate in change, and to reach out to 'ordinary' people, focussing on less intimidating local issues, small group discussions rather than interventions at mass meetings, exchanges that are supportive rather than competitive, analyses that are concrete rather than abstract, and not treating work as the sum total of working class life – 'making the personal political.' In going beyond the workplace, this kind of politics has also suggested routes that move the household beyond the private, to its connection with the community and to the relations between generations. No strategic debates about socialism can exclude the insights, nuances, and attention to process that the women's movement has rightfully insisted be part of any universalizing movement.

Utopia and Agency:
From Doing Other to Becoming Other

The trajectory of André Gorz's work reflected an honest ambivalence about the leadership potentials of the working class in radical change. Even though he said '*Farewell to the Working Class*' in the early eighties, he could not help in his later writings like *Critique of Economic Reason*[41] but return to the trade union movement as the core element of political change, not least in sustaining those varied radical social movements which had grown up 'outside work':

> [Their] campaigns of resistance to the professionalization, technocratization, and monetization of our lives are specific forms of a wider, more fundamental struggle for emancipation. They contain a radical potential which has repercussions on workplace struggles and they mould the consciousness of a growing number of people... The fact that the trade-union movement is – and will remain – the best organized force in the broader movement confers on it a particular responsibility; on it will largely depend the success or failure of all the other elements in this social movement. According to whether the trade-union movement opposes them or whether it seeks a common alliance and a common course of action with them, these other elements will be part of the left or will break with it, will engage with it in collective action or will remain minorities tempted to resort to violence... The attitude of the trade union movement towards the other social movements and their objectives will also determine its own evolution.[42]

Unger's suggestion, raised earlier, that unionization be mandated across the entire workforce may seem to reflect a similar recognition of the importance of unions. But in Unger's case this is less an acknowledgement of their importance than an expression of a desire to settle the issue of recognition and move on to the real vanguard of innovative firms. The focus he and others have placed on changing the nature of the capitalist firm, while more substantive than the communitarianism fashionable among philosophers today, tends towards a depoliticization of both the firm and the union. What this approach underestimates is the social power of capital and the oppositional politics necessarily involved in changing it. We must begin not with the firm, but with changing the role and nature of workers' organizations themselves, their potential as sites of capacity-building and democratization, and especially their scope for moving *beyond* the workplace. Once we approach the issue of class and transformation as being about overcoming dependency on capitalists to the end of developing full human capacities, further expectations emerge around what unions, as the front-line economic organization of workers, might possibly do. And this in turn implies a different kind of unionism in terms of how it chooses and structures its struggles, applies its resources, defines internal democracy and participation, responds to its role as producers and service providers, and relates to the community, political parties and the state.

The problem with unions is not, as Unger and so many others seem to think, that they have been too defensive but that in most cases they have not been defensive enough or at least not defensive in a way that allows them to get beyond merely being reactive. To be defensive doesn't mean to be static. A trade unionism committed to mobilizing its defensiveness would be committed to developing a 'culture of resistance', and nothing is more important to the future possibility of socialism than the current existence of a working class that is determinedly oppositional, organizationally independent, self-conscious of its subordinate position, ideologically confident in the legitimacy of its demands, creatively ready to take on and lead struggles, and insistent that its own orga-nizations be democratic and accountable so as to embody this spirit of popular activism and militancy. In addition to aggressively fighting for traditional demands, the content of union demands would take on new dimensions and be linked to generalizing, within the union, the capacity of members to partic-ipate and thereby develop their over-all political and administrative capacities. Examples include: pushing to take productivity gains as time off from the job and for education both at and away from the workplace; linking health and safety issues to debates and demands about how work is organized and the priorities of technology; negotiating learner-driven training; developing, through internal union educational programmes, the confidence and therefore the capacity to participate amongst all members; and extending the collective capacity to discuss and disagree – to debate – *before* the arrival of those moments of crises when external pressures reinforce tendencies to define all internal opposition to the leadership as sabotage.

In contrast to a defensiveness that is part of building a culture of resistance, there is a set of union alternatives that co-opt the language of 'capacity-building' and economic 'empowerment' to the same ends of the supply-side defeatism we discussed earlier. They operate comfortably within the existing framework of power and their emphasis on the 'progressive' in 'progressive competitiveness' is expressed in proposals for 'jointness' in production, part-nerships for competitiveness, alliances for jobs, worker representation on corporate boards, and most discussion of the use of pension or labour funds for social investment purposes. Since they assume what labour and capital have in common is more important than any differences, they are oriented to placing worker representatives alongside management in 'problem-solving'. What emerges are not alternative capacities, but only practices which echo capital (e.g. learning to run businesses and funds like capitalists do); and even these are restricted to a small handful of worker representatives and officials who partic-ipate in keeping information from their members because of 'corporate confidentiality.'[43] The actual access to influencing decisions is, not surprisingly, extremely limited since it is not won through mobilization but offered to *limit* mobilization. The trade-offs made for that access – material concessions and the symbolic distancing of the leadership from the members – carry dangerous insti-tutional implications with regards to rank-and-file suspicions and leadership credibility. And finally, even if there is something positive that comes out of initiatives such as access to information and input into certain decisions, this can generally be achieved at less cost and with more long-lasting results through the very mobilization this approach pushes aside.[44]

While such so-called alternatives can only take us backwards, they do raise the issue of responding to working class insecurity about their jobs. Although the prime function of unions has been the terms and conditions of the sale of workers' labour power, an increasingly crucial concern of their members has been that of retaining their jobs – something that unions, apart from trying to negotiate the sharing of work through reduced work-time, have been ill-positioned to guarantee. Taking on this defensive concern involves the strategic challenge of unions contributing to workers seeing themselves as not just workers but producers and providers of services, and therefore capable of addressing not only how many jobs are needed, but the nature and purpose of those jobs. This would take private sector unions beyond the workplace and the single firm to thinking in terms of a whole economic sector; and it would take public sector unions beyond their role of representing 'civil servants' who do things *for* others towards mobilizing *with* the people they 'serve' to expand the range and access to social rights and spaces. Worker and consumer councils at the level of whole economic sectors, in contrast to single companies driven by accumulation and competition, would be better able to associate production with use values and with technological linkages across the economy, and would be able to address developing the collective capacities to govern the economy democratically. Public sector councils, for their part, would begin the difficult process of eroding the distinction between public sector workers and their 'clients' as well as between their work and the very different 'consumption' of that work than is involved in the consumption of commodities.[45]

The point of addressing jobs and services in this way is not so much that this is an immediately viable strategy for the gradual encroachment on and eventual takeover of capital and the state, but rather that it involves a gradual development of new capacities and vision, an independent sense of how unions could be 'doing-other' to the end of 'becoming-other': negotiating with employers with a new confidence of workers' potential as opposed to demanding a voice for union leaders on various boards; introducing demands on the state such as access to government departments in terms of expanding the range of information they collect and provide, and state funding of unions' research; organizing meetings of workers in and across sectors to develop their ability to analyse their situation in the economy and society as a whole; and addressing the creation of new political and economic structures to implement this direction, ranging from job development boards and municipal ownership to democratic public financial institutions for controlling and allocating capital flows.

This kind of capacity-building on the part of the labour movement also opens the question of a new relationship to the community – if only, at first, stimulated by the concern in these particular times to avoid isolation. What is involved here is the broader strategic challenge to position unions as potential centres of working class life. This is not simply a matter of finding support for unions in the community through linking workers to 'others', but of high-lighting the fact that workers are more than just 'workers' and addressing their needs in ways that value such glimpses of their potential as their limited experience of 'citizenship' now affords, and raising their expectations of becoming fuller human beings than their social status as workers now allows. For this relationship to the community to be substantive rather than rhetorical (which invocations of 'the community' by many union leaders often are, no less than by many academics and politicians), it must affect the kinds of demands unions make on employers and the state. What this means is that issues like the environmental implications of a work-site, reduced work-time to share jobs and ending the inferior status of part-time jobs must become priorities in collec-tive bargaining; and that the nature of union structures must change as well such as by opening up local union committees to include teenagers and spouses to mobilize for changes in school education, urban and regional planning, health administration, etc.. Such a new unionism, committed to enhancing local community life, would inevitably have to play a leading role in joining with other movements to engage the state at every level, from both inside and outside, to force the development of the kind of democratic administration implied by both the sectoral and community aspects of the radical union strategy outlined here.

In both their militant defensiveness and in expanding their role beyond the workplace it is therefore clear that unions, in 'doing-other', must inevitably engage the local and national state in ways that go beyond lobbying and support for electoral allies. The struggle to democratize the economy is ultimately about collapsing the distinction between economics and politics in a very particular way: one that alters the nature of the state so that the state does not stand external to everyday economic life as a bureaucratic regulator, but is integrated in the struggles to transform social relations – which is the condition for 'becoming other', whereby people and institutions change themselves in the process of changing the nature of the economy.

THE ACCUMULATION OF CAPACITIES: REKINDLING SOCIALIST IMAGINATION

Twentieth century Marxists like Lenin and Gramsci addressed the need for restructuring the state almost exclusively in relation to what would be done *after* coming to power. But if we are to develop the democratic administrative capacities and confidence in our abilities to govern ourselves, we must find ways to constantly engage the existing state. This means that the socialist project can't advance without rethinking anew the relationship between democracy and the state. In the popular mind, the existing capitalist state embodies the democratic idea, however imperfectly, and declarations that because it is a capitalist state it is undemocratic – while true – won't change this. Analytical and rhetorical criticisms of this flawed democracy can score points, but without practical experiences that both reveal its limitations and show that something else is possible, they come up against a resigned acceptance that in a complex society this is as good as democracy can get, or mere cynicism. Our criticisms have to be tied to practical steps – aimed at changing not just what the state does, but how the various elements of the state function, showing that democratic and other gains *can* be made, instilling confidence that elements of a different and richer democracy are possible, and at the same time revealing that such gains remain limited unless we keep going further in linking democracy and economic and social transformation.

These dimensions – the need for engagement with the state, structuring that engagement so it has a socialist purpose, accumulation of the resultant capacities, the development of new means of ensuring accountability – raise all the old questions of political organization and class consciousness. But proclamations about praxis and intervention by a revolutionary party are not particularly helpful. The argument that at unique moments of deep capitalist crises and intensified struggles, a socialist consciousness and vision will explode onto the stage of history is unconvincing or, at best, incomplete. What would sustain such struggles and prevent their intensity from burning out, or prevent the severe implications of the crisis from unnerving the movement? Without a socialist culture *already* in existence – which necessarily includes, amongst other things, already committed socialists, a socialist vision and the everyday capacity building we have stressed – there would be nothing for the militants to plug into during moments of crisis and struggle, and therefore no reason to expect these militants, through 'praxis', to suddenly adopt a sustained coherent revolutionary perspective. We are therefore back to the question of the source of socialist culture. To say at this point we need a revolutionary socialist party to build that culture again only begs the question. New parties will be needed to give political coherence to labour and other social movements as well as to get elected and to prioritize the institutional reforms and experimentation required to engage the existing state in the process of social transformation. But what exactly would such parties do to develop a socialist culture within capitalism?

Developing socialist theory and clarifying socialist vision are essential first steps to building new parties capable of developing popular strategic, democratic and administrative capacities. At issue here, in other words, is not only the politics of the socialist project but its theoretical underpinnings. Marx's main critique of bourgeois political economy was that its boundaries stopped at capitalism's boundaries. It created a sense of the end of history, whereas Marx wanted to open that history up. To this end, he created a better social science. But the socialist project needed something more. Because the socialist project swims in an ill-defined sea of potentialities, because it depends on nothing less than subordinate classes setting out to create a new society, it requires a more comprehensive means of integrating the science of what is to the possibilities and strategic considerations of what might be. It is not a matter of rejecting or abandoning Marxism, but neither is it just a matter of correcting or improving on Marx. It is about adding a new conceptual layer to Marxism, a dimension formerly missing or undeveloped. Amongst other things, this means a theoretical framework that is centered on the concepts of capacities and potentials. Socialism really is about the development of productive forces, but these 'productive forces' include historically new capacities, above all the collective capacities to govern democratically everyday life, the economy, civil society and the state. Without the development of productive forces in this sense, people couldn't run a society even if power was handed over by the ruling classes.

This means that in addition to analysing the accumulation of capital, we also have to analyse the accumulation of capacities. This requires rethinking the units of analysis and social relationships we focus on. As long as, for example, we limit ourselves to the capitalist firm, we fail to focus on discussions about use values (what should entire economic sectors be doing) and coordination (planning links within and between sectors), in other words, about needs and our capacities to address those needs. Or, to take another example, if the unit of analysis isn't the individual worker, but the household which, through an internal division of labour produces and reproduces labour, sells labour power, and consumes, then not only do we have a better opening to address the capacities of women but we can better locate men and women in a context that bridges work and non-work and therefore their full human potentiality or its frustration. Since both production and households are physically located within communities, this also better facilitates addressing the issue of cross-generational class consciousness and the impact of restructuring on class capacities. And the emphasis on 'democratic administration' as a productive force raises questions of simultaneously politicizing the economy (rather than leaving it to the market) and thinking through what kind of state structures at every level might be involved in such a politicization if it is to conform to developing democratic collective capacities.

The cognitive, strategic and inspirational purpose of such a theory is to help us conceive how to inhabit capitalism while building bridges to those individual/institutional capacities to get socialism on the agenda. What the socialist project needs today, therefore, is not so much the details of how socialism would work or what we would do if we took state power, nor just more measures of why capitalism is not good enough. Rather it needs something transitional between these, beginning with a commitment to developing capacities to keep 'the utopian goal clearly visible', as Bloch put it. To that end the motivating vision, incorporating a utopian sensibility with a concern with capacity- building, must encompass at least the following ten dimensions:

1. *Overcoming alienation.* This is not a matter of escaping work in order to fulfil our lives but rather transforming the nature of work as well as giving people outside of the world of work 'the possibility of developing interests and autonomous activities, including productive activities' so that they are no longer 'passive consumers of amusements.'[46]

2. *Attenuating the division of labour.* The principle at the heart of the socialist project – the potential of each of us to become full human beings – cannot be achieved in the context of hierarchical structures 'that obstruct participation or deny equitable access of all workers to equal opportunities for fulfilment and influence.'[47] Because this won't be easy socialists are obliged to begin this process in their own parties, unions, movements, NGO's, offices, plants, universities, etc.

3. *Transforming consumption.* Socialists must recognize that any 'transformation of the relations of production and the organization of work would be conditional on a number of other, equally dramatic, changes of life-style and mode of consuming.'[48] This is not only a matter of ecological sanity but of connecting consumers to the decisions about what is produced, the development of capacities for diverse enjoyments rather than the consumption of homogenized commodities, and the expansion of accessible and generally more egalitarian spheres of public and collective consumption.

4. *Alternative ways of living.* The household as a space where glimpses of socialist capacities are afforded suggests that experiments with more communal forms of living that have the potential of extending 'intense, affectional bonds' to a broader supportive community beyond the nuclear family and other forms of household relations can provide 'a compelling point of entry for a prefigurative politics which proposes new kinds of sharing relationships and new kinds of public places.'[49]

5. *Socializing markets.* Bringing decisions about capital allocation into the democratic public sphere, alongside transformations in modes of consumption and ways of living, allows us 'to envision ways of reclaiming and transforming markets and money, so that they become a means of facilitating mutually beneficial exchange based on a mutually beneficial division of labour in an economy with an egalitarian distribution of economic power.'[50] Only these kinds of markets and social relations will allows us to escape the steel bonds of competition that entrap so much of what passes for utopian thinking today.

6. *Planning ecologically.* The socialist project means developing the capacities within each state for the democratic allocation of time and resources and the quantitative and qualitative balance between production and consumption. The goal is to 'maximize the capacity of different national collectivities democratically to choose alternate development paths… that do not impose externalities (such as environmental damage) on other countries, by re-embedding financial capital and production relations from global to national and local economic spaces.'[51]

7. *Internationalizing equality.* Envisioning this type of planning at the national level means developing international alliances and, eventually, an interna-

tional system that facilitates rather than undermines these efforts. In turn, developing the consciousness and capacities that allows for the building of egalitarian social relations within states must include a growing commitment to a solidaristic transfer of resources from rich to poor countries and to facilitating the latter's economic development via common struggles to transcend the geopolitical barriers to the development of socialist capacities. This not only means recognizing the existence of contemporary imperialism but coming to terms with the 'geographical conditions and diversities' of working class existence and learning how to 'arbitrate and translate' between these diversities and spacial scales in reviving socialist politics.[52]

8. *Communicating democratically*. Socialists need to give priority to developing a vision and strategy for a diverse, pluralist communications media in place of the commodified market-driven media today, so as to allow for the capacities for intelligent collective dialogue to grow as well as to nurture the capacities for rich cultural development. 'For a renewed collective debate about the fundamental principles of social organization to be possible, and for a new socialist project to be articulated and get a hearing, a new media order is needed.'[53]

9. *Realizing democracy*. The whole point of a socialist project conceived in terms of developing individual and collective capacities is to make the deepening and extension of democracy viable. This entails the most serious commitment to conceiving and trying to establish the types of representation and administration that contribute to breaking down the organizationally reinforced distinctions between managers and workers, politicians and citizens, leaders and led, and to overcoming the barriers that separate what we are from what we might become.[54]

10. *Omnia sint communia*. Progressive intellectuals in our time have devoted enormous energy to trying to get around what was obvious to many pre-Marxist utopians, that is, that you simply cannot have private property in the means of production, finance, exchange and communication and at the same time have an unalienated, socially just and democratic social order; and that you cannot begin to approach a utopia on the basis of the acquisitive and competitive drive. There is no way of rekindling socialist imagination so long as this basic principle is obscured, not least because doing so avoids all the difficult questions about making democratic collectivist capacities into real potentialities.

Socialists are living through a unique period: the collapse of communism and the complete abnegation by social democratic parties of any vocation for radical change has left us, for the first time in over a century, with no organizational focus for our goals. The lacuna we consequently face is, not surprisingly, accompanied by a great deal of pessimism. But overcoming that pessimism is not a matter of asserting a new, yet equally short-sighted optimism. Rather, it means drawing inspiration from the continuity between the utopian dream that pre-dates socialism and the concrete popular struggles in evidence around the world as people strive, in a multitude of diverse ways, to assert their humanity. It means drawing encouragement from the activist left's broadening of its political project to encompass many of the ideals we have set out above. And above all, it means apprehending what the very power of capital is inadvertently proclaiming as it over-runs, subordinates, and narrows every aspect of our lives – that capitalism is 'the wrong dream', and that only an alternative that is just as universal and ambitious, but rooted in our collective liberating potentials, can replace it. Rekindling the socialist imagination and accumulating the capacities to develop that alternative are not only necessary but possible.

NOTES

1. Arthur Miller, *Death of a Salesman*, London, Penguin, 1998, pp. 111-2. The famous Beijing production in the early 1980s, just as China's Communist capitalism was being launched, had already demonstrated the play's growing relevance.
2. Ernst Bloch, *The Principle of Hope*, translated by N. Plaice, S. Plaice and P. Knight, Cambridge, Mass., The MIT Press, 1986, p. 198. Largely written during his in exile in the USA between 1937 and 1949, the first two volumes were first published in East Germany in 1954-5 and the third volume in 1959. It is worth noting, in light of the use made here of *Death of a Salesman*, that Bloch regarded theatre as a 'paradigmatic institution' in terms of its ability to 'influence the will of this world, in its real possibilities.' (p. 424) He saw in theatre proof of people's 'mimic need... connected positively with the... tempting desire to transform oneself.... The Curtain rises, the fourth wall is missing, in its place is the open proscenium... From the life we have had the narrowness disappears into which it has so often led...' (pp. 412-3) For an insightful appreciation of Bloch's work by a former student, see chapter nine of Stephen Eric Bronner's *Of Critical Theory and Its Theorists*, Cambridge, Mass:Blackwell, 1994. Cf. Jamie Owen Daniel and Tom Moylan, eds. *Not Yet: Reconsidering Ernst Bloch*, Verso, New York, 1997.
3. Ibid., pp. 445-6.
4. See *The Principle of Hope*, pp. 530, 582.
5. Ibid., pp. 519-20.
6. See *The Principle of Hope*, esp. pp. 148, 197-8, 209, 622-3.
7. Ibid., p. 444.
8. Ibid., p. 622.
9. *A Philosophy of the Future*, translated by John Cummings, New York: Herder and Herder, 1970, p. 92.
10. See Leo Panitch, 'The State and the Future of Socialism', *Capital and Class*, no. 11, Spring 1980 (reprinted as Ch. 9 in *Working Class Politics in Crisis*, London, Verso, 1986), and 'Liberal Democracy and Socialist Democracy', *Socialist Register 1981*. It needs to be noted that Bloch himself tended, at least through the 1930s and 1940s, towards a 'premature harmonization' of the contradictions he discerned in the Soviet Union.
11. The richest attempt to explore this lacunae ('the question before us is – why did Marx ever think that workers could go beyond capital?') is Mike Lebowitz, *Beyond*

Capital, New York: Macmillan, 1995.

12. See *The Principle of Hope*, pp. 232-3.

13. *The German Ideology*, Moscow: International Publishers, 1972, pp. 56-7.

14. Barbara Kingsolver, *Animal Dreams*, New York: Harper Collins, 1990, p. 133.

15. James C. Scott, *Seeing Like a State: How Certain Schemes to Improve the Human Condition Have Failed*, New Haven and London: Princeton University Press, 1998.

16. Ibid., pp. 6-7, 88-9, 101-2, 342-4. At the same time Scott recognises that 'Revolutionaries had every reason to despise the feudal, poverty-stricken, inegalitarian past that they hoped to banish forever, and sometimes they also have had reason to suspect that immediate democracy would simply bring back the social order... Understanding the history and logic of the commitment to high-modernist goals, however, does not permit us to overlook the enormous damage that their convictions entailed when combined with authoritarian state power.' Nor does he go so far as some others do in his critique of the enlightenment and modernism which '... has provided us with a knowledge of the world that, for all its darker aspects, few of us would want to surrender. What has proved to be truly dangerous to us and our environment, I think, is the combination of the universalist pretensions of epistemic knowledge and authoritarian social engineering.' pp. 340-1.

17. Ibid., pp. 8, 327.

18. Hilary Wainwright, *Arguments for a New Left*, Oxford: Blackwell, 1994.

19. Erik Olin Wright, Preface to S. Bowles and H. Gintis, *Recasting Egalitarianism: New Rules for Communities, States and Markets*, New York: Verso, 1998, p. ix. Wright is not sure himself whether Bowles and Gintis's model is advanced 'in the spirit of a thoroughgoing institutional redesign of society' (p. 87), but neither is it at all clear that the two previous volumes in this series – on a guaranteed annual income and associational democracy respectively – would qualify by this test. In fact, by focussing on a redistribution of property rights, albeit within a competitive market economy, Bowles and Gintis clearly see themselves as challenging the limitations of those volumes.

20. *Recasting Egalitarianism*, p. 364.

21. Ibid., p. 48.

22. To compensate for the latter (presented mainly in terms of inducing workers not be risk-adverse when it comes to borrowing and investment), the state would provide self-financing unemployment insurance (only limited payments would go to those whose 'own actions' – including, it appears, failure to work hard enough to raise productivity – are 'implicated in their joblessness') and bankruptcy insurance (it is unpersuasively claimed that it would be not be difficult to insure firms on a self-financing basis against 'exogenous' risks like economic down-turns and to distinguish these from 'controllable' risks like bad management or investment decisions). *Recasting Egalitarianism*, pp. 50-1.

23. See Bertell Ollman, ed., *Market Socialism: The Debate Among Socialists*, New York: Routledge, 1998.

24. An excellent early overview and assessment of this literature was provided by Pat Devine in his essay on 'Market Socialism or Participatory Planning' in the special issue on 'The Future of Socialism' in the *Review of Radical Political Economics*, vol. 24, nos. 3 & 4, Fall & Winter 1992. The most creative contributions were Devine's *Democracy and Economic Planning*, Cambridge: Polity Press, 1988; Diane Elson's 'Market Socialism or Socialization of the Market?' *New Left Review*, no.

172, November/December 1988 and, especially for the attention they paid to attenuating, if not entirely transcending, the division of labour in a complex economy, Michael Albert and Robin Hahnel's *Looking Forward: Participatory Economics for the Twenty-First Century*, Boston: South End Press, 1991.

25. All they have to say by way of elaborating on the worker-owned firms being 'governed by their elected representatives' is: 'We assume that workers direct the managers of the democratic firm to select investments, systems of work monitoring, and other policy options to maximize the workers' welfare.' *Recasting Egalitarianism*, p. 37.

26. *Recasting Egalitarianism*, pp. 390–91.

27. They ignore Barrington Moore's retort to those who relied on assumptions of cultural inertia: 'To maintain and transmit a value system', he wrote, 'human beings are punched, bullied sent to jail, thrown into concentration camps, cajoled, bribed, made into heroes, encouraged to read newspapers, stood up against a wall and shot, and sometimes even taught sociology.' And these days, we might add, supply-side economics. See Barrington Moore, Jr. *Social Origins of Democracy and Dictatorship*, Boston: Beacon, 1967, p. 486.

28. As one of their critics puts it: 'Bowles and Gintis are… so busy making a pitch for egalitarian policies to soft-hearted efficiency worshippers that they risk inviting their readers to forget what egalitarianism is all about. It is not about Nintendo games in every home and more trips to the Mall. It is about self-respect, fairness, equal respect and fraternity…. The fundamental mistake is that they fail to ask what economic growth is for, and they surrender all thought of questioning, let alone controlling, the future that markets dictate to us. Even if Bowles and Gintis are right that those concerned with efficiency should support egalitarian policies, egalitarians… should keep their distance from supply-side economics.' Daniel M. Hausman, 'Problems with Supply-side Egalitarianism' in *Recasting Egalitarianism*, p. 84. It is one of the virtues of Verso's Real Utopia series that each volume also contains such critical essays followed by a response by the main authors.

29. Roberto Mangabeira Unger, *Democracy Realized: The Progressive Alternative*, New York: Verso, 1998, p. 9.

30. Roberto Mangabeira Unger, *False Necessity*, Part I of *Politics: A Work in Constructive Social Theory*, Cambridge, U.K.: Cambridge University Press, 1987. pp. 392–5.

31. Ibid., pp. 406–9, 438. At the time this was written in the mid-1980s, this could be seen as a theorization of the kind of political practice that had already been articulated by the activists who created the Workers Party in Unger's own Brazil, or by Tony Benn and the activists of Greater London Council in the early 1980s. (Unger himself was associated not with the Workers Party but aligned with Cardoso in the formation of the less radical Brazilian Democratic Movement, PMDB. See Eyal Press, 'The Passion of Roberto Unger', *Lingua Franca*, March 1999.) At the time he wrote *False Necessity*, Unger's hope was that the proponents of 'empowered democracy' would be able to work loosely within reform, labor, socialist and communist parties as well as within 'the extrapartisan grassroots movements most open to their vision'(p. 409). By the time of *Democracy Realized* over a decade later, however, Unger seemed much less confident about where to find 'the missing agent of an inclusive politics' (p. 245).

32. *Democracy Realized*, pp. 1, 213–15, 263ff.

33. Ibid., p. 174.
34. Ibid., p. 43.
35. André Gorz, *Strategy for Labour: A Radical Proposal*, Boston, Beacon: 1967, p. 7.
36. 'The condition of post-Marxist Man is that the meaning Marx read into historical development remains for us the only meaning that development can have, yet we must pursue this independent of the existence of a social class capable of realizing it.' *Critique of Economic Reason*, p. 96.
37. *The German Ideology*, p. 104.
38. See Sam Gindin, 'Socialism with Sober Senses', *Socialist Register 1998*.
39. See Jerry Lembcke, 'Class Analysis and Studies of the U.S. Working Class: Theoretical, Conceptual, and Methodological Issues' in Scott G. McNall, Rhonda Levine and Rick Fantasia eds., *Bringing Class Back In*, Boulder: Westview Press, 1991.
40. Henri Lefebvre, *Critique of Everyday Life*, Volume 1, London, Verso: 1991 (1947), p. 33.
41. *Farewell to the Working Class*, Boston: South End Press, 1982; *Critique of Economic Reason*, London: Verso, 1989.
42. *Critique of Economic Reason*, pp. 232-3.
43. One of strongest examples of union involvement in decision-making is co–determination in Germany. However, when Daimler made the decision to merge with Chrysler, this was not discussed at the board level where the German metalworkers were involved; it was deemed too sensitive and the worker input was to ratify it after the fact. Similarly the issue of outsourcing, which is so crucial to German workers is not dealt with at the board level because it would be too 'controversial'. In Canada, there has been a mushrooming of government-subsidized 'labour worker investment funds' to allegedly give the labour movement some control over jobs and the direction of the economy without the capacity to control any particular project, invest in directions which may meet criteria other than profitability, or insist that the jobs created include unionization. For a detailed critique of the latter, see Jim Stanford, *Labour Investment Funds*, Toronto: CAW, 1999.
44. For instance, demanding, through collective bargaining and legislation, reports from the company that are accessible to non–accountants, resources for independent technical assistance in interpreting information, time during working hours to get updates and raise questions of management, union approval of work re-organization or outsourcing decisions, and input through sectoral councils as discussed below.
45. See Greg McElligott 'An Immodest Proposal, or Democracy Beyond the Capitalist Welfare State', *Socialist Studies Bulletin*, no. 52, Winnipeg, (April-May-June1998), pp. 24-48.
46. Gorz, *Critique of Economic Reason*, p. 231.
47. Albert and Hahnel, *Participatory Economics*, p. 35.
48. See Kate Soper's essay in this volume. Cf. the debate on Juliet Schor's 'The New Politics of Consumption' in *Boston Review*, 24: 3-4, Summer 1999.
49. See Johanna Brenner's essay in this volume.
50. See Diane Elson's essay in this volume.
51. Greg Albo, 'The World Economy, Market Imperatives and Alternatives', *Monthly Review*, December 1996, p. 19. And see also Albo's ten point

programme in his 'A World Market of Opportunities? Capitalist Obstacles and Left Economic Policy', *Socialist Register 1997*.

52. David Harvey, 'The Geography of Class Power', *Socialist Register 1998*, esp. p. 70.
53. Colin Leys, 'The Public Sphere and the Media: Market Supremacy versus Democracy', *Socialist Register 1999*.
54. See Greg Albo, David Langille and Leo Panitch, eds., *A Different Kind of State*, Toronto, Oxford University Press, 1993.

UTOPIA AND ITS OPPOSITES

TERRY EAGLETON

THERE IS SOMETHING strangely self-undermining about the idea of utopia. Since we can speak of what transcends the present only in the language of the present, we risk cancelling out our imaginings in the very act of articulating them. The only real otherness would be that which we could not articulate at all. All utopia is thus at the same time dystopia, since it cannot help reminding us of how we are bound fast by history in the very act of trying to set us free from that bondage.

So much is obvious if one thinks of the accounts one hears these days of abductions by aliens. What renders these tales so suspect is not the strangeness of these beings, but exactly the opposite. It is the farcical familiarity of these creatures, their laughably non-alien alienness, which gives the lie to the agitated reports of their victims. Apart from an extra limb or two, the absence of ears, a disagreeable odour or a few feet of additional or subtracted height, they look much like Bill Gates or Tony Blair. Their speech and bodies are grotesquely different from ours, except for the fact that they have bodies and can speak. They fly in craft which can negotiate black holes but unaccountably spin out of control in the Nevada desert.

Aliens are inconceivably different from us, since they apparently steer such craft with extremely short arms, and speak in sinisterly monotone voices. Beings who hail from civilizations perhaps millions of years in advance of our own nevertheless display a prurient interest in human dentures and genitals. Their messages to our planet are couched in nebulous platitudes about world peace worthy of a United Nations' secretary general, and they will be no doubt be coming up with a few vague ecological observations in the fullness of time. The spurious spookiness of extraterrestrials is dismal testimony to the paucity of the human imagination. Any alien which is able to abduct us is by definition not an alien.

Much the same is true of literary utopias in the eighteenth and nineteenth centuries. What is striking about most of these texts, with a few honourable exceptions, is just how absurdly incapable they are of imagining any world definitively different from their own. It is this, not some farrago of outlandish fantasies, which is most unreal about them. In Lady Mary Fox's *Account of an Expedition to the Interior of New Holland* (1837), the inhabitants of utopia have broken so completely with Victorian middle-class convention that they hold casual buffets rather than formal dinner parties. In Sarah Scott's *A Description of Millenium Hall* (1778), utopia is a country house in Cornwall, an anodyne English pastoral in which female midgets play the harpsichord and tend the shrubberies. For the English, the ideal social order needs to have an old orchard and a couple of herbaceous borders.

The ideal society of Charles Ryecroft's *The Triumph of Woman* (1848) is a drearily high-minded regime full of wholesome puddings, docile, state-funded artists and one pew per person in church. Douglas Jerrold's *The Chronicles of Clovernook* (1846) a tale which becomes peculiarly excited at the prospect of little boys rending their trousers while climbing for apples, enthuses over an imaginary society which still has taxes, prisons and poverty. John Kirkby's *The Capacity and Extent of the Human Understanding* (1745) presents us with a noble savage on his paradisiacal island who has figured out more or less the whole of English eighteenth century religion, almost down to country parsonages, simply by attentively observing the natural world around him. All of this reaches its apogee in Daniel Defoe's *Robinson Crusoe* (1719), in which Crusoe finds his way around an exotically familiar environment by exercising a brisk, very English common sense. The novel thus permits us the pleasures of the unknown, while defusing and domesticating its potential menace. It is enheartening for the eighteenth-century reader to watch Crusoe chopping wood and staking out his enclosure, for all the world as if he were somewhere in Surrey.

Something similar is true of Jonathan Swift's *Gulliver's Travels* (1726), where the joke is that giants and microscopic creatures turn out to be a lot more like us than their appearance might lead us to expect. Gulliver, too, domesticates the outlandish, as in his indignant rebuttal of the charge that he has had sex with a woman only a few inches high. *Gulliver's Travels* is among other things a Tory smack at the radical notion that there could ever be a world significantly different from the one we know. By no means all utopias or dystopias, in short, belong to the political left, as the anonymous *Great Britain in 1841, or The Results of the Reform Bill* (1832) well illustrates. The narrator of this troubled tract falls asleep in 1831 and wakes up ten years later, to find his brother bending over him looking forty rather than a mere ten years older than when he saw him last. The cause of this premature ageing is the Reform Bill of 1832, which has allowed the state to confiscate their father's property and forced him into exile. The government has likewise grabbed the funds of the universities of both Oxford and Cambridge; England and Ireland have been dissevered, the king has fled to Hanover, the rioting populace is carrying out summary executions, and the narrator's mother has died of a broken heart.

In a great deal of utopian fiction, alternative worlds are simply devices for embarrassing the world we actually have. The point is not to go elsewhere, but to use elsewhere as a reflection on where you are. Most literary utopias are covert political journalism, constructing their ideal kingdoms simply to promote some parochial obsession in the present. No form of fantasy could be more provincial and prosaic. This apparently most earnest, abstract of literary forms is also one of the most topical and ephemeral. Nothing is more grittily realist than their high-minded idealism. The more urgently relevant to our own political concerns such fictions are, and so the more vivid and powerful, the less utopian they become. By the end of the nineteenth century, after William Morris' great classic *News from Nowhere* (1891), the task of projecting an alternative universe would pass to science fiction, which performed it with a good deal more panache. Though as far as *News from Nowhere* goes, one might recall Perry Anderson's observation that it is one of those exceedingly rare socialist utopias which actually portray the process of revolutionary change as well as the outcome of it.

A good many literary utopias before Morris depicted a future world which only a dedicated masochist would want to inhabit. They are for the most part odourless, anti-sceptic places, intolerably sensible and streamlined, in which the natives jaw on for hours about the efficiency of their sanitary arrangements or the ingenuity of their electoral system. They remind one, in short, of Marx's scornful strictures on the utopian rationalists of his day, whose abstract speculations provided him with a convenient anvil upon which he could hammer out his own rather different political reflections. Marx was quick to spot the futility of what one might call the subjunctive mood in politics – the kind of 'wouldn't it be nice if' fantasies which any progressively-minded intellectual with time on his hands could get up to precisely because such imaginings were utterly unconstrained by material fact.

For Marx himself, the opposite of utopia was not of course some kind of pragmatic realism. Indeed nothing could be more idly utopian. There are two kinds of starry-eyed idealist: those who believe in a perfect society, and those who believe that the future will be pretty much like the present. Those with their heads truly in the sands or the clouds are the hard-nosed realists who behave as though chocolate chip cookies and the International Monetary Fund will be with us in another three thousand years time. Such a view is simply an inversion of *The Flintstones*, for which the primeval past is just American suburbia plus dinosaurs. The future may well turn out to be singularly unpleasant; but to deny that it will be quite different, in the manner of *post-histoire* philosophizing, is to offend against the very realism on which such theorists usually pride themselves. To claim that human affairs might feasibly be much improved is an eminently realistic proposition.

The opposite of utopia for Marx was not the pathological fantasy that the

present will merely perpetuate itself, but what is generally referred to as immanent critique. If Marxism has traditionally set its face against utopia, it is not
because it rejects the idea of a radically transfigured society, but because it
rejects the assumption that such a society could be, so to speak, simply para-
chuted into the present from some metaphysical outer space. It could not be
that everything we know could suddenly grind to a halt, and something inconceivably different take its place, because we would not even be able to identify
what this difference would consist in, having left behind the very language in
which we might describe it. If the notion of utopia is to have force, it could
only be as a way of interrogating the present which unlocks its dominative logic
by discerning the dim outline of an alternative already implicit within it. If talk
of utopia is not to be logically incoherent or idly self-indulgent, we have to be
able to point, now, to the kinds of activities and capacities which might
prefigure it. Authentic utopian thought concerns itself with that which is
encoded within the logic of a system which, extrapolated in a certain direction,
has the power to undo it. By installing itself in those contradictions or equiv-
ocations in a system and where it ceases to be identical with itself, it allows that
non-identity to reveal itself as the negative image of some future positivity. If
'immanent critique' is the traditional name for this operation, 'deconstruction',
in its institutional rather than narrowly textual sense, is one contemporary
synonym for it. Grasped in this light, utopia is what dismantles the opposition
between a future which is merely extraneous or supplementary to the present,
and the bleak post-modern assumption that there is no 'outside' at all. It recognizes, on the contrary, that the forces which might break the system open also
break open the very opposition between 'inside' and 'outside'. Something like
this, presumably, is what the young Marx means by speaking of the working
class as one which is 'in' civil society, but not 'of' it.

If a transformed future is not in this sense anchored in the present, it quickly
becomes a fetish. If we need images of our desire, we also need to prevent these
images from mesmerizing us and so standing in the way of it. Walter Benjamin
understood that the Jewish prohibition on fashioning graven images of God was
among other things a ban on making a fetish of the future, manipulating it as a
magical totem in the cause of your present interests. For Benjamin, the Messiah
might enter history at any moment, which meant that the future was perpetu-
ally open. (He also believed that the Messiah would transfigure everything
simply by making minor adjustments.) Projecting the future may just be an
attempt to control and manipulate it. The true clairvoyants of our age are those
experts hired by capitalism to peer into the entrails of the system and assure its
rulers that their profits are safe for another twenty years. But constructing imaginary futures is also self-defeating, since it can end up absorbing the very energies
which might have been devoted to realizing them in practice. The opposite of
the clairvoyant is the prophet, who contrary to common belief is not concerned
with predicting the future, but simply with warning the present that unless it
changes its ways that future is likely to be exceedingly unpleasant.

But if Marxism has had little to say of utopia, it is also because its task is less to imagine a new social order than to unlock the contradictions which forestall its historical emergence. Seen in this light, Marxist thought itself is rooted in the epoch which it is aiming to surpass, and will be superannuated by what it helps to bring into being. There will be no radicals in the New Jerusalem, because no need for them. Such phenomena belong to the present just as much as the language of patriarchy or man-management. There would be also be a great deal less pity around in a transformed society, since a great deal less to pity.

But if there will be no political radicals – if socialists, feminists, eco-warriors and the like will be, thankfully, no more than a dim, antediluvian memory – there will surely be tragedy, which rules out the more perfectibilist currents of utopian thought. One should think twice before expressing the apparently generous-hearted wish to live in a social order which had passed beyond tragedy. For it is by no means clear that you could root out tragedy without extirpating the sense of human value on which it depends. Tragedy is deeply interwoven with our freedom, relatedness and autonomy, and it is hard to see how it could be abolished, as some more hubristic strains of utopianism have imagined, without eradicating these too. Herbert Marcuse liked to imagine a future in which human beings were so changed that the very act of offering physical violence to each other would make them sick. One would just have to hope that this did not prevent surgery too.

In his work *Modern Tragedy*, Raymond Williams argues two kinds of socialist-humanist case against the orthodox ideologies of tragedy. The first, 'democratizing' case is that tragedy should not be regarded a privileged, exceptional event, the death of princes or the fall of heroes, but part of the texture of common social life. It is a smash on the roads, a broken relationship, a futile death. The second, 'politicizing' case he advances is that tragedy is an historical phenomenon – the long tragedy of class-society, for example – which is in principle capable of being resolved. The problem is that these two arguments are exceptionally hard to reconcile with one another, unless you imagine that futile deaths and broken relationships can also be somehow definitively transcended.

The problem is also that the abolition of oppressive political systems does not itself diminish the tragedy of their dead and discarded victims. Whatever the historical outcome for their successors, that experience remains, so to speak, absolute and irreparable for the victims themselves. When Benjamin remarks that it is memories of enslaved ancestors which drive men and women to revolt, not dreams of liberated grandchildren, he finds a way of using or (in a Brechtian phrase) 'refunctioning' the dead themselves, summoning their shades to the service of the political present through the rituals of mourning and remembrance. For Benjamin, even nostalgia can be a revolutionary force, just as the conspicuous consumption of the bourgeoisie could be made, in a daring dialectical twist, to prefigure the material abundance of a socialist future. But he does not imagine that such re-functionings of the dead could ever retrospectively justify the indignities they suffered.

If Marxism is anti-utopian, then, it is also because – except its wilder, more 'cosmic' flights of fancy – it does not allow itself to be entranced by the dream of a society from which all conflict would have vanished. On the contrary, once some of the eminently engineered conflicts of the present have been resolved, we might be better able to identify what our true contentions really are. Once we have left behind the absurdity by which such ultimately unimportant human differences as gender, ethnicity, national identity and the like have been turned by our rulers into terrains of political battle, we may be able to clear the air a little and spot what genuinely divides us. If socialists may feasibly have hope, one reason is because the contradictions to which they address themselves are, for all their formidable power and centrality, much more modest, transitory affairs than, say, death or physical suffering or moral humiliation. This is not, needless to say, to suggest that they will be resolved – just that they fall into the category of things which in principle can be. 'Bad' utopia persuades us to desire the unfeasible, and so, like the neurotic, to fall ill of longing; whereas the only authentic image of the future is, in the end, the failure of the present.

Utopian thought is hardly in fashion in these sceptical, politically downbeat days, though a certain strain of post-modernist thought has peddled a particularly grotesque brand of it. This is the diseased fantasy that we no longer need to look to a future because the future is here already, in the shape of a perversely idealized view of the capitalist present. It is not so much that the future is infinitely deferred, but that it is with us already, perhaps without our recognizing it as such, in the guise of the hedonistic subjects and libidinal circuits of contemporary consumerism. To pronounce history at an end is in one sense to call the future off, declare it cancelled for lack of interest; but it can just as well be seen as the claim that the future is here already, since the only future we shall ever witness will be a repetition of the present.

This, to be sure, is a very different view of the future from that of the revolutionary avant-gardes earlier in our century, who also saw the future as somehow already with us, since only that which quite literally did not exist – future time – could be an adequate image of the transformation of the present. The word 'futuristic' thus comes in common parlance to mean, ironically, the very latest thing – to function as a description of the present, not of that which will supersede it. In a revolutionary epoch, it is as though the present can only be grasped in its lack of self-identity – in the way that it is even now trembling on the brink of some absolute negation which brims it full of meaning even as it drains it of substance. The future, in the 'pure' temporality of modernism, is just a way of describing the present's lack of coincidence with itself, the way its truth lies in its ceaseless self-surpassing. For Marx, similarly, the 'truth' of socialism lies not in some steady state of the future, but in the way in which a self-divided present is even now struggling to go beyond itself.

A post-modernist scepticism of utopia, however, is generally less because some ideal future is thought to have already arrived, than because – capitalist reality being now global and apparently immovable – the best we can do is decorate our cells, rearrange the deck chairs on the sinking liner, prise open the odd fissure in this otherwise seamless monolith into which a stray beam of freedom or enlightenment or gratification may infiltrate. This, need one say, is to pay an extravagant compliment to one of the most sickeningly fragile systems which history has ever witnessed. It is to confuse the question of the formidable power of capitalism with the question of its stability – to fail to grasp that in one sense the capitalist system is as unstable as it is precisely because of its power. Any form of life with a built-in dynamic to universalize itself is bound to ensnare itself in its own strength, since the more it proliferates, the more fronts it breeds on which it can become vulnerable. For a system to intermesh so many different regions of reality is for it to spread its sway only at the cost of multiplying its potential points of breakdown.

The idea that there is anything graven in stone about this roller coaster of a system is laughable enough; but so is the assumption that its victims are now so spiritually lobotomized, so passive and docile, that they would be unlikely to twitch an eyebrow were the Second Coming to take place in their front gardens. This may be the view of some jaded cultural theorists, but it is certainly not the view of Whitehall or the White House. If there is one moral certainty in all this, it is surely that people will rise up against the system the moment it is rational for them to do so. That is to say, the moment when it becomes tolerably clear that there is nothing any longer in the system for them; that the perils and discomforts of disaffection outweigh the meagre gratification of conformism; that sheer apathy is no longer materially possible; that even an obscure, untested political alternative would be better than what they are landed with; and that anger at the unjust way in which they are being treated is more powerful than fatalism and fear.

Such moments don't of course come often, since it is rational not to rebel against a social system, whatever its grave deficiencies, as long as it is still capable of delivering you just enough gratification to outweigh the risk and laboriousness of seeking an alternative. Once it is not capable of this, however, men and women will take to the streets as surely as night follows day. But though they may take to the streets, they may well not take to socialism – perhaps because, in the view of some commentators, the days of the doctrine are now strictly numbered, so that it won't be around by the time this upheaval happens, if indeed it ever does. But this, too, is an unlikely ground for political pessimism. It is quite probable that socialist ideas will survive, given their historical tenacity and political relevance. And their survival is important in at least one respect, which is that without them – without some kind of socialist organization and direction – a good many more people are likely to get hurt in periods of mass disaffection than might otherwise be the case. There are many things to be said against mere anarchy, one of the more pertinent being that it wreaks a lot of unnecessary human havoc. If we are to minimize the human cost of such social upheaval, we need some idea of how to channel those energies most constructively. And whether this could be done or not is extremely unclear. If there is any ground for political scepticism, then, it is surely here, not in the fantasy that the capitalist system is omnipotent or that the working class will never care for anything but cable television or that the only radicals left around in ten years time will be soft-bellied social democrats.

What is most truly utopian about the thought of Marx, so one might claim, is its distaste for the instrumental. Marx is pained by the notion that what he calls human powers and capacities should be subjected to a dreary means/ends rationality, and looks to a social order in which men and women would be able to realize such powers and capacities as self-delighting ends in themselves. They would no longer be called upon to justify themselves at the lofty tribunal of History, *Geist*, Duty, Party or Utility, but would live instead as though their energies were self-grounding and self-legitimating, which for Marx, as a good Romantic humanist, they are. To attend to the use-value of persons, rather than to their exchange-value, is just another way of putting the same point. Human beings for Marx do indeed, by virtue of their 'species being', have a sort of function, which is to realize their powers and faculties as sensuous ends in themselves. But this is in a way to claim that their function is to be functionless at least if you see 'function' as the abstraction from the particularity of a thing for the sake of some end external to it. It is one of Marx's most precious insights (though by no means one unique to his work) that what we call morality just *is* this constant unfolding of creative human powers and capacities, not some grim set of strictures hedging it round. In this, indeed, he is a thoroughly traditional moralist in the tradition of Aristotle, as opposed to a Kantian moralizer.

One of the many ironies of Marx's thought, however, is that in order to achieve a society in which the grip of instrumental reason might be somewhat relaxed, we stand in need of the most rigorously instrumental forms of thought and action. A few men and women, to be sure, may try to live in this utopian, anti-instrumental style now; but as one of their number, Oscar Wilde, candidly recognized, this can only be a valid rather than offensively privileged form of life if it somehow comes to prefigure a social order in which this life-form would finally be available to everyone. The theme of Wilde's magnificent essay *The Soul of Man Under Socialism* is that the only good reason for being a socialist is that you don't like having to work, and that those like Wilde himself privileged enough not to have to labour are thus 'reminders' of a time when labour will exercise less of a fetishistic power over us all. It is a necessary insight, as well as a mischievously self-serving one: just lie in bed all day and be your own communist society. But it has somehow to be reconciled with the unavoidably instrumental procedures necessary to achieve socialism – a process in which the means would seem to run counter to the ends. Those who most faithfully strive to bring about a new social order may thus not be the best images of that order themselves. What if the process of bringing it into being is in contradiction with the very values it represents?

The problem with leftists used to be that they were so taken up with political means that they were at some risk of forgetting or even obliterating the ends which those means were meant to serve. One might well feel a mite nostalgic for this error, since what we have nowadays is more commonly the reverse: a radicalism which is enthralled by the end-in-itselfness of pleasure, *jouissance*, and the like, but which is distinctly less enthused by the rather more prosaic business of laying the ground by which they might be available to more than a few privileged souls. In this situation, a dash of vulgar instrumentalism might well not come amiss. But there is no reason to imagine that these two dimensions of socialism, the utopian and the instrumental, can be always and everywhere harmoniously united. In this respect at least, the left has always been a broad church which spanned the shaggy-haired prophets and the buttoned-down committee folk, the wild-eyed visionaries and the horny-handed barricade builders. It is unrealistic to suppose that these will always be synthesized within the same body. Blake and Rimbaud were not good committee men, and we do not look to James Larkin for neo-Platonic illumination.

There is one aspect of this tension between the utopian and the instrumental which has not been much examined, but which is especially relevant to our own less-than-sanguine political situation. One of the more creative forms of dissent from the instrumental principle has been a certain leftist faith that, politically speaking, one does what one has to do in a certain disregard for the likely historical outcome. This is largely because the historical outcome in question, given the forces which the left confronts, is likely more often than not to be fairly bleak. This, surely, is part of what Walter Benjamin meant by blasting an event in the struggle of the dispossessed out of the continuum of history. He meant among other things that we should suspend for a moment the historical failure to which the event actually led, snap if off, so to speak, from its less than triumphal consequences, so as to attend all the more vigilantly to the powers which the event incarnated.

If this is what it means to think non-teleologically, rather than (as in a certain post-modern fancy) the notion that history is a chain of aberrations, then one can see its force. And one can see its force not least in a political epoch when the left's chances of success have become notably constricted. It would of course be fatal to use this non-instrumental, non-teleological form of thought simply to rationalize our failures. For Benjamin, this anti-teleology is finally in the service of political achievement, as we redeem these scattered moments in the revolutionary imagination, constellating them into a pattern which forms an alternative to the ruler's image of history and which plays its part in political action in the present. The opposite to the crass triumphalism of our rulers is hardly a squalidly masochistic cult of failure. What the left pits against the power of the right is not failure, but a transfigured concept of power. But just as revolutionary eras highlight certain kinds of socialist value which are obscured in less affirmative times, so the reverse may also be true. In more barren political periods, it is possible for us to retrieve what one might call the more Kantian side of Marxism: the deontological imperative that one does what one considers to be politically right even if it is unlikely to bear much political

MINIMUM UTOPIA: TEN THESES

NORMAN GERAS

I OFFER HERE SOME REFLECTIONS on utopia. I make no extravagant claim for them. They do not trace out a history of the concept, nor do they attempt to explore its thematic range and variety. They are simply one person's thoughts on the subject as we approach a new century and millennium. I have arranged them into ten summary theses.

1. SOCIALISM IS UTOPIAN

As a goal socialism is, and it always has been, utopian, including in its most influential version to date, namely Marxism. This is despite Marx and Engels's attempt, in the *Communist Manifesto* and elsewhere, to take their distance from utopia as mere abstraction or speculation, to ground their own thinking in present tendencies, in an analysis of real historical possibilities and of the social and political agencies for bringing them about. Everyone knows that in this sense the Marxist tradition sought from the beginning to be resolutely *anti-*utopian. Re-read the relevant passages from the *Manifesto*. Of some of their predecessors – Saint-Simon, Fourier, Owen – Marx and Engels say that, faced with a proletarian class not yet sufficiently developed, faced likewise with material conditions still insufficient for the emancipation of the proletariat, these thinkers could but invent in place of what they lacked, and so they invented 'fantastic pictures of future society'.[1]

This was not to be the way of the founding thinkers of historical materialism. Indeed it was the source of one of classical Marxism's great strengths that, committed to the goal of a fundamentally different kind of social order, it sought to provide a political economy, a sociology and a politics of the present and the emergent future. This is, too, what its numberless detractors have most deeply begrudged it. For, whatever the changing fortunes of the movement for socialism, taken all in all there is still no more compelling theory of society than historical materialism, even once all the necessary qualifications to it have been made.

Notwithstanding any of this, however, it remains true that from the outset socialism was utopian. It was a distant land, another moral universe. It was radically *other* vis-à-vis the order of things it aspired to replace. And that is what it still is. A society beyond exploitation is in the realm of the ideal. Furthermore, so far from being any kind of inevitability, its achievement is an unsolved problem and – not to beat about the bush – the very possibility of it is in question. In this way socialism partakes also of one of the pejorative meanings of utopia. Until its realization establishes otherwise, it partakes of the meaning of being an unattainable ideal. We may hope that it can be achieved, but we do not yet know that it can. Nor do we yet know how.

2. WE SHOULD UNASHAMEDLY EMBRACE UTOPIA

We should be, without hesitation or embarrassment, utopians. At the end of the twentieth century it is the only acceptable political option, morally speaking. I shall not dwell on this. I will merely say that, irrespective of what may have seemed apt hitherto either inside or outside the Marxist tradition, nothing but a utopian goal will now suffice. The realities of our time are morally intolerable. Within the constricted scope of the present piece, I suppose I might try to evoke a little at least of what I am referring to here, with some statistics or an imagery of poverty, destitution and other contemporary calamities. But I do not intend to do even this much. The facts of widespread human privation and those of political oppression and atrocity are available to all who want them. They are unavoidable unless you wilfully shut them out. To those who would suggest that things might be yet worse, one answer is that of course they might be. But another answer is that for too many people they are already quite bad enough; and the sponsors of this type of suggestion are for their part almost always pretty comfortable.

3. THERE HAVE BEEN TWO INGREDIENTS OF SOCIALIST UTOPIA

I distinguish from within the Marxist tradition two broad elements of the socialist vision, which, simplifying, I style maximum and minimum ingredients. Informing discussions of the socialist future there has been, on the one hand, a dream or promise of ultimate liberation, one not generally filled out in very much detail but present nevertheless in certain pregnant words and phrases. It might be, from Marx's early works on, the dream of disalienation, of all-round individual self-development. Or it might be the promise in the slogan 'to each according to their needs', lavishly interpreted. It might be the implicit vision of a world of peacefully resolved conflicts without any need of policing or enforcement, or an anticipation of what used to be called 'fraternity'.

One should take care not to exaggerate. The influential thinkers of Marxism were serious people, not fools. They did not believe – as, in that caricature of the 'smiling Marxist' so dear to many critics, they are often represented as having believed[2] – in the possibility of a world free of all limitation and difficulty. They did not expect heaven on earth. Still, the image was there of a condition of uncoerced social peace and of free and ample individual self-realization, with the sign against it of the radically, the incomparably different. Not as in an 'end of time' or a realm of concurring uniformity; this is merely part of the same caricature. But as in a fundamentally new beginning, the self-conscious history of humankind as opposed to a previously opaque prehistory.[3]

On the other hand, there was also – a mark, this, precisely of the materialism – the conception of a simple *sufficiency* of the means and conveniences of life. It was contained in the socialist demand for a release from extreme want and toil, a demand based on the elementary fact (which pro-capitalist liberals typically disguise from or soften for themselves) that the possibility of individual flourishing is seriously undermined by poverty and grave need, as it is by the tedium of a lifetime of unwanted forms of labour. Within, or perhaps behind, any greater was this more modest objective: of providing everyone with the proper platform for a life of free self-development. Might each member of our species one day rise to the level of an Aristotle, a Goethe or a Marx? I don't know, although Leon Trotsky famously asserted so.[4] But the hypothesis was predicated on having to bring about an underlying sufficiency for all.

4. MAXIMUM NOTIONS OF UTOPIA HAVE THEIR INDISPENSABLE PLACE

People will continue to long for what may be beyond their reach. Yearnings of this kind are merely the other face of finitude and limitation, of the regular troubles and the harsher oppressions of the world. As, in the normal way of things, fear of death, protracted pain or illness, close bereavement; and loneliness, disappointed love, personal betrayal or other inner hurts; more generally, excessive burdens and wretched long-term predicaments, are a cause of suffering, so do they also prompt ideas of a release from it. Here the reconstructive capacities of human thought – abstraction, projection, imagination – can always move through various levels of conceivable improvement right up to the furthermost negation. Hence, eternal life, ultimate redemption and the like, as well as some of the more common fictions of many a personal existence. Hence, the most ambitious utopias.

At the same time, elements of the transcendent are lodged within mundane experience, thereby nourishing in a more positive way, too, visions of a radically different human realm. For if the extraordinary is already within the ordinary, why may it not be extended? And why may it not be extended again? Great art – or just good music, of all kinds – could be invoked at this point to exemplify the way in which the aesthetic, the elevating or powerfully affective, inhabits the quotidian world. But another less often used example demonstrates as tellingly how even within the ordinary, at the most seemingly unremarkable sites, there are moments of grace, joy and excitement capable of lifting those present and transmuting the quality of their experience. I refer to the example of modern sport, not much reflected on in meditations about utopia. It is a mistaken neglect, in my own view, since sport today gives as much genuine and memorable pleasure to millions upon millions of people as can be claimed for most other human pursuits. In the unexceptional context of what are no more than idle games, and for all of the accompanying ugliness currently to be found there – abusively exaggerated hatreds, boorishness, the corruptions of a rampantly invasive commodification – there is a communal enjoyment of competitive effort, and there are feats of impressive, sometimes breathtaking skill, and uniquely specific moments of great beauty under pressure not repro-ducible in any other setting. This is on top of the more common enjoyments of time passed shooting the breeze with friends. C. L. R. James already said it many years ago: 'the popular democracy of our day, sitting . . . watching Miller and Lindwall bowl to Hutton and Compton [or, for that matter, watching Edwards, Bennett and J. P. R. Williams, or Cantona, Beckham and Giggs] . . . in its own way grasps at a more complete human existence'.[5]

There could be other examples still: of feelings of deep or intense love, outstanding acts of friendship, compassion, courage. But from both kinds of cause, whether the psychological and moral needs arising from suffering, or possibilities faintly discerned within the lived experience of the real, we will continue to long for what may be beyond our reach. We not only will continue to, we also should. For, set against this wider human–natural background, maximum notions of utopia can be seen to have their value. This value is in the very dream of deliverance. It is in the liberating fantasy that yields a different vantage point from the one confining us and claiming the privilege, all too often, of being the sole *realistic* reality. We have to think about the seemingly impossible in order to be able to discriminate what is genuinely possible. There are few things as bizarre anyway, as Terry Eagleton observes elsewhere in this volume, as the futurist vision trapped within assumptions of a putative realism. 'Those with their heads truly in the sands or the clouds are the hard-nosed real-ists who behave as though chocolate chip cookies and the International Monetary Fund will be with us in another three thousand years time.'

5. POLITICALLY, WE SHOULD BE GUIDED AS SOCIALISTS BY THE AIM OF MINIMUM UTOPIA

These above considerations notwithstanding, the political thought of socialism should now be centred, not on notions of ultimate liberation or of other too distant ambition, but on a world cured of its worst remediable deprivations and horrors. The goal should be modest or minimum utopia. This is a thesis I have suggested in passing once before in the pages of *Socialist Register*, defining minimum utopia as a form of society which could gener-ally provide for its members the material and social bases of a tolerably contented existence, or (put otherwise) from which the gravest social and political evils familiar to us have been removed.[6] Several reasons can be offered for thus limiting the horizon of left programmatic thinking for the time being.

The first and most important of these is simply that, could it but be achieved, minimum utopia would be a remarkable good in itself. To me the most compelling thing in Marxism – along with the broad truth of historical mate-rialism – has always been, not its most far-reaching perspective, but its most basic one. Today more than ever it provides a good enough vision to be getting on with. The world as it is and as it has been presents us with a picture of cruelty, slaughter, gross forms of exploitation and oppression, dire need. If we could hope to achieve merely – *merely* – a condition in which people had enough to eat, adequate water, shelter, health care, and the fundamental rights of expression, belief and assembly; and in which they were free from arbitrary imprisonment, torture, 'disappearance', threat of genocide; now wouldn't *that* be something. Even to articulate the thought is to bring home how remote this objective is. But why should any human being have to settle for less? Remote therefore as it may be, it is indeed the minimum, even while being utopia in a more than powerful enough meaning of the concept. To have only this: it would be humankind's most magnificent accomplishment. Note that insisting on minimum utopia as a political guideline, a sufficient practical objective, does not in itself entail any renunciation of the more maximal ingredients of the socialist vision. These can either wait, or some of them may take care of them-selves more or less. Others may turn out to have been misconceived. The question can just be left open. Relatively, it is of less importance.

A second reason is that we should not frame our projection of possible futures in terms that exclude the less benign, the more troublesome, features of the human make-up as it has revealed itself historically. Since I have argued this point before at length, I will be brief about it here. It is not a matter of denying the extent to which human beings can and do change – individually, historically, culturally – nor the scope there might be, consequently, for a radi-cally different human type, with different social and moral traits, in the dwellings and on the streets of a better future world. It is only a matter of cautioning against a too presumptive optimism in this regard: of drawing atten-tion to how much there is in ordinary and extraordinary experience alike, from the most familiar situations of daily life to the torture chambers and the killing fields, to suggest some enduring human limitations such as could continue to blemish and unsettle even the best-placed social order.[7]

Third, there is a more general reason for scepticism towards any vision composed only of shades of light and nothing darker. For it comes to us from the two extremes of reflection about the social world, both from thinking about utopia itself and from thinking about the lowest depths humanity has sunk to, that we cannot fully comprehend an idea of perfect or complete happiness, let alone deliberately aim for it. This is why pure utopias can seem so flat and dull, whatever the intentions of those designing them. They lack the necessary contrasts that in any actual world make the goods of life what they are, to be valued and striven for against the bads. It is a point that was argued by George Orwell in a pseudonymous essay about notions of utopia recently traced to his authorship: happiness is scarcely conceivable except by way of its juxtaposition – in life as in thought – with more problematic and ambiguous states.[8] At the same time Primo Levi, pondering for his part on his experiences at Auschwitz, expressed a similar truth in terms of mundane finitude and complexity. Perfect happiness and perfect unhappiness are equally unattainable, he wrote, the obstacles to them deriving from the human condition itself 'which is opposed to everything infinite'.

> Our ever-insufficient knowledge of the future opposes it: and this is called, in the one instance, hope, and in the other, uncertainty of the following day. The certainty of death opposes it: for it places a limit on every joy, but also on every grief. The inevitable material cares oppose it: for as they poison every lasting happiness, they equally assiduously distract us from our misfortunes and make our consciousness of them intermittent and hence supportable.

The elusive nature of happiness, Levi also wrote, arises from an incomplete knowledge of 'the complex nature of the state of unhappiness':

> so that the single name of the major cause is given to all its causes, which are composite and set out in an order of urgency. And if the most immediate cause of stress comes to an end, you are grievously amazed to see that another one lies behind; and in reality a whole series of others.[9]

The point of adverting to these observations is emphatically not one of fatalistic pessimism: as would seek to encourage, on account of run-of-the-mill facts of daily life, a resigned countenancing of the vaster avoidable evils that have plagued humankind. The point is only to get more sharply into focus that it is eliminating *these* evils, or levelling them as far as we can, that should be the prime contemporary objective of socialist thought and politics, and this does not require any whitened vision of a future existence frankly unrecognizable to us, if it is indeed desirable. Enough, for now, the known and more easily imaginable forms of human fulfilment.

6. MINIMUM UTOPIA IS A REVOLUTIONARY OBJECTIVE

The use of the language of 'minimum' and 'maximum' in the present context makes it necessary to forestall one possible misunderstanding that could arise from an older meaning of that distinction. Minimum utopia, as here envisaged, entails so fundamental a transformation of the existing structures of economic wealth and power and of the distributional norms relating to need, effort and reward that it is revolutionary in scope. This must be made explicit against an argument I anticipate roughly as follows: that formulated within, for example, a discourse of human rights, minimum utopia loses all socialist specificity; there is nothing in it that speaks against capitalism as such. For the achievements of capitalism, it will be said, and the reforms it has already accommodated, when set against the disasters witnessed in this century under the banner of socialism, make capitalism the better ground for minimum utopian aspirations.

Different lines of response are possible here, among which these. First, the comparison reverses an admonition of J. S. Mill's by contrasting actual (so-called) socialism with an idealized capitalism.[10] The latter's undoubted achievements are given to us as admirable and wholesome by the simple ruse of editing out of the picture the rolling catastrophe that capitalism has been for uncounted numbers of the world's population and continues to be to this day. It in no way minimizes the moral and political calamities for which the left – broadly, and despite its many currents and subdivisions – is answerable, to say that capitalism and its apologists are answerable for as much and of their own. Second, the presentation of this socio-economic form, virtually always by well-shod beneficiaries of it, in the guise of achievement and reformability is a piece of rank complacency that should be a cause for shame. Indeed it would be a cause for shame for most of them if its defenders ever had to stand naked, so to say, justifying their apologetic view to an audience of severely disadvantaged others, without benefit of the mediations and distances that usually protect them from this sort of encounter. So much, at least, is the force of contemporary 'discourse ethics', whatever its other problems. Third, with the complacency goes a manifestly one-sided form of patience: I mean patience towards a type of economic relation that has been with us for a few hundred years, unceasingly dealing out human misery together with its achievements, when the prospects of socialism, on the other hand, are discounted after one inauspiciously-placed and historically much briefer experiment gone wrong.

For the rest, the crucial issue here, concerning feasible economic models of minimum utopia, is one I cannot handle and so leave to others. The claim that there could not be, even with all the burgeoning facilities of today's information technology, anything better than capitalist economic organization and capitalist markets, I am content to meet with a simple counter-assertion. I don't believe it.

7. Minimum utopia is to be conceived not only as socialist but also as liberal

The aim of a minimum utopia is, then, anti-capitalist, but in so far as there are tenets of liberalism not indissolubly bound up with capitalism it should not be anti-liberal. This is a thesis likely to discountenance some socialists. Either they will associate it with an outlook that essentially redefines socialism as a reformed capitalism, an outlook, as I have just made clear, I do not share. Or they will have in mind other associations more repugnant still, thinking of liberalisms – the dominant ones in fact – with a tolerance for vast poverty and inequality, and which find it no problem that a footballer, rock musician or director of companies should be able to earn in the fraction of a life what most working people cannot hope for in a lifetime.

It has to be said, nevertheless, that liberalism historically has also been about trying to set limits to the accumulation and abuse of political power, about protecting the physical and mental space of individuals from unwarranted invasion, and about evolving institutions and practices, political and juridical, that contribute to such ends. That even here a concern for capitalist property has been amongst the motivating objectives does not undermine the more general value of these institutions and practices, and they should not be lightly set aside, whatever other institutional discontinuities may turn out to be necessary in achieving a more democratic and egalitarian social order. They should not be set aside, in particular, on the basis only of a present confidence in some future spontaneous harmony. The great evils we hope to be able to remedy include precisely evils against which liberal institutions have given some protection.

8. Embracing utopia means embracing an alternative ethics

A different moral culture would be required to create and sustain a condition of minimum utopia. In some ways this point will seem so obvious as not to be worth stating. Inhabiting a world used by millennia of practice and acculturation to the 'normality' of some people being able to live by the efforts of others, used, and ever more used, to the most flagrant inequalities, the coexistence of widespread want and suffering with an overflowing luxury, we look towards the possibility of a different and better world, one that would have set its face against this kind of thing and whose watchwords would encompass at least a rough equality. How even to formulate the contrast without supposing a marked change in the moral culture?

The point is only less obvious to the extent of there having been a resilient left tradition, for which Marxism bears much of the responsibility, of diminishing the place of specifically ethical discourses and ethical advocacy within the wider struggle for socialism. It may simply be noted, therefore, that if attempts to reshape moral consciousness are likely to be by themselves insufficient – a thought that was at the heart of classical Marxism in giving the priority it did to analysis of the social tendencies and agencies which might bring socialism about – it does not follow from this that attempts to reshape moral consciousness are unnecessary. In fact the task of finding a path from where we presently are to a planet on which some moderately decent norms have at last come to prevail is unthinkable without a transformation of values. It is improbable, too, that that transformation could be wholly the effect, and not also a contributory cause, of other necessary changes, social, economic and political. This is too mechanical a supposition. The very business of trying to identify, persuade and mobilize the more likely social constituencies of wider change is bound to involve fostering new forms of social consciousness, given how much present forms of it are influenced by prevailing practices. How can it make sense to envisage the desired change of consciousness as not centrally including a change in moral thinking? No serious case for socialism can now bypass the most direct and careful effort of moral persuasion.

I go on, finally, to propose what I see as two components of a minimum-utopian moral philosophy.

9. The moral universe we inhabit is (as if) governed by a contract of mutual indifference

The first component is negative. It consists of a critical characterization of the existing state of affairs. Here I put forward the gloomy proposition that we live in a world not only replete with injustices large and small and the most appalling horrors, but, what is nearly as bad, also oversupplied with a tolerance for such things on the part of most of those not suffering from them. I have tried to encapsulate this idea – the great tolerance people have for the sufferings of others, the living comfortably with them, the attitude of practical unconcern – in the hypothesis of a *contract of mutual indifference*. According to this, the relationship holding between most of the earth's inhabitants may be thought of as governed by the implicit agreement, 'in exchange for being released by you from any putative duty or expectation calling upon me to come to your aid in distress, I similarly release you'.[11] The core argument for imputing this agreement to people may be stated as follows. If you do not come to the aid of others who are under grave assault, in acute danger or crying need, you cannot reasonably expect others to come to your aid in similar emergency; you cannot consider them so obligated to you. Other people, equally, unmoved by the emergencies of others, cannot reasonably expect to be helped in deep trouble themselves, or consider others obligated to help them. Imagine, as a limit position, a world in which nobody ever came to the aid of anyone else under grave assault or cognate misfortune. Even though no formal agreement had been made between the individuals of this world to the effect that they owed one another, under threat or misfortune, nothing in the way of aid or care, the case for imputing such an agreement to them would be compelling. For, given their bystanding dispositions, no one could reasonably entertain a contrary expectation towards the generality of his fellows: along the lines, for example, 'even though I shall do nothing for others very unfortunately placed myself, nevertheless I think they would be obliged to help me and I shall look forward to their help should I ever need it.' No one could persuasively defend such an expectation to other people.[12]

Now, I do not say that the actual world is exactly like the one just described. There are obviously qualifications needed to that description. The most important of them is that people do also act altruistically; they act, at times, in sympathy or solidarity with others; they come to their aid or rescue. I have myself written about some brave examples of this.[13] I claim, even so, that the idea of a contract of mutual indifference captures rather too well the moral logic operating in the world in which we live. Most people, most of the time, do not do enough to oppose or remedy the moral enormities and enduring forms of wretchedness which they know about.

This is not an uplifting thesis, and in proposing it at length I have made a point of emphasizing that it is not.[14] Its unedifying character is evident from one type of response which it has elicited: namely, expressions of a plain scepticism and reluctance towards it. They are based – so far as any reasons have been articulated – on questioning the notion of an *imputed* agreement; and on questioning whether it is plausible to represent people as willing to accept a potentially self-damaging agreement like the one I hypothesize. Nobody venturing this response has yet troubled, however, to answer the argument set out above: to say how, doing nothing or very little to help others in grave difficulty when she could do something or a lot, a person might convincingly defend an expectation of help for herself when in grave difficulty.

The moral logic is discomfiting all right, but the mere discomfiture cannot show that it is not compelling in its way. Minimum utopia would have to rest upon an alternative moral logic.

10. MINIMUM UTOPIA PRESUPPOSES A PERVASIVE CULTURE OF MUTUAL AID

To achieve a minimum utopia we would need to find ways of overturning, reversing, the contract of mutual indifference so that a different ethic, an ideal of multivious care, could come to prevail. To be sure, some notion of this kind has always been implicit in socialist versions of utopia, whatever socialism's more unilaterally 'scientific' adherents might have reckoned to the contrary. The contrast between a society that would give proper weight to individual need and one regulated at every level by deep inequalities of wealth already tells us this to a degree. All the same, to the extent that the strategic focus of much socialist theorizing has been on economic and political structures and institutions and on how to change them, not enough attention has been devoted to exploring the specific contours of a socialist ethic. My final thesis is that the latter would have to incorporate – integrally – duties of aid and rescue, though I do not have space here to address the question of the scope and limits of such duties.[15]

We should not simply assume that the institutional framework, or a 'spontaneity' of attitudes arising from it, would suffice to result in the requisite behaviour on the part of individuals in a future utopia, all doing what was necessary to keep each other safe and well. Any set of projected minimum-utopian institutions is open to potential ruin if these are not actively supported and surrounded by a rich moral consciousness of the duty of care. This is in fact the principal burden of my hypothesis of the contract of mutual indifference: it brings out just how the structural and procedural provisions of a utopia, a projectedly good or well-ordered society, are rendered nugatory – actually ineffective, morally uncompelling – by the absence of a vigorous culture of reciprocal help to meet the threat and the incidence of violation. Such a vigorous moral culture will need a corresponding institutional framework in order to flourish, the framework of, among other things, a robust and self-active democracy; but the institutional framework will likewise depend upon the moral culture. Without it, it will either not come into being or not survive.

Intellectually, the road to minimum utopia goes by way of looking into the moral darkness.

CONCLUSION

In an essay composed now more than sixty years ago, Herbert Marcuse gave expression to a clear tension within left utopian thinking. Writing with Nazism triumphant in Germany, with Stalin's baleful regime consolidated in Russia as well as in the misguided loyalties of much of the international left, he posed a question that is unavoidable for anyone thinking inside the Marxist tradition, and so for 'critical theory', his chosen idiom there. 'What, however, if the development outlined by the theory does not occur?' Marcuse asked. 'What if the forces that were to bring about the transformation are suppressed and appear to be defeated?' He answered this question by continuing to insist, on the one hand, that critical theory 'always derives its goals only from present tendencies of the social process'; but by affirming also, on the other hand, that critical theory has no fear of accusations of utopia. It has no fear of them, he said, because what cannot be realized within the established social order 'always appears to the latter as mere utopia'. However, this very transcendence speaks in its favour rather than against it. 'Critical theory preserves obstinacy as a genuine quality of philosophical thought.'[16]

One must be careful, naturally. Obstinacy can be blind. But an obstinate utopianism is much needed against the potent forces of privilege and indifference. The issue – that is, the outcome between utopia and the brute persisting power of injustice – is ever uncertain. Still, Marcuse's answer remains more attractive half a century on than is a style of thought which, beginning from supposedly neutral general assumptions, ends by landing you in the thinker's own back yard. To be for hope.[17]

NOTES

1. Karl Marx and Frederick Engels, *Collected Works*, volume 6, London 1976, pp. 514–5.
2. See my 'Seven Types of Obloquy: Travesties of Marxism', in Ralph Miliband and Leo Panitch (eds), *Socialist Register 1990: The Retreat of the Intellectuals*, pp. 1–34.
3. Karl Marx, 'Preface' to *A Contribution to the Critique of Political Economy*, London 1971, pp. 21–2.
4. Leon Trotsky, *Literature and Revolution*, Ann Arbor 1960, p. 256.
5. C. L. R. James, *Beyond A Boundary,* London 1963, p. 206.
6. See Norman Geras, 'Socialist Hope in the Shadow of Catastrophe', in Leo Panitch (ed), *Socialist Register 1996: Are There Alternatives?* p. 259 (the essay's title is wrongly given on the cover and the contents page). Reprinted in my *The Contract of Mutual Indifference: Political Philosophy after the Holocaust*, London 1998 – see p. 116.
7. 'Socialist Hope in the Shadow of Catastrophe', pp. 239–63.
8. The essay appeared in *The Observer Review* for 28 June 1998. It was first published,

under the title 'Can Socialists Be Happy?', in the Christmas 1943 issue of *Tribune* and is included in Peter Davison (ed.), *The Complete Works of George Orwell*, London 1998.

9. Primo Levi, *If This is a Man, and The Truce*, London 1987, pp. 23, 79.
10. See John Stuart Mill, *Principles of Political Economy*, Book II, chapter 1, section 3
11. The present section draws on my *The Contract of Mutual Indifference: Political Philosophy after the Holocaust* (hereafter *CMI*), especially pp. 25–48. For the quoted formulation, see p. 43.
12. *CMI*, pp. 28–9.
13. See 'Richard Rorty and the Righteous Among the Nations', in Ralph Miliband and Leo Panitch (eds), *Socialist Register 1994: Between Globalism and Nationalism*, pp. 32–59. Reprinted in my *Solidarity in the Conversation of Humankind*, London 1995, pp. 7–46.
14. *CMI*, pp. 1, 40–41.
15. See *CMI*, pp. 49–77, where I do address this question.
16. 'Philosophy and Critical Theory', in Herbert Marcuse, *Negations: Essays in Critical Theory*, London 1968, pp. 142–3.
17. The positions taken in this essay draw on long (mostly e-mail) discussions and disagreements with my friend Eve Garrard, whom I accordingly thank.

ON THE NECESSITY OF CONCEIVING THE UTOPIAN IN A FEMINIST FASHION

Frigga Haug

THE FOLLOWING CONSIDERATIONS on the relationship between feminism and utopia are not presented as definitive. Feminism is far too diverse and utopian thinking far too disputed, to allow for this. Rather I approach the topic by pondering the specific importance of feminist ideas for political action and the importance specifically of feminist ideas in envisaging another society. In my opinion feminism needs to be understood in the context of liberation theory, and the utopian in the context of critical socialism and revolutionary 'realpolitik'. Being a resident of the previously divided, currently old and new Germany, requires me also to consider certain local particularities.

In addressing the relation between utopia and feminism I find myself in a paradoxical situation because feminism is for me already a political utopia, the idea of abolishing domination and the wish to do so, to reach a goal where what everyone has in common is also common to everyone. The fact that I naturally identify feminism with utopia may seem peculiar. Doesn't utopia have to do with wishes, visions, that is, with irrationality and, if this is true, do reasonable plans, suggestions, and criticism not suffice when we are dealing with societal changes, especially in the case of women? The answer seems to me as certain as the interconnection between feminism and utopia: the situation of women today is so muddled and patriarchy is so solid, so alive and well, that improvements in the here and now do not suffice. We have to look back and devise something new, and then from this different perspective, we will be able to make suggestions for today and tomorrow. As Virginia Woolf put it in her novel, *The Three Guineas*, '. . . we can best help you prevent war not by repeating your words and following your methods but by finding new words and creating new methods.'[1]

1. From Early Utopias to Scientific Socialism

We need to be aware of the development of utopian thought in order to have a platform from which – and in contrast to which – we can think about the utopian in a feminist fashion. We need at least a somewhat clear under-standing of the relation between desire, illusion, and realistic, reasonable politics. Committed to the tradition of liberation theory, I am concerned with the relationship of utopian thought to scientific analysis and criticism, in order to locate the feminist in this context.

Due to adversities in their everyday lives, human beings (women as well as men) flee in their dreams to more desirable worlds. Early utopias (More, Proudhon) portray a simple reversal of the customary: eternal youth, an abun-dance of food, luxuries without value, and gold and gems which are no longer the basic unit in terms of which worth is measured. Wise conversations, perpetual festivities, the portrayal of beauty, and, most importantly, the abolition of suffering born of domination and exploitation. Criticism of this world flies in the imagination to another place, a non-place or utopia, which at the same time should be home. This occurs in fairy tales, stories, paintings, and utopian novels.

The first criticism of utopian thought which can be taken seriously, and which I need to call to mind in my search for the specifics of feminist-utopian thought, came from Marx and Engels. In their attempt to mobilize the current forces in society, they shifted the focus and intention of utopian thinking. Socialism as the turn 'from utopia to science' had two purposes: to integrate fleeting wishes with precise criticism, and to examine both history and life in order to determine what was humanly possible. They intended to discover the 'elements of the new society' in the old one, and to discern the making of an emancipated society out of the contradictions of present conditions; and what they discovered and discerned was to be supported. For this they required a scientific approach. Political strategies need prior analysis and critique. The wings of desire were to be linked to human action. This of course included criticism of these desires as criticism of present conditions, since even dreams bear the traces of domination and subjugation; i.e., criticism of the conditions of individuals in their ties with the quotidian. Wishes should fall from the weightless heavens to be mobilized for the remodelling of society. One concentrates no longer on setting and imagining the specificities of a new social order but instead begins collecting the building blocks for new paths to a new order. Only vague contours, or rather intentions, are specified: freedom from domination, the unfolding of human nature in its various manifestations, collective self-determination and great wisdom.

2. Farewell to Socialism?

What became of the critique of political economy in 'official' Marxism is generally well-known: a self-assured confidence that one was on the right path. Abandoning utopia in favour of 'science' came to mean reducing the abun-dance of desires to what had already been achieved. The solution was: they are always fulfilled. One way of achieving this was by disciplining desires to conform with the reasons of state, for example through the medium of television, which brought the far-off into the living room.

In protest at how the designers of 'actually existing' socialism dealt with the utopian, Bloch wrote early on: 'It appeared that one had already discovered the tendency of being, that is, that one had already arrived beyond it.'[2] Bloch's *The Principle of Hope* attempted to merge the force of human desires with analytic, scientific critique. Anticipation, walking erect, liberation, fulfilment, references to utopia, dreams of the future, and the 'shining through' of what was to come – Bloch's work is full of evocative words that seek magnetically to hold open the possibility of liberation in the 'not-yet'. Bloch was expelled from East Germany. The country collapsed a little more than a quarter of a century later.

Conventional talk about the loss of political utopia as a consequence of the collapse of the 'actually existing' socialist regimes is characteristically at odds with the actual course of events, even if this is in some ways understandable. Even if we ignore the difference between utopian and scientific socialism, talk about the loss of utopia mourns the fact that the 'hereafter' has been stolen, or that the chance of creating another world has been done away with for good, whereas in reality we are dealing with a much more unusual situation, namely that the utopian has ceased to appear grounded in this world. Or to put it another way: the collapse of the formerly socialist countries frees desires and wishes which were confined to those petty conditions and restores them to the status of hopes for a shining future and plans for liberation; and last but not least, the force of scientific analysis is also set free. The critique of capitalism becomes more urgent than ever, both questions about what causes crises and catastrophes, and where elements of a new humane, just, and ecologically benign society may be found. Social development would once again be driven by the hope and fantasy of a world in which it would not only be possible to live, but even desirable.

The question of why we need political utopia seems easy to answer. Without the hope that the world can be changed and without being able to place oneself in a movement for change, it is difficult to live; at most it is merely possible to survive. The continuous present, a life without future expectations, becomes stifling apathy. People have to be sure of their history in order to ensure their future. But as soon as we leave the abstract generality of humankind and enter the concrete arena of two genders, several urgent additional questions appear in this almost-too-simple account of the necessity of utopian political thought.

3. UTOPIA IN GENDER RELATIONS

I read literary feminist utopias. Dreams of liberated reproduction stand obstinately in the foreground. Children grow on trees, being a mother is a matter of collective welfare without biological limitations, freedom from domination is guaranteed (there are no masters of destruction), female cultures thrive in sensuous abundance. Borders and walls alone bear witness to the existence of another world, proof that liberation has not been possible for all humankind.

Whereas in these novels the walls are supposed to prevent the onslaught of the unfree, since the fall of the Berlin Wall in 1989 it appears that those who were formerly locked up have access to the utopia of the promised land of the West. Capitalism as utopia? In the general confusion attending the collapse of 'actually existing' socialism, it seemed necessary to make a rush for the good life. Yet women still seem to be at a loss on both sides of the former borders. How is it possible that the 'realization' of utopia in 'actually existing' socialism and the more recent 'realization' of capitalism could end in a double defeat of the female sex? Where did the desire for liberation lead to, and where will it end up?

Let us begin the other way around. Can feminist utopia gain anything from the collapse of the old 'actually existing' socialist utopia? Dealing with such questions is difficult because our thoughts must execute complicated leaps: moving backwards and forwards between the critique of the botched reforms of 'actually existing' socialism and the critique of both its and capitalism's blindness as regards gender relations.

Nationalization, by focusing on the abolition of the ownership of the means of production, caused other forms of domination to become invisible. The expression 'command-administrative' tried to capture the impossibility of liberation in a system of production and administration in which decisions were imposed from above on the desires of the subordinated. But this expression contains no criticism of the maleness of such a system, nor does its implicit utopia point to the emancipation of women. Yet in the collapse of this system some images become visible. They point to a more radical and all-inclusive political utopia. We can learn from this.

The fate of women in the transition from 'patriarchal-administrative' socialism to capitalist conditions is in many ways characteristic. As Westerners we know what awaits women in our own society; and we also knew that the position of women in the other system was no worse than ours, rather they possessed confident expectations for the future. Women were, for example, economically independent of male providers, and there was also a cultural climate that was decidedly less sexist than ours. When we now realize that in the general chaos patriarchal patterns are taking root again in the East, we complain about the lack of a resistant feminist utopia. Yet writers in the GDR articulated far-reaching feminist plans – Irmtraud Morgner, Christa Wolf, Monika Maron, Helga Königsdorf, just to name a few. Why was there then no widespread feminism, or too little thereof?

4. Feminism and Utopia

It is time for me to better define my understanding of feminism: it represents a complicated and specific stand-point, yet at the same time it includes a universal human perspective. The feminist point of view questions equating humankind in general with maleness, and it challenges the assumption that the particularity of the female means that the female is naturally separated from the rest of humankind. Nevertheless, a new perspective which includes both sexes can only be formulated taking this ascribed particularity into account, because false universalism has to be disproved and replaced by a real universalism. In this way feminism becomes a transcendent political utopia which also leaves its traces in the here and now.

My claim is this: one of the effects of the development of 'patriarchal–administrative' socialism was to make the equation of humankind with 'man' invisible in such a way that socialist perspectives not only were reduced to 'it is fulfilled', but also concealed the narrow-mindedness of such an equation. The wreckage of 'actually existing' socialism also unveils this aspect of domination in the 'not-yet'.

The system perished not only due to economic problems but also due to a lack of democracy. Initiative began to flag. Another sign of decline was the decay and dilapidation of the cities and the fact that ecological problems had assumed alarming proportions. Many share this criticism. From a feminist perspective I query whether all of these problems are not simply the necessary corollary of patriarchal structures and whether the continuous reproduction of these structures can be prevented by anything other than the liberation of women. Universal tutelage begins with the justification of tutelage over women. This is part and parcel of societies whose ruling principle is the ever more efficient production of the means of life, and not the humanization of life, rather than ones for which such economism would be a means to an end, but not an end in itself. This reversal of priorities has caused damage to humans and their natural surroundings for which brigades of repairers are desperately needed. But an ecological response that merely reverses such economism would mean a government that made decisions so that the earth could be protected for generations to come, but also a continued tutelage over women so that they were willing to selflessly care for human beings and their environment without thought of personal gain or wage benefits.

Although Marxist utopian thought intended to 'resurrect the body', to unfold the senses, to reach the highest level of individuality, to revoke the state, and to create a human-to-human relationship which was to be made visible in the relations between the sexes, this intention was reduced to a concrete analysis of domination. In *Capital* Marx saw how the former money-owner, now a capitalist, striding towards the factory 'smirks self-importantly and is intent on business' as Marx aptly described it; and behind him the worker, who only owns his capacity to work, is 'timid and holds back, like someone who has brought his own hide to market and now has nothing else to expect but – a tanning.'[3] Yet Marx was here only observing the work-place outside of the home, otherwise he would have noted that the procession was not over at this point and that behind the worker, off to one side, stood his wife, carrying the household shopping, a baby on her arm.[4] And we have also to add the fact that behind the smiling capitalist stands *his* wife as a cultural creation whose bodily existence lets him forget his own bodilyness to the extent that in his focus on growth and profits he can be indifferent to life.

Even those who adopted a socialist perspective in the labour movement after Marx did not put all human beings and the care of their offspring and future in the foreground. In so far as women were worth a political effort, this only involved making them similar to men, improving their efficiency and performance and including them in gainful employment. Industrialization of the household was the most progressive maxim; later an attempt was made to improve house-work with technical appliances and to demand the substitution of state-run organizations for the household so that women could combine career and family. This entailed not only representing and administering women, it spoke from the male point of view and from the perspective of industrialized production when considering women's work and women's lives. Just as the husband reluctantly does a few chores in the household, in the same manner industrialization of the household was conceived as taking care of a duty, not as humanization. The dream of a humankind that is loving, that acts in solidarity with one another, and that is creative and sensual, disappears in the effective fulfilment of the necessary. There is no time for anything above and beyond this.

It is clearly not enough just to pull women out of the domains in which they do the unrecognized and unrewarded work of keeping us human in order to make possible such a one-dimensional productive world – all of society like a single factory. It would be equally senseless to look for a solution to the problems of humankind merely by merging the gender roles. In their limitation to one gender each both men and women are deficient. A utopia that sees itself as feminist aims at the abolition of 'genders', just as a socialist utopia would hope for an abolition of classes. On the individual level this means that feminine human beings must experience themselves first as humans before they can relate as women to others; culturally it means destroying the whole network of gendering which cuts across our societies; and structurally, it would then be time to join the diverse interests, represented at present by the single genders and which are usually seen as separate domains, in such a way that social, ecological, and cultural development becomes the goal and not an unlikely by-product. This is the only possible transformational work – and at the same time the only kind of work indispensable for our survival – that requires utopian thinking. For this reason utopia enters the realm of reality. It can only be formulated through a feminism that is both resistance and at the same time, a pursuit of happiness. 'Between the deadly end of history and the utopically-visualized end of the humanity's prehistory stands the necessity of interventionary thinking/acting that is militant-optimistic, that critiques ideology yet is utopian, that is conscious and willed, that is realistic yet hopes for the possible, and that is anti-capitalist/anti-patriarchal.'[5]

5. LACK OF UTOPIA: MEMORY OF THE FUTURE

'Heretics/Witches: encourage humans not to let themselves fall into the movement of catastrophe, but to give their individual life shape in the chaos, and to confront the chaos with this shape day by day.'[6]

The case for feminist-utopian thinking collides with the reality of contemporary disillusionment. A threat that long seemed speculative has now arrived: commodity society and its restrictions have corroded the capacity for dreaming and conceiving of utopia.

Let us remember where we came from, where we intend to go, and who we are. Justice is one thing for which we long: for this we need solidarity; and the greatest thing of all, joy, requires love. Our wishes are not immodest, yet still they shrink in the course of our lives, appear too great; the conditions for reaching them appear unachievable, and our own interventions hard to conceive. Who are we as women, who should be responsible for love and solidarity, that we have so little power to accomplish and assert these goals?

Renouncing our wishes, cutting them back to a degree of mediocrity, and resignation, are poor companions for necessary and desirable interventions. What good does the spirit of utopia do us today? Can we place hope in the power of anticipatory wishes? How great is our disappointment over the worsening reality that mocks such wishes as mere dreams when they are just beginning to be envisioned.

I have tried as a teacher to encourage students to envision their own utopias. The result: the wishes that they expressed went no further than hoping that the most urgent problems of their everyday lives could be solved. Kindergartens, a functioning and inexpensive public transportation system, enough affordable apartments – it is as if, in the absence of social democracy for over a decade, social democratic reforms have taken the place of utopias. What remains is the fact that even the ability to conceive of something utopian has to be relearned. A possible means of remembering the future is reading literary utopias. Let us take a second look.

6. FEMINST-UTOPIAN LITERATURE

Instead of giving an overview of several feminist utopias, I will explain and theorize just one, in order to sharpen our thoughts and stimulate our fantasies. In this way I would like to suggest a 'utopian project' which I have named *Joy and Justice*, and which should be understood as both utopia and relevant to the here and now. I will be dealing with the novel *He, She and It* (1997) by the American author Marge Piercy. I will be concentrating on the role of the future, the past, and of women; in addition to this I will consider gender relations as relations of production.

The Future

I do not enjoy reading science-fiction novels in which the development of computers is linearly and fantastically extrapolated: they usually end up being dystopias, or stories about the inhumanity of technology and the perfecting of domination and control. There is no way out. In addition to this, they often confirm my 'feminine' prejudice that home must be found in the 'natural' and not in the 'technical'. In this way Piercy's book has somewhat of a shock effect.

It is the year 2059. Due to a terrorist assault the accumulated human arsenal of weapons has exploded. The earth is almost entirely devastated and contaminated. Twenty-three corporations ('multis') have divided up the rest of the earth and share several satellites that afford artificial living-spaces. These are air-conditioned and protected and are only inhabited by technical experts who are in charge of running the place and furthering the development of the multis. The rest of humankind, as far as it still exists, vegetates and works in the contaminated zones. The companies' satellites are completely computerized and controlled, right down to the design of humans, who are not only all subjugated to the same culture of business but who also are made to look alike, as well as be as fit and youthful as possible, through surgical intervention. Gender relations are organized differently than today. Both sexes have the same jobs and the way in which one reproduces is up to the individual: that is, they can opt for test-tube babies or women can decide to carry through with a pregnancy. Espionage, ruthless competition, and crime prevail in the struggle between the multis.

The Past

One of the contrasting scenarios in the novel is of the survivors of the Jewish ghetto in Prague. Piercy travels back to the end of the sixteenth century and tells the story of the constant persecution, imprisonment, and expulsion of the Jews and of the wishes and dreams of many, and of the wisdom of a few. The way the story is told begins to change. The short bytes of the computer language are left behind and we come to the stuff of myths and legends and the dream that humans will some day be able to create other humans that possess much-needed and sought-after abilities. This is of course a male dream, in which the twenty-first century is directly linked to the sixteenth: a creature of spirit and earth, combined and formed in the right way, could be entrusted with the most important duties, could solve the most urgent problems, and could relieve suffering. The wise man of the twenty-first century is an engineer, the oldest in this modern earthly ghetto which is organized in a seemingly socialist way. He adapts to the expansionist drive of the multis by producing software for them. His ancestor in the Prague ghetto was able to create a Golem who possessed extraordinary physical strength; the engineer of the twenty-first century has constructed a Cyborg that is similar to a human being but is unlimited in his ability to learn and in his thirst for knowledge, who needs no sleep and is so intelligent that he can protect the community single-handedly. Juxtaposing a history of the future after ecological catastrophe and the consummation of the microelectronics age to the history of the Jews in Prague has a strange effect. The past becomes familiar, and in this way so does the future.

The spirit of utopia, so we gather from the story, gains its strength from the 'not-yet' of the past, both in relation to the unfulfilled desires of the past, and in relation to the domination that began then. Its vision of the future includes the memory of the costs of human experience in the past as a historical force that must enter our consciousness.

Gender Relations

Piercy's point of view is feminist. In this way she can uncompromisingly link the development of humankind to the history of patriarchy. It is one of her encouraging strengths that she neither displays patriarchy as something purely evil nor pretends it doesn't exist; rather she portrays it as a solution to the problems of regulating life in a community which has now arrived at a catastrophic finish. The wise Maharal of the sixteenth century created a Golem who, with his extraordinary strength, was able to fend off enemies like a 'one man army'. In the twenty-first century a Cyborg needs extraordinary intelligence. At the same time, the inventor fulfils his wish, as a father, to have a son who, unlike his real one, has not fallen prey to the realm of illusions but, having no needs of his own has only one desire, that is to learn and accumulate abstract knowledge. The same intelligence that brought forth these inventions finally becomes flesh and blood. In order to be accepted and recognized as human (which is necessary in order to serve as a guardian), the Cyborg needs social virtues. Piercy lets a woman appear on the scene who is the engineer's equal, and who, in addition to the abstract masculine virtues, programmes the Cyborg with a bit of feminine 'confusion' for good measure. She teaches the Cyborg to love and to focus his eagerness to learn as emphatically on human beings as on abstract knowledge.

A necessary dimension of any dream of liberation must be the overturning of patriarchy. In Piercy's novel the solution to this problem is even somewhat humorous because she combines the one-sidedness of the sexes in such a way that the original goals are subverted. The child of masculine rational omniscience and the already-realized domination of technology becomes irrational thanks to feminine technological prowess; the price technology has to pay in order to fulfil its goal is its own demise. The logic of pure technical domination needs to be overcome. Competence combined with equal rights for both sexes, the preservation of a certain difference, and the skilful combination of both will make this possible.

Women

Three women are central figures in Piercy's novel: the grandmother, the mother and the daughter. Each of them is entwined in societal chores, each is sensual in her own way, each lives under different conditions. All three are unbelievably competent and qualified, so that they can invest their energies with enthusiasm; without some sort of activity they would most likely lose their sense of purpose. All three actively resist the power of the multis in different ways. The grandmother builds security systems and develops the much–needed software which is the small commune's primary export product. The mother, a name for her that is so inappropriate that it constantly causes one to rethink what mothers are, is an 'information pirate', or hacker. She is a much sought-after criminal, because she frees information from private ownership and makes it available to the general population – for example the formulae of medicines, etc. In an unusual way the daughter represents romantic love, the longing for a family, and in doing so develops a project, out of love for a Cyborg, that makes it impossible for machines to be created with emotions.

An indispensable element of feminist utopias appears to be that positive female figures populate the society: women who are not merely role models, who are not merely active, interventionist, clever, attractive and strong, but women who also take on the dreams and longings that we have today, and live them and fuse them together, so that we can imagine ourselves in these figures.

Relations of Production

Piercy's novel is poetic and theoretically consistent. Domination, control and profit are the goals of the multis, armed with an apparatus of knowledge. The competitive logic of capital has apparently come to an end and yet capital continues to determine the lives of those who have jobs in accordance with the goals of profit – everyone else is human garbage, organized in anarchic, murderous gangs and at the mercy of the ecologically devastated earth. In this way the novel plays out the victory of neoliberal politics to its disastrous conclusion. Even on this destroyed earth there are signs of resistance. But since the old patterns of gender relations are used in order to achieve domination (for example the form of marriage with the possibility of allowing a company to raise one's child) liberation is not possible until both sexes unite their respective strengths as equals.

The present is not devalued in favour of a fictional future; rather the author makes it possible to extract something useful from everyday life. The various and overlapping systems of dominance, as well as the continuing desire of humans for love and justice over several centuries, are made visible. The strength of this literary utopia is, last but not least, the loving and passionate attitude of the author to the world. In this way history and future become present, old-age can be deciphered as experience and wisdom, and the different and the common are deciphered as a force with which our dreams can be transformed into interventionary praxis.

7. POLITICS FOR A NEW GENDER CONTRACT

Finally, I will attempt to anchor the utopian in 'realpolitik'. For this I have chosen the politically discredited liberal concept of the contract. My claim, but also my hope, is that when both sexes begin to view critically the relations in which they live, they will also realize that not only their own, but that all social relations, need to be urgently changed. This sentence assumes the following: (1) that in the dynamic of gender relations lies the possibility of change breaking out; (2) that changes in the relations of production and in the relations between the sexes are worth striving for from the point of view of both sexes; (3) that a revolt in the societal and political landscape is, after all, imaginable.

Since the market seems to have become the only instrument that has universal validity for regulating global society, and since this development has caused a continuous weakening of politics and the welfare state, at least in the western industrial countries, the theorem of the social contract, like the idea of the contract in general, gains relevance once again. The discourse of the social contract refers to the sphere of the political, that is, to the assumption that under conditions of conflicting interests a good society requires consensus, compromises and concessions on the part of its members. The focus on the market does not exclude the idea of a social contract; on the contrary, market and exchange are based on contracts freely made between those who deal on the market. The idea of the contract is liberal and seems to work best when the contract partners are understood as free individuals. But those contracts which in the course of the last decade have entered into a state of crisis are collective contracts, namely those between generations, between labour and capital, between present and future and, finally, between the sexes. In so far as a social contract cannot be articulated in neoliberal thinking, this is the moral deficit of the neoliberal project.

The struggle surrounding the social contract, despite its conservative flavour, contains dimensions of disobedience and resistance. This will certainly become clear when labour and other movements which defend the welfare state are strengthened by incorporating the problem of gender relations – although doing so will also cause them problems. For it is incontrovertible that the genders are locked in a contract embodied in both material and cultural practices. Gender relations today are essentially based on a kind of division of labour, allocating to each separate competencies and responsibilities in society; in the current state of unrest, these relations can be modernized and become a putative solution for socially-produced contradictions. On the one hand the so-called 'house-wife' of Western Europe seems, since the 1970s, to have made way for more dynamic models resulting from women's demands for employment and autonomy. On the other hand these shifts seem to have remained rather superficial because the general consensus is that increasing unemployment should be accepted without significant protest and in large part at the expense of women. In Germany at least, the word 'double earner' is used in connection with the refusal of jobs to women who already have a husband who has one. Not only does the resistance to quotas (also a form of contract) for women in politics, economics and science remain stubborn, but, conversely, the fight for quotas is weakened by a general cultural consensus that we have more important, more existential problems. And in the deregulation undertaken by all western governments for the purpose of improving national competitiveness – otherwise known as the dismantling of the welfare state – it is, as we have already said, silently assumed that in the ensuing social calamities, the nurturing figures of unemployed women will turn up to take care of children, youth, the elderly, the handicapped, the sick, the unemployed, the mentally disabled, etc., etc. Against all probability, the hope and consensus remains that women have such a sense of responsibility for the living and that they can and should honour it. To the extent that women continue to submit themselves to this without any significant resistance, they contribute to accepting as a humanly tenable social project the current practice of subordinating society to the economic imperatives of a tiny minority.

Under a new gender contract the social project would have to be discussed anew in order to reap the present from utopia. I don't imagine that division of labour contracts will be concluded, nor that gender relations are ready for reinvention, but rather that current gender relations, because they help to block a change in a social order striving for profits and unsustainable growth, will be put back on the public agenda. It is first of all a question of concluding a contract with the future, of making the question of the next generation – the reproduction of the human species and the problem of how and under what conditions the next generation should grow up – into a political question. What the next generation will be like is extremely important for civil society, since that generation represents not only the far off future but is already part of the present. The responsibility for the coming generation, as in the current domestic division of labour, should under no circumstances be left to women, since the latter can in no way bear such responsibility. This is so because in the last analysis this responsibility comprises questions of education, nutrition, the environment, resources, and city planning, etc. We can concretise the problem by equating it to all questions of the political and economic which are now regulated in ways that are largely incompatible with the future of humankind. Cancelling the existing gender contract in which women are absurdly made responsible for the future, although they in no way have the requisite competence or power, does not mean that they should simply be fitted into the wage labour sector, with equal entitlements, leaving undone all unpaid, voluntary, and neglected work. After us the flood. It means rather really taking over these responsibilities and conquering the corresponding domains of power and competence in order to do so. What we now need is another division of power and labour that must negotiate another vision of society, set new priorities and situate the genders in a different way. It seems to me indisputable that men must take part in attaining this different goal. This would be just the beginning of a humane society.

Public discussions which could take place practically everywhere should be utilized as a learning process so that a general plan for a society in which it would be worth living would be made more concrete, with the addition of realistic and individual demands. A good beginning would be to come to an agreement about socially necessary work, which must include the care of offspring, and for this reason also the environment as one of the living conditions of future generations. In any case it would be a society that was politically different, with different priorities which, as we know from earlier utopias, would hold the mirror up to the current state of things with inventive and socially critical intentions.

The concept of the contract would be useful in more ways than one. In a socially critical sense it is a utopian perspective which admonishes current politics. If we radicalize and sharpen current problems by including gender relations in our critique in a fundamental way, there appears on the horizon a society that distinguishes itself completely in its goals and in negating everyday domination.

The essential criteria of regulation would no longer be profit and growth but rather priorities that dealt with our present and future life, and with the reproduction of the species, that is, with questions of the future. The way time is used becomes an essential question, although the concept of 'usage' loses its utilitarian content and becomes a question of the quality of life. The division of labour becomes a question of justice and variety. It would be senseless to turn all work, including domestic work, into wage labour; instead we should separate all work from income. The possibility that in a society in which everyone works there would be still be those who could not support themselves, becomes unthinkable. Quotas, which used to be a political aim, would become a perfectly natural premise of a society in which the decoupling of work and income would be internalized by its members and would lose its dogmatic character. On this basis it becomes possible to envision a society which is both a women's project and a utopia. There are enough sources of inspiration. In current 'realpolitik' the concept of the social contract becomes a form of compromise and of state intervention. In the vision advanced here, there would be quotas for women in every area of work, and quotas for men in areas of reproduction and social work – including the right of both sexes to work and take part in politics, as well as to the education and training needed to be able to do both.

Since every previous analysis has assumed that the sexes have differing standpoints and positions in society, and that gender relations are intertwined with the relations of production, we must also assume that the sexes are collective actors that must consensually negotiate a new social contract. In doing so both sexes may have to win and lose some things in order for the society as a whole to survive. The negotiating of such contracts, the struggles and the planning would politicize the public sphere. But this need not mean a tug-of-war between the sexes. The current crisis needs to be discussed in such a way that the fact that current social relations – in this case relations between the sexes – are complicit in the unsustainable conditions that have led to it becomes obvious – just as obvious as both sexes' potential for participating actively in the remaking of society. The prerequisite is that we realize that we actually live in a patriarchal capitalism which has now even made survival into a private affair. This is what needs to be turned from standing on its head back on to its feet – and this would be feminist utopia.

NOTES

1. Woolf (1938: 143)
2. Bloch (1953: 27)
3. Marx (1977: 280)
4. See Hartsock (1983: 234)
5. Barbara Holland-Cunz (1988: 12)
6. Irmtraud Morgner (1988: 154)

REFERENCES

Bloch, Ernst, 1953: *Prinzip Hoffnung,* Berlin; 1973: Frankfurt/M, Suhrkamp Verlag; 1986: *The Principle of Hope,* Oxford, Blackwell Publishers.

Hartsock, Nancy, 1983: *Money, Sex and Power. Toward a Feminist Historical Materialsm.* New York, London.

Haug, Frigga, 1990: Tagträume. Dimensionen weiblichen Widerstands. In: Dies. Erinnerungsarbeit. Berlin und Hamburg; 1990: 2. Aufl.; 1994: Argument-Verlag.

Holland-Cunz, Barbara, 1988: *Utopien der neuen Frauenbewegung. Gesellschaftsentwürfe im Kontext feministischer Theorie und Praxis.* Meitingen, Corian-Verlag Wimmer.

Königsdorf, Helga, 1978, 1990: *Meine ungehörigen Träume:* Geschichten, Berlin/Weimar, Aufbau-Verlag; 1989: *Respektloser Umgang,* Berlin/Weimar, Aufbau-Verlag; 1989: *Die geschlossenen Türen am Abend.* Erzählungen, Frankfurt a. Main, Luchterhand Literatur-Verlag.

Le Guin, Ursula, 1981: *The Dispossessed,* München; neue überarbeitete Ausgabe, Hamburg 1998: Argument-Verlag; 1979: *Planet of exile,* London, Gollanz.

Marx, Karl und Friedrich Engels, *Deutsche Ideologie,* MEW 3 dies., Der Sozialismus von der Utopie zur Wissenschaft.

Marx, Karl, *Manuskripte 1844,* MEW EB I.

Marx, Karl: *Das Kapital.* MEW 23; 1977: *Capital,* Volume One. New York, Vintage.

Morgner, Irmtraud, 1973: *Leben und Abenteuer der Trobadora Beatriz nach Zeugnissen ihrer Spielfrau Laura,* Aufbau Verlag Berlin/DDR; 1983: *Amanda, Ein Hexenroman,* Aufbau Verlag Berlin; 1998: *Das Heroische Testament.* Roman in Fragmenten. Aus nachgelassenen Papieren zusammengestellt, kommentierend begleitet von Rudolf Bussmann, Luchterhand, München.

Piercy, Marge, 1996: *Frau am Abgrund der Zeit.* Neu überarbeitete Übersetzung, Berlin und Hamburg; 1979: *Woman on the Edge of Time,* London, Women's Press; 1993: *Er, Sie und Es.* Berlin und Hamburg, Argument-Verlag; 1991: *He, She and It: A Novel,* Ballantine Books.

Wolf, Christa, 1975: *Nachdenken über Christa T.,* Aufbau Verlag, Berlin und Weimar, engl. *The Quest of Christa T.,* London, Virago Press; 1983: *Kassandra,* Darmstadt und Neuwied, Luchterhand; 1984: *Cassandra a Novel and Four essays,* London, Virago Press; 1996: *Medea,* Luchterhand, Gütersloh; 1998: *Medea,* London, Virago Press.

Woolf, Virginia, 1938: *Three Guineas,* London, Harcourt.

SOCIALIZING MARKETS, NOT MARKET SOCIALISM

DIANE ELSON

NOW, MORE THAN EVER, we are in need of visions of a different kind of future, a future in which people are liberated from the restriction, distortion, and exploitation of their capacities; and can develop new, egalitarian, forms of community, solidarity and democracy. But we have to steer a difficult course between heroic fantasies, on the one hand, and mechanistic blueprints, on the other. We need imagination – but imagination that has not lost touch with the practical realities of everyday material life.

We want to create new forms of collectivity – but the history of our century has taught us terrible lessons about how collectivities that are not rooted in respect for individual human rights create new forms of restriction, distortion and exploitation of human capacities. So we need to envision a better future in a humble and sober spirit, building upon the glimpses of alternatives that are rooted in our current experience, rather than all-encompassing schemes for social engineering. But at the same time, we need to resist the limitations of the present and the fantasy that an accommodation with big business can deliver a fully human society.

Socialism has always abounded in visions of a life free from the pressure of capitalist market forces, whether in self-sufficient local communities or in democratically planned economies. However, on the whole those visions have not sufficiently taken into account the limitations of small communities or the problems of democratic planning of whole economies. One response has been to construct blueprints of market socialism, in which property is collectively owned or distributed on an egalitarian basis, but enterprises engage in market transactions pretty much as they do in capitalist economies. Another response is to explore ways in which market transactions can themselves be reshaped, and markets can be socialized, so that people are not confronted with anonymous, uncontrolled, market forces, but can nevertheless enjoy the benefits of decentralization that market transactions can bring. A focus on decentralization is particularly important for envisioning ways in which new forms of community, solidarity and democracy can be international. A series of autarchic local or national economies would constrict and confine people in the development of their capacities. The problem with 'globalization' is not that it is international, but that it is a one-sided internationalism that operates mainly in favour of big business.

This paper is a contribution to the exploration of the path between *the plan* and *the market*, to envisioning not blueprints for market socialism, but possibilities for socializing markets. Markets and money are potentially useful social inventions that predate capitalism, but they always bear the imprint of structures of economic power. During the course of capitalist development, markets and money were subordinated to the dynamic of production for profit and capital accumulation. Markets became institutions through which surplus value is appropriated and realized as private profit. Money became a form of capital, and prices came to incorporate a mark-up, over and above costs of production, so as to generate an unearned income for the owners of capital. Commodities appear in this circuit primarily as vehicles for capital accumulation, not as use values. Money values dominate. This paves the way for the development of purely financial markets, in which financial instruments (shares, bills, bonds, derivatives) are traded at prices which may bear little relation to the underlying situation of the real economy.[1]

The way forward in the twenty-first century is not to dream of schemes for eliminating markets and money; but to envision ways of reclaiming and transforming markets and money, so that they become a means of facilitating mutually beneficial exchange, based on a mutually beneficial division of labour, in an economy with an egalitarian distribution of economic power. This means embedding markets in egalitarian social relations, which in turn means exploring ways of transforming the property relations that underlie and shape the current configurations of market institutions. This will require building upon already-existing contradictions and dissonance in capitalist markets, and developing already-existing creative initiatives to socialize markets.

These claims are controversial, and already some readers will be bristling with indignation, or shaking their heads in disbelief ('what can the editors be thinking of to publish this?'). Let me reassure them that if they read on, they will not find an argument for envisioning markets (in whatever form) as the principal, and predominant form, of organizing relations between producers and users; but rather an argument for recognizing that for some goods and services, relations between producers and users will be better organized through socialized markets than through other means. For instance, we certainly need a vision that includes, for each country, a national health service, free at the point of delivery; but a national clothing service would be absurd.

The perceptive reader will have realized that I have been referring to 'markets' not 'the market'. The point of departure for my argument is that we must get away from the monolithic abstraction of 'the market', and instead talk of markets (in the plural), which can be organized through a variety of institutions, to serve a variety of ends.[2] This enables us to distinguish between markets which are commercially organized, typically linking anonymous producers with anonymous consumers so as to make as much profit for shareholders as possible; and markets which are socially organized so as to realize mutually agreed egalitarian objectives, respecting the need to care for people and for the environment. I must emphasize that when I talk of 'socializing' markets, I do not simply mean state regulation of markets (though effective state regulation is important); but going beyond that to embed market transactions in egalitarian social relations, so that they can serve democratically agreed social ends. This requires both a transformation of property rights, so as to fundamentally shift the balance between the right to the exclusive use of certain resources and the right not to be excluded from the enjoyment of common resources. This will entail an enlargement of the role of egalitarian collective associations in the economy. I hope to show that socializing markets is not the same as creating what is conventionally described as 'market socialism'.

It is a decade since I first wrote of socializing markets.[3] That decade has seen both a victory for capitalist market forces, with the collapse of planning in the former Soviet Union and Eastern Europe and the opening up to foreign investment in China and Cuba; and also a widespread undermining of belief in the legitimacy and effectiveness of capitalist markets forces, as financial crisis and recession have swept around the world: South East Asia, Russia, Brazil. But in the most powerful countries in the world the power of capitalist markets – especially the power of financial markets – continues unabated. As I write the boom on Wall Street continues, and European financial markets are reported as jubilant at the resignation of the one European finance minister who repeatedly questioned the wisdom of financial orthodoxy. Nevertheless the last decade has also been a decade of experiments, small-scale but growing in strength, in the socialization of certain markets, and the creating of new markets which are socially embedded, in the sense of being organized to serve peoples' needs, rather than to maximize profits.[4]

Since this volume of the *Socialist Register* is meant to be visionary and forward looking, I will not keep referring back to my earlier writings on these issues; and I will adopt neither the convention of a 'reply to my critics' nor the convention of an 'autocritique'. Those with a taste of such things will be able to work out where I have changed my mind and where I have not; where I have formed new ideas and where I have continued to rely on ones I had already developed. Nor will I provide a 'review of the recent literature'. Rather, I want to encourage the reader to think less abstractly, and more concretely, about economic life. Following the activist principle of going forward from where you stand now, I want to begin to flesh out my argument by considering a market in which I, and many readers, participate – the market for the *Socialist Register*. Some readers will be reading a library copy, or a copy they borrowed from a friend, or a photocopy of this particular essay. But the *Socialist Register* depends on there being large numbers of readers who bought their copy – through subscriptions, left bookstores, stalls at conferences. Money changed hands – and the *Socialist Register* could not survive if it did not. The editors and publisher have to be concerned with marketing, with keeping existing markets and developing new ones – in order to sell enough copies to cover the costs of producing each volume.

However, the market for the *Socialist Register* has different characteristics from the market for a magazine produced by a commercial publisher to make as much profit as possible. Those involved in writing for the *Register*, editing it, publishing it, and distributing it, make their contributions out of commitment, not for commercial reasons. The editors and publisher do not treat the *Register* as their private property but as something they hold in trust for a wider movement. Many people give freely of their time to produce and distribute the *Register*. Some are supported, in making their contributions, by a job in an organization which allows them to count some of their contributions as part of their paid workload – for instance, this is possible for writers who are employed as teachers and researchers in publicly-funded institutions. For others, like the publisher, and the staff of left bookstores, their contribution to the *Register* must in turn be reciprocated by a financial contribution that will go towards enabling them to make a living, albeit with lower financial returns than they would make if they chose to engage in publishing and selling a different type of book. This has to be factored into the price of the *Register*, as do the costs of paper, printing services, packing and transportation. But the aim of those who produce and distribute the *Register* is not to maximize financial returns, either for themselves, or for a group of shareholders. The price does not include a mark-up to generate pure profit. Moreover, those who buy and read the *Register* tend to do so as part of a collective intellectual and political practice, in which they will enter into a dialogue with the editors and authors – indirectly, in discussions, or the production of new writings, commenting upon articles in the *Register*; or directly, by e-mailing the editors and authors. The readers, writers, editors, publisher and distributors of the *Socialist Register* are part of an informal association.

Thus, a market relation between the *Socialist Register* and many of its readers exists – but it is a market relation which is socially embedded in the practices of the socialist movement, not an anonymous financial transaction. It is a socialized market, and readers and writers, publishers and sellers are part of a dialogue as well as a market. This socialized market is, of course, squeezed and constricted by the pressure of commercial market forces. Small left-wing bookstores find it hard to survive in the face of the market power of the huge commercial booksellers. Small left-wing publishers find it hard to survive in the face of the market power of the multinational publishing corporations. The tastes of potential readers are shaped by media conglomerates, so that many people come to expect 'sound bites' and 'infotainment', rather than a dialogue that requires sustained and serious attention.

The editors and publisher try to keep the price 'affordable' but its affordability can be dramatically changed by factors quite outside their power to influence – for instance, massive currency devaluations take the local price far beyond the pockets of many potential readers in South East Asia and Brazil; and high unemployment in much of Europe puts the price beyond the reach of others, especially of young people.

But do we envision a future in which the editor and publisher will have to negotiate with a planning committee (or series of such committees) for an allocation of paper, or access to printing services or distribution channels? And in which potential readers will have to negotiate with planning committees about how many, and which, books they will be allocated each year? Suppose the majority of the members of the democratically-elected committees with which we have to negotiate do not find the *Register* an interesting or worthwhile publication? Tastes will surely vary – and I am sure that no one wants a dull uniformity.

An alternative approach is to envision a future in which all the forces which distort and inhibit the flourishing of the socialized market that links the producers and readers of the *Register* have been overcome; and in which more people are able to afford time to help produce the *Register*, time to read it, and money to pay for it. In this paper, I shall try to explore some of the conditions for such a future.

Let us first situate the *Register* more fully in the context of the economic structures of the societies in which it is produced and read – societies in the plural, because the *Register* is produced and distributed through a process of international collaboration and its readership is international. The national economies in which the production and distribution of the *Register* takes place are not monolithic, though they are dominated by commercial market forces. Somewhat schematically, one might distinguish a capitalist, commercial sector (called the 'private sector' in much economic discourse); a state sector (called the 'public sector' in much economic discourse); and a domestic sector, comprising households in which women and men, boys and girls, consume the goods and services of the private and public sectors. (It is in the domestic sector that unpaid care for their members is produced, more especially by women and girls – something which is ignored in most conventional economic discourse about how economies operate, but which has been highlighted by feminist economics.)[5] And there is also yet another sector, in which I think we can locate the production and distribution of the *Socialist Register*, which I shall call the associative sector. This sector is recognized in much economic discourse – but only in terms of what it is not. Conventionally, it is termed 'non-governmental'; or 'not-for-profit'; or the 'third sector' (with the private and public sectors being the other two sectors, and the domestic sector left out). Money and markets play a role in the functioning of associations because they require financial resources (grants, membership dues, revenues from sales) to function and provide services for their members and the wider society; and they employ paid, as well as unpaid, labour. But associations are formed around social rather than commercial objectives.

All of the sectors demarcated here are internally heterogeneous. Within the public sector, there are differences between units in terms of size, function, relation to citizens and relation to government. Some units provide services free at the point of use, while others provide services for which user charges are levied; some units are primarily concerned with effecting income transfers (taxes and benefits); while others are primarily concerned with regulating society (making and upholding laws). Within the private sector, there are wide differences between enterprises in terms of their ownership structure (joint-stock, co-operative, family, individual) and the extent to which they are regulated by the state ('formal' or 'informal'); their size and scope (small and local or huge and international); their success in covering their costs and making a profit. Within the domestic sector, there are many differences between households in terms of size and age structure, reason for household formation, extent of kin and neighbourly links with other households, income and assets of household members, degree to which resources are pooled and shared, egalitarian or non-egalitarian gender division of labour. Within the associative sector, there are many differences between different forms of association: unions, clubs, movements, with differing objectives and scope, differing degrees of formality and differing degrees of internal democracy and commitment to egalitarian goals.

The rationale for aggregating these diverse units into four sectors must rest on some similarity between the functioning of the units in each sector. One possible similarity is in terms of the motivation of individuals within each sector. As Humphries points out, neo-classical micro-economics has tended to depict the motivation of individuals in the public sector and private sector as that of self-interest, while the motivation of decision makers in households has been depicted in terms of altruism.[6] Feminists have found this too arbitrary, as the majority of individuals live in both the world of the household and the work of paid work for a good part of their lives. Why should they be only altruistic in the one and only self-interested in the other? Why not allow for complex mixtures of altruism and self-interest in all areas of life, shaped by cultural norms as well as personal idiosyncrasies?

Another possible common feature of units within a sector is in terms of the mechanisms they use to co-ordinate their internal activities. It is perhaps tempting to see private enterprises as co-ordinated through financial mechanisms, public sector organizations as co-ordinated through plans and rules, associations as co-ordinated through meetings and households as co-ordinated through social norms. But again, reality is more complex, with finances, meetings, norms, plans and rules playing some role in co-ordination of all four sectors. Moreover, command and hierarchy, and mutuality and reciprocity, can characterize the internal organization of units in all four sectors. The family is no more unequivocally 'the heart of a heartless world' than the commercial firm is unequivocally the servant of mammon or the government bureau a subdivision of Leviathan, or the association a prefiguration of a socialist utopia. The internal operation of units in all four sectors is better characterized in terms of 'co-operative conflicts',[7] in which their members stand to gain from co-operation in production but often have conflicting interests on the terms of the distribution of the benefits.

We might also examine the conditions of reproduction of each unit – what do they have to do to sustain their normal functioning? Private sector enterprises have to sell enough to at least cover their costs, and if they are joint stock companies they must also make a profit for their shareholders that at least matches that of comparable firms. Public sector organizations are not constrained in the same way since their costs may be ultimately financed by taxation rather than sales. But the power to tax depends upon the government retaining its power to make and uphold the law, its legitimacy. If the public sector operates in ways that are not considered legitimate, then the power of the state to support it through taxation is likely to be undermined. Households have to meet the needs of their members for food, shelter and clothing, and companionship. We might sum this up by saying that the private sector is structured by a dynamic of sales and profit; the public sector by a dynamic of legitimation; and the domestic sector by a dynamic of provisioning. Associations must sustain their membership (formal or informal) – and this means they must mobilize resources to cover their costs, through subscriptions, donations, grants, and also sales – as well as recruit new members. To a degree, they must be 'business-like', but they must be able to attract gifts, of time or money or other resources, without the demand for a commercial rate of return. Perhaps this might be described as a dynamic of solidarity – though by no means always a solidarity in support of social justice.

The different sectors are inter-connected through a variety of circuits that channel the flows between them. In traditional political economy the emphasis has been on markets as the most important type of circuit, with goods, services, money and labour flowing through them. The role of the state has been generally posed in terms of intervention in markets (which are run by the private sector), to widen, narrow or choke off flows through them. In debates about the most appropriate forms of intervention, and the relative weight of market failure and bureaucratic failure, it has often been forgotten that the state plays a constitutive role in making markets work – supplying an infrastructure of rights and regulations without which no orderly market is possible. Recognition of this enables us to see that markets are public circuits as well as private circuits, co-determined by economic and political structures. Markets do not just link sectors within national economies – they also link them across national economic boundaries. International markets are governed by inter-state systems of regulation such as the World Trade Organization.

The markets which states sustain and which link the private sector to the public, domestic and associative sectors in present-day economies are overwhelmingly capitalist markets dominated by commercial forces. But these are not the only type of markets which currently exist. We have already discussed the *Socialist Register* market as an example of a socialized market embedded in the loose egalitarian association which links all those participating in producing, distributing and using the *Socialist Register*. Many other egalitarian associations organize socialized markets, from bake sales to the international direct trading networks of the Fair Trade movement, which affirm non-economic values, even while operating in markets.[8] These really are markets which could be represented as an exchange of use values, mediated by money, in which the prices are determined by social, not commercial, objectives, subject to the constraint of covering the money costs of production. The people employed in the associations running such markets often give their labour on a partially voluntary basis – working for lower wages than they could obtain in the private or public sectors, putting in long hours of unpaid overtime. Some community associations not only create socialized markets, they also create and regulate their own form of money to facilitate exchanges of goods between members of the association.[9] It is interesting to reflect on why such associations do create a measure of value and medium of exchange to facilitate their transactions, even when these transactions are very localized and face-to-face, often between people who already know each other. These range from the problems of organizing barter exchanges when needs and wants do not coincide (I want to trade my baked goods – but not for car maintenance; you want to trade your car maintenance services – but not for baked goods); to the problems of keeping track of transactions that necessarily take place at different times; to the problems of establishing a uniform 'rate for the job'. An agreed measure of value and medium of exchange makes it easier to have flexible decentralized transactions. It does not make for a very relaxed life if people have to plan all their activities for months ahead. If all this is true at the local level, then how much more so when egalitarian associations cross national boundaries.

But all these socialized markets, just like the market for the *Socialist Register*, are constricted and distorted by the pressure of commercial market forces. For instance international Fair Trade networks are squeezed by changes in interest rates and exchange rates brought about by the private financial sectors' pursuit of maximum profit. Community currency schemes are squeezed by the time pressures of jobs in the private and public sectors and by the need to 'import' goods and service from outside the community.

Of course, the various sectors of an economy are not only linked by commercial markets. Within each national economy, they are also linked via citizenship obligations and entitlements, the circuit of taxes and benefits, the latter including both income transfers and enjoyment of physical and social infrastructure (roads, police stations, law courts, schools, hospitals) free at the point of use. In contrast to markets, in the circuit of taxes and benefits, flows of money payments and receipts of goods and services are not offset against each other in each and every transaction. For protagonists of the commercial market, this is the great weakness of the circuit of taxes and benefits, and leads to scrounging, waste, inefficiency of all kinds. But the circuit of taxes and benefits can deal much better than either commercial or socialized markets with the provision of public goods; that is, goods which by their nature cannot easily be parcelled up and charged for separately – such as street lighting, clean air, and services where there are strong 'spillover' effects, such as health and education, where one person's ill-health can be contagious, and one person's lack of adequate skills can reduce the performance of a whole team. The circuit of taxes and benefits can also in principle provide a common resource, a social security system, which can offset the inability of market circuits to guarantee everyone an adequate living. However, the effectiveness of circuits of taxes and benefits is limited because they are confined to national economies. There is no international governance system to provide support for the provision of global public goods.[10]

A well-functioning circuit of taxes and benefits does not just depend on the legitimacy, probity and effectiveness of the state and of political structures. It also depends on borrowing in some form or other, because the inflow of public revenue cannot be guaranteed to exactly match the outflow of public expenditure, either in timing or in total magnitude. Where government borrowing largely takes place through the mediation of private sector financial institutions, this circuit can be widened, narrowed or choked off, not only by the changing sentiment of voters and political parties, but also by the changing sentiment of bankers. Today, finance ministers pay more attention to what analysts in financial institutions, and traders in financial markets, will think of their fiscal policies, than what parliamentarians, or the electorate, will think. In this way, capitalist market forces structure and distort even those citizenship linkages between sectors that are not based on commercial markets.

A third linkage among sectors is the circuit of financial grants, donations and subscriptions – linking the associative sectors with all the other sectors. This circuit has something in common with the taxes and benefits circuit, in that the flows of money and receipts of goods and services are not offset against each other in each and every transaction; and something in common with market circuits, both commercial and socialized, in that the payments are voluntary rather than enforced by the state. This type of circuit, in which transactions have strong elements of gift transactions, can be particularly effective for financing transformative activities, and to provide things, such as knowledge, which people do not yet know that they might want; in general, to enlarge the scope of human experience and ambition. As the example of the *Socialist Register* illustrates, such circuits operate between national economies as well as within them.

All of these circuits involve money (in terms of which the flows through them can be quantified). But there is also another type of circuit connecting all the sectors – a circuit of communication in which what flows is information, ideas, images, values, meanings, often as much implicit as explicit. Without some degree of shared understandings, transactions in all the other types of circuit would be impossible. Through communication networks, each sector transmits a series of messages which are marked by the organizing dynamic of each sector. The private sector transmits commercial values; the public sector, regulatory values; the associative sector, solidaristic values and the domestic sector, provisioning values. There are negative and positive aspects to the values each transmits – commercial values are venal, and often crass and opportunistic – but they may also be thrifty and innovatory; regulatory values may be petty and bureaucratic, as well as sustaining capitalist social relations and commercial markets – but they may also promote human rights and democracy; provisioning values are associated with caring and giving – but they may also be patriarchal and small-minded; solidaristic values are often assumed on the left to be radical, empathetic and altruistic – but they may also be conservative, exclusive and inward-looking. The messages are inflected with the specificities of different societies, but increasingly also inflected with cosmopolitan values, both capitalist and egalitarian.

The sectors, and the circuits that link them, are gendered structures; that is, they do not just contain within them male and female individuals; their very modes of operation are built upon the prevailing, unequal, gender order. This is obvious in the case of the domestic sector because kin relations are gender-ascriptive relations; that is, 'mother', 'father', 'son', 'daughter' are categories which explicitly denote gender. However, categories like 'employer', 'employee', 'seller', 'buyer', 'citizen', 'tax-payer', 'benefit-recipient', 'grantor', 'grantee', 'volunteer', 'writer' and 'reader' do not explicitly denote gender; and are thus often assumed to denote gender-neutral positions and activities.

Much feminist scholarship over the last two decades has been devoted to showing that much of what may appear to be gender-neutral is in fact a 'bearer' of gender, inscribed with prevailing patterns of gender inequality. There is no space here to report on all the ways that this happens. We shall just highlight some prime examples. For instance, the hierarchy of employment in both public and private sectors is a gendered hierarchy in which male authority is still the norm, and female authority the exception. Moreover, the rules and norms of not only the private but also the public and associative sectors are predicated upon the assumption that the care and nurture of the labour force on a daily and intergenerational basis is primarily a female task, and should be treated as fundamentally external to the operations of the sector, even though none of those sectors can be sustained in the long run unless such unpaid domestic labour is undertaken.[11]

The circuits are also gendered. This is most apparent in the taxes and bene-fits circuit, where obligations and entitlements are frequently structured quite explicitly upon assumptions that women are, or should be, dependent upon men.[12] In addition, communication networks frequently transmit stereotyped or demeaning messages about women. Commercial markets may seem more culturally egalitarian – since it appears that the only thing that matters is how much money you have, not whether you are a man or woman. But the structuring of commercial market transactions is gendered in a way that frequently disadvantages women; sometimes overtly, in that women are not allowed to enter into commercial contracts of certain kinds, or are excluded from certain commercial market places; frequently, and more subtly, in terms of how bargaining is carried out; how risks are perceived and shared; how goods are organized into 'lots' for sale; how information about prices is disseminated.[13] And most women are at a fundamental disadvantage as compared to men – they have less money. Even socialized markets are bearers of gender – women too frequently provide the voluntary labour, while men make the decisions.

Of course, the sectors and circuits are not co-equal. The private sector and commercial markets dominate, undermining the values and ways of functioning of public services, voluntary associations, and family provisioning. The most basic needs of hundreds of millions are not met, while a few millions live in luxury. The discussion of what we want to put in the place of this destructive system still tends to be polarized into plan vs. market.[14] The productive roles of the domestic sector and the associative sectors are largely ignored. Those who are sceptical of the contribution that markets can make to a socialist economy, worry that if decision making is decentralized via markets, then state enterprises and workers' co-operatives will behave, in a short while, just like capitalist enterprises, with the profits now appropriated by the managers of the public enterprises and the members of the workers' co-operatives; and with comparable damage to the planet and to human beings. I agree the role of markets must be approached with caution. But the fundamental problem comes not from the use of markets but from the structure of property rights. Socialists are right to emphasize that a better life for the majority of people on the planet requires a fundamental change in property rights. But the socialist tradition has placed most emphasis on a transfer of the means of production from private corporations to ownership by the state or workers' co-operatives, and in doing so has failed to pay enough attention to the fact that all three types of ownership have an important similarity: they are all forms of corporate property.[15]

Of course, private ownership of the means of production can be a property right held by an individual, but it is the corporately held rights that dominate the private sector, and which socialists are mainly concerned about, rather than small, individually owned businesses. A workers' co-operative is obviously also a form of corporate ownership – the difference being that the corporate rights are held by the employees rather than by shareholders. Both types of ownership confer upon the owners a right to exclude anyone else from the enjoyment of the property which they own. Moreover, ownership of property by a state enterprise similarly gives the state enterprise a right to exclude anyone else from the enjoyment of the property which it owns. Individual citizens do not have direct individual rights to use means of production held by state enterprises. But individual citizens do have direct individual rights to use common property – for instance, common land, public parks and squares, city streets, public libraries. A right to common property is a right to be included, a right not to be excluded; whereas a corporate property right, whether held by shareholders, co-operatives, or a state enterprise, is a right to exclude.[16] Common property is increasingly under threat and the exercise of corporate rights is being concentrated in fewer hands, all over the world.

In thinking about how to organize a socialist economy, we have not paid enough attention to the balance between the common property rights of individuals, the individual property rights of individuals, and the corporate property rights of state enterprises and workers' co-operatives; nor enough attention to the ways in which spillover effects mean that all three types of rights need to be limited and qualified in various ways in order to promote the common good. The lesson of the experience of the regimes of Communist parties in the twentieth century is surely that the foundation of a democratic socialism must be the careful specification and protection of rights, both individual and corporate; and the balance must be weighted strongly towards the individual rights of household members to common property. A socialist economy must be built on a foundation of common property, that is on the rights of individuals not to be excluded from the use of designated resources. It does not make sense to extend this in terms of a right not to be excluded from use of *all* resources. Large-scale production of many goods and services can only be done effectively if certain groups of people do have the right to exclusive use of certain means of production for lengthy periods of time – the workers' co-operative, the state enterprise. Moreover, if individuals and small groups are going to invest their time and energy in creating something new, they need to be able to exclude other people from the use of their equipment and premises, to safeguard their work-in-progress. (Remember that time someone else used your computer when you were away, and you returned to find crucial files had been somehow deleted?) So individual ownership of small businesses, subject to democratic regulation, should be welcomed as a vital source of innovation and diversity.

The right not to be excluded is most effectively strengthened in terms of the individual rights of members of all households to key public services, delivered free at the point of use, such as education and health care; and in terms of the right of each individual to a basic income,[17] a sum of money with which individuals can purchase the basic requirements for sustaining a modest level of consumption. (In terms of our sectors, this means strengthening the common property rights of the household sector.) It would not make sense to give people a standard 'shopping basket' of goods, free of charge, because different people have different tastes. To allow people to meet their specific and individual needs, it is much more useful to provide a basic income in the form of money and allow them to purchase the particular combination of goods that they choose, subject to democratically agreed laws limiting or forbidding sales and purchases which encroach upon the dignity and integrity of the human subject (such as sexual services and body parts). Indeed, they might choose to buy means of production and operate a small business as the route to meeting their basic consumption needs.

The common property right not to be excluded is not an unqualified right. For instances, to protect the environment, it is often necessary to ration access to space (car use restrictions in city streets, areas of public parks reserved for different activities). Moreover, the right to a basic income should be qualified by the obligation to accept certain unpaid, part-time duties of citizenship, such as jury service, and participation in designated community associations, for instance to provide care in the community for those in need of care; or tend community gardens; or run youth clubs. People could, of course, use their basic income to support their participation in any other association, provided their obligations were met. Such a foundation of common property rights (and duties) would strengthen the domestic sector and the associative sector; it could do much to reduce gender inequality and would fundamentally transform the labour market. It would mean that money could not exercise *command* over labour power. Enterprises, whether public, private or co-operative would need to attract people to work in them by offering rewards unavailable in the domestic and associative sectors – such as higher incomes, and opportunities to participate in a wider range of activities in ways that develop rather than distort their capacities.

Rights to enjoy common property need to be constituted at both national and international levels, building upon existing rights in national and international law. The Declaration of Human Rights, and associated human rights instruments such as the Covenant on Economic, Social and Cultural Rights, provide an overarching framework which needs to be strengthened and given more substance. In particular, the relation between human rights and property rights needs clarifying. It is difficult to see that much progress can be made in strengthening individual rights not to be excluded from common property without a substantial extension of collective ownership of corporate property. Substantial private ownership of corporate property undermines the capacity of the state to raise revenue to provide basic services and income by buttressing a powerful lobby for lower taxes; and it perpetuates the commercial values that undermine respect for common property.

An important and difficult issue is the question of who should have the right to enjoy territorially specific common property. If the point of socialism is to create economic justice, then surely this should extend across national boundaries. So why not extend the common property rights to anyone who wants to come and enjoy them? The problem is that supporting and managing a socialist economy will require a series of accountable, democratically elected, territorially-based forms of government. Opening the borders all at once in those countries which can afford to provide a higher level of basic income may generate such large immediate flows of migrants that society would be destabilized. A phased process of gradual relaxation of controls on migration from other socialist countries, together with a massive enlargement of grants from rich to poor societies, and vigorous processes of fostering a shared socialist culture across international boundaries, and of deepening intergovernmental co-ordination seems likely to have more chance of staying on track.

The scenario I envision does have markets in which goods and services are brought and sold and markets in which labour power is bought and sold – so what is to prevent collectively-owned corporate property, such as public enterprises and workers co-operatives, from behaving like capitalist enterprises, and seeking to commodify more and more of life and to make as much money as possible? Without any wider social accountability outside the enterprise, such enterprises would be free to behave like capitalists, in so far as they could retain and distribute surplus income; or could reinvest their cash in new activities. The criteria of success would still be in terms of making money, and satisfaction of human needs would only enter the process indirectly through the mediation of buying and selling.

One important check on commercialism would be to abolish the market in corporate property rights themselves, so that enterprises could not be merged or taken over by a process of buying and selling shares. But to completely break the circuit of capital, a process of social control is required at the points of metamorphosis, so that enterprise performance has to meet certain social criteria before goods and services can be sold or bought, surplus income retained and reinvested, or loans obtained. In the scenario I envisage, all enterprises (private, co-operative and state) would be responsible and accountable for the investment, production and financial decisions they took – but in order to put those decisions into effect, they would have to show that they were fully complying with social standards, as specified by democratic processes, on issues such as equal opportunities, disclosure of information, environmental protection, health and safety at work, consumer protection and worker's rights to join a trade union.[18] Rather than being able to proceed with operations unless ordered to cease trading by a relevant government inspectorate, enterprises would have to show that they were fully complying with social standards *before* they could trade. This would, in effect, mean that the corporate rights over property enjoyed by enterprises, whether privately, co-operatively, or publicly owned, would be *conditional* in the sense that freedom to appropriate and reinvest surplus would depend on a satisfactory social evaluation of performance against a set of democratically agreed standards. Social control would cut across the financial flows, forming a series of checkpoints. Perhaps the most important checkpoints would be in relation to enterprise plans to borrow and to invest, which would require social as well as financial evaluation by publicly controlled financial institutions, but enterprises could also could be required to present a certificate of satisfactory social performance in order to be able to buy and sell goods and services, and hire labour power. This could be applied to international trade as well as to trade within a country. Thus, firms wishing to import goods into a country could be required to show that the goods were produced under conditions that met agreed social standards. Countries could work towards the harmonization of social evaluation standards through international negotiations. Some social standards (such as the right to join a free trade union) should be applied to all countries; others might vary, according to the different levels of income of different countries. For instance, it would not be fair to stipulate the same level of minimum wage for rich and poor countries.

To avoid over-reliance on the state, the process of social evaluation should involve the associative sector as well as government inspectorates. While the government inspectorates would be responsible for certification, and for prosecuting law breakers, associations committed to social justice (trade unions, consumer groups, environment groups, women rights groups, etc.) would play a major role in carrying out investigations; publicizing shortcomings in associated media; representing complainants, in negotiations with enterprises or in legal processes; and advising on how enterprises might improve their performance. Grants, financed by taxation, would be available to support associations in this work. This would be a system of participatory regulation, in which citizens can not only participate in the political process of setting standards, but also in the process of enforcing them. The right to information would be fundamental to this process.

In such an economy, the distribution of the surplus would depend on the structure of prices. Hence, there is a case for some social checks on the price formation process. One might envisage a price commission which would directly set the prices of a limited number of basic goods, in particular the prices of utilities (gas, electricity, telecommunications, etc.). For all other prices, the price commission would have power to audit and regulate price formation, i.e., enforce disclosure by enterprises of the basis used for price formation and enforce changes in prices and price formation procedures where they are not in line with social standards. The associative sector would play a major role in investigating and publicizing price policies, and presenting cases for action to the price commission.[19]

It may be objected that these social controls will slow down the economy and inhibit competition leading to losses in productivity. But rapid change and uninhibited competition also have costs, and their supposed benefits in terms of increases in productivity are often illusory. Our accounting systems have been set up so as to capture the increases in sales but not the human losses that so often accompany rapid economic growth – loss of free time, depletion of health and strength, erosion of provisioning values. If we account for the social as well as the economic consequences, then a slower paced, less frenetic economy will be seen to have benefits.

To really embed markets in egalitarian social relations, it is also necessary to extend and deepen communication circuits, creating an obligation for enterprises and associations to share information, and promoting dialogue so as to enable decisions made by enterprises and members of households to be more public-spirited and less atomized. Transformative associations have a catalytic role to play here, mediating between enterprises and households, bringing buyers and sellers into contact with one another to pursue shared social objectives beyond a narrow immediate interest in getting the best bargain in the next transaction. New information technology can play a positive role here by facilitating dialogue across time and space. It would be important to develop a culture in which the government gave grants to transformative associations which are helping to build socialism, while at the same time respecting their autonomy.

The macroeconomic framework for an economy organized along these lines would need to be set by a democratically accountable planning commission that would recognize the productive roles of the domestic and associative sectors, as well as the public and co-operative sector. It would determine overall levels of taxation and public expenditure (on operations of government, free-of-charge public services, basic income and grants); financial parameters, such as rates of inflation, rates of interest or foreign exchange rates; and parameters for human development and environmental protection. Major, large-scale, new investment projects would be centrally co-ordinated, and designed using social indicators as well as financial indicators. Membership of the planning commission would include elected representatives from the legislature, and also representatives of public enterprise and co-operatives sector, the public services sector, the small business sector, the associative sector and the domestic sector. Most importantly, the financial system would be directly under the central control of the planning commission, with lending and borrowing subject to social standards. The major markets that would need to be abolished are the markets for corporate control and financial derivatives, which are the major supports of monopoly power and sources of economic instability. These are the markets which are now under criticism from very wide sectors of opinion all around the world. The challenge is to build upon that criticism to decisively change the balance of power between financial capital and ordinary people whose lives are being distorted and even destroyed, by money in pursuit of yet more money.

In doing that, alternative visions of the future are important. But after the failures, and worse than that, horrors, of the twentieth century, it is vital to create non-authoritarian visions, rooted in individual rights and decentralized decision making, with checks and balances against centralized corporate power of all kinds. Markets, if they are transformed and socially embedded in egalitarian social relations, are vital to that vision, helping to support the autonomy of households and associations. My vision is not a 'market society' but not a 'bureaucratic society' either;[20] it is a society in which democratically accountable state agencies structure markets so as to give a much greater chance for households and associations to flourish – surely the best conditions for the *Socialist Register* to flourish too.

There is much more that needs to be developed in this vision. But my aim was not a blueprint, more a set of principles or guidelines. I wanted to get beyond the sterile debate on the market versus the plan to suggest that we need a vision of socialist economies that rests on a foundation of strong individual rights to enjoy common property and collective rights over corporate property; that recognizes that households and associations are part of the economy; that understands the cultural dimension of economies, the values and norms that are communicated by economic practices; and that recognizes the useful role that socialized markets – markets embedded in egalitarian social relations – can play in facilitating both decentralized decision making and cosmopolitan decision making, freeing our vision of socialist economies from the straight jacket of the national economy organized by the state.

I have said nothing much about how we get from here to there – producers of utopias rarely do. But a necessary utopia should at least signal some ways in which connection can be built between movements of resistance to capitalism, movements to create alternatives, and fissures and cracks in capitalist power structures. Let me suggest three ways. The first is to strengthen the movements demanding greater accountability in the use of economic power, both the power of states and the often much greater power of private business corporations. The watchword is democratizing the economy rather than liberalizing the economy. The second is to strengthen the movements that are seeking in various way to transform markets, to embed them in egalitarian social relations, through social entrepreneurship and through participatory setting and monitoring of social standards. The third is to build links between the realization of human rights, the right to enjoy common property, and the exercise of collective rights over corporate property.[21] Though socialism may have been marginalized today, the ideals of democracy and human rights enjoy widespread support. We have to show how the full realization of the latter still depends upon an economic transformation, while making it clear that what we mean by that is a transition to a slower, kinder, gentler, more inclusive economy – one that really embodies, in this sense, the ideals of socialism.

NOTES

1. For further discussion see Adam Tickell, 'Unstable Futures: Controlling and Creating Risks in International Money' and Wally Seccombe, 'Contradictions of Shareholder capitalism: Downsizing Jobs, Enlisting Savings, Destabilizing Families', both in *Socialist Register 1999*, London, Merlin, 1999.
2. This point has been stressed in a number of contributions in feminist economics See for instance, Maureen Mackintosh, 'Abstract Markets and Real Needs' in Henry Bernstein et al., *The Food Question: Profit vs People*, London, Earthscan, 1990; and also 'Dialogue: Interrogating Markets/Interrogating Gender', *Feminist Economics*, Vol. 2, No. 1, Spring, 1996, especially the contributions by Lynn Duggan and Jennifer Olmsted (pp. 86–89); Richard Wilk (pp. 90–93) and Linda Robertson (pp. 98–113).
3. Diane Elson, 'Market Socialism or Socialization of the Market', *New Left Review*,

No 172, Nov/Dec, 1998, pp. 3–44.

4.   These can be local, such as Local Exchange Trading Systems and other commu-
     nity currency systems (for a brief overview, see Susan Meeker-Lowery,
     'Community Money: The Potential of Local Currency', in Jerry Mander and
     Edward Goldsmith (eds), *The Case Against the Global Economy*, San Francisco, Sierra
     Club Books, 1996; or international, such as the 'Fair Trade' arrangements which
     are putting peasant producers of goods like coffee and cocoa in touch with
     European Consumers (see for instance, Michael Barratt Brown, *Fair Trade*,
     London, Zed Books, 1993).

5.   See, for instance, special issue of *Feminist Economics*, Vol 2, No. 3, 1996 and Diane
     Elson, 'The Economic, the Political and the Domestic; Businesses: States and
     Households in the Organization of Production', *New Political Economy*, Vol. 3, No.
     2, 1998, pp. 89–208.

6.   Jane Humphries, 'Rational economic families? Economics, the family and the
     economy', in Georgina Waylen (ed) *Towards a Gendered Political Economy*,
     London, Macmillan. Forthcoming.

7.   The term has been widely used by Amartya Sen: see for instance his 'Gender and
     co-operative conflicts' in Irene Tinker (ed), *Persistent Inequalities*, London, Oxford
     University Press, 1990.

8.   A good example is Twin Trading, established in London in 1985, which develops
     fair trade links between European consumers and co-operatives of small scale
     growers of coffee and cocoa in Africa and Latin America.

9.   For a discussion of such associations see Susan Meeker-Lowry, 'Community
     Money – The Potential of Local Currency' in Mander and Goldsmith, *The Case
     Against the Global Economy*.

10. For more discussion of this issue, see Inge Kaul, Isabelle Grunberg, and Mark Stern
     (eds), *Global Public Goods*, London, Oxford University Press, 1999.

11. This has been explored in some detail by Nancy Folbre, *Who Pays for the Kids?*,
     London, Routledge, 1994 and Jean Gardiner, *Gender, Care and Economics*,
     London, Macmillan, 1997.

12. For further discussion, see for instance, Ruth Lister, *Citizenship-Feminist
     Perspectives*, London, Macmillan, 1997.

13. These issues are explored in depth by Barbara Harriss-White, 'Female and male
     gain marketing systems – Analytical and Policy Issues for West Africa and India',
     in Cecile Jackson and Ruth Pearson (ed), *Feminist Visions of Development*,
     London, Routledge, 1998.

14. See for instance, David Schweickart, James Lawler, Hillel Ticktin and Bertell
     Ollman, *Market Socialism – The Debate Among Socialists*, London, Routledge, 1998.

15. This similarity is emphasized by C. B. Macpherson, *Property*, Oxford, Basil
     Blackwell, 1978.

16. This point is also due to Macpherson, *Property*.

17. There is a large literature on the pros and cons of basic income, much of it dealing
     with the problem of incentives and 'free-riding', on the assumption of population
     of myopic, amoral, self-centred individuals, unmovable by collective deliberation,
     unable to devise ways of creating a mutual assurance to contribute. I think we have
     to take the risk of assuming that people are capable of more far-sighted and reci-
     procal behaviour, given appropriate conditions, such as the strengthening of the
     public sphere, (on the latter point, see Colin Leys, 'The Public Sphere and the

Media: Market Supremacy vs Democracy' in *Socialist Register*, London, Merlin, 1999); and the validation of women's 'different voice', rooted in caring for people (see Lourdes Beneria, 'Gender and the Constitution of Global Markets, 'Paper presented at Women and Development Conference, City University, New York, October, 1998).

18. This list is not meant to be exhaustive, but merely illustrative The social standards would embody a further set of common property rights.

19. The experience of regulating the privatized utility companies in UK has relevant lessons, although the powers of the UK regulators are very limited by the market for corporate control of the utilities.

20. As Polanyi put it 'the end of market society means in no way the absence of markets'. Karl Polanyi, *The Great Transformation*, Boston, Beacon Press, 1957, p. 252.

21. A particularly important topic is the exploration of the variety of ways in which collective rights can be exercised over corporate property. Here I have referred simply to public enterprises and workers' co-operatives. But there can be a variety of governance structures of workers co-operatives, some more conducive to social accountability than others.

THE CHIMERA OF THE THIRD WAY

Alan Zuege

Trapped between a shifting social base and a contracting political horizon, social democracy appears to have lost its compass. In such altered conditions, is it likely to undergo a new mutation? Once, in the founding years of the Second International, it was dedicated to the general overthrow of capitalism. Then it pursued partial reforms as gradual steps towards socialism. Finally it settled for welfare and full employment within capitalism. If it now accepts a scaling down of the one and giving up the other, what kind of movement will it change into?[1]

THE REALIGNMENT OF IDEOLOGY and policy in left parties over the past two decades leaves increasingly little doubt as to the kind of movement social democracy has become. But judging from recent social democratic discussions about alternatives – not to mention ongoing struggles over the direction of left governments and parties – one could well form the impression that social democracy still has more potential than simply adding a sugar coating to the bitter pill of neo-liberal austerity. Reformists may, as Perry Anderson suggests in the quotation above, have lost their compass. But a growing body of work by left intellectuals has emerged intent on setting a new course for social democracy, hoping to construct a hegemonic project appropriate to the 'new times' ushered in by recent political and economic transformations. The electoral successes of left-of-centre parties in the mid to late 1990s, breaking the momentum of the political right, are thus presented as an opportunity for the moderate left to reinvent itself.

It would be premature to attempt to assess what Britain's Tony Blair or

Germany's Gerhard Schröder mean by the 'Third Way' and it is not yet clear if their policies really amount to a distinctive break with neo-liberalism. What can be assessed at this point, however, are the various policy frameworks set out in recent years by social democratic intellectuals which share the premises of the third way in their reliance on a revitalized discourse of 'partnership', while explicitly offering strategic alternatives to both neo-liberalism and the old post-war social democracy. It is the purpose of this essay to critically examine these alternatives, and to consider whether they are capable of providing the substantive grounds for social democracy's 'New Way'.

SOCIAL DEMOCRATIC ALTERNATIVES: FROM GOLDEN AGE TO LEADEN AGE

In the advanced capitalist countries, the prosperity and stability enjoyed during the post-war Golden Age formed the backdrop to the development of domestic class compromises. In an expansionary climate marked by rapid economic growth and relatively autonomous national markets, social democrats espoused a 'utopia' of class harmony administered by a Keynesian welfare state. Left political parties, with their special relationship to organized labour, won elections on the promise that they could deliver wage restraint, industrial growth, and labour peace to capital, and full employment, rising standards of living, and an enhanced policy-making role to workers. In the management of this class compromise, neo-corporatist incomes policies and economic planning structures – suffused with the ideology of partnership – were often key instruments, particularly in the 'model' social democracies of northern Europe.

Many of those trying to chart a new course for social democracy base their case for breaking with the past on the disappearance of the conditions which once favoured these institutions of class compromise.[2] Two in particular are singled out: the end to the Fordist system of mass production and the dismantling of the Keynesian national policy framework. According to these accounts, both were crucial for the 'organized', national capitalisms of the post-war period, allowing workers, employers, and the state to exercise their proper functions in a corporatist order. Workers could be organized into strong, centralized trade unions in the context of large, dominant, and stable firms. Peak-level bargaining with strong employers' associations helped guarantee wage and benefit increases for workers proportionate to productivity advance, while states had the capacity necessary to manage levels of aggregate demand and ensure the absorption of the scale of goods produced.

In accounting for the factors contributing to the decline of this organized capitalism, one line of argument focuses on the adoption of 'post-Fordist' flexible technologies and work practices in advanced industry.[3] The saturation of mass consumer markets in the capitalist core is said to have destabilized post-war growth and diminished the role of Keynesian state policies and trade unions in securing effective demand. The Swedish experience, among others, is used to illustrate how this shift has been accompanied by employer demands for wage flexibility, the increasing fragmentation of the working class, and the experimentation with greater cooperation in the workplace, all of which disrupt stable patterns of coordination between business, labour, and the state.[4] An alternative perspective emphasizes the effects of the expansion of global markets.[5] The integration and mobility of capital is said to pose severe limitations on the traditional range of options available to left governments, faced now with the combined threat of imports from low-wage economies, relocation of international investment, and a spectacular growth in the volume of mobile financial assets. In such a global setting, aggressive national policies of expansion will result in benefits 'leaking' abroad and vigorous opposition from investors and financial markets. The fate of France's 'Mitterrand experiment' in the early 1980s is widely accepted as proof positive that globalization has eliminated the option of Keynesianism in one country.[6]

With challenges to the national Keynesian and corporatist orthodoxies gathering momentum through the 1980s, there arose a number of proposals on the left for an alternative accumulation strategy appropriate to these 'new times'.[7] Strategies for full employment and social welfare increasingly looked to the international level for ways to moderate the effects of flexibility and globalization, by raising labour standards or by reinstating Keynesian policies at a higher level through more broadly representative supranational institutions or coordinated macroeconomic expansion. The popularity of the Social Europe project and the strategic emphasis placed by labour movements on social clauses, side agreements, and social charters are testimony to the influence of these ideas. However even with interest growing in supranational forms of governance, the institutional conditions for winning progressive reform through inter-state negotiations and cross-national bargaining remain weak.[8] This has contributed to an increasing focus on the need to develop national and regional strategies which would restore the fortunes of social democracy on the basis of new bargains struck between capital, labour, and the other 'social partners'.

This search for a new corporatism tends to fall into three distinguishable, though frequently linked, strands: (1) those calling for some sort of productivity pact, which links progressive outcomes to improvements in the competitive capacity of labour and industry – 'supply-side corporatism'; (2) those seeking a new distributional bargain, which recasts social and incomes policies to spread the benefits and sacrifices of economic growth within international constraints – 'open-economy corporatism'; and (3) those urging a broader social compromise, which aims at improving both competitive and distributional outcomes by extending participation in all spheres of social life – 'corporatist social governance'.

At the level of political calculation, each of these strategies relies heavily on restoring the institutions and ideology of social partnership, but with a new twist. The post-war pattern of social corporatism was principally (though not exclusively) focused on managing aggregate demand in the context of relatively closed national economies. By contrast, the first strategy of supply-side corpo-

ratism emphasizes productive forms of 'concertation' in its search for a collab-
orative path to competitive advantage. The second strategy of open-economy
corporatism encourages coordinated bargaining to spread the burdens of
competition and the benefits of growth within limits imposed by international
markets. The third strategy, corporatist social governance, seeks out alternative
modes of organization and inclusion – beyond labour and capital, market and
state – to develop local social cohesion, long-term commitment, and economic
dynamism. Programmatic statements on the Third Way as such, issued from
sources closer to centre-left governments, tend to be less specific than each of
these approaches, but the rhetoric and many of the general commitments are
the same: competitiveness and the global market; 'active' welfare states and
'public-private partnerships'; 'social entrepreneurship' and 'harnessing local
initiative'.[9] Yet for all their modernizing rhetoric, the emphasis on cross-class
trust and partnership remains at the core, and is replete with contradictions such
as have beset all corporatist schemes for class harmony. The social democratic
case for each of the new strategies will now be examined before turning to a
discussion of these contradictions in the second half of this essay.

The case for 'supply-side corporatism'[10]

The first approach calls for a new industrial politics linked to alternative
models of growth which emerged in the late 1970s and 1980s. As unemployment and balance of payments pressures mounted during this period,
increasingly reinforced by sensitive international financial flows, attention
turned to the performance of the export sector.[11] The 'competitiveness
debate' which ensued reinterpreted economic performance in terms of the
notions of dynamic efficiency and competitive advantage. In doing so it
provided an analytical basis for justifying active intervention and institutional
solutions to overcome market barriers and to shift production into higher
skilled, higher value-added manufacturing.[12] While the priority of the global
market was assumed – above all in the overriding commitments to financial
stability and exposing sectors to the 'stimulus' of external competition – the
emerging growth models theorized that rapid rates of export-led growth could
be achieved to ease employment and trade pressures without generating inflationary problems.

'Supply-side corporatism' is based on the idea that a gentler, more humane
mode of integration into the world economy is possible. It tries to balance an
embrace of the world market with the maintenance of high local standards of
equity and justice. Internationalization and flexible production are seen to limit
the effectiveness of traditional policies for growth and employment. But internationalization is also believed to open up an alternative in supply-side measures
to improve the availability and efficiency of local factors of production. While
intervention at the supranational level may provide useful supports for such a
strategy, the 'progressive competitiveness' position is primarily centred on
measures to boost the productive capacity of sectors exposed to international

markets.[13] By achieving competitive success through industrial innovation, a skilled workforce, and quality products, it is believed, states can 'earn' their way to expanding jobs and welfare.

This model of development calls for states and institutions to play a significant role in building the technological and organizational capabilities of economic actors. It finds support in several currents of political economy which challenge the neo-classical view of institutions as mere distortions of efficient market allocation. The 'new corporatism', however, goes beyond the old corporatist focus on the formal organization of labour, to encompass a wider set of variables that are seen as contributing to successful adjustment and relative economic performance. These include frameworks of financial intermediation, business organization, skills-formation, industrial relations, and state-society linkages.[14]

On the basis of these proposals, politically-conscious reformers went a step further. Connecting the emerging export-led growth model to an explicit class bargain designed to restore the fortunes of the left, supply-side corporatists have argued for new industrial politics along distinct localist and national trajectories.[15] Local pluralists argue that globally-integrated economies allow (or even enhance) the potential for egalitarian initiatives based on strong coordination among local states, firms, and community actors.[16] This contrasts with those who identify particular national sectors and industries as the appropriate sites of intervention, where actors can collaborate to push economic activity into a 'virtuous circle of upmarket industrial restructuring'.[17] Both localist and national corporatist variants profess to being 'ultimately *politically motivated*'. Their objective is to establish 'a similarly productive role for egalitarian redistribution in the creation of *effective supply* as was provided for in the Keynesian model of effective demand'.[18]

The strength of the left's bargaining position on such terms is considerable, we are told. Union participation is indispensable to securing collective inputs that are poorly provided for by the market but which are necessary for quality competition, such as the industrial peace and workplace flexibility necessary for continuous innovation and rapid adjustment to changing markets; education and training systems to enhance the value-adding capacity of workers; and standards around working conditions and wages which foster cooperative networks of flexible firms and mobile workers.[19] In return, firms are to increase investment, shift production away from low-skilled sectors, encourage workplace involvement, agree to floors on conditions and wages, and accede to a more equitable distribution of the gains from increasing competitiveness.

Supply-side concertation thus operates on multiple levels. Within the firm it is intended to facilitate technological change and workplace reorganization; while beyond the level of the firm, the goal is to negotiate shifts in resources between industries, sectors, and regions. The role of left parties is to mobilize the requisite ideological and political support for this strategy, and to oversee its terms while in government. Local and national states can thus, to varying extents, help foreclose the 'low road' (competing on costs) and consolidate the 'high road' (competing on quality). They are able to accomplish this by strengthening labour and environmental regulation, cultivating worker representation through works councils or other means, and softening the impact of restructuring through active social and labour market policies. But how left governments and union leaders might actually go about winning the progressive side of these reforms in the face of capital's resistance is rarely addressed.

The case for 'open-economy corporatism'[20]

The second approach's response to the impasse of left alternatives attempts to breathe new life into distributional arrangements. The dilemma these reformers face is how to overcome the obstacles that came to confront the coordinated welfare state without abandoning its perceived commitments to redistribute wealth and risk, accord a prominent role to labour, and secure relative social and economic stability. The strains on the leading European social democracies are often acknowledged, but advocates of the new distributional politics claim that the point is to adjust, not abandon, traditional principles. What is needed then is 'a feasible open-economy model of corporatism' which can create a 'virtuous circle between domestic egalitarianism and international openness as a political economic model for the world.'[21]

Strategies for an 'open-economy corporatism' set out a double-sided programme. First, they look to use tax, wage, and social policies to renew growth through targeted public investment or improved export performance. Second, they seek to find new means of sharing out the burdens and rewards of sustaining that growth in the face of international and domestic constraints. Policies at the national level may supplement the strategies for international cooperation and competitive capacity-building outlined above, or serve as an independent basis for egalitarian policy. For example many who look to coordinated macroeconomic expansion to overcome the constraints on open economies (usually in the European context) argue that 'income restraint would [still] fall to national governments' to accomplish, since the obstacles to constructing successful systems of wage bargaining at more central levels appear insurmountable.[22] Redistributive policies are also critical for those advocating a supply-side corporatist model, since these can help translate the gains of international competition into further productivity advance and/or prevent excessive wage demands from precipitating a loss of competitiveness. For others, centralized bargaining structures can play a more direct role in reviving progressive politics.

A 'return to incomes policy' is proposed as the most effective means, as Colin Crouch has put it, 'to get a grip on a labour market that is either inflationary or too costly' by international standards.[23] For many of these new corporatists, domestic wage inflation is still the ghost that haunts capitalist economies. Even unemployment, disproportionately high among unskilled workers, cannot prevent skill bottlenecks and hence exorbitant wage increases in high-productivity, post-Fordist industries; nor can it effectively dampen other forces from triggering an inflationary spiral.[24] As globalization has further weakened the already blunt instruments of fiscal and monetary policy, which discipline labour only at a high cost to investment and employment, incomes policy is still seen as a powerful tool in the hands of left governments.

Yet for these new corporatists, institutionalizing wage restraint represents more than a technical fix to an intractable problem of capitalist economies. It is also presented as a positive means of creating space for economic stability and progressive policy.[25] At a minimum, wage restraint is supposed to make possible a relaxation of fiscal and monetary policy, with the potential to create jobs and growth. At best, it can be the pillar of a more assertive national program for full employment. A few left economists, like Andrew Glyn and Bob Rowthorn, argue that the publicly-financed expansion of labour-intensive, non-traded sectors, together with wage subsidies and associated measures, are the best means of addressing sluggish private investment and high unemployment. In this strategy of 'employment spreading', although the priority is placed on over-coming domestic constraints, there is an implicit recognition of the limits imposed by internationalization.[26]

Less ambitious but more commonplace in open-economy corporatist models is the call to reconstruct incomes and social policy to 'get a grip' on labour and social costs in the face of competition. The proliferation of 'social pacts', especially in eastern and southern Europe, is even thought by some to represent a countervailing tendency to pressures to converge on a 'lean welfare state' model.[27] A move to find negotiated responses to international challenges has led to the restoration of broad coordination between unions, employers, and governments, from a series of agreements in Ireland covering pay restraint and social reform to a tripartite framework for incomes policy in Italy.[28] Although often motivated by 'the search for "least bad" solutions by all part-ners concerned in hard times', these efforts are said to help strengthen cooperative institutions of policy-making while tailoring policy outcomes to the external demands of regional integration and economic competitiveness.[29] Workers trade-off wages or benefits for some commitment to jobs and various forms of social protection. The new mix between centralization and decen-tralization of bargaining favoured by the centre-left is reflected in these agreements, as well as in the growing interest in the way the Danes, Dutch, and Austrians have altered their corporatist systems to the perceived demands of flexibility.[30] Welfare states also must adapt to the modern demands of an aging population and the growing visibility of social costs. Even the most ardent supporters of the Scandinavian alternative are now resigned to the need for public sector wages to fall, tax and benefit systems to incorporate stronger incentives to employment, and equality of outcome to further give way to equality of 'opportunity'. The rationale offered, even by welfare state defenders such as Gösta Esping-Andersen, is that short-term pain will eventually yield long-term gain.[31]

Growth strategies based on open-economy corporatism will depend, like its supply-side counterpart, on a set of political preconditions. On this view, social democrats must broker a new distributional bargain favourable enough to induce domestic capital to increase local investment and support high levels of wage solidarity, social services, and public sector growth consistent with its position in international markets. This, in turn, depends on the ability of left parties and trade unions to mobilize the cooperation of labour. The appeal to long-term self-interest with the promise of future gain is clearly one element necessary to the success of this mobilization. But a strategy of eliciting workers' active consent through other means may be just as important if the resort to compulsion is to be avoided. The 'willingness to redistribute' thus becomes a critical variable in the success of egalitarian policy, and developing an ideology of restraint and reciprocity a means of cultivating it.[32] Appeals to 'altruism' and 'patriotism' are seen as necessary and progressive alternatives if, as Andrew Glyn has put it, the costs of these strategies are to be 'willingly shouldered' by labour.[33]

The case for 'corporatist social governance'[34]

The third approach in the social democratic search for a third way calls for a broader social compromise to accompany the new directions in industrial and distributional politics. This compromise involves tapping into available social resources in the form of institutional networks and community activism. Various strategies further aim to expand these resources by extending 'associative', 'stakeholding' or 'communitarian' forms of social participation across economic, political, and cultural spheres. Through civic engagement, reformers hope to address the problem of 'social exclusion' by giving voice to marginalized groups, and to unleash the benefits of increased social dynamism by improving the flow of information, commitment, and trust within expanding social networks. Non-market coordination, they believe, can serve to socially embed market-based adjustment and lessen reliance on competitive forces. Although the models differ in emphasis they converge on the claim that densely organized social environments can contribute to democracy and efficiency in a flexible and globalized world.

Promoters of 'corporatist social governance' are at great pains to distinguish their own partnership models from post-war patterns.[35] Many are quick to recite the problems of cumbersome bureaucracy, a passive citizenry, and an impoverished group politics which came to be associated with the Keynesian welfare state, and few support the kind of 'organized' social economy that flourished during the boom. In place of big labour, big business, and big states they foresee a more 'porous' state, a more heterogeneous organizational politics, and a higher level of popular participation. In other words, corporatist policy-making should move beyond the confines of economic negotiation between an exclusive set of peak associations, and encompass a broader array of social actors, a wider scope for negotiation over public goods, and more possibilities for deepening democratic practice within organizations.

The rediscovery of the 'third sector', the 'social responsibilities' of individuals, and alternative modes of economic and political 'governance' are different aspects of the reconceptualization of civil society.[36] Yet they are also bound up with the left project of repositioning and are linked closely to the new industrial and distributional politics which define it. The success of productivist bargains, for example, is increasingly understood to hinge on the building of an appropriate social infrastructure. Those institutional resources which, as we saw earlier, are supposed to confer competitive advantage in high quality production – the appropriate organization of industrial interests, finance, labour relations and public-private partnerships – may themselves depend on broad framework conditions which make local cohesion, commitment, and coordination likely in the first place. High-trust economies which facilitate a density of interaction and flow of information in turn promote innovation through learning by using, doing, and interacting.

Distributional bargains are to have new roots in civil society. The 'willingness to redistribute' and the culture of trust and reciprocity on which it rests, it is argued, must be reproduced through appropriate social institutions. Moreover the universal welfare state is said to be giving way to a 'mixed economy of care' in which the private and voluntary sectors take over functions previously administered by the state. The devolution of powers to community and regional bodies promises to improve the efficiency of service delivery and the responsiveness of social provision. An expansion of the third sector financed out of taxes is also proposed as one (if not the most politically acceptable) alternative to public sector growth as a means of mopping up surplus labour.[37]

The social democratic articulation of a new social compromise also serves ideological and strategic purposes. The promotion of intermediate social forms (including the centre-left's renewed interest in 'the family') is designed to chart a third way between the unfettered market and bureaucratic state associated respectively with the New Right and Old Left. Further, the more popular style and broader appeal of these societal projects are meant to help link emerging accumulation strategies, built around productivist and distributional bargains, to a more encompassing and explicitly hegemonic project for the left.[38]

One crucial building block of this discourse has been the 'social capital' thesis.[39] Social capital refers to sturdy norms of mutual reciprocity shaped over time by interactions between collective actors. Corporatist social governance theorists argue that besides the formation of physical and 'human' capital which productivist and distributional bargains attend to, a sufficient 'stock' of social capital must be generated if economic and political success are to be assured. As one study of regional prosperity in Italy concludes: 'economic actors embedded in local economic orders possessing dense but relatively egalitarian socio-political networks were able to share information, form alliances, build trust, and resolve conflicts through negotiation… and hence negotiate the process of industrial adjustment.'[40] While early formulations of the social capital thesis assumed the relative immutability of socio-political endowments, finding them anchored in deep-seated cultural traditions, other reformist models contest this view. Anglo-American intellectuals in particular, inspired by the examples of dynamic economic zones in Italy, Japan and Germany, have contemplated ways to produce the societal raw materials of corporatist bargaining in their own countries through conscious institutional design.

'Stakeholding' is one approach which puts forward an assortment of reforms guided by the principle that the interests most affected by institutional decisions are entitled to representation or other forms of protection when those decisions are made.[41] Political measures, it is argued by proponents like Will Hutton, should be taken to improve democratic procedures and enforce rights to information. Economic measures should encourage firm-level consultation and develop skills and other relevant capabilities necessary for participation in the labour market. And social measures should promote inclusiveness and activism in civic life. Working in combination, these reforms will foster a culture of interdependence and cooperation by giving people a greater 'stake' in the community.

'Associational' models take a similar tack.[42] They seek to enhance the quantity and quality of productive social intercourse by creating an environment conducive to self-organization. States should provide civic associations with public status and delegated powers, and in exchange, those associations are to bring their internal practices into compliance with democratic standards. In the end, it is hoped, a parallel system of functional-associational representation will supplement the existing territorial-electoral system. Civic groups based on cooperation will relate to each other through negotiation: the invisible hand of the market and the visible hand of bureaucracy will be complemented by what Bob Jessop calls the 'visible handshake' of democratic associationalism.[43] Participation, accountability, and social cooperation are to be enhanced through these deliberative processes while public policy is rendered more efficient by reducing transaction costs and improving information flows.

Stakeholding and associationalism respond as well to the new social democratic concerns for the constraints imposed by economic flexibility and globalization. First, it is suggested that the erosion of state capacity can be minimized with the positive-sum gains of state-society partnerships, anchoring that capacity in diverse institutional networks.[44] Second, strategies that multiply the cross-commitments of existing actors (e.g. producers, suppliers, consumers, public officials) and attract new investment to vibrant economic zones are also advanced to 'fix' capital in particular places.[45] Only through such a process will firms be constrained by some level of territorial commitment and so persuaded to use their 'voice' instead of 'exit'. The local ties between these actors can then be strengthened and deepened. This process of 'thickening' may be stimulated by a variety of initiatives: regional industrial banks and measures to combat 'short-termism' in financial markets, incentives for firms to decentralize or enter strategic alliances, and support for mutually-owned enterprises or stakeholding companies.[46] In general, greater local commitment and interdependence, it is alleged, will encourage capital to be more 'patient', plan for innovation, and result in greater cooperation between management and labour.

Stakeholding, associationalism, and similar models propose additional foundations to labour–capital partnerships for a third way programme. They fill a few more gaps in an evolving intellectual and strategic framework which envisages multifold changes to industrial, distributional, and civic politics.[47] As political strategies, the prospect of drawing a wider set of social partners into corporatist bargains makes them particularly appealing. Even apparently more radical approaches have tried to incorporate their hegemonic and participatory insights: witness how they also crop up in models of market socialism, the 'negotiated economy', progressive financial reform, and pension fund schemes.[48] Yet as we shall now see, the new social democratic models of partnership are fraught with tensions similar to those of the old and, under the existing balance of class forces, are less likely to ground a counter-hegemonic path of progressive advance than to be subordinated to the increasingly ruthless path of capitalist restructuring.

CONTRADICTIONS OF THE THIRD WAY: THE REAL POLITICAL CONTEXT

The left's case for realignment rests on the claim that corporatist-style politics contributed to stability and growth in the post-war period, but the imperatives of technological progress and global economic expansion now demand their fundamental adjustment. Such assumptions are misleading. On the issue of corporatism, conventional accounts relying on selective history and static correlations gloss over the actual experience of *recurrent* conflict and state coercion.[49] Far from eliminating the contradictions of capitalism corporatist institutions displaced them onto other levels. On the one hand, the commitment to full employment and rising consumption posed a growing constraint on accumulation. On the other, the incorporation of profitability criteria created fissures in the organizations of the working class. Gösta Esping-Andersen was quite correct when he used to argue:

> The contradiction in the corporatist arrangement… is that in order for the corporatist state planning to be insulated from mass pressures, the leadership must be sufficiently isolated from its mass base – causing it to lose its legitimacy. If the leadership is well integrated into the working class and remains a legitimate expression of working class interests, then corporatist planning in the interest of capital accumulation will be undermined to the extent that it is forced to accommodate working class demands.[50]

Corporatist arrangements not only fostered new partnerships, they also fomented new divisions: between the industrial and political wing of the labour movement; within social democratic party structures; and within trade unions.

These tensions worsened as the crisis of overaccumulation generalized and deepened in the Leaden Age.[51] Increasing capitalist competition and working class militancy contributed to deteriorating conditions of profitability, stirring more radical challenges to corporatist arrangements from both right and left. Internationalizing capitalist classes began withdrawing from cross-class redistributional bargains for full employment. At the same time the economic downturn and capitalist mobilization prompted social democratic leaders to ward off more radical challenges within their own movements, embodied in initiatives like the Alternative Economic Strategy in Britain, the Common Program in France, and the Meidner Plan in Sweden. This period of protracted class struggle culminated in an offensive by state managers and capitalist classes to impose flexibility on the workplace, and international competition on national markets. Neither of these was a simple consequence of the forward march of technological progress or expanding markets, as social democratic intellectuals of the post-Fordist and globalist persuasions suggest. Although formulated as responses to mounting systemic pressures, both the employers' offensive and state-administered globalization took shape as explicitly political projects, intended to unleash downward pressures on workers through programmes of austerity and to discipline governments through the 'constitutionalization' of neo-liberalism in inter-state treaties.[52]

The deflationary bias of the crisis and the neo-liberal cast of regional integration projects have helped to undermine left initiatives at the supranational level. The failure of the Social Europe project has brought this home most clearly.[53] At the same time, efforts to recast social democratic alternatives at national and local levels have had to operate in the political landscape bequeathed by intensified exploitation and a new phase of class conflict. With left defeats at the hands of a globalizing bourgeoisie and modernizing party elites, reformers committed to social democratic renewal have turned their attention to the overriding objective of appeasing business. Even those with more radical inclinations who remain unwilling to challenge the prerogatives of global capital are forced to adopt a strategy of enticing capital with the sacrifices of workers. Restated in these terms, the corporatist bargains now on offer represent little more than social democratic means to intensify work, shift income shares to capital, and appropriate the energies of civil society.

'Supply-side corporatism' and the global productivity race

Capitalist competition and industrial militancy, forces which undermined the post-war corporatist bargains, reappear as equally powerful obstacles to supply-side corporatism, and make both the practical feasibility and the alleged progressive potential of this accumulation strategy highly dubious.[54] Under prevailing conditions of excess capacity and weak demand, the supply-side alternative has little hope of solving problems of unemployment and slow growth.[55] Productivity increases in the manufacturing sector will not produce more employment but, in the context of stagnant output and limited demand for manufacturing products, will serve only to reduce the total number of high-wage jobs globally.[56] Leading growth sectors cannot be expected to take up the slack given their capital-intensive nature. Employment strategies centred on training and education are equally feeble. Most are premised on the implausible notion that a skills mismatch and imperfect information in the labour market are the principal sources of mass unemployment, rather than the global crisis of overaccumulation and the neo-liberal project it spawned.

Victory in the race to capture an increasing share of world markets has become increasingly elusive as more and more states adopt the same approach. Export-led debt servicing in the South and the competition for employment in the North drive a near universal agenda of constraining domestic demand and promoting sales in foreign markets. This in turn has contributed to the global crisis of demand amidst falling household consumption, decreasing private investment, and cuts to public expenditure since the 1970s.[57]

All this has meant that as outlets for exports narrow, and low-wage competition remains fierce, supporting egalitarian policies through a strategy of competitiveness becomes increasingly difficult. Where it can be achieved, the productivity growth necessary for export success must not be eaten up by wage increases. But without a socially acceptable sharing out of these gains, at the very least for workers in the export sector, the material basis of the 'trust' which underpins continuous technological change and speedup of the labour process will be undermined. For the global pursuit of competitive advantage is constantly raising the 'productivity bar', forcing technological change and intensification of work. As a result, states must jump ever higher simply to maintain their respective position in the international value-added hierarchy. Increasing output per worker is not enough; to win better living standards, it must be raised faster than in competitor economies.[58] Participation in the global productivity race thus translates into unrelenting pressure to intensify work.

Yet even for technological leaders there are few guarantees that real wages and working conditions will not be eroded. Cut-throat competition and mass unemployment give employers significant reason and opportunity to withhold productivity gains from workers. The post-Fordist faith that quality production for niche markets can be insulated from downward pressure on prices and costs inspires little confidence that wages can be kept out of competition. This fallacy rests on a truncated understanding of the competitive process, and a limited appreciation of the contemporary integration and mobility of capital across sectors and regions.[59] The encroachment of transnational firms on the 'flexibly-specialized' small-firm sectors of Italy and the pressure of Japanese lean production on the 'upmarket industrial restructuring' of Germany seem to reinforce this conclusion.[60]

The contradictions of international competitiveness are only one side of the picture. Under supply-side corporatism the role of organized labour must also be reoriented, so that 'national unions prevent skilled workers from disrupting cooperative shopfloor relations by harnessing their demands for higher wages, exerting sanctions on local union officials, and educating their members on the importance of export success.'[61] Unions may also assume a role in planning shifts in resources between industries, sectors, and regions, moving economic activity from lower to higher value-added production. But these adjustments are more difficult in circumstances of stagnation and unemployment, where there is less hope of redeploying displaced workers. Those who cannot directly contribute to the competitiveness agenda are likely to be left behind, increasing social polarization. In these and other ways, the strategy of supply-side corporatism threatens to harden divisions between workers, as unions are charged with controlling their most militant members and administering uneven development in an export-led growth model dependent on the intensification of labour.[62]

The downward logic of 'open-economy corporatism'

'Open-economy corporatism' confronts a similar set of obstacles. Social democratic arguments notwithstanding, the space for distributional politics has progressively shrunk with the slowdown in growth, internationalization of capital, and intensification of competition. The post-war pattern which in some contexts modestly redistributed income and services *to* the working class now appears to be increasingly ruled out by capital's rejection of binding corporatist bargains. In prominent cases like Sweden and Germany, as elsewhere, business has moved investment off-shore and driven collective bargaining down to industry and company levels.[63]

Unable to impose distributional settlements on capital, more left-wing social democrats propose a different kind of bargain which would redistribute work and income *within* the working class. Under Leaden Age conditions, however, this strategy is likely to be very difficult to sustain.[64] Capitalists will oppose it to the extent that solidaristic bargaining conflicts with the competitive pressure to link wages and conditions more closely to local productivity. Workers will oppose it to the extent that the burden of supporting full employment with lower incomes and higher taxes becomes too high. In reality, with redistribution from capital to labour off the agenda, and redistribution within the working class difficult to maintain, corporatist polices are increasingly used to shift income shares *from* labour to capital.[65] As Leo Panitch anticipated, corporatist structures have become a primary 'vehicle for engineering, legitimating and administering the increase in exploitation... necessary to sustain capital in the crisis.'[66]

With durable and egalitarian distributional bargains apparently on the decline, reformers' enthusiasm for the rise of social pacts is understandable. Although more ad hoc and less binding in nature on the whole, these concertation processes have led to the resumption of tripartism in some countries. A closer look at these pacts reveals a great deal about the changing function of corporatist politics. In many cases, governments have actively forged them to meet treaty obligations arising from participation in regional economic integration. In Europe, states have commonly drawn upon the Maastricht Treaty and the Growth and Stability Pact for 'external' authority to force restructuring on domestic social actors. After voluntarily tying their hands in these international agreements, governments then invoke their binding authority and appeal for 'consensus' on how best to implement them. In this way, states simultaneously push globalization forward while appropriating national structures of concertation to achieve political outcomes that might otherwise be too costly.[67]

Social pacts are also formed as strategies for adjusting to declining competitiveness. If these national concertation processes could be stabilized over time, active coordination across the Euro-zone might become a way of inducing more expansionary policies for growth and employment. But the combined effects of the deflationary bias of the world economic crisis and the restrictive macroeconomic regime adopted in Europe (now enforced by the European Central Bank) make more menacing scenarios of the kind recently described by Andrew Martin rather more likely:

> social pacts… would not necessarily aim *only* at keeping cost growth from exceeding those in other states. They could just as well be aimed at increasing competitiveness by keeping cost growth *below* what it is in their trading partners. …The effort to gain competitive advantage by labor cuts would proceed by collusion instead of coercion. Rather than relying on the weakening of union bargaining and political power by market forces in the context of high unemployment to enable employers (and governments) to impose cuts, cuts would be negotiated. But the understanding of common, or coinciding, interests on which 'competitiveness alliances' are based in any individual states can readily include an interest in cuts relative to those in other states sufficient to gain competitive advantage. To the extent that this logic operates in any of the states in which competitive corporatism is achievable, it would seem difficult for the national actors in any of the other states to avoid seeking cuts to at least restore relative competitiveness if not to gain competitive advantage, whether through national social pacts or not. Thus, a deflationary vicious circle of competitive internal depreciations or labor cost dumping would be as likely to be set in motion by a re-nationalization of wage bargaining as it would in the absence of the national social pacts through which the re-nationalization is manifested. The ensuing increases in unemployment and insecurity seem bound to undermine the legitimacy of the social pacts and the unions that enter into them, accelerating union decline.[68]

Thus a 'return to incomes policy' may indeed be on the horizon, but not for the reasons social democratic intellectuals profess. Whether existing corporatist institutions are being redeployed to raise the rate of exploitation, to drive globalization forward, or as a potential weapon in the competitive struggle over who will bear the brunt of devalorization through the crisis, they are being steadily adapted to the changing and contradictory needs of international accumulation. Administering austerity in this fashion involves a new politics of incorporation. Various ideological appeals have been issued by social democratic leaders around the world to legitimate the sacrifices asked of their memberships: class solidarity, national competitiveness, global determinism, and the myth of 'collective profligacy' are just a few. Where these prove insufficient, the compulsion of the state or market will once again be required. The organizational consequences of such a sustained downward adjustment of living standards secured through corporatist structures and partnership ideologies would not be the virtuous circle of productivity gain and social reform promised by advocates of the third way but its opposite, most likely followed, if historical precedent is any guide, by the further disorganization and renewed demobilization of the working class.[69]

The contradictions of 'corporatist social governance'

Social democracy's efforts to reconfigure civil society represent another contradictory response to the growing demands of participation in a stagnant and integrating capitalist economy. Strategies to promote civic 'engagement' and 'embedded' accumulation reconceive of the community sector as a vehicle for policy implementation and economic development. Unlike the political right though, which favours an increasing reliance on these agencies as a means to shrink the state and 'do more with less', many on the soft left are naively optimistic that measures aimed at improving organizational integration and social cohesion will generate returns to democracy and living standards in the context of a strong partnership state. But in their concern to accommodate capital these societal projects will do little to reverse the wider administrative and economic context wrought by neo-liberalism. Without confronting capital's power more directly, they face the same dangers encountered by the other models of social partnership, of incorporation as subsidiary elements in the global logic of competitive austerity.[70]

The idea of community sector participation in public policy is not new, of course. The ranks of civic organizations have long played a modest role mediating the delivery of social services. Policy consultation and group funding under the Keynesian welfare state also created room within the state for social activists to organize and advocate on behalf of social concerns. As the economic crisis unleashed renewed domestic conflict, and fiscal and political pressures on welfare regimes reached the breaking point, this political presence came to be seen as a barrier to restoring accumulation. Capital's agenda of restructuring the state, to reimpose discipline on workers and facilitate its global ambitions, meant sources of political opposition from workers, social activists, and consumers of social services first had to be minimized. In the ensuing struggle governments have defunded and delegitimized adversarial groups, marginalized state agencies associated with community and social services, and progressively withdrawn from the commitment to social protection of the disadvantaged.[71]

The financial, administrative, regulatory, and ideological framework of the neo-liberal state favours a new mode of incorporation.[72] The retrenchment of

the public sector in the context of growing social need has created new potential for third sector agencies to fill the void, but an increased responsibility for
the delivery of declining services may not be accompanied by greater influence
over the direction of policy. In the words of David Osborne and Ted Gaebler,
whose theories have shaped administrative restructuring around the world,
'entrepreneurial governments have begun to shift to systems that separate policy
decisions (steering) from service delivery (rowing).'[73] For all the social democratic discussion of giving genuine public voice to a diversity of collective actors
the real underlying momentum of policy, especially evident in the rise of
contract-based funding patterns, in fact relegates them to the task of 'rowing'
while reserving for public managers strategic 'steering' decisions such as the
allocation of resources and setting of performance targets. The growth of
public-private 'partnerships' has done little to deflect these trends as bureaucrats
are reluctant to cede authority and tend to dominate them.[74] The emerging role
for associations endorsed by the state is that of compliant service provider, not
the political advocate, public educator, and community organizer envisioned
by left theories of social governance.[75]

Strategies to re-embed development in dynamic social and economic
networks also exaggerate the potential of local and community-based schemes.
They overestimate the capacity of governments to create and maintain local
comparative advantages in institutional and knowledge infrastructures, and
underestimate the limits imposed by global integration on attempts to harness
them for progressive aims. Where extensive economic and social linkages have
not been developed over time and penetrated deeply into the institutional fabric
of a region it is difficult to imagine how they can be constructed *ex nihilo*, as
institutionalist arguments sometimes concede and any number of failed government-sponsored 'science parks' illustrate. Even where successful 'systems of
innovation' have formed, they no longer necessarily respect national and
regional boundaries. The comparative mobility of highly-skilled labour, the
fluidity of information, and technological diffusion through transnational
production systems now extend these systems across borders.[76]

While it may be true that spatial competition gives rise to increased differentiation between regions and makes investment decisions more sensitive to
institutional and even cultural differences, the international mobility and integration of capital still determines the *grounds* for this differentiation. Adjustments
to local socio-economic networks to attract mobile capital must encompass an
ever-wider range of variables informing investment decisions in highly competitive markets. These include not simply the ostensibly beneficial aspects of
high-quality, cooperative, and innovative manufacturing, but all the conditions
of stable and competitive production, from 'favourable' regulatory standards,
tax burdens, wage rates, and working hours to an 'appropriate' work ethic and
managerial culture. As Dick Bryan argues, 'the effect of a globally integrated
economy is to place these socially specific conventions under scrutiny'.[77] The
terms of social democratic discourse around the 'learning economy', 'active

welfare states', and 'social capital' unfortunately appear increasingly receptive to the demands of cultivating such an all-encompassing competitiveness.

Even if increasing flows of capital can successfully be drawn in, social ties of interdependence will do little to hold these regions together or facilitate their egalitarian development under competitive pressures. By tapping into integrated financial markets, 'embedded' firms and community initiatives too are subjected to the disciplinary effects of an internationally-determined rate of return on economic activity, a rate which social democratic governments cannot guarantee.[78] The alternative financial systems offered by stakeholding-type models seem to be rapidly losing their credibility, as firms are increasingly able and willing to bypass intermediate financial sources to borrow directly from integrated capital markets, and evidence accumulates that the social market models of Germany and Japan are in real trouble.

Community-based models of reform exhibit the same disregard as the other partnership models for the contradictory location of corporatist-type structures within the dominant set of economic relations and state determinations. The rhetoric of civic engagement can provide needed legitimation for downloading services onto communities and individuals in the interest of cutting costs and depoliticizing their provision. Shifting activities to the voluntary sector with its lower wages and unionization rates also appeals to state managers concerned to boost competitiveness and reduce the power of organized labour. Finally, civic organizations may add legitimacy and spread responsibility for capitalist restructuring as civic leaders indeed develop a 'stake' in the process.

This dark side of 'community participation' strategies illustrates the serious threat posed to social organizations drawn into them. Barring a major transfer of funds from government, the task of assuming an increasing burden of social service delivery would place tremendous strains on the financial and organizational capacity of third sector agencies. As associations take up the administration of state services in a period of fundamental class restructuring they also risk becoming more directly embroiled in managing social conflicts, internalizing the contradictory demands of social need and administrative efficiency, and creating further splits between leaders and their mass bases. The same dynamic tension between the insulation and integration of organizational leaders vis-à-vis their memberships noted by Esping-Andersen in the neo-corporatist context would be generalized across the associations participating in the governance of capitalist societies. Additional pressures to professionalize, formalize, and bureaucratize their organizational structures would inevitably arise from closer interaction with the state.

These tensions are anticipated in both the theory and incipient practices of corporatist social governance, as they seek to reconcile increasing popular participation with capitalist social relations. Associational theorists like Philippe Schmitter, no doubt informed by his past research as the leading advocate of neo-corporatism, expresses an awareness of the problems of increasing participation *within* the organizational vehicles of capitalist policy. Most proponents defend associative governance at one and the same time for its participatory character – raising the standards of democracy within organizations – and its contribution to 'effective' policy implementation – through efficient means of internal enforcement. Notably Schmitter envisions associational intermediation becoming a sort of 'service industry' for politics, embracing an elite model deliberation which maintains that 'public-regardingness will be maximized if the leadership and staff of associations can be ensured some degree of autonomy from the immediate preferences of their members.'[79] In a related fashion, when stakeholding advocates like Andrew Gamble and Dominic Kelly are pushed on the issue of increasing participation *across* organizations, multiplying the number of stakeholders represented in institutional decision-making, they too make concessions at the cost of democracy. As far as stakeholding in corporate governance is concerned, fearing a gridlock in decision-making, they propose that 'other stakeholders might be given a right to consultation, and possibly beyond that a right to compensation, but the executive autonomy of the firm would be preserved.'[80]

The evidence from community-based models of political and economic reform put into practice is equally uninspiring. Cynthia Cockburn's classic study of local government responses to mounting fiscal pressures and community struggles in England during the 1960s and early 1970s is indicative. Cockburn revealed that the project to incorporate community organizations within the apparatus of the local state was initiated and dominated throughout by state officials; that cooperative groups were forced to adapt their organizational structures to communicate with government, while the most militant groups which challenged the terms of participation were crushed with state repression; and that tensions emerged within participating organizations as increased interaction between organizational elites and local officers pulled leaders away from their bases.[81] In the very different context of Québec in the 1990s, even with its richer institutional legacy, the 'Social Economy' project to build a progressive model of community-based development has thus far been little more than a means of 'reducing the social and wage costs that the competitive export-sectors are asked to bear.'[82]

The theoretical and practical dilemmas of the social governance strategy point clearly to its inadequacy as a hegemonic project for the left. Incapable of transforming the balance of class forces crystallized in the neo-liberal state and globalized market, it is powerless to lead the programme of civic renewal and political democratization it espouses, and risks being appropriated by a very different hegemonic formation that William Robinson has called 'promoting polyarchy': low-intensity democracy supported by elite management of popular pressures within civil society.[83] Similarly, the move to harness the economic potential of community actors holds little promise of embedding a more humane path of development, but harbours the significant threat of institutionalizing those actors' role as caretakers for the social and ecological waste left behind in the race for global position.

Conclusions

The economistic foundations of the left's 'New Way' bear remarkable resemblances to those of the old ways of classical social democracy: attempting to rebuild its political project on the social relations called forth by its 'progressive' economic forces of flexibility and globalization, and the pursuit of an elusive cross-class bargain with a progressive fraction of the bourgeoisie.[84] In declining to challenge the unconstrained power of global capital, even social democratic intellectuals who might offer some substance to the rhetoric of the third way leave few options but to entice capital with the sacrifices of workers. Social democracy will no doubt continue to position itself as the movement uniquely situated to secure the sacrifices capital now demands with the least threat of political disruption, drawing on its relationships to organized labour and community groups much as it has in the past. But exploiting these same relationships would seem to bring further advantages today in the competitive drive to lower costs on accumulation. Wage, welfare, and social reproduction costs remain for the most part nationally-specific variables – variables distinguishing rival investment sites within global chains of production – which may be altered through programmes for reform. The social democratic agenda increasingly targets these variables as it seeks to adapt not just industrial and political structures, but social structures as well, to the imperative to compete and win in global markets. In pursuit of this agenda, the so-called modernizing left asks workers to trade away what remains of their post-war entitlements for the chimerical promise of participation in a global knowledge economy, and to buy into the new industrial, distributional, and civic accords which purport to make it possible. But with the legacy of overaccumulation still unravelling and the ravages of international competition unyielding, these reformist 'bargains' amount to little more than a 'negotiated' path to austerity.

The contradictions of the third way may come quickly to a head when exposed as little more than social democracy's path to the downward adjustment of domestic living standards and the export of unemployment abroad. For it is difficult to imagine how the effect of third way reforms can be anything other than that of 'ratcheting down the playing field on which the next round of competitive struggle will then be played out… further alienating electorates already highly sceptical about mainstream politics.'[85] The hope, then, must be that socialists will find ways to move into the political space opened up by the repositioning of social democracy and the false alternatives it now peddles, and put real alternatives back on the agenda.

NOTES

I would like to thank Greg Albo, Murray Cooke, Colin Leys, Chris Mohr, John Peters and Leo Panitch for their kind help.

1. Perry Anderson, 'Introduction' to Anderson and P. Camiller, eds., *Mapping the West European Left*, Verso, London 1994, pp. 15-16.

2. Joel Rogers and Wolfgang Streeck, 'Productive Solidarities: Economic Strategy and Left Politics', in D. Miliband, ed., *Reinventing the Left*, Polity, Cambridge 1994; Charles Sabel, 'Bootstrapping Reform: Rebuilding Firms, the Welfare State, and Unions', *Politics & Society*, vol. 23, no. 1, March 1995.

3. Michael Piore and Charles Sabel, *The Second Industrial Divide*, Basic, New York 1984; Arndt Sorge and Wolfgang Streeck, 'Industrial Relations and Technical Change: The Case for an Extended Perspective', in R. Hyman and W. Streeck, eds., *New Technology and Industrial Relations*, Basil Blackwell, Oxford 1988. Broadly speaking, the post-Fordist approach may be seen to encompass the flexible special-ization and diversified quality production theses, as well as variants of neo-Schumpterian, institutionalist, and regulationist theories; cf. Winfried Ruigrok and Rob van Tulder, *The Logic of International Restructuring*, Routledge, London 1995, ch. 1.

4. Torben Iversen, 'Power, Flexibility, and the Breakdown of Centralized Bargaining', *Comparative Politics*, vol. 28, no. 4, 1996.

5. Fritz Scharpf, *Crisis and Choice in European Social Democracy*, Cornell University, Ithaca 1991; Paulette Kurzer, *Business and Banking*, Cornell University, Ithaca 1992; John Gray, *After Social Democracy*, Demos, London 1996.

6. It should be noted that the thesis of the declining capacity of the state finds expres-sion among those who stress post-Fordist shifts as well. See Franz Traxler and Brigitte Unger, 'Governance, Economic Restructuring, and International Competitiveness', *Journal of Economic Issues*, vol. 28, 1993, especially p. 17; Andrew Sayer, *Radical Political Economy: A Critique*, Blackwell, Oxford 1995; J.R. Hollingsworth and R. Boyer, eds., *Contemporary Capitalism: The Embeddedness of Institutions*, Cambridge University, Cambridge 1997. For a critique see Jamie Gough, 'Theorizing the State in Local Economic Governance', *Regional Studies*, vol. 32, November 1998.

7. Helpful surveys of social democratic thinking about strategic alternatives include: George DeMartino and Stephen Cullenberg, 'Beyond the Competitiveness Debate: An Internationalist Agenda', *Social Text*, no. 41, 1994; Aram Eisenschitz and Jamie Gough, 'The Contradictions of Neo-Keynesian Local Economic Strategy', *Review of International Political Economy*, vol. 3, no. 3, 1996; Greg Albo, 'A World Market of Opportunities? Capitalist Obstacles and Left Economic Policy', *Socialist Register 1997*, Merlin, London 1997; and David Coates, *Models of Capitalism: Growth and Stagnation in the Modern Era*, Polity, Oxford, forthcoming.

8. Existing barriers include the relative weakness of international labour organizations and the unflinching opposition of key sections of international capital and the US state. The intensification of national rivalries within a stagnant and integrated global economy also works against coordinated macroeconomic expansion, creating a 'free rider' problem as countries which minimize expansionary measures stand to benefit at the expense of others continuing to expand. Many have tried to account for the mechanism of this 'deflationary bias' within a world

economy characterized by slow growth and international capital mobility. See, for example, the early and accessible restatement of the Keynesian critique focusing on the role of financial markets: Michael Stewart, *The Age of Interdependence: Economic Policy in a Shrinking World*, MIT, Cambridge, Mass. 1984.

9.   Anthony Giddens, *The Third Way*, Polity, Cambridge 1998; Tony Blair, *The Third Way*, The Fabian Society, London 1998. *The Economist* glibly but fairly accurately describes the experience of engaging with these semi-official statements: 'Trying to pin down an exact meaning in all this is like wrestling an inflatable man. If you get a grip on one limb, all the hot air rushes to another', December 19–January 1, 1999, p. 73.

10.   Samuel Bowles, Robert Boyer, Herbert Gintis, Michael Piore, Charles Sabel, David Soskice and Wolfgang Streeck have been leading advocates of this position.

11.   Dick Bryan's thoughtful work explaining the ascendance of the international competitiveness agenda places a strong emphasis on current account imbalances and the way they came to be constructed in economic discourse. The sum total of these imbalances (surpluses and deficits combined) among the larger industrial countries jumped from a level below 100 billion per year before 1982 to over 300 billion in the second half of the 1980s, a level representing over 2% of aggregate GDP. Bryan, 'International Competitiveness: National and Class Agendas', *Journal of Australian Political Economy*, no. 35, 1994, pp. 2–3.

12.   Dick Bryan, *The Chase Across the Globe: International Accumulation and the Contradictions for Nation States*, Westview, Boulder 1995, ch. 9.

13.   As Britain's Commission on Social Justice puts it, 'while demand management remains a fundamental issue at the European level, it is under-investment – and our capacity to export – rather than under-consumption that is the foremost economic problem', *Social Justice: Strategies for National Renewal*, Vintage, London 1994, p. 103.

14.   Peter Hall, 'The Role of Interests, Institutions, and Ideas in the Comparative Political Economy of the Industrialized Nations', in M. Lichbach and A. Zuckerman, eds., *Comparative Politics*, Cambridge University, Cambridge 1997.

15.   Based in part on initial divisions within post-Fordist research, two theoretical positions emerged which drew inspiration from different empirical referents: either the 'Third Italy', characterized by local concentrations of small and medium firms producing exports for niche markets and held together by strong 'informal ties' and the shared provision of collective services; or the 'Rhenish model' distinguished by larger firms producing high-quality products in differentiated but high-volume markets, ordered by more formal legal and institutional arrangements.

16.   Influential writers making such arguments include Charles Sabel, Michael Piore, Paul Hirst, Jonathan Zeitlin, Alan Scott, Michael Storper, Philip Cooke, David Wolfe. This tendency is comparatively suspicious of the nation state, trusting of informal ties and community values for enforcing cross-commitments, and appeals more to the small- and medium-sized business sector. See the extensive critical work by Aram Eisenschitz and Jamie Gough on the 'local pluralists': *The Politics of Local Economic Policy*, Macmillan, London 1993; 'Theorizing the State in Local Economic Governance', *Regional Studies*, 32, November 1998.

17.   Streeck, *Social Institutions and Economic Performance*, p. 54. See also Philippe Schmitter, 'Sectors in Modern Capitalism: Modes of Governance and Variations in Performance', in R. Brunetta and C. Dell'Aringa, eds., *Labour Relations and*

Economic Performance, Macmillan, London 1990 and the contributions to J. Roger Hollingsworth, Philippe Schmitter, and Wolfgang Streeck, *Governing Capitalist Economies: Performance and Control of Economic Sectors*, Oxford University, Oxford 1994.

18. Wolfgang Streeck, 'On the Institutional Conditions of Diversified Quality Production', in E. Matzner and Streeck, *Beyond Keynesianism*, Edward Elgar, Aldershot, 1991, pp. 28, 48.

19. Wolfgang Streeck, 'Training and the New Industrial Relations: A Strategic Role for Unions', in M. Regini, ed., *The Future of Labour Movements*, Sage, London 1992; Rogers and Streeck, 'Productive Solidarities: Economic Strategy and Left Politics'; Charles Sabel, 'Can the End of Social Democratic Trade Unions be the Beginning of a New Kind of Social Democratic Politics?', in S. Sleigh, ed., *Economic Restructuring and Emerging Patterns of Industrial Relations*, W.E. Upjohn Institute for Employment Research, Kalamazoo, Mich. 1993.

20. Andreas Boltho, Colin Crouch, Robert Dore, Gösta Esping-Anderson, Geoffrey Garrett, Andrew Glyn, Ton Notermans, Martin Rhodes, Bob Rowthorn, and Frank Vandenbrouke take up diverse political positions in this literature.

21. Geoffrey Garrett, 'A Virtuous Global Circle', *Boston Review*, vol. 22, no. 6, December 1997/January 1998 and *Partisan Politics in the Global Economy*, Cambridge University, Cambridge 1998.

22. Grahame Thompson, 'The Death of a Keynesian Europe? Prospects for Expansion and Political Constraints', in J. Michie and J. Grieve Smith, eds., *Creating Industrial Capacity*, Oxford University, Oxford 1996, p. 187.

23. Colin Crouch, 'Incomes Policies, Institutions and Markets: An Overview of Recent Developments', in R. Dore, R. Boyer and Z. Mars, eds., *The Return to Incomes Policies*, Pinter, London 1994, p. 186.

24. See the essays in Boyer and Dore in ibid. The creation of the European Central Bank is even seen to have possible inflationary consequences to the extent that national central banks no longer possess the credible threat they once wielded to hold wage demands in check. See Andrew Martin, 'EMU and Wage Bargaining: The Americanization of the European Labor Market?', Center for European Studies, Harvard University, September 1998, pp. 22-6.

25. Dan Corry and Andrew Glyn, 'The Macroeconomics of Equality, Stability and Growth', in Glyn and D. Miliband, eds., *Paying for Inequality*, Institute for Public Policy Research, London 1994. See also Glyn's 'Social Democracy and Full Employment', *New Left Review*, no. 211, May-June 1995 and 'Egalitarianism in a Global Economy', *Boston Review*, vol. 22, no. 6, December 1997/January 1998; Geoffrey Garrett, *Partisan Politics*; Frank Vandenbroucke, *Globalisation, Inequality and Social Democracy*, Institute for Public Policy Research, London 1998.

26. Glyn's notion of a 'non-free-lunch-Keynesianism' acknowledges the need to finance initiatives through higher taxes and wage moderation, instead of government deficits which could prompt a backlash from financial markets, and to maintain the competitiveness of the export sector through targeted public spending which contributes to productivity growth. See Albo's discussion of 'employment spreading' in Albo, 'A World Market of Opportunities?'.

27   International Labour Review, 'Perspectives: Experience of Social Pacts in Western Europe', *International Labour Review*, vol. 134, no. 3, 1995; Martin Rhodes, 'Globalization, Labour Markets and Welfare States: A Future of

'Competitive Corporatism'?', in M. Rhodes and Y. Mény, eds., *The Future of European Welfare: A New Social Contract?*, Macmillan, London 1998; Geoffrey Garrett, *Partisan Politics*.

28. Charles Sabel, *Ireland: Local Partnership and Social Innovation*, Organisation for Economic Co-operation and Development, Paris 1996; M. Regini and I. Regalia, 'Employers, Unions and the State: the Resurgence of Concertation in Italy?', *West European Politics*, vol. 25, no. 1.

29. Rhodes, 'Globalization', p. 195.

30. Franz Traxler, 'Farewell to Labour Market Associations? Organized versus Disorganized Decentralization as a Map for Industrial Relations' and Colin Crouch, 'Reconstructing Corporatism? Organized Decentralization and Other Paradoxes' in Crouch and Traxler, eds., *Organized Industrial Relations in Europe: What Future?*, Avebury, Aldershot 1995.

31. 'The most logical solution… is that we rethink the idea of redistribution and rights: accepting inequality for some, here and now, but guaranteeing at the same time that those who fare less well 'here and now' will not always do so; that under-privileged will not be a permanent feature of anyone's life course. This kind of dynamic, life-chances commitment to equality is arguably a positive-sum solution in that it stresses a social policy more explicitly designed to optimize the self-reliant capacities of the citizenry… the core of such a model's social citizenship guarantee would combine education and proactive income maintenance.', Gösta Esping-Andersen, 'After the Golden Age? Welfare State Dilemmas in a Global Economy', in Esping-Andersen, *Welfare States in Transition*, Sage, London 1996, p. 10.

32. Vandenbrouke discusses the importance of the 'willingness to redistribute' in *Globalisation, Inequality and Social Democracy*, pp. 43–51. A growing literature attempts to link cooperative industrial relations and efficient inter-firm relations to conditions reciprocity and 'trust'. See most recently the 'Special Issue on Contracts and Competition', *Cambridge Journal of Economics*, vol. 21, no. 2, March 1997; Charles Sabel, 'Constitutional Orders: Trust Building and Response to Change', in Hollingsworth and Boyer, *Contemporary Capitalism*; Christel Lane and Reinhard Bachmann, eds., *Trust Within and Between Organizations*, Oxford University, New York 1998.

33. Glyn, 'Social Democracy and Full Employment', p. 55. Dore argues: 'The history of incomes policies is… the history of attempts (a) to deploy these three argu-ments – the self-interest argument, the patriotism argument and the altruism argument – (b) to generate levels of mutual trust which assured those who were swayed by those arguments that others would not take advantage of them, and/or, where trust was weak, to back them up with statutory instruments and legal sanctions', to which one might add the direct compulsion of the market. 'Introduction: Incomes Policy', p. 8.

34. Leading progressive intellectuals calling for social renewal based on greater community and local participation include stakeholding advocates like Will Hutton and Andrew Gamble; associationalists like Joshua Cohen, Paul Hirst, Joel Rogers, Charles Sabel, and Philippe Schmitter; economic sociologists of the 'socio-economics' and 'embeddedness' approaches like Amitai Etzioni and Mark Granovetter; progressive geographers like Ash Amin, Michael Storper, and Philip Cooke; as well as left proponents of strategies to develop 'social capital' and 'third sector'.

35. Many expressly reject the corporatist label: Will Hutton, 'An Overview of Stakeholding', in G. Kelly, D. Kelly, and A. Gamble, eds., *Stakeholder Capitalism*, Macmillan, London 1997, p. 7; Joshua Cohen and Joel Rogers, 'Solidarity, Democracy, Association', in Cohen and Rogers, *Associations and Democracy*, E.O. Wright ed., Verso, London 1995.

36. The notion of a 'third sector' attempts to distinguish analytically the sphere occupied by voluntary, non-profit and cooperative organizations from the 'public' and 'private' sectors.

37. Jeremy Rifkin's defence of this strategy has been influential. See *The End of Work*, G.P. Putnam's Sons, New York 1995.

38. The current lack of political enthusiasm for left strategies based on industrial and incomes policies, especially in the Anglo-American countries, is well recognized. The difficulty of winning their popular acceptance without wrapping them in a more appealing and accessible social package has been noted by, among others, William Tabb, 'Vampire Capitalism', *Socialist Review*, vol. 22, no. 1, January/March 1992. See Colin Leys, 'A Radical Agenda for Britain', *New Left Review*, no. 212, July/August 1995, pp. 9–13 on the example of stakeholding as a hegemonic project.

39. Key texts include James Coleman, *The Foundations of Social Theory*, Harvard University, Cambridge 1990; Robert Putnam, *Making Democracy Work*, Princeton University, Princeton 1993; Peter Evans, 'Government Action, Social Capital and Development: Reviewing the Evidence on Synergy', *World Development*, vol. 24, no. 6, 1996; Simon Szreter, 'Social Capital, the Economy and the Third Way', http://www.nexus.org/debates/3wayecon/library/socialcap.htm.

40. Richard Locke, *Remaking the Italian Economy*, Cornell University, Ithaca 1998, p. 175.

41. Major works include John Kay, *The Foundations of Corporate Success*, Oxford University, Oxford 1993; Will Hutton, *The State We're In*, revised edition, Vintage, London 1996; Gavin Kelly, Dominic Kelly, and Andrew Gamble, *Stakeholder Capitalism*; Bruce Ackerman and Anne Alstott, *The Stakeholder Society*, Yale University, New Haven 1999.

42. Basic sources include Wolfgang Streeck and Philippe Schmitter, Philippe Schmitter, 'Corporative Democracy: Oxymoronic? Just Plain Moronic? Or a Promising Way Out of the Present Impasse?', mimeograph, Stanford University, Stanford 1988; Hirst, *Associative Democracy*; Charles Sabel, 'Learning by Monitoring: The Institutions of Economic Development', in N. Smelser and R. Swedberg, eds., *Handbook of Economic Sociology*, Princeton University, Princeton 1994; Cohen and Rogers, *Associations and Democracy*; Ash Amin, 'Beyond Associative Democracy', *New Political Economy*, vol. 1, no. 3, November 1996; and Philip Cooke and Kevin Morgan, *The Associational Economy: Firms, Regions, and Innovation*, Oxford, Oxford 1998. Associational research has proceeded along two somewhat distinct trajectories, a post-corporatist one and a local pluralist one. This mirrors the above noted split in post-Fordist thought. For the former tendency, see Streek, Schmitter, Cohen and Rogers; for the latter, see Sabel, Hirst, Cooke and Morgan.

43. Bob Jessop, 'The Governance of Complexity and the Complexity of Governance', in A. Amin and J. Hausner, eds., *Beyond Market and Hierarchy*, Edward Elgar, London 1997, p. 117.

44. Jeffrey Hart, *Rival Capitalists*, Cornell University, Ithaca 1992; Peter Evans, 'Government Action, Social Capital'.

45. Ash Amin and Nigel Thrift, 'Living in the Global', in Amin and Thrift, *Globalization, Institutions, and Regional Development in Europe*, Oxford University, Oxford 1994; Paul Hirst and Grahame Thompson, *Globalization in Question*, Polity, Oxford 1996, pp. 144-7; and Boyer and Hollingsworth, 'From National Embeddedness' all make arguments to this effect.

46. Amin and Thomas, 'Living in the Global', p. 275; Cooke and Morgan, *The Associational Economy*.

47. Efforts to bring some of these intellectual strands together include, David Miliband, 'The New Politics of Economics', in C. Crouch and D. Marquand, eds., *Ethics and Markets: Co-operation and Competition within Capitalist Economies*, Blackwell, Oxford 1993; Hall, 'The Role of Interests'; Jessop, 'The Governance of Complexity' and the various contributions to Hollingsworth and Boyer, eds., *Contemporary Capitalism*.

48. On market socialism see Erik Olin Wright, 'Political Power, Democracy and Coupon Socialism', in J. Roemer, *Equal Shares*, Verso, London 1996; on 'negotiated economy' models, see Ash Amin and Damian Thomas, 'The Negotiated Economy: State and Civic Institutions in Denmark', *Economy and Society*, vol. 25, no. 2, May 1996; on associational monitoring as an aspect of financial reform, see Robert Pollin, 'Financial Structures and Egalitarian Economic Policy', *New Left Review*, no. 214, November/December 1995; and on pension funds schemes, see Robin Blackburn, 'The New Collectivism: Pension Reform, Grey Capitalism and Complex Socialism', *New Left Review*, no. 233, January/February 1999.

49. Leo Panitch, 'The Tripartite Experience', in K. Banting, ed., *The State and Economic Interests*. University of Toronto, Toronto 1986; Simon Clarke, *Keynesianism, Monetarism and the Crisis of the State*, Edward Elgar, Aldershot 1988; and Paulette Kurzer, *Business and Banking* expose different dimensions of this instability. Garrett, *Partisan Politics*, is a blatant example of the weakness of contemporary social democratic analysis, attributing much of the current troubles of social corporatism to mistaken policy decisions.

50. Gösta Esping-Andersen, Roger Friedland and Erik Olin Wright, 'Modes of Class Struggle and the Capitalist State', *Kapitalistate*, nos. 4/5, Summer 1976, p. 197.

51. For detailed Marxist accounts of the present crisis see the different perspectives offered by Michael Webber and David Rigby, *The Golden Age Illusion*, Guilford, New York 1996; Robert Brenner, 'Uneven Development and the Long Downturn: The Advanced Capitalist Economies from Boom to Stagnation, 1950-1998', *New Left Review*, no. 299, May/June 1998.

52. For efforts to theorize this process, see Stephen Gill, 'The Emerging World Order and European Change,' *Socialist Register 1992*, and Leo Panitch, 'Globalisation and the State,' *Socialist Register 1994*.

53. Bernard Moss summarizes the recent experience of European workers: 'whatever unions may have gained from the EC – training schemes, works councils, health and safety legislation – they have lost through EC sponsored deflation and deregulation.', 'Is the European Community Politically Neutral? The Free Market Agenda,' in B. Moss and J. Michie, eds., *The Single European Currency in National Perspective: A Community in Crisis?*, Macmillan, London 1998, p. 161.

54. For detailed theoretical and political analysis, see the evolving critique of the

progressive competitiveness position in and around the *Socialist Register* since 1994. See also Bryan, *Chase Across the Globe*; Eisenschitz and Gough, 'The Contradictions of Neo-Keynesian Local Economic Strategy'; George DeMartino, 'Industrial Policies versus Competitiveness Strategies: In Pursuit of Prosperity in the Global Economy', *International Papers in Political Economy*, vol. 3, no. 2, 1996; Hugo Radice, '"Globalization" and National Differences', *Competition and Change*, vol. 3, no. 4, 1998 for other important perspectives.

55. Awareness of the impending dangers is much higher in the financial press than it is among social democratic leaders and intellectuals: 'the global "output gap" between actual and potential production will, by the end of 1999, be at its widest since the 1930s. If the economies of America or Europe were to take a sudden lurch downwards, the world might easily experience outright depression, with prices and output falling together, just as they did 70 years ago', *The Economist*, February 20-26, 1999, p. 15.

56. Eileen Appelbaum and Ronald Schettkat, 'Employment and Productivity in Industrialized Economies', *International Labour Review*, vol. 134, nos. 4-5, 1995.

57. Edward Nell, 'Stagnation, Volatility, and the Changing Composition of Aggregate Demand', in J. Eatwell, ed., *Global Unemployment*, M.E. Sharpe, Armonk 1996. See Greg Albo, '"Competitive Austerity" and the Impasse of Capitalist Employment Policy', *Socialist Register 1994*, on the general logic at work.

58. Dick Bryan, 'International Capital and the Valuing of Labour', *Journal of Contemporary Asia*, vol. 27, no. 4, 1997, p. 78.

59. See especially Howard Botwinick, *Persistent Inequalities*, Princeton University, Princeton 1993 and Bryan, *Chase Across the Globe*.

60. Ash Amin and Nigel Thrift, 'Neo-Marshallian Nodes in Global Networks', *International Journal of Urban and Regional Research*, vol. 16, 1992; Birgit Mahnkopf, 'Between the Devil and the Deep Blue Sea: The German Model Under the Pressure of Globalisation', *Socialist Register 1999*; Coates, *Models of Capitalism*.

61. Kathleen Thelen, 'Beyond Corporatism: Toward a New Framework for the Study of Labor in Advanced Capitalism', *Comparative Politics*, October 1994, p. 121.

62. Albo, 'A World Market of Opportunities?', p. 20.

63. The level of outward foreign direct investment more than tripled in Sweden and Germany during the last half of the 1980s and the push by employers to decentralize bargaining in both countries has also been well documented. Stuart Wilks, 'Class Compromise and the International Economy: The Rise and Fall of Swedish Social Democracy', *Capital and Class*, no. 58, Spring 1996, p. 101; Brenner, 'Uneven Development and the Long Downturn', p. 229.

64. See the discussion in Greg Albo, 'Canadian Unemployment and Socialist Employment Policy', in T. Dunk, S. McBride and R. Nelsen, eds., *The Training Trap*, Fernwood, Halifax 1996.

65. This is now accepted by many social democrats as the unavoidable consequence of economic globalization. See Scharpf, *Crisis and Choice* and Evelyne Huber and John Stephens, 'Internationalization and the Social Democratic Model', *Comparative Political Studies*, vol. 31, no. 3, June 1998.

66. Leo Panitch, *Working Class Politics*, p. 204.

67. See Andrew Martin, 'EMU and Wage Bargaining', pp. 26-34.

68. Ibid., pp. 28-9.

69. See Panitch, *Working Class Politics*, ch. 4 and p. 204 on the effects of the British

Labour Government's 'social contract' negotiations in 1975–6.

70. Leslie Pal, 'Civic Re-alignment: NGOs and the Contemporary Welfare State', in R. Blake, P. Bryden and F. Strain, eds., *The Welfare State in Canada*, Irwin, Concord 1997; John Shields and B. Mitchell Evans, *Shrinking the State: Globalization and Public Administration 'Reform'*, Fernwood, Halifax, 1998; Paul Nelson, *The World Bank and Non-Governmental Organizations: The Limits of Apolitical Development*, Macmillan, London 1995; Patrick Bond and Mzwanele Mayekiso, 'Developing Resistance and Resisting 'Development': Reflections from the South African Struggle', *Socialist Register 1996*, and Ben Fine, *The World Bank and Social Capital: A Critical Skinning*, unpublished paper.

71. In Toronto, for instance, studies conducted in 1995 and 1996 found that the 293 community-based social service agencies surveyed had lost $11 million from government sources, creating a funding crisis in that sector. Jamie Swift, *Civil Society in Question*, Behind the Lines, Toronto 1999, p. 76. Funding for Canadian social movement organization has also been cut, assisted by an ideological campaign to portray these groups as 'special interests'.

72. Pal, 'Civic Re-alignment'; Shields and Evans, *Shrinking the State*, ch. 5.

73. David Osborne and Ted Gaebler, *Reinventing Government*, Reading, Mass: Addison–Wesley, 1992, p. 35.

74. Shields and Evans, *Shrinking the State*.

75. Paul Leduc Browne, *Love in a Cold World? The Voluntary Sector in the Age of Cuts*, Canadian Centre for Policy Alternatives, Ottawa 1996.

76. Radice, '"Globalization" and National Differences', pp. 16–18.

77. Dick Bryan and Michael Rafferty, *The Global Economy in Australia*, St. Leonards, Allen & Unwin, Australia 1999, p. 71.

78. Dick Bryan, 'National Economic Strategies and International Finance', *Journal of Australian Political Economy*, no. 39, 1997.

79. Schmitter, 'Corporative Democracy', p. 26.

80. Andrew Gamble and Gavin Kelly, 'Stakeholder Capitalism: Limits and Opportunities', http://www.dar.cam.ac.uk/nexus/gamkel.html, p. 5.

81. Cynthia Cockburn, *The Local State*, Pluto, London 1977.

82. Peter Graefe, 'The High Value-Added, Low-Wage Model: Progressive Competitiveness in Québec from Bourassa to Bouchard', paper presented to the Third Annual Great Lakes Conference in Political Economy, York University, Toronto, May 8, 1998, p. 20.

83. William Robinson, *Promoting Polyarchy*, Cambridge University, Cambridge 1996.

84. Simon Clarke, 'The Crisis of Fordism or the Crisis of Social-Democracy?', *Telos*, no. 83, 1990, pp. 76–7.

85. Coates, *Models of Capitalism*, Conclusion.

OTHER PLEASURES: THE ATTRACTIONS OF POST-CONSUMERISM

KATE SOPER

THERE ARE TWO main reasons, both of them accountable in one way or another to the legacy of Marxism, why socialists in the twentieth century have tended to be cautious about embracing utopian ideas. One lies in the sense that a responsible socialist politics cannot be content with moral posturing about desirable futures, but must relate its aspirations for social change to the potentials for this already immanent in the existing order of society. Here, the anti-utopian argument comes in the form of a rejection of voluntarism, and its longstanding influence on the left owes a great deal to the polemic sustained by Marx and Engels against idealist conceptions of the revolutionary process. Communism, as they explain in the much quoted passage from *The German Ideology*, is not a state of affairs to be established or an ideal to which reality will have to adjust itself, but 'the real movement which abolishes the present state of things', and 'the conditions of this movement result from the premises now in existence'.[1]

The second, and related, reason for socialist caution about utopianism derives from Marx's resistance to inductive arguments about the future: his refusal to allow claims about the present character of human beings to have any bearing on what might be possible in post-capitalist society. Elements of this argument (which comes in effect to operate as a kind of veto on any blueprinting of the communist mode of existence) are to be found in *The German Ideology*, the *Critique of the Gotha Programme* and other texts. But it is given particularly forceful expression in the *Grundrisse*, where it is implied that inferences drawn from human nature as it now is offer little gauge for judging what it can or will become, and that the future is in this sense unmeasurable by any present yardsticks:

> When the limited bourgeois form is stripped away, what is wealth other than the universality of individual needs, capacities, pleasures, productive forces, etc., created through universal exchange? The full development of human mastery over the forces of nature, those of so-called nature as well as of humanity's own nature? The absolute working-out of all his creative potentialities with no presupposition other than the previous historic development, which makes this totality of development (...) the end in itself, not measured by a *predetermined* yardstick? Where he does not reproduce himself in one specificity, but produces his totality? Strives not to remain something he has become, but is in the absolute movement of becoming?[2]

There is a good deal to be said in support of both these types of objection to utopian speculation. Marx is right to warn against indulging in purely wishful visions of the future, and one cannot but endorse his strictures (and they could extend today to some 'unreconstructed' Marxists themselves) against those who fail to relate their conception of how things ought to be to conducive factors or potential agents of transformation in the present. One also needs to be wary of the paternalist – even totalitarian – implications of confident pronouncements on what is wrong in the present, and what needs to be done to correct it in the future. Overly rigid and detailed projections of future economic and political 'needs' and forms of human self-realization are certainly not without their dangers, and have resulted in some disastrous forms of fanaticism. A post-structuralist sensibility of the kind exercised by Derrida in his *Specters of Marx* towards what he sees as the overly ontologizing impetus of a Marxist-socialist theory has in this sense some rationale. Yet as I myself have argued in the context of a discussion of *Specters of Marx*, it is precisely in his projections of communism as a society unmeasurable by future yardsticks that Marx comes closest to the spirit of these Derridean recommendations; but also here, too, that he tends to expose most clearly the risks of exercising too many scruples about the specification of future political forms. For too little ontology can be just as dangerous as too much; and one could argue that in his failure to be more specific about the conditions of realization of a genuinely democratic and egalitarian post-capitalist order Marx left open a dangerous vacuum in the theory of communism: a vacuum that in the event came to be filled by a totalitarian form of politics.[3]

Moreover, ready as Marx was to rebuke the 'utopian socialists' for their lack of realism in failing to appreciate that the only possible future form of society is that already latently inscribed in the present, he failed himself to see the force of this argument in relation to his own claims about human nature. A society whose gains could not be assessed by reference to any present moral or emotional yardsticks would seem no less open to the charge of idealist projection than one envisaged in complete abstraction from already existing levels of productivity and technical development. It is true that Marx expected human nature to be 'purged' and transformed in the process of revolution itself, and that the latter can have a dramatic impact on the feelings and outlook of those caught up in its making. All the same, some minimal continuity between the existing bourgeois structures of needs and moral sensibilities and those developed under communism would seem a condition of the emergence of the political will to revolution in the first place.[4]

RE-ENGAGING WITH UTOPIAN ARGUMENT

The Marxist position on utopian thinking, one may therefore argue, was never quite as coherent as some followers made out, and in the light of these limitations alone there is reason for socialists to reconsider the impact of its legacy. But there are additionally a number of more concrete and historically specific factors that might today invite a more positive conception of the political role of utopianism.

In the first place, some form of alternative, utopian vision is a prerequisite of the socialist critique, and alone renders it self-consistent. Socialists themselves will no doubt differ in their opinions about the extent to which the realization of a democratically organized, egalitarian, non-capitalist global order remains a realistic political goal. They may have different opinions, too, about whether it is possible to remain socialist in the absence of belief in the coming of a socialist order. The more orthodox Marxists will no doubt think of it as contradictory to defend a socialist form of critique without a correlative faith in the possibility of socialist progress. Others are likely to regard it as quite consistent to profess their socialism as a form of dissent from, or moral witness to, the iniquities of capitalism without sustaining any great hopes of advancing its political principles and programmes. But in either event, the vision of an alternative society is essential to the coherence of the commitment, and dispute will be over the degree to which this is ceasing now to figure as a realizable 'utopia' and becoming a 'utopia' in the more literal (and Marxist-pejorative) sense of being unrealizable – of figuring as a merely regulative ideal outside the parameters of a conceivable historical eventuation.

These reflections may strike some readers as odd, even shockingly unorthodox – which indeed in a sense they no doubt are. But they are not without their precursors in the socialist tradition, most notably in the argument of the Critical Theorists, in so far as this recognized the progressive disappearance from the political stage of the agents who might have been motivated to advance the form of social transformation to which it continued critically to aspire. For Adorno, Horkheimer and Marcuse, the utopian gesture towards redemption – however hopeless it might be of realization – remained crucial to the maintenance of their own critical position.[5]

Moreover, even those who today hold a similarly despairing view of the chances of the global capitalist order being replaced by some democratic-socialist mode of production will yet recognize the differential impact of different policy options, and the need to encourage support for those more conducive to social justice and ecological sustainability. This is to work to a rather more gradual and modest agenda of political improvement than some revolutionary Marxists would think definable as 'socialist'. But it is nonetheless the most realistic option at the present time, and also the programme within whose framework a certain form of utopian projection can enter as a constructive and efficacious force for change. It is in this context that utopian thinking can figure as something more than a regulative ideal or transcendental gesture to the needed but impossible 'beyond' of the place and time of the actual. It is where a certain form of utopian blue-printing or elaboration of a new 'political imaginary' can have a shaping impact on political objectives and motivations in the present. At any rate, in what follows I want to elaborate on my sense that utopian visions are 'necessary' not only as the sublime 'other' to those insisting, Fukuyama-style, on the 'end of history'; and not only as a logical counter or implication of any socialist critique of capitalist modernity; but also as stimulants of desire, and hence as contributing to the development of new forms of political subjectivity. In support of this claim, I shall in the first instance offer some reflections on my conception of the links between desire, agency and utopian imagining.

UTOPIAN PROJECT AND THE AGENTS OF CHANGE

In matters concerning poverty, injustice and ecological devastation, it is very much easier to expose the sins and the sinners than it is to point to the means and the agents of correction. Anyone with eco-socialist sympathies will be able to list the industrial practices and modes of consumption immediately responsible for these evils, and to indicate the underlying sources of the problem in the structures, institutions, social relations and consumerist culture of the capitalist economy.

But what can contemporary, democratically committed, eco-socialists cite as the possible sources of transformation of these causes of destruction? In raising the question I am not denying the extensive global networks of socialist opposition outside the first world orbit, or the many left-leaning popular movements and non-governmental organizations campaigning around the world on issues of poverty, race, feminism and environmentalism. But it would in my opinion be foolish and wishful (not to say un-democratic) for socialists within the industrialized nations of the West to aspire to some sudden and revolutionary dismantling of the capitalist system, rather than to seek in the first instance to promote a left-wing social-democratic agenda by means of a parliamentary mandate. My question in this sense is about whether we have any grounds for supposing that pressure for this kind of agenda might over time lead to the democratization of the electoral process and the emergence of substantial support for a political party committed to a radical green programme of action.

Or, to re-pose the question in somewhat starker and more abstract terms: do we have any good reasons to suppose that a significant check will be exercised in these societies on the processes of capitalist globalization and the ever more intensive forms of economic competition and ecological exploitation to which nation states, or alliances of states, are now committed? After all, it is only by means of their relatively high levels of consumption of planetary resources, and at the expense of the more impoverished sectors of the global community, that the affluent countries of the First World have managed hitherto to sustain their privileged status; and it is only by persuading voters of their capacity to continue to command those resources and to enhance growth rates and standards of living that their political parties, whether of the right or of the left, have hitherto managed to secure sufficient electoral support for government. Why should we suppose any willingness in the future to alter this long-established politics of national self-interest and the hierarchical structure of global resource distribution that it perpetuates?

No one could deny that there are very few signs at the present time of any imminent shift away from these growth-oriented and self-regarding political commitments. Yet one may concede this while continuing to believe that there are reasons not to despair altogether of increased support in the longer term for something closer to the eco-socialist agenda. In the first place, we may cite the very real alarm that is now felt about ecological attrition and the vast disparities of wealth and privilege that are the consequence of the successes of global capitalism. Many today are repelled by an order which allows the wealth of some 500 dollar billionaires to exceed the combined annual income of half the world's people. They are uneasy about the ways in which the pursuit of first world affluence protracts and exacerbates deprivation elsewhere. They know that continuing along the current paths of untrammelled growth and consumerism will mean ever increased exploitation of the poorer economies, and ever more fascistic policies on immigration in the richer – and some are fearful that this could lead over time to the wholesale collapse of any sense of collective human morality and solidarity. Alongside the emergence of these more general forms of anxiety, one may also point to signs of greater public concern with specific issues (the international arms trade, for example, the disposal of nuclear and other industrial waste products, agribusiness, genetic engineering and food modification) which have hitherto been regarded as the preoccupation of a minority of activists.[6]

There is, then, some fairly widespread concern to reduce global inequalities and to promote a more sustainable, more peaceful and fairer use of resources, although it would have to be admitted that had a compassionate concern for the misery and injustices incurred by the capitalist order been more predominant in the past, we would not be contending with the currently prevalent forms of social misery and ecological collapse. These motives are therefore very unlikely in themselves to issue in any substantial shift of political allegiances, or even in any very radical transformation of consumer habits.

On the other hand, there are some grounds to believe they will be reinforced in the future by growing disaffection and anxiety with the conditions obtaining within affluent society itself. Those who are now more or less permanently unemployed, or very vulnerable in such work as they do have, to the shifting demands of a deregulated economy and its ever more 'flexible' contracts; the many victims of cultural and economic discrimination; the single mothers and other groups who are being deprived and scapegoated through the erosion of welfare services; the teachers, health workers, and others in the public services who are caught up in the aggressive commodification of their professions: all these, frequently overlapping, categories may be said despite their differences in immediate priorities to have a longer-term common interest in a more left-leaning political agenda. One might mention here, too, the politicizing impact of some of the more negative effects of the consumer society. Many forms of pleasure and convenience consumption which were previously unquestioned (for car travel, air-flight, disposable goods, instant foods, etc.) have now been compromised by alarms about their ecological side-effects, their impact on health or their anti-hedonist repercussions for the affluent life itself. Anxieties of this kind are, of course, by no means universal, and tend at present, for obvious reasons, to be largely confined to those in the middle and upper income brackets. They will also very often be experienced in conflict with other, more immediately pressing, concerns over employment security. Those who are dependent for their livelihood on the less eco-friendly forms of production and consumption will not find it so easy to be enthused about any ecologically prompted fall-off in demand for these commodities. Yet despite these countervailing influences and their partial and fluctuating impact on the enthusiasm for green measures, we can still point in recent times to higher and relatively diversified levels of public support for anti-pollution legislation, more organic modes of food production, and curbs on road building or airport extension. We are witnessing, we might argue, the emergence of a new, more contradictory structure of consumer needs whereby consumers are looking to alternative life-styles in order to escape the unpleasurable by-products of their own formerly less questioned sources of gratification. Associated with these shifts in patterns of consumption there is a growing interest in 'life politics' issues, less faith in the expertise of the 'experts', and less readiness to accept official versions of what constitutes progress and how to promote it. There is a sense – by no means universal as yet, and certainly not much articulated, but a sense all the same – that the key political issues, which are really concerned with the purposes of human activity and the quality of human happiness, are not being seriously addressed by official party politics; and that the cynicism and disaffection which is often expressed about the political process itself is symptomatic in this respect.

What are the implications of this type of analysis of the likely sources of support in the future for a programme more radical and green than anything currently on offer from the official parties of the Left? A first point to make, perhaps, is that despite the general option in favour of the market economy, the scale and nature of public anxieties about the future would seem to indicate that there is rather little faith in the capacities of the global capitalist order to guarantee collective human welfare in the long term, or to deliver us from impending perils and crises. Indeed, one can argue that the dearth of support for a more radical green agenda at the present time has its cause not so much in any heady public enthusiasm for global capitalism, or belief in its powers to secure a just and peaceful world order, but rather in the degree of distrust and hostility felt at the present time for the forms of socialist alternative that have hitherto been experienced. The current demise of socialism should not, in this sense, be interpreted as evidence of a complete disowning of its fundamental values, or shift in the levels of potential support for the promotion of a more just and egalitarian order. It is better interpreted, in part, as an index of the level of public scepticism about the feasibility of a non-totalitarian alternative to the capitalist market, and as reflecting the fear of the disorder and personal costs that would seem associated with any move in that direction.

Given this context of fear and distrust of alternatives, it will be important for socialist economists to continue to expose the limitations of market methods of attempting to control and repair ecological damage, and to provide blueprints of the economic and political institutions that might help to ensure a more egalitarian and ecologically viable world order.[7] It will also be important for the advocates of such policies to meet the arguments of those who insist that the deregulated market itself promises to provide the most sensitive and efficient mechanism for checking pollution and developing alternative resources and more eco-friendly technologies. But an excellent case can be made for arguing that the kinds of reform and cosmetic changes that are consistent with obedience to capitalist priorities will not be enough to protect even the more affluent societies from the impact of progressive ecological depletion, let alone ensure stability on a global scale, and that it is only if market forces are submitted to greater and more democratic political control, that we might hope ultimately to stave off ecological disaster and its potentially horrendous social consequences. What needs to be emphasized in the context of such arguments is the unique potential of such alternative forms for reconciling the cause of nature conservation with that of social justice and universal human well-being. Where capitalism will immiserate increasing numbers in the interests of sustaining the affluent lifestyle of a privileged minority, socialist measures promise to conserve nature by removing it from the grip of social exploitation. It can be argued, too, that environmental protection will be much better served by a more public and collective provision of a whole range of primary needs. It is increasingly recognized across the political spectrum that current policies on transport and energy use are not only ecologically absurd and irresponsible but counter-productive even in purely economic terms because of their impact on human health. Implicit in these forms of awareness is an understanding that the uncontrolled pursuit of private profit, and the continued expansion of the modes of consumption it encourages, are on a collision course with certain objective natural limits on growth.

At the same time, as indicated above, these appeals to reason and morality can be complemented by those addressed to a more directly hedonist self-interest, where the stress falls less on the pain and displeasure to be avoided for others and more on the enhanced forms of self-realization that a less market-driven and consumerist culture would be able to offer to individuals. Compelling arguments for radical change will thus need to dwell as much on the pleasures of consuming differently as on the sheer deprivations that will be made good by doing so. Looked at from this perspective, one might argue that the communications of the radical writer or theorist must necessarily assume a utopian aspect in the sense that they will seek to convey by all means possible (and not simply in theoretical writing) the seductions of life after consumerism.

ALTERNATIVE HEDONISMS

One way of looking at this kind of utopian task is in terms of the projection of other modes of satisfying our distinctively human demands for innovation, creativity, and self-distinction to those currently on offer. For what we call 'development', Western 'civilization' and its capitalist–consumerist culture, can in the most abstract sense be viewed as the narrowly constraining and inegali-tarian structure of needs and consumption within which we have hitherto been forced to pursue cultural transcendence (the desire for more than material satis-faction) and to gratify the aspirations of what Rousseau termed *amour propre* (our emulative and competitive self-love which seeks the recognition and esteem of others). The alarm over 'ecological crisis' can, for its part, and in the most abstract sense, be viewed as the awakening to the destructive and ultimately unsustainable nature of this 'civilized' vehicle or mode of transcendence.

According to some elements within the environmental movement – some of the deep or eco-centric ecologists, for example, and those working under the Heideggerian call to 'authentic dwelling' – the solution to the 'crisis' is conceived in terms of a 'return' to nature, the restitution of some 'lost' but more 'genuine' relationship to it, or harmonious co-existence with it. Though the forms of social organization and socio-economic arrangements permitting this 'return to nature' are often pretty sketchy and under-developed in these argu-ments, the general implication is that it is a return to a 'simpler', less technologically reliant mode of being: restoring ecological harmony means committing ourselves to a more cyclical-reproductive and traditional way of being. We would ourselves get 'closer' to nature by learning to exist in a more 'natural' manner: a manner more akin in its immanent mode of being in nature to that of other animals. To put it very crudely and reductively, for this vein of ecological politics, if humanity is to become more eco-friendly it must become less distinctively human, less driven by its forms of *amour propre* and the quest to break with all 'natural' or presupposed limits of existence and self-expression.

This is an injunction, however, which is not only utopian in the bad 'idealist' sense of being unrealizable (except, possibly, for a few isolated communities of a kind which in fact already happily exist in the interstices of modern life); it is also dystopian in its aspirations. For it is not so much the return to the confines of tradition, simplicity and 'animal' immanence to which we should aspire, but the advance beyond the limiting, partial, in many respects anti-hedonist and ecologically irresponsible forms of transcendence furnished by modernity.

As Marx already recognized in the nineteenth century, the drive of capitalism had exposed the limitations of 'all traditional, confined, complacent, encrusted satisfactions of present needs, and reproductions of old ways of life,' and there was no going back from that relative sophistication and disenchantment.[8] As Marx saw, too, under the pressure of universal exchange and commodification, individuals would increasingly become, as he put it, 'objectless' or 'naked in their subjectivity': severed from the presuppositions of selfhood which came from being linked to a specific, place, community and social role, and thus no longer anything like so existentially predefined.'[9] But so long as these de-traditionalizing and dis-embedding processes remained caught up in the straightjacket of capitalist ownership and distribution, they would be bound, Marx predicted, to be experienced as alienation:

> In bourgeois economics – and in the epoch of production to which it corresponds – this complete working-out of the human content appears as a complete emptying-out, this universal objectification as total alienation, and the tearing-down of all limited, one-sided aims as a sacrifice of the human end-in-itself to an entirely external end. This is why the childish world of antiquity *appears on one side as loftier*. On the other side, it really is loftier in all matters where closed shapes, forms and given limits are sought for. It is satisfaction from a limited standpoint; while the modern gives no satisfaction; or where it appears satisfied with itself, it is *vulgar*.[10]

Today, moreover, we are better placed than Marx to see how far, in fact, the processes of Enlightenment liberation have been perverted or distorted under the pressures of continuing commodification and its profit-oriented, shopping mall provision for need-fulfilment and self-extension. Freed though they may have been from earlier, 'encrusted' limits on satisfaction, for all too many this has been only to confine them either to boring, and often rather futile, forms of work or to the dreariness of a life on the dole. And to these limitations have been added the more universally applicable deprivations of contemporary existence: too little time, too little space, too little beauty and freedom from air and noise pollution, especially in the built environment where most now live. In this sense, as Horkheimer and Adorno argued some time ago now in their *Dialectic of Enlightenment*, industrial development, technological mastery, and the ever-increasing productivity of labour have served not to free people from the tyranny of the work ethic and its associated forms of misery and injustice, but to confirm them in an essentially 'primitive' dedication to toil and hedonist deprivation. 'Nature', which could have been the beneficiary of human civilization, has become its victim. The narrow and puritan habits of mind, the failure of self-development, the social oppressions that marked the archaic stage of the 'struggle' against nature: much of this has in essence been carried over, albeit in altered form, into the economic structures and culture of the most developed societies of the Western Enlightenment. In the process, moreover, the gratifications afforded in compensation for the pains of a more 'primitive' existence – the 'simpler' life, an unspoilt environment, a secured place within the community – have also been sacrificed. The civilization which might have allowed us the best of both primitive 'simplicity' and modern 'complexity' has given us too little of either of those potential benefits.[11] One might note, too, in this connection, the more directly biological impact of this negative dialectic, where it is almost always the more impoverished and exploited victims of capitalist modernity who become further removed from the security and comforts of doing things in 'nature's way', while the latter, on the other hand, becomes the luxury of the richer and more privileged.[12]

If we are ever to unravel the dystopian web of contradictions in which the marginalized and least privileged peoples of the capitalist world are now so deeply entrammelled, a major transformation of current patterns of resource use and consumer dependency will be needed within the more affluent sectors. For us today in the West, the utopian aspiration must be to establish a *modus vivendi* which uncouples our pleasures and modes of self-expression from reliance on global exploitation, both social and environmental: which can reconcile the *ecological* and *egalitarian* needs for a more cyclical and reproductive (more 'natural' or 'immanent') mode of interaction with nature with the more distinctively *human* and *individualist* needs for continuous cultural creation and productive innovation (with the demands of transcendent being). Can we find ways of living rich, fulfilling, complex, non-repetitive, lives without social injustice and without placing too much stress on nature? Can we find ways of not 'going back to nature' but advancing to a more assertively human and ecologically benign form of future?

One of the challenges of such a project will be to disencumber the more positive political aspects of the Enlightenment – the commitment to pluralism, racial equality, democracy, gender parity, mass education, cosmopolitanism – from its altogether less emancipatory forms of economic rationality and ecological complacency. It will be to find ways to conserve the environment and to remain in some kind of ecological equilibrium while resisting any regression to the hierarchical and patriarchal cultural and social divisions that have traditionally always accompanied more reproductive and ecologically sustainable societies. Another will be to develop the means of enjoying novelty and the stimulus of 'progress' – of enhancing our lives with strange and unexpected experience – but without the spur of new material goods and without the constant recourse to ever more time-saving and space-contracting modes of transport and delivery.

In both instances, one may argue, progress can only be made through release from the current dominance of the work ethic and a move towards a more rational division of work and leisure, and a more democratic, because more universally applicable, ratio of the one to the other in day-to-day life. In this sense, the reduction and fairer redistribution of work must be placed at the centre of the utopian political imaginary. Under the current economic dynamic, people are either being forced out of work altogether into the demoralizing dependency and penury of unemployment, or finding work only by joining the expanding group of contingent and highly flexible part-time workers without benefits or job security; or else, where they are in full-time employment, are being pressurized into ever more intensive and 'workaholic' routines. This is an allocation of work and rewards which does little to reduce economic and social divisions within the nation state. Global justice and ecological conservation will not be advanced by employment structures which depend on the continuous diversion of human material resources to wasteful and luxurious production and ever more sophisticated technological expansion within the more privileged economies; nor, with the exception of a privileged minority, will human pleasure and self-development, since neither the jobless nor the contingent workers who have the time but not the money or security, nor the employed who have the wage but all too little time, have been placed in a position seriously to enjoy rich and diverse modes of existence. On the contrary, they are all victims in differing ways of an economic imperative which is as ecologically wasteful as it is insensitive to what it is squandering in terms of human pleasure and fulfilment.

In short, economic procedures which are defended across the official left-right political divide as viable and essential to human well-being are in reality committed to an irrational and immoral division of time, labour and wealth, which many now fear could issue ultimately in social and ecological breakdown. Hence the importance the greens have rightly attached to the campaigns for the reduction of the working week without loss of income or security, and for a shift on the same basis to part-time work and job-share schemes. Hence, too, the inspiration that can be drawn from those who have centred their utopian argument around the relief from work, the extension of free time, and the severing of the supposedly indissoluble link between being in employment and enjoying reasonable conditions of existence.

Very relevant here right from the beginning were Marx's observations on the dialectic of necessary and surplus labour time in a post-capitalist society, and the extent to which this could in principle release surplus labour from embodiment in material, resource-consuming commodities and allow it to be realized in the form of idleness and free time. It is true, of course, that Marx's position on the expenditure of surplus-labour in a socialist economy was not explicitly 'green' in the sense of specifying that this would be spent either literally doing nothing or only in ecologically sustainable ways. But in a formal sense it certainly lends itself to such a development, and the utopian thinking of Herbert Marcuse, Walter Benjamin and André Gorz on the liberation from work could be cited as significant contributions to the 'greening' of historical materialism along these lines.[13] Of these three, however, it is only Gorz who makes any serious attempt to address the practical problems of transforming the structure of work in a modern complex industrial society. Where Marcuse is content to speculate on the role of fantasy, eroticism and play in liberating us from a repressive Reality Principle, and Benjamin opts for a Fourieresque model of work as play, Gorz more realistically – and compellingly – insists on the necessary heteronomy of much work in contemporary society.[14] Indeed, not only does Gorz regard the alienation of much work done for a living within modern industrial conditions as ineliminable, he is also insistent, in his later writings, that the economic rationality of the market is the most efficient form of organization for certain areas of production.[15]

It may reasonably be objected, however, that in the current climate even Gorz's more pragmatic and feasible proposals on the liberation from work remain 'utopian' in view of the range and intransigence of the obstacles in the way of their realization. Certainly, it would be foolish to deny the extent of the internalization of the work ethic, and the alarm experienced by many at the prospect of a reduction in their work routines, even were this to incur no loss of remuneration. In asking whether the attitude engendered by capitalist societies to work and its rewards can be replaced by systems of work and pleasure having less ecologically and socially exploitative consequences, we are asking whether entrenched forms of monetary greed, compulsive modes of behaving, and deep-seated habits associated with class and gender divisions can, indeed, find their gratification in alternative ways of being, and this is by no means certain. Idleness may be eco-friendly, but it will also require people to find ways of enjoying it, and of breaking in the process with very engrained patterns of living.

Indeed, in a culture so dominated by the profit motive, in a culture, that is, where time is money, and accumulating money (saving time) the prime desideratum, the joys of idleness scarcely any longer count as such. Loitering, being lazy, slowing down, passing time: the negative connotation of these alternatives to working says a good deal about our current resistance to the pleasures of *not* saving time. But we may imagine that our attitudes to time expenditure would be very different in a society in which heteronomous work had been cut by a third to a half, and the great majority worked only some four hours a day, or had one out of every three weeks off work, or a month off out of every four. Individuals in such a society would be much freer to choose their hours of relative activity and relaxation, to pack their free days with the former or to hand them more fully over to the latter. With far fewer commuting into work and more staggered times of arrival and departure, the rush hour would become a thing of the past, and many more days could have a tranquil beginning, with time to read or talk or write, to exercise, to prepare and eat food, to be with children, to play an instrument, to make love. The remainder of the daytime hours could also be spent in more diverse ways than is currently possible for all but the richest and most privileged: in part they would be devoted to work, certainly, but not so intensively as to prevent a visit to a cinema, or gallery or concert or swimming pool or other place of culture or recreation; and even then, there would still be time left over for study, for drinking with friends, for roaming around, for romancing, for sitting still, for reading, thinking, dreaming.

It is true that any such transformation of the relations of production and the organization of work would be conditional on a number of other, equally dramatic, changes of life-style and mode of consuming. It should be emphasized, too, that none of these will be achieved without some sacrifice of pleasure or convenience. But they are changes nonetheless whose hedonist gains arguably outweigh their losses, and all of which would have the great benefit of contributing to a more egalitarian and sustainable global order. One such change would be a significant reduction in the provision and consumption of time-saving commodities such as disposable goods, fast food, pre-cooked meals, and other items designed primarily to relieve the stress and burden on the harried and overworked. There would be time again to prepare fresh food, and to linger over it. There would even be time for many more to grow their own food in gardens or allotments. With more time and flexible work routines, people would also be better placed to reduce their reliance on a battery of labour-saving commodities within the private domestic unit: there could be more sharing of machinery within the locality, more communal maintenance of it, and more recourse to collective provision for chores such as laundry. Developments such as these would also have the virtue of helping to reduce isolation and boredom, particularly among the elderly and less mobile. The vastly increased free time available to people, and the shift away from highly consumerist life-styles, will also allow for an explosion of eccentricity and escape from the tyranny of profit-driven fashions and commodity conformism.

Another essential condition of the realization of the eco-socialist utopian future would be a transport revolution resulting in hugely reduced reliance on airflight and the use of the private motor car. This will involve some considerable sacrifice of speed and convenience, and requires adjustments that few show themselves currently to be very willing to make. But in exchange for travelling more slowly, there will be huge gains in safety for all forms of travel, vastly improved air quality, and massive reduction in noise pollution. There will also be much pleasure to be gained in terms of improved health and sense of well-being, since many more will become regular bike users, walkers and riders. Some motor routes will need to be retained for emergency and delivery vehicles, buses and taxis; but for the most part urban space will be reclaimed for cyclists and pedestrians, both of whom will have their own traffic-free routes and be able to proceed in a more or less carefree mode. Pavements and squares can become tree-lined, flower dense areas for strolling, and large parts of them given over to cafes and restaurants, street amusements, sporting activities, chess or other games, and open air concerts or exhibitions. Motorways and other major road systems could be converted into complex segregated bus and cycle routes (with many of the latter being covered for protection against the weather, and enhanced by the provision of music, painting and sculpture). A fast and impeccably efficient train service, and far greater use of ships and river boats would help to cater for longer journeys. People will travel less swiftly and cover less distance for their holidays and trips abroad than currently where they can fly half way round the world for brief break. But in compensation their journey will become less harassed, and will itself constitute a pleasurable and more relaxing component of any trip they make.

Let us note, too, that quite apart from its beneficial ecological impact, a restructuring of employment allowing for more job-sharing and a proliferation of secure part-time jobs will go a long way to help resolve the tensions deriving from the dissolution of patriarchy in Western societies, and the emergence of gender as a site of contestation rather than a sphere of reproduction.[16] For there is no way in which these tensions – which have followed on the feminist challenge to the gender division of labour, and the schism between 'public' and 'private' realms and their respective activities and priorities – can be satisfactorily met through back-tracking attempts to shore up and perpetuate the conventional male-female allocation of roles, status and position. Nor, however, can they be so through the ongoing commodification of the sexual and affective field associated with the nurturing and caring functions still largely performed within the family. For to proceed in that way is to consolidate new forms of elitism between those who can afford to pay for all forms of child-care and domestic servicing, and the under-class of ill-paid (and still largely female) providers of those services; it is also further to commercialize the 'symbolic' domain in ways that are inappropriate to its provision of love and care, and resistant to the pleasure and fulfilment it can offer. They are tensions of the transition from patriarchy which can only be more happily resolved in a society where it has become the norm for both sexes to share more equally both in outside work in the 'public' sphere and in child-care and domestic tasks in the 'private' – and that means, essentially, in a society that has revalued its expenditure of time and adjusted its conception and organization of 'work' accordingly.

On this basis, one can envisage the emergence of a culture of interpersonal relations that had transcended gender oppression, on the one hand, yet at the same time resisted the current drift towards a more narcissistic and self-sufficient mode of sexuality, on the other. This would be a culture in which gender parity would be able to co-exist with passionate forms of personal dependency, intense erotic engagements and enduring commitments, both hetero- and homosexual; a culture which had fought free of patriarchal repressions but without dissolving the messy and emotive but also intensely rewarding bonds that come with being a realized, fully organic, distinctively human being. In this context, personal relations are likely to become more various and less dominated by peer group conformity. One can envisage many more cross-generational friendships and relations; much more co-parenting (which places less stress on lovers, is beneficial for the children and a prime instrument in the dismantling of patriarchy).

The utopian 'erotic' I am advocating here is clearly at odds with the autotelic and rather solipsistic enjoyments of gender 'performance' and self-styling currently advocated by some feminist theorists.[17] Nor does it subscribe to the fashionable celebration of cyberotic sex and the disembodied and transient enjoyments of virtual reality 'couplings'.[18] On the contrary, where the flexibility and de-socializing tendencies of these new modes of sexuality will coexist very comfortably with the very similar imperatives of a work-oriented, highly competitive and anti-collectivist culture, a utopian erotic of passion, dependency and conviviality can figure as an alternative hedonism to it, and should be promoted as such.

Let it be said, however, that in wanting to counter the supposed 'utopia' of cyber-sexuality, I am not denying that there are aspects of the 'net-working society' and the shift to 'informationalism'[19] that have utopian potential from an ecological, educational and hedonist point of view. As with all forms of new technology, these developments in computerization have emerged within hierarchical social and economic structures, whose marks they bear, and which they are serving now to reproduce. It is true, too, that the evidence of such studies as have been carried out on the matter indicate that computerized systems have as yet done little to cut down on the numbers still commuting to work; and that, if anything, 'face-to-face' exchanges have multiplied as a consequence of the increase in electronic communication.[20] So far, then, it seems the new technologies have been used to 'enhance' life in ways that are still dependent on high-speed, high-energy transportation of persons and material goods; to expand and complexify an existing structure of consumption rather than to divert desire into more eco-friendly types of gratification. All the same, the new forms of electronic communication and virtual reality interaction do, in principle, allow us to cut down on the polluting, noisy and high-energy consuming forms of transport involved in 'face-to-face' communications and material transfers in 'real' time-space. They could also allow for an unprecedentedly global and democratic exchange of information; for greatly extended public participation in policy-making and in the informal discourse networks of the public sphere; and for a proliferation of interesting and novel 'conversations'.

Included among these conversations, one would hope, will be many exchanges on utopianism itself: both concerning the extent to which utopian speculation can indeed help to shape and shift desire along the lines I have suggested; and on the more substantive issue of what is, or can be found desirable as the substitute for market-driven life-styles and patterns of work and consumption. I have here thrown out some ideas about the general framework within which affluent societies might begin to revise their thinking on pleasure and consumption and thus help to establish a more egalitarian and ecologically rational global order. But I have done so in the full knowledge that this offering is, indeed, a matter of utopian projection, and thus very vulnerable to realist objections about its unworkability; and also with the embarrassment and diffidence that comes with knowing that all such utopian adumbrations are to some degree problematic in virtue of their very aspiration to speak for or represent the desires of others. Socialists, as suggested earlier, have not always been as sensitive as they might be to this problem of representing collective needs and interests. In defending a role for this representation in the form of speculation on hedonist alternatives, I am also very ready to acknowledge that all utopian dreaming bears the personal imprint of its dreamer, and that it is therefore always in the interests of the collective that the dreams be shared and pooled. So I would, as part of my own defence of the emancipatory role of utopian visions, include the need for an ongoing and democratic 'conversation' on the quality of the good life. At the same time, however, I would also assume that it is indispensable to any *socialist* conception of this that its pleasures begin with knowing that they have not come only at the cost of human misery and ecological degradation. Socialists, in other words, may diverge considerably on the details of what makes for pleasure and right living, but they will agree that all the more subtle, refined and complex pleasures will be grounded in the simpler satisfaction that comes through the elimination of suffering and exploitation. Indeed, in the end, it may even be this more negative grounding, or seemingly mere precondition of utopian existence, which reaches to the limit of a truly utopian aspiration, and constitutes its most expansive form, since it alone leaves all further potentials untold and therefore unimposed. As Adorno says, 'perhaps the true society will grow tired of development and, out of freedom, leave possibilities unused, instead of storming under a confused compulsion to the conquest of strange stars.'[21]

NOTES

1. K. Marx, F. Engels, *The German Ideology*, ed. C. Arthur, Lawrence and Wishart, London, 1970, pp. 56–7; and the theme is repeated in *The Communist Manifesto*, see especially the opening of the section on 'Critical-Utopian Socialism and Communism', in K. Marx, F. Engels, *Selected Works*, Lawrence and Wishart, London, 1970, pp. 59–60.

2. K. Marx, *Grundrisse*, Penguin, Harmondsworth, 1973, p. 488. Cf. Terry Eagleton's discussion of the unrepresentable 'sublime' of Marx's communist projection, *Ideology of the Aesthetic*, Blackwell, Oxford, 1991, ch. 8.

3. 'The Limits of Hauntology', *Radical Philosophy*, 75, Jan–Feb 1996, pp. 26–31, esp. p. 31.

4. Cf. my development of this point in the context of a review of Steven Lukes, *Marxism and Morality*, in *New Left Review*, 163, May–June, 1987; reprinted in *Troubled Pleasures*, Verso, London, 1990, see esp. pp. 132–3.

5. It is their explicit acknowledgement of the potential idealism and self-subverting contradictions of their own critical position (or position *as* mere critics), that differentiates the Frankfurt thinkers from the post-modernist critics of the 'disasters' of the Enlightenment. For even though there are clear affinities between post-structuralist and early Frankfurt theorizations of the Enlightenment and subjectivity, power and desire, where the Critical Theory position differs markedly is in combining its 'will

to happiness' with explicit recognition of the social forms of conditioning that were rendering its aspirations ever more purely utopian; and it is this, too, which allows us to define the Critical Theory position as socialist in commitment.

6. Some more recent indications of this, to speak only of Britain, have been the level of support for the Greenpeace campaign over the disposal of the Brent Spar, the popularity of the jury's 'Not Guilty' verdict on the four women of the Swords into Ploughshares group accused of damaging an aircraft bound for Indonesia; the outcry caused by the discovery that a British company had been supplying arms to Sierra Leone; the support for the elimination policy on landmines; the BSE panic and new levels of sensitivity to food dangers which it has generated.

7. For some examples and discussion, see P. J. Devine, *Democracy and Economic Planning: the Political Economy and the Self-Governing Society*, Polity, Cambridge, 1980; M. Albert and R. Hahnel, *Looking Forward: Participatory Economics for the Twenty-first Century*, South End Press, Boston, 1991 and *Political Economy of Participatory Economics*, Princeton University Press, Princeton 1991; D. Elson, 'Market Socialism or Socialization of the Market?', *New Left Review*, no. 172, November–December 1988, pp. 3–44; E. Altvater, *The Future of the Market*, trans. P. Camiller, Verso, London, 1993.

8. '…capital drives beyond the national barriers and prejudices as much as beyond nature worship, as well as all traditional, confined, complacent, encrusted satisfactions of present needs and reproductions of old ways of life.' *Grundrisse*, op. cit., p. 410.

9. Ibid, pp. 450–6 and cf. the section on 'pre-capitalist economic modes of production', pp. 471–515, and my discussion in *On Human Needs,* Harvester Press, Brighton, 1981, pp. 125–42.

10. *Grundrisse*, op cit., pp. 487–8.

11. Theodor Adorno and Max Horkheimer, *Dialectic of Enlightenment*, Verso, London, 1979, ch 1.

12. Some recent relevant illustration of this is to be found in Donna Haraway, *Modest _Witness@Second_Millenium™FemaleMan©_Meets_OncoMouse™*, Routledge, London, 1997, especially her discussion (pp. 202–12) of Nancy Scheper-Hughes, *Death without Weeping: the Violence of Everyday Life in Brazil*, University of California Press, Los Angeles, 1992.

13. Herbert Marcuse, *Eros and Civilization*, Beacon Press, Boston, 1966, esp Part II; for Walter Benjamin's utopian argument on work as child's-play, see Susan Buck-Morss, *The Dialectics of Seeing: Walter Benjamin and the Arcades Project*, MIT Press, Cambridge, Mass. 1989, esp. pp. 261–66 and 273–80; for André Gorz's argument on work, see *Farewell to the Working Class*, Pluto, London, 1982; *Paths to Paradise: on the Liberation from Work*, Pluto, London, 1983; *Critique of Economic Reason*, Verso, London, 1989.

14. Marx himself, we might note, also rejects any ludic model of work. Criticizing Fourier for thinking that work can be made into 'fun' or 'mere amusement', he advises us that 'really free working such as composing is at the same time the most damned seriousness, the most intense exertion.' (*Grundrisse*, op. cit., p. 611). Even this line of thinking, however, seems less than persuasive in view of the impossibility of converting most tasks performed in the contemporary labour process into anything remotely resembling the composition of music. Writing music is clearly hard work, but it is equally clear that its pressures are very different from those of

driving a train or working in a kitchen or on an assembly line, and that it is impossible for all labour to become 'free' in the sense of being as creatively intensive and rewarding as composing a symphony. Cf. my discussion in *On Human Needs*, op. cit, pp. 196–202.

15. In both *Farewell to the Working Class* and *Paths to Paradise* Gorz acknowledges the necessity of non-autonomous labour but tends to regard it as a wholly negative distraction from more fulfilling forms of 'autonomous activity'. In the subsequent development of his position (see in particular, *Critique of Economic Reason*) Gorz recognizes the importance of paid employment as a means of acquiring a social existence and identity. He also, as indicated, argues for the importance of the market in meeting a certain range of needs in contemporary industrial societies. For an exposition and critical discussion of Gorz's argument on work, see Sean Sayers, 'Gorz on Work and Liberation', *Radical Philosophy*, no. 58, Summer 1991, pp. 16–20. Sayers argues that Gorz is mistaken in his resistance to the rationalization of domestic work and welfare provision, and conservative and backward-looking in his acceptance of the intrinsic alienation of work in the 'public' sphere and in regarding the spheres of private and public as separate and irreconcilable. Finn Bowring has argued, with some justice, that this critique is based on a distorted reading of Gorz's argument, though he himself seems reluctant to recognize that there may be difficulties for women in accepting Gorz's position on caring, nurturing activities and domestic work. See his article, 'Misreading Gorz', *New Left Review*, no. 217, May–June 1996.

16. Cf. Manuel Castells, *The Rise of the Network Society*, Blackwell, Oxford, 1996, pp. 3–4 and *The Power of Identity*, Blackwell, Oxford, 1997, ch. 4.

17. As, for example, in the argument of Judith Butler, *Gender Trouble: Feminism and the Subversion of Identity*, Routledge, London and New York, 1990; *Bodies that Matter: on the Discursive Limits of Sex*, Routledge, London and New York, 1993.

18. See, for example, the articles by Mark Poster and Sadie Plant in Lisa Tickner et al (eds.), *Future Natural*, Routledge, London and New York, 1996, pp. 183–202 and pp. 203–217; cf. Joan Broadhurst Dixon and Eric J. Cassidy (eds.), *Virtual Futures: Cyberotics, Technology and Post-Human Pragmatism*, Routledge, London and New York, 1998. Cf. also the 'cyborg feminism' of Donna Haraway, *Simians, Cyborgs and Women*, Routledge, London and New York, 1991.

19. I take both these terms from Manuel Castells, op. cit.

20. Ibid., ch. 6, esp. pp. 394–8.

21. T. Adorno, *Minima Moralia*, trans. E. N. F. Jephcott, Verso, London, 1978, p. 156. Adorno is here elaborating on his claim that, 'there is tenderness only in the coarsest demand: that no one should go hungry any more'. To quote him more fully: 'If uninhibited people are by no means the most agreeable or even the freest, a society rid of its fetters might take thought that even the forces of production are not the deepest substratum of man, but represent his historical form adapted to the production of commodities. Perhaps the true society will grow tired of development and, out of freedom, leave possibilities unused, instead of storming under a confused compulsion to the conquest of strange stars. A mankind which no longer knows want will begin to have an inkling of the delusory, futile nature of all arrangements hitherto made in order to escape want, which used wealth to produce want on a larger scale. Enjoyment itself would be affected just as its present framework is inseparable from operating, planning, having one's way, subjugating.'

UTOPIAN FAMILIES

JOHANNA BRENNER

Every oppressed group needs to imagine through the help of history and mythology a world where our oppression did not seem the pre-ordained order. The mistake lies in believing in this ideal past or imagined future so thoroughly and single-mindedly that finding solutions to present-day inequities loses priority, or we attempt to create too-easy solutions for the pain we feel today.[1]

IN TWO GREAT UTOPIAN novels of the 1970s, *Woman on the Edge of Time* and *The Dispossessed,*[2] Marge Piercy and Ursula LeGuin drew on anarchist, that is, radically democratic collectivist ideas while exploring in depth those areas of life that have been feminism's particular focus. They imagined how children would be parented and educated, whether gender would even exist, how individuals would experience and express sexual desire, what human relationships would be like. Both novels assumed, as did feminists of the time, that the privatized, heterosexual nuclear family household was antithetical to radically democratic, egalitarian social relations. They imagined worlds where gender was no longer a central social category, where homosexual desire was treated no differently from heterosexual desire, and where monogamous relationships were not mandated but freely chosen. They envisioned children and parents embedded in a supportive, democratic community, men and women equally involved in care-giving, the essential chores/pleasures of daily life (cooking, eating, laundry, etc.) taking place in communal rather than private spaces. Their concepts of parenting and of education challenged dominant ideas about children's need to be protected from the demands of the adult world. Education ought to be based in learning by doing as children participated in meaningful work. They envisioned more democratic, less authoritarian relationships between adults and children. Challenging the idea of a benevolent necessity for adult control, they argued that children had much greater capacities for self-regulation and responsible decision making than adults gave them credit for. They also argued that involving children in productive work had to begin early, so kids would appreciate the pleasures and rewards of contributing to the common good. In a society where labour is organized through profoundly democratic decision making and for meeting human needs, workplace 'efficiency' would encourage, even demand, making a place for apprenticeship – not to mention flexible (and shorter) working hours to free people up for activities of nurture, leisure, and citizenship. These utopian visions grew out of some of the core struggles of second-wave feminism, particularly its radical liberationist wing. Compared to feminists today, feminists then, facing a patriarchal family/household system that appeared firmly entrenched, felt more free to reject the family wholesale. And, in a period of relative prosperity and economic security, they were also more free to experiment with alternative forms of living.

My generation of socialists and socialist-feminists who took part in and were inspired by the great post-war waves of rebellion against exploitation, oppression and colonial rule, have been fundamentally shaped by our historical experience, an experience of enormous political gains but also dashed hopes, profound disappointments, and some bitter defeats. The post-modernists' hostility to 'grand narratives' (feminist as well as Marxist) draws support from not only the bankruptcy of Communism but also the exhaustion of the radical political organizations (Marxist, anti-racist and feminist) of the 'sixties and 'seventies which embodied the revolutionary aspirations of our generation.

The 'pre-figurative' communes and political collectives of the New Left, including feminist groups, who hoped to bridge the present and the post-revolutionary future have almost all splintered and died. Attempts to legislate personal relations and group life, to 'live according to political principle' defined in rigid, narrow terms, bred intolerance, sectarianism, factionalism and splits. Yet the questions we tried to address are still with us. It's time to dust ourselves off and return to those imaginative visions, informed but not defeated by our failures. 'Pre-figurative' communities (political groups, community-based organizations, collectively run workplaces and living spaces) are an important ground for winning new people to socialist ideals. They allow us to practise being in different kinds of relationships, to experience our capacities for co-operation, solidarity, and democracy.

From the perspective of the 1990s, the battle against the bourgeois family, against the stultifying, consumerist, conformist, privatistic, patriarchal household, might seem anachronistic. There are strong political forces attempting to reimpose the traditional male breadwinner/female care-giver family ideal; and we have been forced to spend far too much political energy beating them back. But there are strong counter-currents, appearing perhaps more in how people live than in the political system, where well-organized conservative minorities have influence far beyond their numbers. Many children spend some time in a single parent, generally single-mother, family; in almost 25% of two-earner households in the USA women earn more than men; increasing numbers of blended families create many new kinds of kin relationships; new reproductive technologies are exploding concepts of 'natural' motherhood, and lesbians and gay men are more accepted as parents and more 'out' as families.[3] And in so far as their circumstances allow it, many men and women are trying to break old gender patterns, sharing both income-earning and responsibility for everyday care-giving within their families. It is no longer compelling to assert that only one kind of family is natural, normal, or even preferable. But important as they are, these changes have, if anything, strengthened the family's hold on popular social and political imaginations. While families may be more internally democratic, they are also even more private than ever before, one of the few remaining places people expect to give and receive support.

The harsh political and economic shifts in the society surrounding the family have closed off the space for imagining different kinds of community. Instead of organizing for a revolutionary alternative to welfare state cold-war liberalism, we find ourselves battling to simply preserve a minimal welfare state. But the issues we confronted are still there. If anything, life in this centre of global capitalism seems ever more contradictory: on the one hand, increasing opportunities for self-expression through consumption of a giddy array of commodified identities; on the other, frightening economic insecurity and worries about what the future might hold. On the one hand, increasing sexual autonomy for women, and on the other the abandonment of single mothers and their children, now forced to survive alone in the low-wage labour market. Increasing economic and political opportunities for women, yet a crisis in care-giving inside and outside family households.

The communitarians and religious authoritarians are trying to convince Americans that we have too much freedom and too much individualism. They argue that security, support, and nurture can only emerge when obligation and duty are enforced by social norms, law, and the reallocation of resources to encourage desirable and discourage undesirable individual choices. However much the communitarians may criticize capitalism for its rampant individualism and commodification of every sphere of life, their utopian vision is antithetical to feminism. They denigrate the value of 'chosen' interdependencies (friendship, intentional communities) and privilege bonds of obligation that rest on a bedrock of blood relations – the primordial 'born into' communities whose webs of interdependence are never questioned and therefore never really chosen, only accepted.[4]

Feminists of colour have confronted more directly than white feminists the strengths and weaknesses of 'born-into' communities. Contrasting families in communities of colour to those of the white middle class, Black and Latina feminists argue that the extended kin (and fictive kin) sharing networks linking women and children across families, and the norms of communal responsibility for children, especially strong in Black communities, offer an alternative to the possessive and exclusive relationships of the bourgeois family.[5] This positive re-valuation of disparaged family forms emphasizes the communal values and co-operative institutions which undergird resistance to white supremacy and provide a basis for women to claim authority in their community. However important this analysis as a corrective to the early feminist critique of a suppos-edly universal male breadwinner household, it still left only dimly illuminated another side of racial solidarity in a patriarchal, capitalist society: the suppres-sion of women's sexual desires, the limitations on their exercise of public power, the onerous responsibilities for others that left little room for self, the webs of sometimes overwhelming financial and emotional dependencies, the corrosion of relationships weighted down with too much to carry. In ground-breaking work opening up possibilities for exploring sexism within communities of colour, lesbian feminists of colour explored the painful terrain of their marginalization within their home communities. They described the enforced silences, the regulation and self-regulation of women's sexuality as a political strategy, the fears of betrayal projected on to women's bodies and sexu-ality, the powerful pressures toward conformity and the suppression of individual needs/desires in the name of group solidarity.

> We believe the more severely we protect the sex roles within the family, the stronger we will be as a unit in opposition to the anglo threat. And yet, our refusal to examine all the roots of the lovelessness in our fami-lies is our weakest link and softest spot. Family is *not* by definition the man in a dominant position over women and children. Familia is cross-generational bonding, deep emotional ties between opposite sexes, and within our sex . . . It is sexuality, which involves, but is not limited to intercourse or orgasm. It is finding familia among friends where blood ties are formed through suffering and celebration shared. The strength of our families never came from domination. It has only endured in spite of it – like our women.[6]

In challenging the narrow ground of solidarity that has dominated the culture and politics of their home communities, lesbian feminists of colour have been among the most eloquent voices articulating, in accessible language and with emotional immediacy, the case for a radically democratic anti-racist and feminist-socialist politics in the U.S.

The American public's refusal to be horrified by Clinton's extra-marital affairs indicates that backward looking moralists remain a minority. Yet, conser-vatives have also captured political ground by taking aim at one of contemporary capitalism's weakest points: the pervasive anxiety about how we will take care of ourselves, each other, our elderly, and our children, and a simmering resentment about the toll that this care-giving is taking. Family households are more burdened and perhaps more isolated from other sources of support than ever before. In one of the most blatant examples of political hypocrisy in our time, the last remaining public institutions through which some kind of societal responsibility for our elderly and our children is expressed – social security and public education – are under ruthless attack. In the current political configuration, where government and the public are savaged and the market extolled, the family household remains the only place where people can envision non-contractual relationships, claims on others for support, and an unquestioned right to have one's needs met. The romance of the capitalist market, of a society organized around individualistic striving, can only work if families are there to pick up the pieces.[7] Affluent families are increasingly substituting paid services made affordable by service workers' low wages. Working-class families get by in other ways (drawing on female relatives for child care, working different shifts so parents can trade-off being home, having fewer children). But even with these accommodations, responsibilities for others, in addition to children, remain: the elderly parents, the brother who can't find work, the sister who can't make it alone as a single mother.

The situation produces a downward spiral: the more people must rely on family, the more focused they become on increasing their individual resources and maximizing their own family fortunes, the less willing to support other people's families, other people's children. New, more inclusive ideals of family are contesting compulsory heterosexuality and male dominance within the household. But they do not, in themselves, challenge the ideal of the family household itself as a haven in a heartless world. New, reformed and more democratic family ideals can coexist with an intensification of familistic political ideologies and individualistic survival strategies.

One of the main weak points of the current economy is its failure to support families. So it would seem that one of the best arguments against the assaulting forces of the capitalist juggernaut is to point out the contradiction between corporate power and family needs. Many progressives are taking just that tack: the name of New York State's newest effort at creating a third party, the 'Working-Families Party' is a case in point. To form a politics around 'working families' is terribly limited and ultimately conservative. To be clear, I am not arguing against campaigns, such as the UPS strike, which protested the widespread use of part-timers on the ground that many UPS workers had families to support. But a politics centred on 'working-families' simply reproduces bourgeois morality in which working is a sign of deservingness and family a sign of need – as if single individuals are or ought to be 'self-sufficient.' And it reinforces the ideal of the family/household as the privileged site of economic, emotional, social support and care. Further, a program of demands organized around the needs of 'working families' obscures the ways in which different kinds of communities are systematically disadvantaged. Some communities have more non-working families than others. Finally, assimilating gay/lesbian families to straight families by focusing on their commonalities as 'working' or 'economically productive' or 'stable/coupled', leaves little room for the liberatory demands of sexual politics. This is not simply a matter of including rights of sexual expression as a fundamental democratic demand. A radical vision of community has to recognize the sexual/erotic bases of human connection, challenging both the repressiveness of traditional conservativism and the 'repressive desublimation' of the contemporary sexual order. Queer politics creates a space for articulating this, partly because queer sexuality has not been harnessed so directly as heterosexuality to procreation and thus to the institutions of social reproduction. As lesbian feminists of colour have demonstrated, through writing and political activism, fear of or shame about having the wrong kind of sexual desire fuels a defensive repressiveness which spreads throughout a community. In contrast, appreciation for our unruly desires makes them less threatening, we have less need to regulate ourselves and others, opening up more possibility for empathic connection and thus solidarity.

Familistic politics is attractive in part because communities are weaker than ever before. But 'community' is itself an amorphous concept. We speak, at least in the U.S., of the business community, or the therapeutic community, in the same way we speak of neighbourhoods or socially homogenous spaces. Community as a particular kind of public space, a space for communication, democratic decision-making and co-operation around crucial tasks and decisions, is understandably undeveloped in advanced capitalist societies. In the capitalist political economy, communities are formed primarily out of their common position with regard to markets (e.g., for housing, for jobs) and to various institutions that regulate the distribution of resources (e.g., local government, the welfare department, the education system). Community appears as an arena of voluntary relationships over against the necessary and more obligatory ties of family and the commands of capitalist employers. So while there is a kind of 'romance' of community, and even perhaps a real longing for community, in the U.S.A. today there is little space for people to create or sustain communal institutions. On the other side, in both American myth and historical experience, the potentially arbitrary and repressive power of communities looms large. This can only be countered by a vision of radically democratic communities that allow space for variation in the ways that individuals can live and participate.[8] From a feminist perspective, democratic community is built not only out of particular kinds of political structures, but also by particular kinds of people – people who have the ability to negotiate inevitable tensions between collective demands and individual needs. These capacities are first learned in relation to our early care-givers and continue in how we experience ourselves in relation to others.

Feminists have long argued that child rearing by women within the context of an isolated family/household creates particular kinds of gendered personalities but also fundamental difficulties around dependence for both men and women. The hyper-individualism of bourgeois society is reproduced in personality via family structure. Personality is shaped both directly and indirectly (through how parents, teachers, and other care-givers envision the goals of child development) by a capitalist culture that denigrates dependence and overvalues individual independence (understood as freedom from ties to others). But fears about dependence needs arise also from forms of parenting that especially intensify dilemmas of development. These dilemmas arise out of a human reality – the long period of dependence and inequality of power in relations of infants/children to adults who care for them. Whatever the existential limits or grounding of developmental dilemmas in human physiology, social structures shape both their character and resolution. For children reared by isolated, disempowered mothers and distant fathers in patriarchal family households, developmental struggles centre around individuation from a female care-giver, conflicting desires around autonomy and merger, conflicting fears about being left alone and about being taken over.[9] Having the capacity to bring these fears and desires into some kind of balance, to resolve them in at least a 'good enough' way is necessary for individuals to engage well in the give-and-take of democratic group life – to be able to share power, to recognize others' needs and, at the same time, to be able to assert one's own views against pressures toward group conformity, to tolerate conflict.

Feminists have thought quite a bit about this question, especially about how a rigid, defensive, masculinity constructed through the denigration of the feminine reinforces drives toward domination, expressed in both the micro-politics of relationships and the macro-politics of the economy and the state. Feminists have also at least tentatively explored how women's fears of separation create over-enmeshment, inability to distinguish others' needs from one's own, conflict avoidance and inability to tolerate differences within a group, and projection of aggressive impulses on to sons, husbands, and fathers.[10] These analyses all point toward rearranging family life in very fundamental ways. A key change, feminists have argued, is for men to become equally involved with the daily routines of care-giving for young children. This is important not only to change how boys and girls come to acquire gendered identities . It is also crucial to creating reciprocity and equality among adults who have to negotiate with one another in ways that a more gendered division of labour does not require. And men develop skills – the ability to tolerate and respond to helplessness, to recognize and respond to others' emotional states, to anticipate wants and needs – which carry over into their relationships with adults – with their partners as well as their colleagues and friends.[11]

Feminist utopian visions, though, go further than re-arranging the gender division of labour within the household. They reject family households as the basic unit of social reproduction, of reciprocal exchanges of emotional and physical caring necessary to renew life. The reasons are both social and psychological. First, more collective forms of everyday living expand the sphere of social solidarity and exert a countervailing pressure against the privatistic and exclusivist bonds of sexual/affectional partnership and parent-child relations. Second, although it is important for children to have intense, affectional bonds with some particular others, it seems that these ties can be made more problematic where parents don't share care-giving with other adults. In more communal forms of living, children can use other adults as a buffer in negotiating conflicts/tensions with their parents. And, participating in a broader supportive community, parents may find it easier to treat their children as separate individuals rather than extensions of themselves. In other words, situated within a broader caring community, children and parents might not experience conflicts around autonomy/separation and dependence/merger as intensely as we do today. Further, affective ties that extend beyond the mother-child dyad, the oedipal triangle, or even sibling relationships lay the basis for individuals to develop psychic structures incorporating a broader set of social identifications.

Comparative studies of child rearing practice already indicate the importance of culturally produced understandings and the social organization of care-giving for defining paths of child development.[12] Segura and Pierce argue that the particular family constellation within which Chicano and Chicana children are cared for, characterized by non-exclusive mothering and significant cross-generational ties between grandmothers and granddaughters, explains, in part, why Chicanos and Chicanas develop strong group identities.[13] Mahoney and Yngvesson make the point that how a society defines the process of development affects interactional patterns between adults and children. For example, among the Ilongot people of the Philippines the developmental process is understood as a gradual acquisition of knowledge (and thus of increased autonomy) through an extended network of interactions (experiences) with multiple caretakers. In contrast, they argue, among the Anglo-American middle class, development is seen to be a struggle for autonomy envisioned as breaking away from a confining dependence on a primary parent.[14]

What are some implications of these ideas for political action? Instead of a political focus on protecting and supporting families, we should argue for expanding, supporting, and reviving communities, and investing resources in local, democratically-controlled institutions for providing care. The entry (both chosen and forced) of women into paid work has drastically undermined the basis for traditional community: the unpaid labour of women. The crisis of care-giving and the burdens on individual family households are a compelling point of entry for a pre-figurative politics which proposes new kinds of sharing relationships and new kinds of public places: like co-housing, community gardens, day-care co-operatives, democratized schools and recreation centres, etc.

Such experiments and reforms would provide a space for envisioning a rich, local, public life and identifying the kinds of resources individuals will need in order to participate. For instance, parents can't belong to day-care co-operatives if they can't afford to leave work to fulfil the volunteer time requirement. And they can't understand or appreciate what's happening with their older children in public schools, if employers won't pay them for their time off work. Making schools more democratic, and convincing teachers to share power with parents, requires that parents have the time and resources to really participate in the work of the school.[15] Living patterns are constrained by social institutions but also by the built environment. Without capital to renovate old housing, most people can't participate in new kinds of living arrangements, like co-housing. Co-housing communities combine individual households with communal living spaces. Members are expected to participate in a committee responsible for some collective activities and daily life is organized around sharing of responsibilities like providing adult supervision for children after school and cooking dinner. Co-housing communities offer new possibilities for expanding the circle of adults who care for children and for each other. They make it more possible for individuals to participate in child rearing without necessarily producing their own child. And they allow adults to share the burdens and pleasures of caring for each other. Taking the sting out of living single, co-housing community creates a ground for real freedom about coupling up. These experiments should be encouraged and subsidized with public funds, rather than being available only to those who have the money to try them.[16]

Recreating community, rebuilding a supportive infrastructure for care-giving that does not rely on exploiting women's unpaid labour, points in the direction of new kinds of public investment: not only new public jobs (more recreation directors, child-care workers, etc.) but resources for building new kinds of relationships between those who provide services and those who use them. Democratized public schools, day-care centres, and community centres, as co-operative institutions, require workers, parents, children, and other neigh-bourhood residents, to participate and work together. And, because community institutions are part of a larger public system of provision, participatory norms can be extended upward – in a council-type system of governance. This is a particularly important point, for local control can also have a narrow, even conservative side. To counter parochial tendencies, community institutions have to be embedded in a broader set of democratic decision-making rela-tionships with each other. Posing an alternative to the top-down and top-heavy bureaucracy of the capitalist welfare state, the fight for democratic communal caring effectively challenges the rightist ideologues who contend that only privatization can provide real control and choice.

There are many different entry points for the political initiatives I am proposing. In the U.S. some of these would be: the fight to defend the public schools against voucher systems, the movement to shift federal spending from the military to human services, efforts to defend single mothers driven into low-wage jobs, battles about urban development and attempts to reshape the built environment, local government use of federal funds for public housing. In these and many other arenas, we can pose alternatives to the over-burdened, isolated family household through an attractive vision of co-operative, democratic, ways of caring for adults and children.

One of the many ironies of our present is that, at least in the U.S., the expanding space for more inclusive, more diverse, more tolerant and more respectful social relations in personal life coexists with a narrowing space for public democracy, a cynicism about public life. This irony reflects not just the defeats but the successes of the liberatory movements of the 'sixties – their cultural and political legacy. However bleak the political terrain on which we struggle today, we cannot afford to lose the communal, egalitarian visions those movements created nor to suspend attempts to prefigure these visions through the kinds of organizations we build, the reforms we propose, and the ways we argue for them. If, last time around, prefigurative politics informed by utopian visions often became oppressive, we can learn from our mistakes. To defensively turn away from dreaming because we are so afraid of being disappointed, to wish for less because we fear we cannot win more, will impoverish and undermine our efforts to build more radical political struggles. We can speak to the real dilemmas, the practices, and the yearnings of working-class people. The crisis in care-giving haunts everyday life, creating a political space for the left as well as the right. We can enter that space with political discourses and, as far as possible, practical proposals for new kinds of communal institutions that express our vision of deeply and thoroughly *democratic* community.

NOTES

1. Cherrie Moraga, *Loving in the War Years*, Boston: South End Press, 1983, p. 129.
2. Marge Piercy, *Woman on the Edge of Time*, New York: Ballantine Books, 1976; Ursula K LeGuin, *The Dispossessed*, New York: Harper & Row, 1974. The novels are also different. LeGuin's subtitle 'an ambiguous utopia' reflects her exploration of repressive tendencies in communal society, a problem that is not at all fore-grounded in Piercy's novel. The two novels also reflect, perhaps, generational differences in radical post-war feminisms. If Piercy's theoretical touchstone is Shulameth Firestone (*The Dialectic of Sex*), LeGuin's would be DeBeauvoir (*The Second Sex*).
3. Just to be clear: of course the changes have very real downsides. Single-mothers are impoverished; reproductive technologies have opened up new avenues for controlling and exploiting women's bodies, two-thirds of the closing of the gender gap in wages has occurred not because women are making more, but because men are earning less.
4. Michael Sandel, *Liberalism and the Limits of Justice*, New York: Cambridge University Press, 1982, pp. 150–152; Jean Bethke Elshtain, 'Feminism, Family and Community', *Dissent* (Fall, 1982).
5. Patricia Hill Collins, *Black Feminist Thought,* Routledge, 1990, esp Chapter 6.
6. Moraga, pp. 110–11; see also, Evelynn M. Hammonds, 'Toward a Genealogy of Black Female Sexuality: The Problematic of Silence', in *Feminist Genealogies, Colonial Legacies, Democratic Futures*, eds. M. Jackqui Alexander and Chandra Talpade Mohanty, New York, Routledge, 1997, pp. 170–182.
7. Michele Barrett and Mary McIntosh, *The Anti-Social Family*, London, Verso, 1984
8. Much of our thinking about collective living is pre-occupied with the problem of 'free-riders', on the one hand, collective despotism on the other. These are important questions. But that they loom especially large for us says more about our own society than universal human propensities toward domination and exploitation. The evidence from social relations among egalitarian band societies indicates

that they are able to achieve a balance in which individual idiosyncrasy and differ-ential abilities to contribute to the group or engage in the group's social life are tolerated. Conflicts are resolved through dialogue; rifts acknowledged and, at least temporarily, repaired, through games, clowning and communal ritual. See, e.g., Colin M. Turnbull, 'Mbuti Womanhood', in *Woman the Gatherer*, Frances Dahlberg, ed., New Haven: Yale University Press, 1981.

9.   Jessica Benjamin, *Bonds of Love*, New York: Pantheon Books, 1988.

10. Lynne Segal, *Slow Motion*, New Brunswick: Rutgers University Press, 1990, pp. 264–268; Valerie Miner and Helen E. Longino, eds., *Competition: A Feminist Taboo?*, New York: The Feminist Press, 1987, esp. pp. 21–37, 195–208.

11. Scott Coltrane, *Family Man*, New York: Oxford University Press, 1997, pp. 117–120; Barbara Katz Rothman, *Recreating Motherhood*, New York: W. W. Norton, 1989, pp. 223–228.

12. Coltrane, pp. 180–192.

13. Denise A. Segura and Jennifer L. Pierce, 'Chicana/o Family Structure and Gender Personality: Chodorow, Familism, and Psychoanalytic Sociology Revisited,' *Signs: Journal of Women in Culture & Society*, vol. 19, no. 1 (Autumn 1993) pp. 63–91. The authors also explore the relationship between these child-rearing patterns and 'machismo'.

14. Maureen A. Mahoney and Barbara Yngvesson, 'The Construction of Subjectivity and the Paradox of Resistance: Reintegrating Feminist Anthropology and Psychology', *Signs: Journal of Women in Culture and Society*, vol. 18, no. 1 (Autumn 1992), pp. 44–73.

15. David Levine et al, eds., *Rethinking Schools: An Agenda for Change*, New York: New Press, 1995.

16. Kathryn M. C. Cament and Charles Durrett, *Cohousing*, Berkeley: Habitat Press, 1988.

OUTBREAKS OF DEMOCRACY

RICARDO BLAUG

NOWADAYS, EVERYONE'S a democrat. Everyone believes that authority rests on the consent of the governed. Even dictators hold elections, and claim they represent the will of the people. Democracy boasts a moral superiority as well as a unique performance. As the safest, most decent and most effective method of government, it has at last triumphed over its enemies, and now claims to be the only legitimate and viable political form.

This has been a remarkable rehabilitation. For most of its history, democracy was seen as a degenerate mode of politics, much feared for its reliance on a populace seen as foolish and volatile. Yet since the adoption of representation in the eighteenth century, and the provision of an institutional place for democracy at the level of the state, we have laid to rest those dangerous images of noisy and volatile mobs, constant mass assemblies and endless inefficient talk. With the people being ruled by proxy, and periodically consenting to elite rule in elections, we have found a way to combine legitimacy with decency and viability. Now, modern representative forms provide enough participatory input to be legitimate, yet not so much as to damage their viability. As such, it's easy to see why the democratic club is one that everyone wants to join.

Certainly, those who have most recently joined this club, be they Africans, Latin Americans or Eastern Europeans, have made significant improvements on their previous regimes. Yet they also sense a growing disappointment. This is due not only to the increasingly apparent social costs of a free (and unstable) market, but also to the realization that the transition from mass action against authoritarianism to the settled structures of elections and parties involves a significant reduction in political activity. In rising against their masters, people participated in noisy debate and spontaneous action. Now, they have become mere spectators in an elitist game.

There are rumblings, also, within the established democracies. Here we struggle with the inescapable fact that participation is a sham. Falling voter turnout, widespread cynicism and a loss of respect for our representatives is our lot. Elected by a small percentage of the vote, and even this won by the distortion of information, our political and economic elites once again sever any connection they ever had with the people in order to pursue their self-regarding ways. Though our politicians claim our consent, whole sections of the populace have become superfluous. Not only is their participation no longer required, but they are also denied work, resources, public services and opportunities.

So it is that the 'end of history' turns out to be characterized by extraordinary suffering, a global elite bonanza which completely evades democratic control, and a frightening degree of political and economic instability. We face our future unaided by radical theory, and the triumph of representative democracy has been accompanied by a general crisis of utopian energies. It seems we must resign ourselves to our collective addictions: there will be no revolution, no let-up to our cruelty, no stopping our self-destruction. No longer can we imagine a different kind of politics. Recently, the Zapatistas appealed to us in the following way: 'Why is it so quiet here?' they asked. 'Is this the democracy you wanted?'[1]

In fact the demise of radicalism is far from complete. At the margins of both theory and practice there is significant exploration of a different and altogether older kind of democracy. Here, as it was for the ancients, for Rousseau, and for Marx, democracy is not so much a set of procedures and institutions, as a way of life, an ethical ideal, an answer to the question: 'how should we live?'[2] So we find groups, associations, and social movements across the world valuing a quite different quality of participation in their decision-making, one which asserts distinct identities, recovers excluded cultures, and suggests new relationships with our environment.[3]

Often, these activities are deeply suspicious of existing hierarchies and democratic institutions, and are therefore careful to by-pass traditional political channels. Indeed, one of the characteristics of these initiatives is a certain anti-institutionalism. We see this same rejection of institutional politics in right-wing militias and in a range of groups using new technologies to co-ordinate their actions.[4] Even in the voluntary sector, public administration and business management, we see recurrent themes of decentralization, active participation and the flattening of hierarchies.[5]

Available for our consideration, then, is a range of populist, anti-institutional and participatory political activity, some of which is democratic, some of which is not. Our capacity to distinguish between the two is much aided by recent theoretical developments. From across the social sciences, an extraordinary rush of attempts are currently underway to deepen democracy. Communitarians, Habermasians, feminists and post-modernists all draw our attention to the nature of consent required if an authority is to claim legitimacy.[6] According to these accounts, meaningful participation is not just a question of occasionally checking a box beside a person's name. Rather, what becomes of central importance is the process of forming and informing that act of choice, the openness of debate which precedes the act of consent, and the quality of information available to political participants. Discernible here is a distinct vision of democracy, one which rests upon face-to-face deliberation, one which stresses that deliberations be fair. 'Fairness' indicates the absence of coercion, the right for all to participate, to be properly informed, and to have their views taken seriously.[7] Fair deliberation here emerges as the defining characteristic of democracy. It is only this that can confer legitimacy. Of these anti-institutional initiatives outlined above, it is those which aspire to fair deliberation that offer a glimpse of a different kind of democratic politics.

Yet the moment we seek examples, perhaps from the politics of identity, from self-help community groups, or from Do-It-Yourself culture, we confront recurrent criticisms These suggest that such ethical forms of democracy are parochial, idealist and politically irrelevant. More specifically, they have been strongly admonished for abandoning attention to material questions,[8] for their lack of concrete institutional reforms,[9] and for their unrealistic, and possibly dangerous, over-estimation of citizen capacities. It is perhaps for these reasons that fair and anti-institutional democratic initiatives have attracted so little serious scrutiny. Either ridiculed as pubescent (by statist political science), or dismissed as irrelevant to real questions of power (liberalism,[10] Marxism[11]), or displaced in favour of textual analysis (post-modernism, post-structuralism), they are not seen as having contributed to our understanding of crucial organizational and strategic questions.

In response, those seeking to defend this different vision of democracy have argued that its effectiveness cannot be adequately assessed by instrumental means. Historically, moments of fair and anti-institutional democratic action have often had important effects which are indirect: they place issues on the public agenda, they educate and empower citizens.[12] We can hardly, for example, dismiss the 1848 Revolutions simply because they failed to capture state power. By announcing the future centrality of popular opinion in politics, the events of that year were of lasting importance.[13]

Further counter-arguments have been suggested by theorists seeking to deepen democracy. For example, Benjamin Barber and Paul Hirst have offered a range of practical institutional reforms which would allow fair deliberation to be effectively fed into the decision-making processes of the state, so preserving the organizational benefits of a central representational structure.[14] By giving deliberative democracy a 'place', they hope to combine its increased legitimacy with political viability.

Yet these latter suggestions, while going some way toward addressing the issue of political irrelevance, remain strangely transfixed upon the state. Almost none address the problems encountered by participants in real deliberative situations. Democratic theorists have almost always seen themselves as designers of entire political orders. They have sought to show how states could be both legitimate and effective. The theorist, gazing out over the entire institutional landscape, diagnoses ills, and designs institutional treatments. From this elevated perspective, trying to deepen democracy becomes a problem of design, of finding forms which will allow for fair deliberation to be fed into the decision-making apparatus of the state, of suggesting institutional structures to house participation. To be effective, to be politically relevant, deliberative input must be channelled, limited, managed. Otherwise it can not run states.[15]

Yet most of us do not practice statecraft. We do not, in fact, face the problem of reforming an entire political order. Instead, we live everyday lives, in our families and communities. We work, we belong to civic associations and, when sufficiently motivated to overcome our pessimism, we engage in political activism. From the perspective of a participant in everyday collective decision-making, democracy presents a quite different set of problems. Here, now, democracy means fairness and effectiveness in the decision-making process of an actual group.

For all their talk of deliberation, if you ask a democratic theorist questions like: How can our decisions be fair and effective? How can we have more democracy, say, in our place of work? you will be greeted by a loud silence. This is because they are busy elsewhere. Anxious to be seen as politically relevant, they want to show democratic states how to run. Participants would be more impressed if we could learn, first, how to walk.

What, then, can we say about democracy as it appears from the perspective of actual participants? We might start with Wolin's suggestion that 'democracy needs to be reconceived as something other than a form of government,' more along the lines of 'a mode of being'.[16] In so doing, we begin to see that democracy is not so much about 'where the political is located but how it is experienced.'[17] Wolin describes democracy as something that happens to people, something immediate, something characterized not by a form for participation, nor by an institutional design, but precisely by a loss of form, and by a breach of design.[18] It is 'defined by its opposition to existing arrangements rather than by them.'[19]

We are here invited to contemplate democracy as an immediate and transgressive moment which occasionally erupts[20] in our everyday lives. According to this view, democracy is not an institutional form but, instead, something that can occur among particular people in particular situations. In an outbreak of democracy there is a sudden recovery of politics, an awakening, a process of political renewal. There is a moment when we rise above the power-saturated ways in which we normally interact, and something quite different takes place between us.

An outbreak of democracy in this sense, whether on a small or large scale, begins with a sudden challenge to power. It can occur with extraordinary rapidity, and almost always catches us by surprise. Trained, perhaps, by generations of sovereigns and clerics, we now concentrate our attention exclusively on political and cultural elites, and so cannot see the seething activity which at last expresses itself in an outbreak of democracy. Our surprise[21] is then matched by our horror, as it gradually dawns upon us that such disorganised political forms might, in fact, be very effective indeed.

Certainly, democracy as a way of life has always been highly opportunistic. It mushrooms into the political spaces vacated upon the loss of order. Crisis, systemic breakdown and incompetent leadership all favour its spread. Examples of democratic outbreaks, some on a massive scale, are common in the history of religious struggles, agricultural uprisings, labour movements and secessionist rebellions. Against our expectations, they are often very effective in the way they co-ordinate action. Marx had his own preferred examples, especially the June Days of 1848. 'It is well known,' he states, 'how the workers, with unexampled bravery and ingenuity, without leaders, without a common plan, without means, and, for the most part lacking weapons, held in check for five days the army, the Mobile Guard, the Paris National Guard and the National Guard which streamed in from the provinces.'[22]

Garton-Ash stresses just this kind of unexpected effectiveness in his description of the formation of Solidarity,[23] and there are accounts of the development of democracy on the American frontier which stress its ability to co-ordinate action in the absence of law.[24] Others have identified such outbreaks in Russia during 1917, in Paris in 1968, in the American resistance to the war in Vietnam, and in the League of Revolutionary Black Workers in Detroit. Goodwyn details this same combination of fair deliberation and effectiveness in his discussion of the National Farmer's Alliance, Shay's Rebellion, and the Flint Sit-Down strikes of the 1930s.[25] Further glimpses are afforded in the way the Danes, in the face of Nazi power, collectively and overnight placed a yellow star on an entire nation's coats;[26] in striking miners' wives ability to agitate for, and support, their embattled communities,[27] in the mass mobilization of citizens which brought down the puppet regimes of Eastern Europe. There have also been great refusals, like the boycott of the Nike Corporation by black American youth, prompted by Public Enemy's exposure of racist hiring practices, the resistance in Europe to Shell's dumping of Brent Spar and the British city of Liverpool's boycott of the *Sun* newspaper following its reporting of the Hillsborough disaster.[28]

What we see in these examples is, first of all, an alternative form of collective action. It is precisely this form which co-ordinates most things in our everyday lives. Here, beneath the veneer of institutions, activities occur in horizontal, flattened networks of communication, lacking centralized guidance yet somehow with the capacity to effectively co-ordinate. It is precisely this alternative form of action co-ordination, termed 'rhyzomatic ... like crab-grass' by Deleuze and Guattari,[29] that so terrifies those in power. Having claimed that only an institutional politics can be effective, they now confront a way of organizing that they do not understand.

But how does this kind of disorganized democracy actually function? What happens upon an outbreak of democracy? To answer these questions, we must move away from the study of participation as it takes place within institutionalized political science, and instead borrow from empirical work undertaken in social psychology, communication studies, community activism and radical democratic practice.

When the veneer of social order begins to tear, people gather together. Whether in those spaces so carefully hidden from the eye of power – the wood, the street, the public house, the coffee shop – or in places formerly cleansed by surveillance and legalised force, such as the town square or the theatre, people get together and they talk.[30] The temperature of this new interaction is hot, there is energy and noise, there is debate. The same thing occurs when existing power-saturated and hierarchical groups in civil society suddenly find their structures subjected to suspicious interrogation and open discussion.

Accounts of such moments repeatedly note that speech becomes animated, that people are keen to be heard; they listen to others with interest and there is a heightened concern to elicit all views. Another early indication is that people become highly suspicious of all forms of existing authority. The women's movement in particular found that one of the effects of this suspicion was that women identified new ways in which they were oppressed. In short, during open discussion, people become politicized. As republican theory has always claimed, participants are able to broaden their interests to include those of others,[31] and even to include the common interests of the group. As the forum continues to meet, friendship, vitality and rapid learning all draw people in.[32] Now, to use Rousseau's phrase, they 'fly to the assemblies'.[33] In an outbreak of democracy, the benefits of participation far outweigh the costs.[34]

Social psychologists have found that what seems to drive these processes, to give them their extraordinary energy, is that in an outbreak of democracy conflict *works*.[35] It somehow generates cohesion, it causes people to re-evaluate their preferences and needs,[36] it brings about consensus. There are disagreements, and these are acted out – often in highly dramatic ways. Livy's history of early Rome has many good examples of such political drama, and it was precisely this energizing conflict to which Machiavelli attributed the vitality of that republic.[37]

A further characteristic of democratic outbreaks is that participants seek ways to deliberate which are seen to be right and fair. This means they regularly evaluate their decision-making process to check that it is as fair as circumstances allow. In judging the quality of their own democracy, they must necessarily make appeal to a common understanding of fairness, be it a universal ideal or a social construction. Whatever its epistemological status, the ideal of fairness is interpreted differently in different cultures, and participants bring their own ethical and aesthetic understandings to bear on such judgments.[38] Accounts of democratic outbreaks illustrate this great variety of style, while at the same time reflecting a common democratic core. In most cultures, argumentation is not something stilted and rational, but includes the use of rhetorical devices such as irony, ridicule and *ad hominem* arguments. In the sometimes playful mass debates of democratic Athens, for example, to abuse a speaker's ancestry was considered to be a valid part of criticizing their views. Yet Athenians certainly watched their democracy with care, subjecting their decisions to constant reassessment and complaint.[39]

Upon an outbreak of democracy, leadership is no longer based on social roles, but becomes more fluid: its functions divided and shared. Where it does accrue to particular individuals, it is because the group benefits from his or her abilities. Whether the benefits of leadership outweigh its dangers is a constant topic of discussion for the group. On those rare yet inevitable occasions where ostracism is necessary, it tends to be practised against those more powerful members of the group who are widely seen to be actively working against the collective interest.[40]

As the forum continues to meet, networks emerge, group boundaries harden, and adversarial postures are adopted towards the institutions of power.[41] The group develops in-jokes, stereotypical images of opponents and symbolic representations of its cohesion. Nevertheless, a characteristic of fairness is openness of membership, and informal and un-bureaucratic procedures to include new arrivals.

Generally, activity remains frenetic, people make extraordinary sacrifices and act in uncharacteristic ways.[42] A great deal of emotion continues to be expressed, both positive and negative: people can't sleep, they fall in love, and what they are able to achieve surprises both others and themselves. In recovering their collective power, participants report an extraordinary sense of euphoria and a heightened confidence in their own ability.[43] Drawing now on many different points of view, the group's deliberations often result in highly creative decisions. When implementing such decisions, people act with responsibility and commitment. This is another important way in which 'rhizomatic' democratic action is particularly effective. In more hierarchic forms, implementation of decisions (made by others) always entails a collective loss of energy, due both to foot-dragging and to the necessary costs of enforcement.[44]

Such moments of fairness enjoy some successes: power is challenged, its ways revealed.[45] If outbreaks become extended and networked together, new rights can be won, and sometimes even governments fall. But usually there is failure.

Failure has multiple causes, both external and internal. Externally, one of the most significant difficulties faced by any genuinely democratic network is the unbridled hostility of the state and other institutions of power. Usually, outbreaks can be safely ignored, ridiculed, denied resources and allowed to peter out. Should they manage to survive and network together so as to present even a symbolic threat to existing structures of power and property distribution, other strategies, such as informants, pay-offs and dirty tricks are used. Finally, if even these prove inadequate, states (democratic as well as authoritarian) will resort to violent repression in order to restrict the growth of democracy.[46]

Further difficulties arise when an outbreak expands and finds it must develop new administrative structures. As the scale of activities increases, contacts with the institutions of power become more frequent and the network finds it needs delegates, proxies and spokespersons.[47] Subsequently, the selection and control of representatives comes to occupy more and more of their time and energy, necessitating new levels of institutional structure. This process often follows upon a group being offered much-needed resources, or perhaps the attention of the media or powerful decision-makers. Such resources invariably come with strings attached, and the nature of these strings can pose significant organizational difficulties for the group. Asked now for written constitutions, due processes of accountability and proof of representativeness, networks find they must evince structures which fulfil conditions for the raising of resources. This can entail having to learn new languages for the expression of their activities and adopting particular self-descriptions which fit the conceptual categories of the resource provider. This is an important institutional moment in the life of a democratic outbreak, and it can strongly affect the texture of interactions taking place within it. At such points, discussion is, to use Habermas's phrase, gradually 'colonized' by instrumental forms.[48]

Here then we witness the generation of specialized teams, sub-groups of representatives and support and briefing structures for those increasingly active outside the original group. The danger with this secondary layer of structure is that it tends to move decisions away from direct discussion and interrogation. Representatives find ways of acting that seem to offer efficiency gains, they develop new expertise in getting things done. Yet if this learning is concentrated in sub-groups and individuals, if it remains uninspected by the original group, if it begins to sediment into distinct intra-group cultures, then it becomes damaging to the discursive ability of the group as a whole. We witness just this in various Green parties,[49] within the women's movement and when self-help groups apply for charitable funding. The colonization of the democratic outbreak, and the institutional structures this brings into being, ineluctably erode its face-to-face quality.[50] Now, what was once done by talking is taken over by individuals with particular abilities, displaced by bureaucratic procedure, rendered static by hierarchic institutional solutions.

At last, if it has not fizzled out or been repressed, the outbreak is co-opted and fully institutionalized.[51] Participants now find themselves mere spectators of a process that was once their own. So domesticated, discussion returns to its more common, power-saturated and 'normalized' form.[52] If the outbreak was widespread and prolonged, its slogans will be adopted hypocritically, aped by politicians and used to advertise clothing to teenagers. Now declared a 'Triumph of Democracy',[53] the revolutionary moment is finally contained in a constitutional form. Here, participants in a successful outbreak find themselves subject to that most seductive of ends: death by liberal democracy.

Internal causes of failure are easy to identify. Stress and exhaustion, fear of repression, frustration, resignation, repeated narcissistic injuries and withdrawal are among them.[54] Often, these take the form of group divisions that increasingly constrain discussion, or the emergence of a faction or leader whose methods undermine fair communication. Old power differentials reappear, so that once again men dominate the discussion, experts automatically take on tasks which become invisible to the group, and the more confident members, now doing all the talking, complain about the level of participation of the less active. Riven by conflict that is now destructive,[55] the noise at last begins to abate. As the cost of participation rises, people no longer attend with the same frequency. When democracy ends, apathy returns, as does the exclusive concern with self-interest and the prevalence of 'free-riding'.[56] Instead of agreeing to disagree, as they might have done during the democratic outbreak, conflict goes underground, and consensus becomes, once more, a sham.[57]

Now the recriminations begin. People start to 'pathologize' those who hold views different from their own, and to see that difference as sabotage.[58] Ostracism becomes a weapon to be used against less powerful members of the group. The process becomes increasingly divisive, and as the ideology of the network hardens further still, a kind of micro-Thermidor occurs, one characterized by 'group think' and the enforcement of conformity.[59] Now, in a parody of self-rule, participants take on the task of oppressing themselves. With the eclipse of fairness, leaders and sub-groups police deliberations, thus resurrecting the negative side of direct 'democracy', in which individual freedom is effectively denied.[60] Such an occurrence is then greeted with gleeful shouts of 'I told you so!' by those threatened by the outbreak.

Whatever the combination of causes, democratic outbreaks seem to have a discernible life cycle: they burn brightly, then either fizzle, are repressed, become profoundly unfair, or are co-opted and institutionalized. They can last for moments, or for months, but eventually they come to an end.[61]

What use, then, are such extraordinary and ephemeral moments? We have noted their capacity to educate citizens, to renew ordinary politics, and to effect change. In assessing their value, we should also recognize that the many problems democratic outbreaks must overcome, if they are to extend their activities and remain democratic, are not necessarily without solutions. All the various pressures identified above, be they internal or external, have been overcome by particular democratic outbreaks in the past. What we can say, however, is that no single outbreak has managed to overcome them all in order to build a genuine anti-institutional democratic movement which has been sustained over time.

Yet the fact that this has so far not occurred in our political history does not preclude its future possibility. If groups succeeded in mobilizing, networking and co-ordinating their activities on a large scale, perhaps adopting some second layer structures which are carefully controlled, sustaining their democratic character across periods of lesser energy, taking on everyday organizational functions, it is still conceivable that an accumulation of democratic outbreaks could constitute a different kind of politics.

Assessing the value of such ephemeral events therefore presents us with significant difficulties, not least among them being the question of whether the past can be used to predict the future. To assert that democratic outbreaks will always only be ephemeral would require a law-like explanation (and thus, prediction) of their necessary failure, something that is entirely beyond our present knowledge of such events. Not only do we lack such an explanation, we also lack the capacity to adequately evaluate the effects of such outbreaks. Where these might include indirect effects, such as pressures on elites to make concessions and lasting images of struggle, we are never sure precisely what is to be valued, nor over how long. Indeed, for how long must an ephemeral activity be sustained before we designate it as important? Five years? Ten? Surely, it needs to be at least seventy-five years, for otherwise, each of our individual lives becomes unimportant. Yet we cannot insist that an event must last for more than a hundred years for it to be important, for otherwise, liberal democracy itself appears to be of little value. The charge of ephemerality, and the easy dismissal of fair and anti-institutional democratic initiatives it seems to allow, is a numbers game we do not know how to play. Certainly, democratic outbreaks are ephemeral. But that does not mean they always will be, nor that they thereby lack importance.

There is one deficiency of democratic outbreaks, however, that cannot be denied: they are unable to provide a stable supply of deliberative input for a state. Simply, democracy from the participant's perspective may not be the kind of thing that can be accommodated in an institutional design. To see why this is so, we must recall that the basic building block of democratic legitimacy is fair face-to-face deliberation. What makes an outbreak of democracy legitimate, and, importantly, what keeps it so, is the ceaseless energy with which its members are suspicious of unfairness. Only by talking, arguing, celebrating, can participants be sufficiently vigilant to extend the duration of their democratic moment. Subject to significant pressures on their time and resources, participants often face the need to compromise their fairness in order to make gains in effectiveness. They need to agree to methods of quick decision-making which may not involve the whole group, to temporary hierarchies, to reliance on a particular person's skills, and generally to a number of practices which are in fact unfair.

What we are considering with such trade-offs is the addition of a second layer of organizational structure, a minimal increase in formalized procedure. Participants in democratic outbreaks face an unending array of difficult collective judgments which will determine whether they remain democratic or not. Somehow, they must recognize the need for a gain in effectiveness, agree to a reduction in their own participation, and remain vigilant that the resulting trade-off does not become permanent. While fairness is difficult enough in itself, it becomes even more so when we try to manage and control this second layer. As the empirical evidence shows, even minimal reliance on proxies and bureaucratic procedures can be hard to reverse. Often, it results in permanent damage to the deliberative capacities of the group.

Those who participate in outbreaks of democracy thus confront legitimacy as ephemeral and entropic, as requiring constant reassertion. Good judgment is, therefore, characterized by an ongoing suspicion, not only of all forms of authority, but also of those subtle shifts in texture that occur in groups as they interact with existing institutions of power.[62] Groups show poor judgment when they succumb to the temptations of institutional solutions and lazily allow their processes to lapse back into illegitimacy. Discursive assessment, rapid and suspicious, is required before the group can legitimately adopt some institutional relief such as the selection of a delegate, the adoption of a procedure, or some other hierarchical arrangement which secures an easing of the discursive load.[63] Vigilance is a virtue democrats must have in abundance; they must be non-believers, active in their ambivalence, wide awake. In this way, they can constantly scrutinize the effects of their trade-offs upon the deliberative capacities of the group, and so legitimately adopt and control a second layer of organizational structure.

One recurrent difficulty with this second layer pertains to our understanding of how and why representatives become separated from those they represent.[64] This phenomenon has been inspected by democratic theory, though usually in order to show that any serious engagement with existing structures of power necessitates the adoption of hierarchical and perhaps oligarchic methods. So we find Michels analysing the Social Democratic Party in Germany and concluding that its efforts to organize inevitably generated oligarchy.[65] The explanation for democratic degeneration is here given in terms of a spatial metaphor: it is the *distance* between the representatives and the people that results in the former's transformation into 'oligarchs.'[66] Distance, however, is more descriptive of this process than it is explanatory. What we really require is a deeper understanding of the subtle ways in which institutions, even democratic ones, gradually distort the experience of democracy. Group representatives, in their efforts to do business with elites, seem ineluctably to internalize a different set of norms and values, finally becoming socialized into a more institutionalized view of participation: one which seeks to manage it effectively in order to serve the needs of the elite. The danger here, then, is that the representatives of the people become co-opted into a quite different project from the one that originally generated their mandate.

A further obstacle to the evaluation of democratic breakouts arises from the contradictory nature of the criticisms so often levelled at apparently disorganized political forms. The history of such outbreaks would seem to indicate that the simple charge of ineffectiveness is misplaced, and is likely to be more ideological than substantive. It cannot be the failure of democratic outbreaks to co-ordinate action that accounts for the refusal by political science to take anti-institutional initiatives seriously, nor does it explain the lack of sustained study of how we might stimulate and nurture such activities, develop ways for groups to network together and thereby to overcome the problem of partiality which always besets local actors.[67] Rather, at the heart of this disinterest is the fear that rhizomatic action is *too* effective, dangerously so, and thus prone to violent disorder. As such, it must be controlled. Otherwise, and here is the rub, it cannot provide the safety and stability required by elites to maintain their power, in other words, the state. Any radical politics that cannot run a state is thereby seen as deficient.[68] To say that democratic outbreaks are unimportant because they are dangerous, ineffective, and ephemeral, is therefore, to evaluate them in a purely instrumental way; purely instrumental, that is, for the maintenance of existing state power.

And of course, outbreaks of democracy cannot run states. Indeed, running a state is not, after all, a suitable task for the spontaneous and ephemeral, nor for the joyful, the committed or the autonomous.[69] It's not the sort of thing one would do if wide awake, if suspicious of illegitimacy, if wanting to be involved in processes of actual democratic judgment. It is clearly true that an outbreak of democracy can co-ordinate collective action. It can effectively provide for both material and social needs. It can defeat centralized structures of power in the field. It can take over a whole area, culture, way of life, so fast it takes the breath away. But it cannot run states.

This is because we cannot, as the designing theorists would suggest, simply stack democratic layers on top of one another, and then, in a great leap of faith, switch to a representative structure at the level of the state. Above the second layer, the texture of deliberation is inexorably changed. Here, face-to-face interaction is replaced by a corrupting politics of proxy, by bureaucratization and ossification of procedure, by institutionalized mechanisms geared solely to effectiveness. Above the second layer, and sometimes even within it, fairness is not only lost, it is also forgotten.

How, then, could there ever be such a thing as a democratic state? In the liberal democracies, we live with significant trade-offs of participation for effectiveness. But, again, it is not the presence of unfair practices that signals illegitimacy. It is the lack of deliberative agreement to such trade-offs. Where no serious effort is made by the state, or even by a major political party, to seek meaningful deliberative input into the making of collective decisions, then such trade-offs must be seen as illegitimate. And of course, even if a state did seek such input, it could only do so by attempting to provide institutional forms which, as we have seen, are not conducive to fairness as it is experienced by participants. We must conclude therefore that newly democratic states have joined a club of non-democrats. It is for this reason that they are disappointed, it is for this reason that they find themselves in (our) brave new world of political silence and carefully managed participation.

This, though, is not to remove all possibility for a deepening of democracy. Historically, participatory rights are not given by suddenly generous elites. They are taken by emerging oppressed groups. Only as groups learn to operate their own procedures with fairness and effectiveness, only as they find ways to network with other such groups while retaining their democratic core, can they begin to challenge the existing structures of power.

Yet it is precisely when we begin to consider the possibility of such a challenge that we reveal the extraordinary lack of knowledge we have accumulated over our history regarding what it actually means to rule ourselves. We know so little about how to behave fairly in groups, how we might nurture and network democratic break-outs and thus begin a genuinely democratic movement. When suitably humbled by this lack of knowledge, the question of how we might deepen democracy escapes from the hands of the designing theorist and becomes one that participants can only ask themselves. Do we want to be autonomous citizens? Do we want to have fun, to make noise, to act on our growing mistrust? Or do we want merely to watch as those forces which work against democracy increasingly colonize our lives and perhaps even destroy us completely?

Deepening democracy could, quite suddenly, and quite alarmingly, become something more than an unlikely possibility. Any significant outbreak can be relied upon to rapidly generate a great number of very angry and very active citizens, and would certainly, eventually, challenge for greater democratic control of the market. At such a point, participants would find themselves trying to discursively evaluate what must surely be one of the greatest 'non-decisions' and the least deliberated trade-offs of democracy for effectiveness in human experience – the subordination of democracy and social justice to market supremacy. An outbreak on such a scale would be tantamount to revolution, and as history shows, no violence is ever spared to protect the market from the demands of justice.

'Once you have citizens,' Rousseau said, 'you have all you need.' At present, we have few citizens. Liberal democracy studiously fails to produce them. For the most part there is apathy, cynicism, extraordinary hardship and also, possibly, impending infrastructural breakdown. Yet, where a political structure relies for its stability on systematic de-politicization and the exhaustion of utopian energies, it is always vulnerable. There is much dry wood. There are many outbreaks of democracy. Just because our elites cannot see them does not mean they do not occur. After all, the democratic project of basing authority on the fair and considered agreement of those affected has always been one that has threatened to grow out of control.

NOTES

1. Zapatistas, *Communiqué*, 4 February, 1994
2. R. Shusterman, 'Putnam and Cavell on the Ethics of Democracy', *Political Theory*, 25, 1997: 193–214.
3. See, for examples, B. Epstein, 'Radical Democracy and Cultural Politics: What about Class? What about Political Power?', in *Radical Democracy*, D. Trend (ed.), London: Routledge, 1996: 127–139; *Differences*, Special Issue, Vol. 6, 1994; and ongoing editions of *SchNEWS*.
4. M. Castells, *The Power of Identity*, Oxford: Blackwell, 1997: ch. 2.

5. D. Burns et al., *The Politics of Decentralization*, London: Macmillan, 1994; M. Castells, *The Rise of the Network Society*, Oxford: Blackwell, 1996: 167.

6. J. S. Fishkin, *The Dialogue of Justice,* New Haven: Yale University Press, 1992; J. Elster, 'The Market and the Forum', in *Foundations of Social Choice Theory*, J. Elster, J. Hylland (eds.), Cambridge University Press: Cambridge, 1986: 103–132; C. Mouffe, *The Return of the Political,* London: Verso, 1993.

7. J. Habermas, *Moral Consciousness and Communicative Action*, Cambridge: Polity Press, 1992: 89; J. Cohen, 'Deliberation and Democratic Legitimacy', in *The Good Polity*, A. Hamlin, P. Pettit (eds.), Oxford: Basil Blackwell, 1991: 17–34.

8. N. Geras, 'Ex-Marxism Without Substance: Being a Reply to Laclau and Mouffe', *New Left Review*, 169, 1988: 34–62.

9. W. Kymlicka, W. Nelson, 'Return of the Citizen: A Survey of Recent Work on Citizenship Theory', *Ethics,* 104, 1994: 352–381, here at 369, n. 21.

10. Perhaps the classic rejection is presented in R Dahl, E. Tufte, *Size and Democracy*, Stanford University Press, 1974, where it receives an axiomatic proof.

11. Since Lenin's ' "Left-Wing" Communism – An Infantile Disorder', in V. I. Lenin, *Selected Works*, Moscow: Progress, Vol. 3, 1977: 291–369.

12. S. Wolin, 'Fugitive Democracy', *Constellations*, 1/1, 1994: 11–25, here at 17.

13. E. J. Hobsbawm, *The Age of Capital*, New York: Meridian, 1979: 21.

14. B. R. Barber, *Strong Democracy,* Berkeley: University of California Press, 1984: P. Hirst, *Associative Democracy,* Cambridge: Polity Press, 1994.

15. This is Habermas's position, one which severely hampers attempts to conceive of a radical politics arising from his work

16. S. Wolin, 'Norm and Form: The Constitutionalizing of Democracy', in *Athenian Political Thought and the Reconstruction of American Democracy*, J. P. Euben et al. (eds.), Ithaca: Cornell University Press, 1994: 29–58, here at 54.

17. Wolin, 'Fugitive Democracy', 18.

18. See also, H Lefebvre, *The Production of Space*, Oxford: Blackwell, 1991.

19. Wolin, 'Norm and Form', 41.

20. H. Lefebvre, *The Explosion: Marxism and the French Revolution,* New York: Monthly Review Press, 1968.

21. F. Guattari, T. Negri, *Communists Like Us,* New York: Semiotext(e), 1990: 31; J. C. Scott, *Domination and the Arts of Resistance,* New Haven: Yale University Press, 1990: 86, 224.

22. K. Marx, 'The Class Struggles in France: 1848–1850', in *The Marx-Engels Reader*, R. C. Tucker (ed.), London: Norton, 1978: 586–593, here at 589.

23. T. Garton-Ash, *The Polish Revolution: Solidarity*, London: Granta, 1991.

24. R. H. Weibe, *Self-Rule: A Cultural History of American Democracy,* Chicago: University of Chicago Press, 1995: 15, 60, 257.

25. L. Goodwyn, 'Organizing Democracy', *Democracy*, 1/1, 1981: 41–60.

26. J. C. Isaac, 'Oases in the Desert: Hannah Arendt on Democratic Politics', *American Political Science Review,* 88/1, 1994: 156–168.

27. B. Campbell, *Goliath: Britain's Dangerous Places,* London: Methuen, 1993: 319.

28. In 1989, Liverpool football-club supporters died in Hillsborough Stadium in Sheffield as a result of police mismanagement of overcrowding, a disaster for which the *Sun* initially blamed Liverpool supporters.

29. G. Deleuze, F. Guattari, *A Thousand Plateaus: Capitalism and Schizophrenia,* Minneapolis: University of Minnesota Press, 1987.

30. See, in particular, Scott, *Domination*, 64, 118, 121–122, 124; S Moscovici, W. Doise, *Conflict and Consensus: A General Theory of Collective Decisions*, London: Sage, 1994: 48, 60, 64, n. 1; Garton-Ash, *The Polish Revolution*, 51; A. Phillips, *Engendering Democracy,* Cambridge: Polity Press, 1991: 49, 121, 142.

31. What Arendt calls 'enlarged thinking' See S. Benhabib, 'Judgment and the Moral Foundations of Politics in Arendt's Thought', *Political Theory*, 16/1, 1988: 29–51.

32. Phillips, *Engendering Democracy*, 129. That learning is a side-effect of participation is well documented, and has even served to provide justifications for democracy. See e.g. J. Knight, J. Johnson, 'Aggregation and Deliberation: On the Possibility of Democratic Legitimacy', *Political Theory,* 22/2, 1994: 227–296, 295 n. 62. On the 'therapeutic' effects of user participation in mental health service provision, see V. Lindow, 'A Chance for a Change', *Nursing Times*, 89/12, 1993: 33–34.

33. J.- J. Rousseau, *The Social Contract*, Harmondsworth: Penguin, 1968: 140.

34. J. J. Mansbridge, *Beyond Adversary Democracy,* New York: Basic Books, 1980: 9.

35. A. O. Hirschman, *Exit, Voice and Loyalty*, Cambridge, MA: Harvard UP, 1970: 206–211.

36. C. R. Sunstein, 'Preferences and Politics', *Philosophy and Public Affairs,* 20/1, 1991: 3–34.

37. N. Machiavelli, 'The Discourses', in *The Portable Machiavelli,* P. Bondanella, M. Musa (eds.), Harmondsworth: Penguin, 1979: 167–418.

38. J. Habermas, 'Struggles for Recognition in Constitutional States', *European Journal of Philosophy*, 1/2, 1993: 128–155, here at 139, 144.

39. J. Ober, *Mass and Elite in Democratic Athens*, Princeton: Princeton University Press, 1989, 148, cites Isocrates' observation that Athenians tended to 'sit around in the shops complaining about the existing political order.'

40. Phillips, *Engendering Democracy*, 123; Ober, *Mass and Elite*, 74; Garton-Ash, *The Polish Revolution*, 54.

41. A. Pizzorno, 'An Introduction to the Theory of Political Participation', *Social Science Information*, 9/5, 1970: 29–61, here at 44ff.; Phillips, *Engendering Democracy*, 123. Such in-group/out-group distinctions, or, as C. Schmitt describes them in *The Crisis of Parliamentary Democracy*, Cambridge, MA: MIT Press, 1985, 'us and them' mentalities, can constitute important components of group identities as well as exclusionary practices.

42. See Phillips, *Engendering Democracy*, 118: J.-P. Sartre, *The Critique of Dialectical Reason,* London: NLB, 1976; Book II, ch. 1; Scott, *Domination,* 209, 222.

43. R. Flacks, 'Reviving Democratic Activism: Thoughts About Strategy in a Dark Time', in *Radical Democracy,* Trend (ed.), 102–116 suggests that political activists' accounts of their successes contradict theoretical denials of their effectiveness, here at 102.

44. Scott, *Domination,* 188; S. Bowles, H. Gintis, *Democracy and Capitalism,* New York: Basic Books, 1987: 200.

45. A. Melucci, 'Social Movements and the Democratization of Everyday Life', in *Civil Society and the State,* J. Keane (ed.), London: Verso, 1988: 245–260.

46. Goodwyn, 'Organizing Democracy', 47.

47. Phillips, *Engendering Democracy*, 134.

48. J. Habermas, *The Theory of Communicative Action*, Vol. 2, Cambridge, MA: Beacon Press, 1987: 355ff.

49. See the discussion of such parties in H. Wainwright, *Arguments for a New Left,*

Oxford: Blackwell, 1994: ch. 7.

50. Wolin, 'Norm and Form', 36.

51. A process described by L. J. Ray in *Rethinking Critical Theory,* 74 as one of 'repressive modernization.' He also draws attention to attempts by the state to 'displace public issues into socially isolated sub-cultures', 66–68.

52. Moscovici and Doise, *Conflict and Consensus,* 62.

53. See Wolin's citations of the western press as they greeted such developments in Poland and Thailand, 'Norm and Form', 30.

54. M. Walzer, 'A Day in the Life of a Socialist Citizen', in M. Walzer, *Obligations: Essays on Disobedience, War and Citizenship,* Boston: Harvard University Press, 1970; H. Kohut, *The Analysis of the Self,* New York: International Universities Press, 1971: 128–134; Moscovici and Doise, *Conflict and Consensus,* 42, 61; J. J. Mansbridge, 'Time, Emotion, and Inequality: Three Problems of Participatory Groups', *Journal of Applied Behavioral Science,* 9/2–3, 1973: 351–368.

55. Knight and Johnson, 'Aggregation and Deliberation', 286.

56. M. Olson, *The Logic of Collective Action,* Cambridge, MA: Harvard University Press, 1971.

57. Phillips, *Engendering Democracy,* 130–133.

58. Phillips, *Engendering Democracy,* 145.

59. Moscovici and Doise, *Conflict and Consensus,* 144.

60. Zuckerman highlights this tendency in 'The Social Context of Democracy in Massachusetts', *The William and Mary Quarterly,* third series, 25/4, 1968: 523–544.

61. This, for Wolin, is what gives it its 'fugitive' character See also, Wolin, 'Norm and Form', 55; Lefebvre, *The Production of Space,* 416.

62. Ober cites the ancient Athenian view that a good judgment preserves the capacity to make good judgments, *Mass and Elite,* 161.

63. The history of constitutionalism, particularly the seminal discussions by Burke and Madison, has often highlighted the energy savings afforded by codified political procedures.

64. P. J. Proudhon, 'Parliamentary Isolation', in *The Anarchist Reader,* G. Woodcock (ed.), Fontana: Glasgow, 1977: 110–11; Guattari and Negri, *Communists Like Us,* 104.

65. R. Michels, *Political Parties,* Glencoe, Illinois: Free Press, 1958.

66. Wolin inspects this distance in 'Norm and Form', 43.

67. Radicalism needs more than the usual discussion of 'coalition politics' if it is to benefit from and maintain the legitimacy of such networks Accounts of international meetings of local protesters in *SchNEWS* 156, 26 Feb., 1998, and 200, 5 Feb. 1999, would suggest that this is an area in which practice is currently forging ahead of theory.

68. For an analysis of this assertion and its role in the history of socialism, see M. Salvadori, *Karl Kautsky and the Socialist Revolution, 1880–1938,* London: Verso, 1990: 226–250.

69. Guattari and Negri, *Communists Like Us,* 143; A. Pannekoek, *Workers' Councils,* Melbourne, 1950: 52.

REAL AND VIRTUAL CHIAPAS: MAGIC REALISM AND THE LEFT

JUDITH ADLER HELLMAN

UNTIL THE UPRISING of 1 January 1994, Chiapas stood at the periphery of the periphery. It was a land marginal to both the Aztec and the Mayan empires and, at the time of independence from Spain, unclear as to whether it would become another miserably poor, nominally independent Central American country, the northernmost province of Guatemala, or the southern-most state – and, in effect, internal colony – of Mexico.

With just over three million people, Chiapas has now become the 'navel of the world' – as the Incas called their capital, Cuzco. It is the setting of events so moving and compelling that they can bring 50,000 Italian protesters into Piazza del Popolo, while the networks of Chiapas solidarity groups ring the world, dozens of websites are devoted to following the ins and outs of events in the Altos de Chiapas, a reported 5,000 foreigners have fanned out over these highlands to participate in one way or another in the drama as it unfolds, and by April 1998, representatives of 45 U.S.-based organizations convened in Washington D.C. to establish a Solidarity Network.[1] In sum, in countries around the globe there are energetic activists for whom a central political and social commitment is solidarity with the Zapatista Army of National Liberation, the EZLN. They consider Subcomandante Marcos and the EZLN to have articulated the most impressive challenge to neoliberalism and they see the Zapatistas as the foremost exponents of a revolutionary way of doing politics through electronic communication.

Why is the drama in Chiapas so compelling? What is the appeal that has led so many progressive people outside Mexico to make it the focus of their atten-tion? In the early days the caustic observations, self-reflexive wit, and biting perception of Marcos held foreigners spellbound, and surprised and charmed millions of Mexicans. But beyond the figure of Marcos – heroic, analytic, rebellious, amusing and solemn by turns – stands the appeal of the events as seen from a great distance. As Pierluigi Sullo, Nino Lisi and Marcello Vigli all note and debate in the pages of the Italian daily, *Il Manifesto*, the vast mobilization around Chiapas in Italy, the avalanche of signatures on the petitions of protest, and the massive participation in the national demonstrations protesting the massacre at Acteal 'mean something important for the left.'[2]

But what, exactly, does it mean? What accounts for the European, Canadian and American left's ferocious attachment, not to say obsession, with Chiapas? Is the appeal to those so far from Chiapas based only on the ease with which Marcos's utterances can be interpreted and reshaped to cover every event, to speak to every personal and collective need? When Michael Lowy writes with enthusiasm, 'It is a movement freighted with magic, with myths, utopias, poetry, romanticism, enthusiasms and wild hopes, with "mysticism" . . . and with faith. It is also full of insolence, humour, irony and self-irony.', he has catalogued many of the elements of the appeal that the struggle of miserably poor, vulnerable people have for those whose circumstances are so different. As he himself notes, 'This ability to reinvent the re-enchantment of the world is no doubt one of the reasons why Zapatism is so fascinating to people far beyond the mountains of Chiapas.'[3]

If the appeal to outsiders is not strictly a search for 're-enchantment', by the disenchanted, is it perhaps an impulse similar to that of Sartre and de Beauvoir who, disheartened by the prospects for revolutionary change in their own society, embraced the cause of revolution in the third world? Is it a contemporary case of involvement with people's struggles elsewhere in the place of participation and personal investment in the struggle at home?

Unquestionably much of the appeal to outsiders of the events in southern Mexico lies in the apparent extremity of the case. It appears as a direct confrontation between the powerless and the powerful, the pure and the impure, the honest and the corrupt. Given the elegant simplicity of these images in a world normally filled with ambiguities (or worse, post-modern relativism), it is not surprising that there are progressive people around the world who would do *anything* to support the struggle in Chiapas *except* learn the confusing details. In short, there is a great resistance on the part of many abroad to acknowledge and integrate into their analysis the immense complexity of the forces at play in Chiapas today.

In this essay I propose to examine a number of the complexities that make the situation at once so explosive and so resistant to resolution. In doing so I will identify the reductionism that produces a simplified version of events that is necessarily misleading. I will then analyse the very mixed role of electronic communication which has, on the one hand, saved countless lives by relaying information on military and paramilitary violence and human rights abuses around the world, but has also provided a remarkably 'flattened' picture of the actors and events in Chiapas. This picture constitutes a kind of 'virtual' Chiapas that is instantly available to us on a computer screen,[4] but which bears only a very partial resemblance to the 'real' Chiapas that Chiapanecans themselves or foreign activists, human rights workers, EZLN sympathizers, or even casual visitors would find on the ground in southern Mexico.

Finally, I will highlight the political perils of intense involvement with a virtual Chiapas. What harm, we might ask, is done if people thousands of miles away seize upon a set of images, symbols, and slogans that consolidate their sense that they form part of an international force that confronts neoliberalism? To be sure, there is no harm in much of this enthusiasm and, indeed, many foreign Zapatista solidarity groups are explicit on the need to support the effort in Chiapas by pursuing struggles closer to home. However, I will show that virtual Chiapas holds a seductive attraction for disenchanted and discouraged people on the left that is fundamentally different than the appeal of the struggles underway in the real Chiapas. Solidarity with the real people who inhabit the real Chiapas requires far greater political maturity and tolerance for ambiguity than the most passionately dedicated support for virtual Chiapas. It reflects a severe problem in the contemporary left's politics that energetic solidarity for Chiapas often seems to require unambiguously downtrodden *indios* who are homogeneously good and pure, not multi-faceted, fully developed people with varied and divisive interests, not to mention complex individual personalities. Understandable as the urge to simplify may be, I will show that it is politically important to distinguish between the Chiapas on our computer screens and the actual situation on the ground.

POINTS OF AGREEMENT

There are, or course, some aspects of the case about which there is little or no controversy. For example, all reliable accounts of the background to the Zapatista uprising necessarily emphasize the ironic and tragic disparity of a land exceptionally rich in resources populated by the poorest people in what is still a country comprised, in the majority, of poor people.[5] In this internal colony, a population that is substantially without proper shelter, adequate food, drinking water, or electricity, 'exports' timber, corn, beans, gas, oil, and hydro-electric power to the rest of Mexico.

Common as well to all serious analyses of the causes of the upheaval in Chiapas is a focus on the recent decades of rapid economic change stimulated by a mass of state-sponsored programmes that followed centuries of neglect by the central government in Mexico City. The populist programme of President Luis Echeverría (1970–1976) required a vastly expanded state presence in Chiapas and precipitated a tenfold increase in public spending in this previously marginal corner of the republic. Within a very brief period, both the political economy and social structure of Chiapas were transformed by ambitious projects: investments in roads, dams, petroleum extraction, cultivation and commercialization of coffee, development of cattle and milk industries, and 'colonization' schemes to move landless peasants from other parts of Mexico and other regions of the state of Chiapas into the Lancandon rainforest. These state policies pushed Chiapanecans into the world economy, even as the wars in Central America and the refugee flows they produced, altered the structure of employment throughout southern Mexico.

Naturally, these transformations touched different groups of indigenous people in different ways, further impoverishing some, while opening to others alternatives to subsistence farming and new sources of income in transport, construction, oil, cattle and dairy production. And soon the disequilibrium produced by these economic and social changes was intensified by the crash of the oil boom that had drawn so many indigenous people from the central highlands into wage labour on the gulf coast.[6] Over the next decade, the social tensions produced by the oil boom and bust were deepened by a series of political and economic shocks: the debt crisis of 1982, the fall of coffee prices, and, finally, the neoliberal programme of President Carlos Salinas (1988–1994) which, for Chiapanecos, principally involved the elimination of price supports to corn and basic grain producers and the alteration of Article 27 of the Constitution, a concession to Mexico's NAFTA partners that spelled the end of the land distribution programme that had been the key element in maintaining social peace in the Mexican countryside.

Thus, the framework for understanding the remote and immediate causes of the outbreak of armed conflict in Chiapas centres on this series of changes. The most useful analyses inevitably set this rapid penetration of capitalist relations and the hyper-involvement and subsequent withdrawal of the state against a background of racist oppression of the indigenous population that began with the Spanish Conquest and continues in most respects unabated to the present day. Moreover, such analyses emphasize the way that the landed oligarchy of Chiapas historically utilized both a racist discourse *and* control of the PRI, that is, the Institutional Revolutionary Party's apparatus in Tuxtla Gutiérrez, the state capital, to reinforce its economic, social, and political domination. Under the circumstances, the intervention of the federal government challenged the hegemony, but ultimately did not undermine the control, of the Chiapanecan oligarchies, while the social upheavals created by the economic transformations of the 1970s and 1980s stimulated a new militancy and consciousness among both indigenous and mestizo peasants. In virtually all accounts of the events, it is this heightened consciousness that provides the precondition for the Zapatista uprising in 1994.

This militancy found two forms of expression. The first grew out of the outreach activities of the Catholic diocese under the leadership of Bishop Samuel Ruíz.[7] Their activities began in the 1960s with the training of catechists who fanned out across the highlands, presenting the Bible and sermons translated into indigenous languages and urging the people to talk about their oppression and to consider their rights.[8] These grassroots efforts culminated in 1974 in the First Indigenous Congress which brought together 1,250 Indian delegates from more than 300 communities. Informed by the new concepts of liberation theology, the congress was sponsored by the Mexican state, but appropriated by Bishop Samuel Ruíz and the catechists as a means to give voice to indigenous communities, encouraging them to select their own delegates and conceptualize their problems in their own words. As Collier notes, the congress 'provided a model of bottom-up organizing upon which independent peasant organizations subsequently drew', and offered the opportunity to give expression to the grievances of indigenous Chiapanecans in terms that precisely prefigured the discourse of the Zapatistas twenty years later.[9]

The second type of militancy took the form of peasant unions, often tied to radical national organizations. Organized in many cases by veterans of the urban student movement that had been savagely repressed in October 1968, these new formations of the left reflected the belief of so many former student activists that only through the long-term, painstaking development of mass movements of the poor in the countryside and in urban shanty towns would it be possible to challenge the hegemony of the political elite entrenched in Mexico City. These organizations appeared in Chiapas shortly after the First Indigenous Congress demonstrated so clearly the capacity of indigenous people to come together across ethnic and linguistic lines and to grasp and articulate their own grievances.[10]

The history of this organizational effort in the 1970s and 1980s is – not surprisingly – a history of alliances and schisms. It is a tale of collaboration and co-operation, but also of rivalry between and among Maoists, Communists, Trotskyists, independent *agraristas,* Catholic missionaries and catechists, and Evangelical Protestants – all set against the co-optive efforts of the Mexican state to sponsor its own competing peasant organizations.[11] The Zapatista movement is clearly an outgrowth of the activities of these predecessor organizations. It reflects the commitment of these precursors to the basic principle of stimulating indigenous leadership and organization from below. However, *zapatismo* also represents a reaction against the compromises with the system in which so many of these organizations eventually became involved.

Thus there is little disagreement about the origins of the Zapatista movement in these two earlier organizational efforts, religious and secular. Moreover, for all the different interpretations regarding the nature of *zapatismo,*[12] there is a clear consensus that a distinguishing characteristic of the movement is the way in which, over a period of more than a decade, it slowly constructed a wide and solid base of support among an assortment of ethnic groups in the highlands of Chiapas. Unlike the classic guerrilla *foco* that hopes to attract a following after revolutionary activity has been launched, the Zapatistas were firmly supported by thousands of adherents in villages throughout their zone of operations. To build this base, the EZLN organizers drew upon long-standing principles of Mexican nationalism and they 'breathed new life into a revolutionary history of Mexico which, for decades had been appropriated by the ruling party'.[13] Drawing on these traditional radical themes, they developed a discourse that spoke not only to the most downtrodden people in Chiapas, but to disadvantaged Mexicans throughout the republic. Eventually, in 1995, with the convocation of activists and supporters from around the globe, the Zapatistas came consciously to represent and to articulate internationally popular critiques of neoliberalism.[14]

It is similarly clear that a defining characteristic of the uprising has been the ambivalent response it has elicited from the Mexican state. While the Chiapanecan economic and political elites rallied quickly to pressure for some definitive action to dismantle the movement, neither Salinas nor his successor, Ernesto Zedillo, has managed to settle upon a policy of accommodation or repression, of negotiation or military action, but rather both have pursued all of these possible responses at different times. This lack of a consistent policy is, in turn, tied to the unprecedented circumstances created by the technology that allows people around the globe to follow events as they unfold and to weigh in as a force of international public opinion concerning an event that the Mexican state would prefer to define as a national or local affair. The revolution in electronic communication and the exceptionally effective communication skills of Marcos have fostered an international solidarity that has, in turn, promoted both the survival of the movement and the personal survival of its members.[15]

THE COMPLEXITIES

Thus we find very little disagreement among analysts about the political, social and economic conditions that gave rise to the rebellion, the largely incoherent response of the Mexican state, or the success of the Zapatistas in reaching beyond the immediate zone of conflict to incorporate other Mexicans and sympathizers from around the world into their broader movement. However, when we turn to the accounts available to this mobilized international community of supporters, we find that what is generally communicated about the situation in Chiapas is a highly simplified version of a complex reality. While this picture is not intentionally distorted, it is ultimately misleading in ways that leave those who sympathize with and support the struggle in Chiapas in a very weak position to understand and analyse the events as they unfold. At times, as I will show below, it even makes it difficult to support the struggle in meaningful ways.

What are some of the politically important complexities of the Chiapanecan situation that have been lost or ignored in transmission to outsiders?

Land tenure

Almost everyone concerned for the welfare of indigenous people and poor peasants in Chiapas has learned that 56% of the land is in private hands. This oft-repeated statistic is misleading because it usually presented in a way that suggests that the private holdings are all concentrated in the hands of a few large landlords. The corollary to this supposition is that these estates could be available for distribution to the landless in 'ejidos' under the agrarian reform law *if* the political will existed to move forward with expropriation of large haciendas and the distribution of land to petitioning peasants.[16]

Unfortunately, this *agrarista* dream cannot come true in the conflict zone in Eastern Chiapas, that is, Los Altos and the Lancandon Selva where the Zapatista movement is based. In this region there is almost no 'distributable' land left in large haciendas.[17] In eastern Chiapas, the *latifundios* and even *neolatifundios*,[18] substantially disappeared in the course of the last three decades. Some land was given as ejido parcels in earlier agrarian reform distributions and in the 1980s, the federal government purchased 80,000 hectares of private land for distribution to 159 peasant settlements. Thus, with the relocation to eastern Chiapas of western Chiapanecans displaced by the construction of the hydroelectric dams from the 1950s onward, the settlement of landless peasants from fourteen other Mexican states and the Federal District in the 1970s and 1980s, and the land set aside for bioreserves (under pressure from the international environmental community and supporters of the Lancandon Maya), so much of the land in the region had been given away in small parcels that the *latifundistas* in the zone found it safer to sell off portions of their land to neighbouring peasants in small lots than to resist the tide of land invasions and expropriations.[19]

Given the enormous pressure of population on land resources throughout Chiapas, the vast preponderance of the 56 percent of all land that is privately held in fact consists of *minifundios* of 5 hectares or less in a region where the smallest ejido plot is set at 20 hectares.[20] Thus, where some outsiders are apt to see a traditional *lucha agrarista* taking shape in which they imagine that landless peasants would be pitted against landlords in rural class struggle, in reality, the '*luchas*' over land in Chiapas are no less bitter but, sadly, they most often constitute a 'war of the poor'. In these events, *ejidatarios* who are trying to expand their inadequate parcels, or younger sons and daughters of *ejidatarios* who cannot inherit the family holdings are locked in conflict with neighbouring *minifundistas* who are fighting to hold onto their pathetically small and poor subsistence plots.

Religion

In the virtual Chiapas with which most internet users are familiar, religious actors have a crucial role to play. The religious actors we encounter on the computer screen are Bishop Samuel Ruíz, the Diocese, the Catholic human rights activists of the San Bartolomé Centre for Human Rights, and perhaps a few Protestants in the form of the U.S.-based Pastors for Peace.

While religion does play a central role in the events unfolding in Chiapas today, the picture on the ground is far more complex than the version on the screen. To begin with, competition for hearts and minds and above all souls, between Catholic and other religious groups has been a key motivating force in all that has unfolded in Chiapas over the last forty years. The transformation of Bishop Samuel, himself, from a traditional conservative into a socially engaged activist was prompted in the late 1960s by his perception of the need for the Catholic Church to become involved at the grass roots *in order to check* the advance of evangelical Protestants among the peasants.[21] As everywhere in Latin America and particularly in Central America, a ferocious competition exists in Chiapas between the Catholic Church and evangelical missionaries for the attention, affection and adherence of the poor. But for all the courage and sincere efforts of the catechists, and the charisma and dedication of Bishop Samuel, today only a bare majority of all Chiapanecans are Catholic, a figure that represents the lowest proportion in any Mexican state.[22]

We might almost say that the downtrodden in Chiapas have never been free to make political choices, but increasingly they have made religious choices. And a great assortment of Protestants, some progressive and some conservative, have attracted converts. Of the Protestant churches, the Presbyterians are the largest and longest established, followed by Pentecostalists (Assembly of God, Charismatics, Elim and Eunecer), Seventh Day Adventists, Sabbaticants, and Jehovah's Witnesses. On the scene as well, but in smaller numbers, are Baptists, Lutherans, Church of Nazarene, the Christian Church or Followers of Christ, Church of God, Light of the World, Prince of Peace, the True Church of Christ, and the Central American Church among others.[23] Most recently Islamic and Mormon missionaries have drawn converts and, in a couple of new settlements composed of Protestants who were expelled from predominantly Catholic communities, Islam will soon become the numerically dominant religious group.[24] Thus the religious map of Chiapas resembles a crazy-quilt of different religious sects, some historically well rooted and others, brand new. And to complicate matters further, these religious affiliations sometimes coincide with and sometimes cut across political identifications with either the official party, that is, the PRI, or the centre-left party of opposition, PRD (Democratic Revolutionary Party).

Thus while Bishop Samuel appears to be – other than Marcos himself – the central protagonist in the virtual accounts of Chiapas, and looms as a towering figure in the versions of events that circulate in France, Italy and Spain, he is not the only important religious actor on the stage. To ignore the other actors is to fail to recognize what many consider to be a low-intensity religious conflict that cross cuts ethnic politics.

The Political Actors

Just as religious players turn out to be more numerous and varied than in the picture we usually see on the computer screen, the panoply of political actors in the drama unfolding in Chiapas is also considerably more complex. While virtual Chiapas is characterized by quite clear categories of good and evil, the more complex reality on the ground features a much larger cast of characters and even some groups that can be more difficult to define and sort out.

In virtual Chiapas, the bad guys are the Zedillo regime, President Ernesto Zedillo himself, his Minister of the Interior, Francisco Labastida, his official negotiator, Emilio Rabasa (scion of an elite Chiapanecan family), the PRI (perhaps disarticulated into branches: that is, 'dinosaurs' and 'reformists'), the Mexican state, the Mexican armed forces, and the U.S. military counter-insurgency forces, or at least the Drug Enforcement Agency, acting in clandestine fashion as a counter-insurgency force. The good guys are understood to be the Zapatistas, indigenous people, a broader category generally referred to as peasants, plus their NGO supporters, and Bishop Samuel and the Diocese.

In reality, of course, there are more players and many different interests at stake. A more complete analysis of the situation requires us to consider the interests of the Chiapanecan State as distinct from the Mexican State and national strategic energy interests as distinguished from regional economic and political power holders within Chiapas. For that matter, we should think of both the PRI and the PRD in Chiapas as having concerns that are far from identical with their national affiliates. In addition to ethnic distinctions among indigenous people – an aspect of the situation that *does* find its way into the electronic version of events since the pluri-ethnic presence of Tzotzil, Tzeltal, Chol, and Tojolabal is such a prominent feature of all Zapatista gatherings – we need to factor in important differences in land tenure that create different interests among poor cultivators as in the conflicts among *ejidatarios*, *minifundistas* and the landless that were discussed above. Moreover, a key group of people who receive only sporadic attention abroad are those referred to in Chiapas itself as the 'army of the displaced', that is, indigenous people who are not Zapatista supporters who have been dispersed as refugees from the highlands to as far away as Tapachula on the coast. These *desplazados* are Chiapanecans from the conflict zone who, in many cases, voted not to take up arms when consulted by the EZLN in late 1993, and who were subsequently expelled from their communities or chose to leave the region for fear of getting caught in the cross fire. Now numbering well over ten thousand, the *desplazados* take centre stage in internet communications when they become victims of violence at the hands of the Mexican army or the paramilitary troops comprised of indigenous men armed by the Mexican state. But the fact that many of the refugees from the conflict zone also reject *zapatismo* does not figure prominently in the internet accounts.

The internet does make constant generic reference to non-governmental organizations as 'civil society' and, indeed, a great deal of electronic communication is, at some point, filtered through NGOs. However the term, civil society, does not seem adequate to capture the variety and diversity of organizations on the ground where, in fact, more than 750 Mexican and international NGOs are operating.[25] For the most part, the NGOs appear on our screens as an undifferentiated mass of progressive foreigners and Mexicans who work more or less in concert to alleviate the pain of the conflict in Chiapas, to stand by the oppressed, and to transmit the truth about what is unfolding in this distant and isolated place. While the internet version of events is largely uncritical of both foreign and Mexican NGOs operating in Chiapas, this attitude is not always shared by the people on the scene. Although those who principally relate to Chiapas on their computers are understandably reluctant to criticize anyone who has actually taken off for Mexico to participate in NGO activities there, NGO activists and others at work in Chiapas are not so reticent.

Interviews I conducted in 1998 among a wide range of NGO workers indicated that a great many of these people do not like, trust, or respect one another and, as a consequence, are not able to collaborate. Many of the Mexican NGO people are former government employees who were downsized when the state was 'streamlined', and some of them have brought to their NGO work the attitudes that informed their relations with poor people when they were part of the state – a tendency for which they are roundly criticized by other NGO workers. Competition for international attention among a very limited universe of donors, turf wars, as well as profound philosophical differences plague the relations between and among NGO workers. For example, Bishop Samuel and the Diocese – so widely admired abroad for their courage by progressive people in general and progressive Catholics in particular – evoke a very different response among NGO women working in Chiapas on women's problems. Many such activists note an ironic similarity between the courageous political stances taken by both Bishop Samuel and Pope John Paul II in contrast with the two leaders' conservative social positions on contraception and abortion and indeed even on women's rights.

Moreover, some NGO workers expressed resentment at the pressure they experience to 'filter' their work, as they put it, through the Diocese, and the most important Mexican human rights organization in Chiapas, the Fray Bartolomé de las Casas Centre, which was founded by Bishop Samuel, but operated as a secular, autonomous organization, was taken over by the Diocese after the 1994 uprising. Relations between the Zapatistas and the Church, as well as between Marcos and Bishop Samuel have had their ups and downs, to say the least, and local organizations in place and struggling for peasants' rights since the 1970s have been denounced by Marcos as '*tercerista*' ['third way-ers'] when their adhesion to the EZLN's appeals seemed insufficiently enthusiastic. As one long-time peasant leader said to me in an interview,

> Marcos is always talking about 'civil society', but who does he think *we* are? He dismisses us as compromised by the relations we have had with the state [agencies] to get the things that peasants need. He appeals over the head of people here to civil society in the rest of Mexico and abroad, as if people farther away from Chiapas have not made their own compromises!

In short the 'civil society' that so many Chiapas solidarity activists see as the focus of their own hopes for solutions to the problems in Chiapas and more broadly in Mexico, turns out to be a more ideologically diverse and conflictive space than it might seem in the messages that circulate on the EZLN web sites and e-mail lists. When the array of actors and interests are examined close at hand, we find, not surprisingly, that there is a very large number of agendas both secular and religious, as well as radical, reformist, and conservative, that are being pursued in Chiapas today.

Indigenismo

The promotion of indigenous identity and the drive for indigenous autonomy seem very straightforward goals when they appear in internet communications. However, given the size of Mexico's indigenous population of 6.5 million,[26] and the centrality of the 'indigenous question' to the development of Mexico as a nation, the issue turns out to be, of course, far more controversial than the current, nearly unanimous international call for autonomous communities would suggest.

Under the circumstances, before weighing in with enthusiastic international support for autonomy, it would seem important to have at least some understanding of the concepts that emerged from the Mexican Revolution (1910–1917) and the public policies to which those concepts gave rise. At a minimum, we would need to acknowledge the historical identification of Mexican nationalism with the indigenous past.[27] In the aftermath of the Revolution, the revival of interest and concern with the indigenous roots of the country, the recuperation of the figure of Cuauhtémoc, the nephew of Móctezuma who led the uprising against the Spanish, the celebration of indigenous history in post-revolutionary intellectual life – whether in the textbooks issued by the new revolutionary regime, or the works of the Mexican muralists like Diego Rivera, David Siquieros, or Jose Clemente Orozco – all provided the ideological foundation on which policy debates took place around the future of indigenous people in modern Mexico.[28]

Unfortunately, however, these discussions took place not within indigenous communities, but rather among '*indigenistas*', that is, *mestizos* or whites who were usually quite unselfconscious about establishing policy on 'Indian affairs'. Not surprisingly, progressive Mexican intellectuals and policy makers have always been deeply divided on the subject. Cultural ecologists, integrationists, and Marxist *indigenistas* (who understood ethnicity as equivalent to class in relations between *indios* and *mestizos*) vied with incorporationist *indigenistas* for control of policy formation. This last group prevailed and implemented programmes for community development and the construction of schools, clinics and roads to bring disadvantaged indigenous people into full participation in the economic, political and social life of the nation. At the same time their vision required the 'preservation' of indigenous culture through the creation of dictionaries of indigenous languages, the stimulation of craft production, and similar programmes.

However, the same drive to incorporate indigenous people into the Mexican nation and market opened the door to their manipulation by the PRI, their gross exploitation by non-Indians, and their increasing dependency on the state. Under the circumstances, given the negative outcomes of integrationist policies, the development of a capacity for autonomous self-government became a principal goal of the Chiapanecan catechists in their missionary activities in the highlands in the 1970s. The composition of new pluri-ethnic communities comprised of indigenous people of various identities governed by structures 'designed to transcend rather than erase ethnic differences' was at the heart of the catechists' efforts in Los Altos. As Neil Harvey describes this movement, 'Community cohesion was not based on native traditions, but rather on political militancy and religious belief. Ethnic identity was recreated as a basis for political unity.'[29]

It is this concept of self-rule that underpins the proposals on indigenous autonomy put forward by the Zapatistas and embodied in the San Andrés Accords, signed by the representatives of the EZLN and the Mexican State in February 1996. The accords call for 'the recognition of the right of indigenous people to self-determination within a context of autonomy, the expansion of their participation and political representation, the guarantee of their access to justice, and the promotion of their cultural, educational and economic activities.'[30]

Inasmuch as the Zedillo regime signed the Accords but then failed to implement them, the EZLN broke off negotiations, and the call for the implementation of San Andrés quickly became the rallying point for Zapatista supporters everywhere. It has also become a mobilizing theme for indigenous people throughout Mexico. To read the accounts on the internet, it would seem that the entire world of progressive opinion is also solidly behind this model, or indeed, as Padre Gonzalo Iruarte, Vicar-General for Justice and Peace of the Diocese of San Cristobal de las Casas said to me in an interview in May 1998, 'only profoundly paternalistic people who do not respect the capacity of indigenous people to govern themselves would be aligned against the principles embodied in this agreement.'

And yet, the idea has its critics. As has always been the case in the debates around the 'indigenous question' in Mexico, profound disagreement characterizes the positions held on the issue. In the interviews I conducted with Chiapanecan political activists and anthropologists involved with indigenous communities in the highlands, the lack of enthusiasm for autonomy was striking. It is notable that the climate of intolerance for alternative perspectives on autonomy was such that those based in Chiapas were very eager to express their views to me, but some were reluctant to speak for attribution. One explained:

> This concept of autonomy is illusory because it suggests that *caciquismo*,[31] the divisive forces of class, religion, political affiliation, and all the corrupt and violent people are external to indigenous communities and can be shut out once the communities gain autonomous control over their affairs. But these forces don't lie *outside* of indigenous communities. They are already deeply rooted *inside* these communities, and autonomous administration will only reinforce the divisions and the dominance of the powerful over the weak, of rich over poor, of men over women.

Another told me:

> Somehow this proposal has garnered great international support, but for

me autonomy is not an answer. I have heard a lot about the 'Canadian model' and it is usually posed as if, applied in Mexico, the indigenous people could close off their communities to outsiders and the vast natural riches of Chiapas will become theirs to exploit! The only problem is that the indigenous people of Los Altos are not sitting on top of the oil or gas or timber or hydroelectric power. These natural resources are in other parts of the state. The resource base in the highlands and the Selva is miserably poor.

What I think is needed is not autonomy but a serious redistributive policy. Autonomy would only mean that these impoverished people would be even more enclosed in their misery. What we should be demanding is that the poorest, disadvantaged regions receive a greater proportion of the national wealth. It's little wonder that this proposal on autonomy is the only part of the San Andrés agreement that the Mexican state was willing to sign on to. It costs the state *nothing* if the indigenous people close in on themselves.[32]

Another interviewee was more directly critical:

North Americans who participate in these discussions seem particularly enthusiastic about autonomous control but often they are bringing their own concepts to the discussion, concepts that pertain to a different reality. Do they think that the Tzotzil are going to set up casinos where well-to-do Mexicans are going fly in to drop millions of pesos at the gambling tables? Do they imagine that this is Canada where the dominant society copes with its guilt by channelling billions of dollars into the construction of a territorial capital for a new territory and supporting autonomous indigenous government at the rate of tens of thousands of dollars per capita?

The real question is not whether foreigners should be discussing the issue, or whether the experiences of indigenous struggles in other countries have bearing on Mexico. Rather it is a question of whether indigenous people in Chiapas are going to be better off with autonomy. Well perhaps they will. Or maybe they will end up no *worse* off than they are today. But in either case, it is not a discussion in which people with an essentialized notion of the *indio* should be participating.

It is this kind of essentialist notion of *el indio* that was expressed when, as in May 1998, 134 Italian would-be human rights observers turned up in Chiapas wearing neon green vests emblazoned with the words *somos todos indios del mundo*, 'we are all Indians of the world'. In examining the international fascination with indigenous people, Alison Brysk writes,

The image of Indian as Other was read differently by Latin American policy makers and the international public. To their compatriots,

Indians' appearance made them threatening, subhuman, or simply invisible; to North Americans and Europeans, it made them fascinating, exotic and romantic.[33]

Those who hold romanticized, essentialized notions of indigenous people in Chiapas necessarily have trouble thinking through the implications of autonomous communities in which minority rights are not guaranteed because, for them, *los indios* are all one undifferentiated mass of people. While these Italians may be familiar with a long history of intolerance, expulsions of minorities, and even ethnic cleansing in Europe, their 're-enchanted' image of *indios* did not admit the possibility of violence or intolerance within indigenous communities in Chiapas. But, in fact, the map of Chiapas is dotted with settlements formed by indigenous people who were expelled from their communities for religious or political reasons. It is remarkable how little appreciation of this problem is part of the discussion on the internet. In his writings, John Gledhill has expressed concern about the 'unresolved tension between constitutional individualism and indigenous communalism'.[34] But, for a great many Chiapas solidarity network members, the issue of minority rights within autonomous communities simply does not arise.

REVOLUTION BY INTERNET?

The relationship of electronic communication to the struggle in Chiapas raises two questions. One, as we discussed in the previous sections, is the way in which the information that circulates about events in Chiapas is simplified, flattened and sometimes, even distorted by its transmission and re-transmission on the internet. This problem, of course, is related to the question of how we learn things on the world wide web. What are the sources from which the information comes?

A separate question is how do we respond to the information that we receive electronically? How do we 'do politics' as an internet community? What does it mean when you can 'participate' in a movement without ever leaving the comfort of your room, without ever standing or marching in the rain?

Sources

Careful examination of the material that is translated, summarized and distributed through a variety of networks reveals that almost all of this material is drawn from the Mexican leftist daily, *La Jornada* which is published in Mexico City. *La Jornada* has had a special relationship to the Zapatistas from the start and the EZLN relies on this newspaper in a number of ways. Although there is a public perception that the Zapatistas are directly wired to the internet and tap out their messages on laptops in the Selva, in fact they count on *La Jornada* to relay their messages. As Lynn Stephen notes,

> In reality, the EZLN is not directly connected to E-mail or to the internet. According to Justin Paulson, Webmaster for the web site

'EZLN.ORG,' EZLN communiques are first faxed to several newspapers including *La Jornada* which publishes them. Different web sites then pick them off *La Jornada*'s web sites. Because of the rapid publication of the EZLN's communiques on the internet, they appear to come directly from the EZLN on to the net. In reality, often when I have visited Zapatista communities, I have brought news to them of what is going on in Chiapas – sometimes just 40 kilometres away.[35]

Not only do the Zapatistas count on *La Jornada* to transmit their messages to the world, but, according to a number of people I interviewed in Chiapas, the newspaper has played a major role in providing feedback to the Zapatistas on how to craft a message that would be better understood beyond the borders of Chiapas or Mexico. Moreover, *La Jornada* has a particular relationship to the Zapatistas that some argue effects its coverage of the news. As one Chiapanecan activist told me in April 1998,

> Here we jokingly refer to *La Jornada* as the '*Chiapas Gazette*' or the '*Ococingo Times*' because it carries more news on Chiapas and the EZLN than on any other place in Mexico, sometimes even the capital! Of course it's convenient for us who live here and get to see two 'local papers'. But I read *La Jornada* and I don't recognize a lot of what I read. I'm not saying that they make things up. But they report things in a very partial way. If two Zapatista sympathizers are found dead in a gully, that's always reported. But if two peasants who were not EZLN supporters are found dead, sometimes it gets no mention at all.

Editorially *La Jornada* is close to some elements on the left and critical of others. And the newspaper's preference for the Zapatista position over other left positions has sometimes led to the exclusion of alternative views from the left. For example, regular contributors to the signed 'Opinion' sections of *La Jornada* have been bewildered to find that their columns were not run when they put forward views more sympathetic to the PRD position which called for fostering electoral participation in Chiapas than to the Zapatista position that elections were fraudulent and served reactionary interests and should not be a priority.

Having participated as an electoral observer in Chiapas in 1994, I would be the last to argue that fraud is not a problem in Chiapanecan elections.[36] Given the Chiapanecan elite's historical use of elections to reinforce its illegitimate hold on political power, it is easy to understand the EZLN's decision to sit out the elections of 1996, doing nothing to mobilize its supporters to vote. However, even if the question of the electoral road *vs.* extra parliamentary activity is a very old debate on the left, it would still seem to be a discussion that is worth having. By 1996 the Zapatistas had settled on a position of indifference to electoral activity at the same time that the Chiapanecan PRD thought it stood an excellent chance to take control of the Chamber of Deputies in Tuxtla Gutiérrez, if only people in the conflict zone would show up at the polls to cast their ballots. In May 1998, I interviewed Gilberto Gómez Maza, head of the PRD in Chiapas who asserted,

> The PRD is organized in all 111 municipalities in the state and if you count the seats we did win, plus the seats we could have gained had people voted in the regions controlled by the EZLN, we would have been able to form a majority in the Chamber of Deputies together with the opposition deputies from the PAN.

The son of two rural school teachers, Gómez Maza studied medicine at the National University and became the first, and for decades, the only pediatrician serving the indigenous people of the Chiapanecan highlands. His experience of the poverty and neglect in Los Altos, propelled him into political activity first as a follower of Heberto Castillo and the Mexican Workers Party (PMT), and later, when Castillo decided to support Cuauhtémoc Cárdenas's bid for the presidency in 1988, in the PRD. 'What we are struggling for is to change the relations of power in this state,' he observed, 'and were it not for the anti-electoral stance of the EZLN,' he insisted, 'we could have gone a long way to accomplishing this goal.'

It seemed to me in speaking with Gómez Maza that foreign activists concerned with the future of Chiapas would at least want to think through and debate these assertions. But a full discussion among foreign Chiapas solidarity groups of the appropriateness of the electoral road would have been difficult based on the information available on most web sites because those speaking in favour of participation in elections generally did not make it into print,[37] or, when they did, theirs were not the features from La Jornada that were relayed around the world.

La Jornada's partiality on the subject would not be a problem if Chiapas solidarity groups outside of Mexico had other sources with which to cross check. But, careful examination of the material that is translated, summarized and distributed through a variety of networks reveals that most of the material available electronically is drawn from La Jornada. To be sure, this is a limitation not so much of La Jornada, which does provide broader coverage of the PRD, the unions and other struggles on the left, but of the way that material is selected and distributed and edited for internet distribution.

It is striking that many people who bring a sceptical attitude to anything they read in the 'bourgeois press' and who are capable of making the proper adjustment for sectarian perspectives when they read material generated by others on the left, accept what they read on the internet with no further critical thought – although this material is also filtered through the lens of particular political perspectives. In interviews with dozens of Chiapas solidarity activists that I carried out in Canada in 1996–1997, I found no one who could tell me who any of the webmasters are (other than their names), what are their politics or why one would feel comfortable with depending on a variety of sites, all of them monitored by just a handful of individuals. Like others around the world,

I feel respect for and gratitude to someone like Harry Cleaver at the University of Texas for the time and effort that he has put into keeping us all informed about Chiapas from the first day of the uprising. But it is nonetheless astonishing that there is so little awareness that most of what we read about Chiapas, and civil society in general in Mexico, has been selected and transmitted by Harry Cleaver or a couple of other people whose political outlook – other than a passionate belief in the power of the internet and its potential to build a 'civil society in cyberspace'[38] – is completely unknown to most.

The problem of unequal access

This brings us to the problem of unequal access to progressive world opinion. The received wisdom about power and communication is, of course, that there is very unequal access to the means of communication. But this is usually proposed as a problem by which progressive opinion loses out to conservative or mainstream interests in media controlled by the rich and powerful. The internet, in most of these discussions, is posed as providing a levelling mechanism, a democratic or popular opportunity that opens the way for the poor and marginalized to communicate on the same terms as the rich and powerful. Through this means, we are told, it becomes possible for us to build links to other progressive actors and to construct a community in cyberspace. It provides, as Cleaver and others have asserted, the possibility to circumvent the censorship of the state, to chop down electronic barriers and to liberate information from corporate and state control.[39]

While this is unquestionably an achievement of electronic communication, there is an argument to be made that progressive organizations within Mexico have very unequal electronic access to public opinion. The Zapatistas have been appropriately hailed as media savvy communications geniuses, but other movements of the left, indeed, other armed revolutionaries like the Popular Revolutionary Army (EPR) that is active in Puebla, Guerrero, and Oaxaca, not only lack an articulate spokesman like Marcos, they have not found their webmaster. And, as a consequence, their perspectives are not before us on our screens, and their activities are rarely reported.

In the case of the most important party of the left, PRD, one Mexican-based media expert explained, 'the traditional left in Mexico is techno-phobic, and has few ideas how to make electronic communication work for them.' Whatever the reason, indeed, the PRD has been very slow to make use of the internet and as a consequence, the party appears in electronic sources largely in terms of its deficiencies which are highlighted in communications from the EZLN. Because of this unequal representation on the internet, few sympathizers around the world are able to debate, based on statements from both sides, the relative merits of each position and the appropriateness of various tactics and strategies.

Vicarious participation

The excitement and satisfaction originally inspired by the opportunity to make political use of electronic communication to connect to a 'community' of fellow activists continues undiminished for many. The posting and reposting, the calls for signatures on petitions, adhesions to protest manifestos, the sharing of experiences of mobilization have all worked to create a sense of 'connect-edness' among progressive people around the world and, in particular, among supporters of the Zapatistas. Indeed, nowhere does the sense of political accomplishment fostered by electronic communication seem keener than among EZLN solidarity activists.

However, much of this sense of connection is illusory because so much electronic communication takes place as a solitary act. When political participation consists of clicking a reply button that adds our name to a list, this act does not necessarily bring people together. Once support of a petition involved face-to-face encounter with another human being and perhaps a monetary contribution to underwrite the cost of a newspaper ad. Declining to sign-on also involved at least a few moments of debate with the person passing around the petition. Now the rejection of a political position can be accomplished in a stroke of the delete button. What is more, it could be argued that the extremely low level of engagement required to participate in this fashion produces a political effect that is equally modest. That is, 'sending a message' in this facile way may create an impression on power holders that is correspondingly reduced when compared to the same message communicated by thousands, or hundreds or even dozens of activists gathered in the same public space at the same time.

Moreover, as internet users we enter discussion groups and chat rooms with '*compañeros*' with whom we will never really need to work out our differences as we once had to do in political groups. We are no longer required to encounter each other, nor to work to persuade others of our position. We can just log off when we tire of the terms of debate on a particular list.[40] The anonymity that is provided to us in this form of political participation, the potential for instant withdrawal from the group, the small degree of effort that is required to express solidarity through these means constitute both the attraction and the limitation of internet activism. Electronic militancy offers a means to be part of a movement and to communicate to downtrodden people around the world that we have them in mind without actually having to bestir ourselves to climb out of our ergonomically correct computer chair to leave the house!

Lynn Stephen, a widely respected figure in the organization of solidarity activities around Chiapas, has noted another limitation of electronic communication and asks if it is not, in fact, 'a roadblock to grassroots activism'.

> Every day, thousands of Americans receive updates from Chiapas, chat with others and feel that they are doing something. They are informed, but the kinds of actions elicited on the net are far from the tactics which often produce major political pressure. Feeling connected on the net

does not often inspire the kinds of high level, continual political pressure that can have a long-term impact on the United States Congress. . . . Meeting in a church basement to work on an information packet to distribute to local congressmen in visits is not the same as sending an attachment to a senator's aid about U.S. participation in the militarization of Chiapas.[41]

Stephen stresses that some types of activity co-ordinated through the internet can actually 'limit grassroots organizing efforts'.

Civil disobedience campaigns on the net, sending a fax, or voting on a Zapatista ballot by e-mail are important, but are not substitutes for face-to-face interaction and grassroots organizing. The fact that it took more than four years for a wide-ranging national meeting to be called of all groups involved in Mexico organizing with a strong basis in Chiapas suggests that the glut of information on the internet may have slowed down the urgency for creating a national network. People felt connected, but this did not result in long-term planning.[42]

Even Harry Cleaver, one of the most enthusiastic proponents of electronic political movement, acknowledges some of the limitations of reliance on the internet:

The limits to [the power of the Net] lie both in the limits of the reach of the Net (as we have seen it does not connect everyone) and in the kinds of connections established. There is already an enormous amount of information in The Net about all sorts of struggle which have not yet been connected, not to the Zapatistas, not to each other. The availability of information and a vehicle of connection does not guarantee either that a connection will be made or that it will be effective in generating complementary action. Even political activists fully capable of tapping all the sources of information about social struggles available on the Net are regularly overwhelmed by the sheer amount of information. As The Net grows, and as the number of groups involved in struggle that are capable and willing to use it grows too, this problem will grow apace . . .[43]

CONCLUSIONS

We have seen that in a variety of different ways, Chiapas solidarity activists have come to depend on the internet to keep themselves informed and to guide their political activities. To a great extent, this new technology has facilitated the international effort to support courageous and highly vulnerable people who are struggling for their rights. However, rather than linking people in ways that strengthen their capacity to influence events, internet activism sometimes creates an illusion of connectedness and political effectiveness where little exists. The version of events that is transmitted and forwarded over and over may leave solidarity activists feeling overwhelmed by the quantity of material at the same time that the information conveyed is often so partial as to be misleading. The highly simplified version of events communicated about Chiapas makes the decision to weigh in on the side of the oppressed relatively easy, but the question of how to proceed from there, or what is to be done, very difficult.

A remarkable number of people around the world are prepared to devote a great deal of their time to support the struggle in Chiapas. The question is whether they might better spend some of that time working to understand Chiapas in all its complexity, the way Chiapas fits into Mexico, and the way Mexico fits into the international order. The impulse to use the 'onrush of neoliberalism' and the 'popular struggle against neoliberalism' as organizing concepts by which to grasp the forces at play in the world is very strong. But these reductionist approaches are bound to lead to the same frustration and failure as the old reductionist models. What is unfolding in Chiapas today is not reducible to 'neoliberal predations' nor even to 'indigenous identity issues'. And we must be wary of approaches that claim this is the case.

Very basic appeals to respect human rights can be launched with no deeper understanding of the specifics of the situation. But any project that is more ambitious requires serious analysis. That a lack of awareness and preparation created by the constant circulation and repetition of a small number of super-ficial ideas about Chiapas has its costs, is illustrated in the backlash that has followed the expulsion from Mexico in May 1998 of 108 of 134 Italian soli-darity activists. The contradictions of the Italians' *somos todos indios* approach quickly became apparent when they marched into Taniperla where they were anxious to express their concern and support for beleaguered *zapatista* women. The Italians were set upon, pushed and shoved by *indios* upon their appearance in the town. These were machete- and stick-wielding *indios* who, as PRI supporters, may fall outside of the all-embracing category that the *somos todos indios* construction proposes – but they were *indios* nonetheless.[44]

For lack of knowledge and appreciation of the depth of post-revolutionary Mexican nationalism the Italians fell into a trap. In the end, the event was portrayed as a 'foreign invasion' in a country that has known foreign invasion, and it gave the Zedillo regime a nationalist card to play, reinforcing the xeno-phobia that has been the regime's only response to international concern for Chiapanecans.[45] This unfortunate outcome was the inevitable result of a kind of solidarity work that is based on a very partial and superficial knowledge of Mexico and Chiapas. It is the kind of solidarity work that comes out of acquaintance only with virtual Chiapas.

To be sure, some may argue that the circulation of a highly simplified or flat-tened version of events is necessary *to avoid* the airing of differences while war is being waged on defenceless people. To some extent they may fear that open discussion of differences on the internet may be exploited by the Mexican state to dismiss progressive pressure from abroad, just as many on the left of earlier generations feared that airing differences over the USSR or China would be misused. This old problem for the left is exacerbated in so far as solidarity activists actually believe that if we do not speak of the conflicts and cleavages among forces on the left, or within indigenous communities, or among NGOs in Chiapas, the Mexican state will not learn of these disagreements and will not have the opening to exploit resentments and schisms in its effort to control the situation and disarm the movement.

In weighing this argument, we must consider that the chief architect of Zedillo's counter-mobilization/counter-insurgency strategy in Chiapas is Adolfo Orive Berlinguer. Through the 1970s Orive was perhaps the single most important figure in the political mobilizations in the highlands and in the co-ordination between the conscientization activities of the catechists and the organizational efforts of maoists. Having studied with Charles Bettleheim in Paris, Orive returned to Mexico and became the leader first of the Popular Politics tendency and later the maoist Proletarian Line – the same movement in which Marcos was formed. Orive came to Chiapas at the behest of Bishop Samuel himself, to organize a peasant-based movement that would bring together maoists, radical school teachers, liberation theologists and labour organizers.[46]

By the end of the 1980s, however, Orive was working for Carlos Salinas and, based on his detailed knowledge of the physical and political geography of the conflict zone, was recruited by Zedillo in 1994 to direct the counter-insurgency in Chiapas. Given Orive's knowledge of every schism, historical or current, it is unconvincing to argue that if we do not discuss frankly and openly among ourselves the differences in perspective among assorted actors in Chiapas, then these disagreements will remain a secret from the regime.

In the end international solidarity is crucial to the survival of the thousands of people who are risking their lives to demand justice. But support is most effectively given by outsiders who grasp the situation at hand, not by those for whom Chiapas is a trope, or those who content themselves with a virtual rendering of events and actors that oversimplifies reality to the point that it bears only a very vague resemblance to the situation on the ground. International concern about Chiapas has, unquestionably, worked to restrain and contain aggression against the Zapatistas and their supporters, undoubtedly saving many lives. But effective human rights work requires, among other things, good and reliable information. In the end we might want to think less about our own 're-enchantment' and more about what is really happening in southern Mexico – even if some of the gritty details are less than enchanting. To do otherwise compromises the crucial role that foreigners can play in protecting the human rights of people at risk.

NOTES

I would like to thank Adolfo Gilly, Silvia Gómez Tagle, Steve Hellman, Peter Ives, Colin Leys, Leo Panitch, Scott Robinson, Emiko Saldivar, Sid Tarrow, and Charles Tilly for their helpful comments; Douglas Chalmers, Luin Goldring, Ron Hellman, and Ken Sharpe for the opportunity to try out these ideas in seminars; and Steve Hellman and Peter Ives for steady encouragement and the materials they collected for this article. I would also like to acknowledge the support of Social Science and Humanities Research Council of Canada for financial support of this research.

1.   See Lynn Stephen, 'In the Wake of the Zapatistas: US. Solidarity Work Focused on Militarization, Human Rights, and Democratization in Chiapas', Paper presented at a conference titled, 'Lessons from Mexico–U.S. Bi-National Civil Society Coalitions', 9–11 July 1998, University of California, Santa Cruz.

2.   *Il Manifesto,* 28 March 1998. The debates appeared in this issue and in *Il Manifesto,* 10 February 1998, and 1 March 1998.

3.   Michael Lowy, 'Sources and Resources of Zapatism', *Monthly Review,* Vol. 49, No. 10, March 1998, pp. 1–2.

4.   Throughout this article, I am using the term 'internet' to refer to the most commonly-accessible sites that people interested in Chiapas would be most likely to find while surfing the world wide web For example, using 'Chiapas' as a keyword on various search engines provided in the most common web browsers (e.g., Excite, Infoseek, Lycos, or Yahoo), I found that a semi-systematic survey of the materials available tends to produce the same sites – and links – over and over. Therefore, the material to which I refer throughout this analysis, would be found on the following sites, or by following the links provided in them:
     Accion Zapatista
     http://www.eco.utexas.edu/faculty/Cleaver/zapsincyber.html#Accion Zapatista
     AMDH Bulletin
     http://www.lanic.utexas.edu/la/region/news/arc/amdh/1995/0000.html
     Chiapas 95 http://www.eco.utexas.edu/faculty/Cleaver/chiapas95.html
     Chiapas 1997 http://mac.theramp.net/Domcentral/justice/chiapas.htm
     Chiapas Index http://www.ifconews.org/chorgndx.html
     Chiapas Menu http://www.indians.org/chiapas/
     FZLN http://www.eco.utexas.edu/faculty/Cleaver/zapsincyber.html#Frente Zapatista de Liberacion National
     Mexico Solidarity Network http://www.mexicosolidarity.org/index.html
     SIPAZ Servicio Internacional para la Paz
     http://www.nonviolence.org/sipaz/sipazf.htm
     ¡YA BASTA! http://www.ezln.org/
     Zapatistas in Cyberspace http://www.eco.utexas.edu/faculty/Cleaver/zapsincyber.html

5.   Thomas Benjamin, *A Rich Land, A Poor People: Politics and Society in Modern Chiapas* (Albuquerque: University of New Mexico Press, 1996); and George A. Collier with Elizabeth Lowery Quarantiello, *Basta! Land and the Zapatista Rebellion in Chiapas* (Oakland, CA: Food First, 1994), pp. 16–7; Neil Harvey, *Rebellion in Chiapas: Rural Reforms, Campesino Radicalism and the Limits to Salinismo* (La Jolla, CA: Center for U.S.–Mexican Studies, UCSD, 1994); and Adolfo Gilly, *Chiapas: la razón ardiente* (México, D.F.: Ediciones ERA, 1997).

6.   Harvey, pp. 10–14; John Womack Jr, *Rebellion in Chiapas: An Historical Reader* (New York: The New Press, 1999), pp. 20–9; John M. Whitmeyer and Rosemary L. Hopcroft, 'Community, Capitalism and Rebellion in Chiapas', *Sociological Perspectives,* Vol. 39, No. 4, pp. 517–38, pp. 528–33); and Richard Stahler-Sholk, *Neoliberalism and Democratic Transition: Looking for Autonomy in the*

Jungles of Chiapas, paper presented at the Annual Meetings of the Midwest Political Science Association, Chicago, 23–25 April 1998, p. 1.

7. Womack, pp. 29–43; Carlos Fazio, *Samuel Ruíz: El Caminante* (México, D.F.: Espasa Calpe Mexicana, 1994), pp. 101–113. Xochitl Leyva Solano, 'The New Zapatista Movement: Political Levels, Actors and Political Discourse in Contemporary Mexico', in Valentina Napolitano and Xochitl Leyva Solano (eds), *Encuentros Antropológicos: Power, Identity and Mobility in Mexican Society* (London: Institute of Latin American Studies, 1998), pp. 41–2.

8. Collier, pp. 62–3; Womack, p. 39.

9. Collier (p 63) juxtaposes the demands presented by Chol, Tojobal, Tzeltal and Tzotzil delegates to the 1974 Congress with the EZLN's Thirty-Four Point Agenda for negotiation proposed in 1994 and shows that they are almost identical. Ibid., pp. 64–5.

10. Neil Harvey, *The Chiapas Rebellion: The Struggle for Land and Democracy* (Durham, NC: Duke University Press, 1998), pp. 86–88.

11. La Botz, pp. 26–38 provides an especially clear and useful summary of this extraordinary period of organizational activity. A particularly useful aspect is his explanation for the great enthusiasm for Maoism among radical Mexican leftists.

12. See the debate around the 'post-modern' nature of the movement, especially Roger Burbach, 'Roots of the Post-modern Rebellion in Chiapas', *New Left Review*, 205, 1994, pp. 113–24; and Daniel Nugent's critique of Burbach, 'Northern Intellectuals and the EZLN', *Monthly Review*, Vol. 47, No. 3, July–August 1995, pp. 124–38. Also see Sergio Zermeño, 'State Society, and Dependent Neoliberalism in Mexico: the Case of the Chiapas Uprising', in William C. Smith and Patricio Korzeniewicz, eds., *Politics, Social Change and Economic Restructuring in Latin America* (Miami: University of Miami, North–South Center Press, 1997) pp. 123–49; Whitmeyer and Hopcroft, Lowy, and Susan Street', *La palabra verdadera del zapatismo chiapaneco*', *Chiapas,* Vol. 2, 1996, pp. 75–94.

13. Lynn Stephen, 'Mexico's New Zapatismo: A Culturally and Historically Embedded Critique of Neoliberalism', Paper presented at the Annual Meetings of the American Anthropological Association, Philadelphia, 2–6 December 1998, p. 3.

14. See EZLN, *Crónicas intergalácticas: Primer encuentro intercontinental por la humanidad y contra el neoliberalismo* (Chiapas: Planeta Tierra, 1996).

15. See Harry Cleaver, 'The Zapatistas and the Electronic Fabric of Struggle', in John Holloway, ed, *The Chiapas Uprising and the Future of Revolution in the Twenty-First Century*, html version from Chiapas95 web page, 1996; María Elena Martínez Torres, 'The Internet: post-modern struggle by the dispossessed of modernity', Paper prepared for the 1997 Annual Meeting of the Latin American Studies Association, Guadalajara, 17–19 April 1997; and Manuel Castells's section titled 'Mexico's *Zapatistas*: the First Informational Guerrilla Movement' in his book, *The Power of Identity* (Oxford: Blackwell, 1997), pp. 80–1.

16. Under the provisions of the agrarian law in place until 1993, this land would have been distributed to landless petitioners in the form of 'ejido parcels' that they would be free to cultivate and pass along to one of their offspring, but that would not be available to rent, sell or mortgage.

17. Until the reform of Article 27 of the Constitution in 1993, a landholding was only

afectable or available for expropriation and distribution to petitioning peasants when it exceeded a maximum size established in accordance with the type of agricultural production pursued on that parcel.

18. That is, illegally large landholding created out of the concentration of holdings that fall within the legal maximum. Typically, a *neolatifundio* is comprised of a number of holdings that have been put into various family members' names, although in the commercial export agricultural zones of Mexico it has also been common for individuals to pay trusted *prestenombres*, or namelenders, to act as the owner of record for a 'neighboring farm' that is, in fact worked as part of a single large estate. Salinas's alteration of Article 27 of the Constitution made this kind of subterfuge unnecessary, to the great delight and relief of large landowners everywhere in Mexico. See Judith Adler Hellman, *Mexican Lives* (New York: The New Press, 1994), pp. 139–41.

19. Collier, p. 48–50.

20. The minimum size of an ejido parcel differs from place to place in Mexico according to the quality, fertility and access to water of the land that is distributed On the subdivision of land parcels into ever smaller holdings under pressure of population growth, see María del Carmen García A. and Daniel Villafuerte Solís, 'Economía y sociedad en Chiapas', in María Tarrío and Luciano Concheiro, eds., *La sociedad frente al mercado* (México, D.F.: Ediciones La Jornada, 1998), p. 352.

21. Collier writes, 'Before 1974, the Catholic Church had already begun extensive grass roots evangelizing in eastern Chiapas, in part to ward off the advance of Protestantism' p. 62. Also see Womack, pp. 36–43 on this Catholic response to the spread of Protestant conversions.

22. INEGI, *Censos Generales de Población y Vivienda, 1990,* cited in García A and Villafuerte Solís, p. 364.

23. *Ibid*, p. 365.

24. In interviews conducted in May 1998, the explanation offered to me for the increase in Mormon and Islamic conversions was the appeal to men of religions that – as interpreted in the Chiapanecan contest – not only tolerate, but sanctify polygamous relationships Now, instead of having an official wife, married in church plus a second *mujer*, and her children 'on the side' in the classic *casa chica,* men can have all their wives and children living with them under one roof.

25. María del Carmen García A, 'Las organisaciones no gubermentales en Chiapas: algunas reflexiones en torno a su actuación política', in Centro de Estudios Superiores de México y Centroamérica, *Anuario 1997* (Tuxtla Gutiérrez: Universidad de Ciencias y Artes de Chiapas, 1998), p. 50.

26. The National Institute of Statistics, Geography and Informatics, INEGI reports only 6.5 million because the standard they use is that a person must speak an indigenous language to be counted as an indigenous person. Meanwhile, the National Indigenous Institute, INI, which has good reasons to avoid under-counting indigenous people, estimates 10 million. See INEGI, *XI Censo general de población y vivienda*, México, D.F.: INEGI, 1992.

27. Cynthia Hewitt de Alcántara, *Anthropological Perspectives on Mexico,* London: Routledge, 1984), p. 53.

28. Guillermo Bonfil Batalla, *México Profundo: Reclaiming a Civilization* (Austin: University of Texas Press, 1996); and Luis Villoro, *Los grandes momentos del indigenismo en México*, tercera edición (México, DF.: Fondo de Cultura Económica, 1996).

29. Neil Harvey, 'La autonomia indigena y ciudadanía étnica en Chiapas', paper presented at the XX Meetings of the Latin American Studies Association, Guadalajara, Mexico, 17–19 April, 1997, p. 10.

30. *Ibid.*, p. 18. Héctor Díaz-Polanco, *La rebelión zapatista y la autonomía* (México, D.F.: Siglo Veíntiuno Editores, 1997); Luis Hernández, 'Ciudadanos iguales, ciudadanos diferentes: la nueva lucha india', *Este País*, febrero, pp. 38–39; Marco Rascón, 'Autonomía para la integración', *La Jornada*, 16 febrero, 1998, pp. xiii–xvi; Gilberto López y Rivas, 'Los significados de San Andrés', *La Jornada*, 16 febrero, 1998, p. xii; Carmen Lloréns Fabregat and Rosa Albina Garavito Elías, 'Esencia de los acuerdos de San Andres', *Coyuntura* 84, enero–febrero, 1998, pp. 33–40.

31. The rule of strong men or *caciques*.

32. This quote is drawn from an interview with Juan Pedro Viqueira, one of the few analysts who spoke for attribution He later elaborated these views in 'Los peligros del Chiapas imaginario', *Letras Libres*, enero 1999, pp. 20–8; 96–7.

33. Alison Brysk, 'Turning Weakness into Strength: The Internationalization of Indian Rights', *Latin American Perspectives*, Issue 89, spring 1996, Vol. 23, No. 2, p. 46.

34. John Gledhill, 'Liberalism, Socio-Economic Rights and the Politics of Identity: From Moral Economy to Indigenous Rights', in Richard Wilson, ed, *Human Rights, Culture, and Context: Anthropological Perspectives* (London: Pluto Press, 1997), summarized in Xochitl Leyva Solano, p. 50.

35. Lynn Stephen, 'Mexico's New Zapatismo', pp. 6–7.

36. Judith Adler Hellman, 'The Mexican Elections: Rush to Judgement', *Globe & Mail*, Toronto, 2 September 1994, p. 8; On the 1994 elections, see Silvia Gómez Tagle and Ma. Eugenia Valdéz Vega 'Chiapas', in Gómez Tagle, ed., *1994: Elecciones en los estados* (México, D.F.: La Jornada Editores, 1997), pp. 179–209.

37. It is ironic that on the subject of elections in Guerrero State, *La Jornada*'s position is quite different and the view that the electoral road might be usefully pursued at the same time as armed struggle has gained the approval not only of the Popular Revolutionary Army, that is, the guerrillas themselves, but also of *La Jornada*. See Blanche Petrich's interview with Arnaldo Bartra, 'En Guerrero, armas y urnas no se excluyen', Sunday 13 February 1999, p. 8.

38. See Cleaver, and Martínez Torres.

39. *Ibid.* Also see Castells, pp. 72–83.

40. A similar point was made by Benjamin Barber with regard to democratic participation in US. politics in 'Internet: A Place for Commerce or a Place for Us?', a presentation to the Columbia University Seminar on the Political Economy of War and Peace, 28 January, 1999.

41. Stephen, 'In the Wake of the Zapatistas', pp. 14–15.

42. *Ibid.*, p. 13.

43. Cleaver, p. 19.

44. In the detailed coverage given to the event in the pages of the Italian daily, see Giani Proiettis, 'L'esercito minaccia', *Il Manifesto*, 7 May 1998. Indigenous people who support the PRI and oppose the Zapatistas are always referred to as *priistas*, that is, 'PRI supporters', and even as *'squadracce priiste.'* This second term is best translated as 'organized squads of thugs' and is usually used in Italy to refer, literally, to fascist gangs.

45. Almost a year later I found Mexican human rights specialists divided on the ques-

tion of the utility of an approach that appears to challenge Mexican sovereignty at the same time that it tests the constitutionality of restrictions on foreigners' activities in Mexico and the rights of free association of Mexicans.

46. La Botz, pp. 32–34. Of Orive, Womack, p. 221, writes, 'The one constant in the movement had been the pre-eminence of its primary intellect and "ideological director", arguably the most remarkable organizer of his generation, Adolfo Orive.'

THE CENTRALITY OF AGRICULTURE: HISTORY, ECOLOGY, AND FEASIBLE SOCIALISM

Colin A. M. Duncan

WHILE MOST SOCIALISTS now more or less habitually make reference to what is called 'the environment', very few have yet fully confronted the immensity of the change in our thinking that is really called for if we seriously acknowledge humankind's historic and ongoing dependence on the rest of nature. But any honest attempt to conceive of a socialist future must acknowledge it; the argument of this essay is that doing so involves reversing the tendency of a hundred and fifty years of socialist thought. To anticipate the conclusion, in any desirable socialism agriculture would be culturally and technically central because industry has to be reduced back to the margins. The time is ripe for reinverting the relationship between humankind and the rest of nature: the accelerating threat posed by capital-oriented growth to ecological integrity, even to the very survival of our species, is becoming more and more obvious to everyone (except, of course, capitalist ideologues). Too few socialists, however, have been very well placed to point this out. Indeed the failure of most socialists to respond effectively to the assertions of the self-styled 'neoliberals' of the last quarter of the twentieth century is not unconnected with a long-standing weak grasp of ecological matters. Certainly we must now rethink our conception of the socialist project in light of them.

From a classical socialist point of view the recent situation has been absolutely ludicrous. Not one of the major problems socialists have been complaining about for nearly two centuries has been solved. Some of the symptoms have altered their global location a bit, but anybody who can read Dickens and has seen pictures of Malaysian slums is capable of getting the basic diagnosis right. It is still perfectly clear overall that an enormous number of very poor people are making things for a comparatively small number of very comfortable people. Absolutely nothing fundamental has changed. With respect to the final decades of the twentieth century it can also be argued that at no previous point in human history have such large fractions of capital been allocated and reallocated amongst so-called 'investments' by people with greater ignorance of the real consequences of their activities. While managers attempting actually to set up or even operate productive facilities could see the damage being done by whip-saw capital flows, few of the distant owners cared, for many became vastly richer without doing a stroke of extra work because mere ownership was an entitlement to shares in immense flows of income undiluted by inflation. Others who likewise have been doing little work recently have not become quite so rich, however, because in many places chronic mass unemployment has returned. Although that was the entirely predictable consequence of changes in policies regulating foreign exchange and credit, the causal linkages were simply ignored. Perhaps they had to be if people were to become persuaded that not even regulation could work, let alone planning. Yet planning was hardly dead. On the contrary, within gigantic corporations it was newly fundamental. While Microsoft employees planned how to integrate trivial human pastimes on a massive scale, government employees were told that nothing of any consequence could be done about serious complex problems. Those who were not cynically pensioned off got to oversee disintegration.

Socialists' general ineffectiveness in face of these multiple absurdities is, of course, not unconnected with the complicity of past socialist thinking with capitalist approaches to production. This has long been fairly widely acknowledged in the case of industry but the problem can be seen to be deeper if one seriously considers agriculture.[1] Yet once the break with capitalist thought about industrial production is made, a much more radical approach to reconstructing the division of labour on socialist lines becomes possible; moreover, it could allow us to solve the problem of the environment at the same time, and solve it at least as well as any other approach on offer. This may already sound encouraging enough, but it gets better still. Unlike other utopian socialist initiatives, the type I propose here does not involve extremely rapid or forceful social change. If environmental problems turn out to be as severe as many fear, they will of course hit capitalist and socialist dreams alike, so, this side of catastrophe, the environmental problem provides an historically unique and socially bearable opportunity for socialism.[2]

What is clear is that capitalism itself cannot solve the environmental problem. Under capitalism wealth cannot be allowed not to grow, and the rate of return demanded by mobile forms of wealth enforces a short time-horizon that excludes ecological reasoning. But even before so much capital was so extremely mobile, the appallingly abstract concept of wealth upon which capitalism depends made it blind to its material consequences. For a long time this did not matter much. Merchant exploitation of price differentials between distant market contexts, and even capitalist production itself, pre-dated the massive use of fossil fuels and prairie soils, and did relatively little harm to the environment. Indeed as I will show in outline below, the most advanced capitalist society for long was based almost exclusively on processing recently living material raised over and over again from soils and tree root systems that had already been reused for centuries. Indeed some capitalists showed people mired in feudal arrangements that locally the environment could be enriched, not depleted, even while great gains in output and living standards were achieved. On the other hand it is ahistorical as well as illogical to assume that socialism has to be still more dependent on fossil fuels and prairie soils than capitalism in its earlier prime. Paradoxical as it may seem now, we must envisage socialism in terms of regaining the technical ground on which capitalism was once based.[3]

To put this more plainly, in Adam Smith's day, long before capitalist production had become reliant on fossil fuels (let alone prairie soils), agriculture (in the broad sense also comprising tree management)[4] was the source of almost all raw materials; but agriculture itself required no raw materials, only land and labour. Not only does agriculture as an ecological activity not itself need raw materials, it can also actually provide them. In that key respect it is essentially more like gathering and hunting and fishing than it is like contemporary industrial production. Industrial production necessarily demands raw materials and fuels from *elsewhere*, and currently demands so much, and of so many kinds, and generates so much abiotic waste, that we now believe we cannot continue on these lines without causing general harm to the planet's own regulatory apparatus. By contrast, the soils of much farmland used to be routinely *improved*, through agriculture, and could be again; only agriculture is thus capable of giving us adequate supplies of food and raw materials without negative consequences. Agriculture has not always been so benign, and much of it currently isn't; the fact remains it alone could benignly supply so many billions with the basics. I do not actually believe 'basics' is a mysterious term, but perhaps I should point out that we cannot include under it enormous stocks of goods with built-in obsolescence. Concerning reasonably durable goods we will of course have to wait and see. But even many 'luxury'-producing activities do not require much in the way of materials: e.g., music-making, fancy food preparation, gossip, poetry, etc. All these are open to the poor, if they have the time, for agriculture can supply all the materials they require.

Seeing these matters in proper perspective calls for a deeply historical sense of the variety of ways we have passed our time on Earth so far; it is important to recognize that environmental problems are not new, nor are the solutions. The problems go back at least as far as the widespread adoption of agriculture, the food 'source' on which 99.99% of us now depend absolutely. The technical practices that could have cured past local mistakes made many millennia ago are essentially the same as those we must adopt today for both local and global problems. For it can be said that we now know that in general, and especially when we farm, we must try to imitate the functional complexity of the rest of nature, not defy it, and this is necessarily a matter of refined local practice.[5] In order not to defy nature we must not deify it either. Nature as a whole is not so bad that we must fear it, but neither is it so good that it will tolerate absolutely any treatment from us. The atmosphere on which we depend, and in which alone our primate ancestors could evolve, was and is the inherently global and joint product of microbes and plants. We are creatures of the air and we must stop the pretence that we could control the living processes in the earth and in the waters of this planet. The only reasonable policy is to leave geo-physiological control up to microbes and plants.[6] With the adoption of agriculture – the practice of interrupting the natural cycle of plant species reproduction to make land constantly produce only a limited number of plant species, above all food grains – humans issued, in effect, a challenge to the rest of life. In those cases where the farming mimicked the complexity of the ecosystems that would otherwise have occupied the field space, probably the damage was absorbed. But the enormous extension of ecologically crude (even essentially anti-biological) farming techniques undertaken in the last century and a quarter has made the problem acute. Now that we see the impending consequences we must resolve to farm in future only by those means that the planet as a whole need not notice.[7] This presents technical problems to socialists and non-socialists alike.

The fundamental point is this: much of the planet's hillsides, grasslands, woodlands and wetlands now need revegetation if its atmosphere, soils and waters are to remain hospitable to us, and it might as well be done with long-lived useful species since we need to be able to get food, fuel, and material from that vegetation, over and over again. During the last century and a quarter a significant proportion of the human population has also been deriving a great quantity of fuel and material from rocks – both from greasy kinds like coal and the more or less liquid substances known as petroleum, and also from mineral types such as iron and nickel. This has implied an ever-deepening spiral of dependency. Not only does getting and working metals require the massive use of fuels, but the opposite is also true. In the last half dozen decades of this recent and truly 'Stone Age', many people have even begun to use petroleum and minerals on a large scale as 'inputs' in a new kind of agriculture. We are now becoming fairly certain, however, both that the greasy rocks ought not to be burned at the high rate they recently have been, and that over the last few millennia human beings have removed too much of the planet's vegetation. These problems clearly exacerbate each other.[8] We need both to restore woodland and wean ourselves from excessive reliance on burning petroleum and/or coal. Either we will be able to get enough material and fuel from sustainable woodland practices (the way almost all peoples for long used to have to), or not. If not, then we will have discovered that the problem simply cannot be solved so long as human populations remain so high, and/or so many people live where fuels are needed so much. With luck we will discover this gradually enough to be able to do something about it without a social catastrophe. So much for fuels and materials.

With regard to food the problem is also serious but probably less so. There is even less inherent incompatibility between our need to use only biologically complicated farming techniques and our need for food. It is true that the bulk of current research expenditure in agricultural science is still being applied to the opposite purpose, namely the further biological simplification of agricultural processes, but that is mostly due to the manifest self-interest of a few dozen corporations. Since we are not obliged to buy any of their products they could in principle be simply marginalized out of existence.[9]

The point that should specifically interest socialists is that both sets of fundamental material problems (fuel/materials and food) can be solved by renovating the division of labour. It is not yet too late to solve all environmental problems simultaneously and all that is technically needed is historical knowledge of past sustainable systems of forestry and agriculture coupled with labour – lots of labour. There are literally scores of past ways of doing things that we know are sustainable because historians can show they were in fact sustained.[10] Very few of the historians whose work establishes the point were even aware of the issue, let alone trying to prove it, so their impartial testimony is as good as it gets. Practically speaking it is just a question of learning again how to grow and tend plants properly. Arguably most men and women alive three hundred years ago knew most of what we now need to know. And since the overall task could accurately be described as a kind of gardening there seems no reason to expect lots of trouble on the labour-process side. The few who cannot find any agriculturally-relevant work they can do or enjoy can do useful research, or entertain with music, or mind babies – whatever truly needs doing.[11]

This is not a futuristic fantasy. If we abstract from the tragic and farcical activities of the last two centuries, and put agriculture, our most important connection with the biosphere, back at the centre of our thinking, we will find that history is on balance mostly on our side with respect to the subset of human problems socialists can reasonably hope to solve. Even the negative lessons support this view because arguably it has been precisely the failure to pay proper attention to the problem of agriculture that has vitiated every major socialist project so far. Partly because of their obsession with new industrial techniques, all 'actually existing socialisms' have had immense difficulties with agriculture, both socially and technically. It might seem that Maoist China ought to count as a partial exception to this rule but it can be argued that total disaster was only avoided there because many Chinese pragmatically persisted in using various tried and true farming techniques of great antiquity,[12] techniques that owed nothing whatsoever to any socialist doctrines, or capitalist ones for that matter. Indeed, the non-socialist world's handling of agriculture this century is curiously analogous to China's. If there have not been actual shortfalls in food supply for the inmates of capitalism, it has only been at the ongoing expense of capitalism's fiscal and intellectual coherence. *In every country that is claimed to be oriented to the integrated market system an exception has been made for farming enterprise.* Everywhere in the world agriculture has been hooked up to state life-support systems for almost three quarters of a century.[13] This is a significant fact, not just an embarrassing nuisance – which it is – for the ideologues of 'free markets'.

But to go back for a moment to agriculture under 'actually existing socialism', as it once was: prairie grain-farming gave a tremendous boost to American capitalism and also profoundly affected most mainstream strands of Marxist thinking. The links between these effects have not often been emphasized and may have been logically merely contingent, but in practical terms the consequences unfolded inexorably. Lenin and Stalin (and Trotsky) saw mechanized harvesting on prairie soil as a sufficient technical basis for building an advanced industrial society, and with unprecedented speed at that. Perhaps things might have gone not too badly if the Bolsheviks had not come to power in a peasant society.[14] But in point of fact the prairies of the Russian Empire, unlike those of North America, were already occupied by *farmers* who had only recently (and for the first time in millennia) gained some real control over the lands they worked. These peasants rightly saw that no immediate benefit for themselves could come from co-operating with the Bolsheviks. Any benefits would be in the distant future and they were not being offered any choice about the type of industrial model anyway. Lenin scrupled enough to back-track. But he also died relatively young, and Stalin tore Lenin's New Economic Policy into shreds as soon as he had consolidated his position as Lenin's successor. The agrarian result was disaster and tragedy,[15] followed by decades of dismal failure. After the era of famines (enforced and 'accidental') a system emerged which combined spectacularly low yields per unit of land area with appalling rates of soil erosion.

That the system rested on fairly high labour productivity was hardly a compensating factor because as American experience showed a single-minded focus on labour productivity is incompatible with good soil management and therefore also ultimately incompatible with sustained yields. With their comparatively small population the Americans for long had little reason to care about yields, or about erosion for that matter. Revealingly it was the incomes collapse and related politico-cultural crisis of farming that made the American public finally pay attention to the emerging Dustbowl;[16] the adequacy of the food supply was never really in question. That was largely because what was genuinely positive in the whole American experience with prairie farming, and what the Russian Communists crucially failed to emulate, was massive investment in storage and transportation infrastructure.[17] So whereas the Americans were able simply to reshuffle their sourcing, the Soviets wasted, year after year, decade after decade, an enormous proportion of what was harvested efficiently from fields carrying only meagre quantities of produce. The farcical – indeed contemptible – later combination of space travel and bread lines did a great deal to eventually destroy the credibility of the Soviet regime. Anyone who examined the disastrous and still dwindling levels of return on investment in Soviet agriculture in the 1970s knew it was just a matter of time before it collapsed.

To solve the food supply problem the regime had to decide in the early 1970s to repeal its own conceptual corn law, so to speak, and commence massive and regular importation from the North American prairies. Entirely unwilling to de-industrialize its mentality, however, it also insisted on continuing to pour technical inputs into the agricultural sector that could ill be afforded. The escalation of the Cold War through the early 1980s turned a chronic problem into an insoluble systemic crisis.

ENGLISH LESSONS?

Only one excuse can be made for the Bolsheviks: hardly anyone else was bothering to understand the modern significance of agriculture either. We, however, can connect history and theory more usefully once we stop being blinded by the glare emanating from industrial phenomena. Marx's analysis of capitalism centred on the English case. On the subject of industrial production he remains the most acute analyst we have ever seen. On questions relating to finance he has arguably been later matched only by Keynes. But when it came to farming Marx was misled by his obsessive interest in changes in industrial production techniques into supposing that labour-saving change is also important in agriculture. He saw little evidence of such change in English agriculture and concluded quite erroneously that it had not improved significantly. He did not understand the agronomy and failed to notice how very differently English estates had been administered compared to those in other European countries.

In England a few thousand families owned almost all the land genuinely worth farming and they had become very wealthy as well as powerful renting it out to capitalist tenant farmers. From the late seventeenth right through to the late nineteenth century this was the normal pattern. An estate was owned by a family and administered by the current living recipients of rents who, however, were rarely absolute owners. Ultimate control of most estates was usually vested in some later generation of the family via the legal device of a strict settlement (a kind of entail). This was done to prevent any profligate generation from ruining a powerful family by running down the real estate. It was also normal for the tenant to be obliged to farm according to time-tested local practice, at the very least during the last years of any long lease. Agriculture done thus – according to the 'custom of the county' as it was called – normally caused an improvement in the condition of the farmland. Production was not merely sustained but usually rose. For many decades on either side of the Napoleonic Wars English agriculture fed one of the most rapidly growing populations ever seen in history and did so on the basis of a system that generated continuously improving yields *without need of external inputs*.

But Marx never investigated all this. Instead he got his opinion of the English agricultural sector from the middle-class Radicals who despised the aristocracy and alleged that agriculture was starved of capital and was consequently underproducing – basically a tissue of lies. Indeed as Adam Smith had laboured to explain some decades earlier (in long and unequivocal passages that most later

readers simply refused to understand), the only real use for capital in agriculture is to hire labour.[18] Once one sees that the system was based in the local
recycling (through sheep and cattle) of locally sourced nutrients, one can see
that labour is the only relevant input. Once a farmer has sheep and wheat seeds,
all that is needed to make more sheep and more wheat seeds is labour. And
there is no evidence that English agriculture was ever starved of capital.[19]
Landlords may have kept an undue proportion of income for themselves, and
thus indirectly 'obliged' their tenants to pay low wages to field-labourers, but
that is a matter of distribution not production. We now know that the key
advances in English farming technique were made in the sixteenth and seventeenth centuries. The so-called 'agricultural revolution' supposedly manifest in
the increasing production of the eighteenth and early nineteenth century was
simply the natural and necessarily gradual result of the earlier self-improving
system being allowed to work in peace, insulated from the pressures of short-
term market and climate fluctuations by the aristocracy's general historic
preference for long leases. This had allowed a great sophistication of agronomic
practice. England is famously geologically varied (a single county, Somerset,
varying more from east to west than all of Russia from north to south, to give
the classic example). As a gradual result of experience, the 'system' of farming
England as a whole was constituted out of a mosaic of finely adapted local variations on some general principles of cattle- and sheep-corn husbandry.
Everywhere the key factor was the tendency of the system to generate steady
and sustainable improvements in land productivity. Most of the increase came
from ever more efficient recycling of nutrients, continuous improvements in
soil structure and pest management integrated into the intricate rotations which
used finely adapted regional breeds of sheep and cattle.

Then, virtually overnight, prairie farming was allowed, even encouraged, to
make this all irrelevant. On the never-before-farmed prairies of North America
a deep and otherwise admirable soil profile was found ready-to-hand. It had
never been made to support centuries of human food production – and it hasn't
yet either. In England (as in ancient China and many other places besides) the
people had learned how to farm with a level of skill that will not regain relevance so long as the prairies are relatively new. In fact we have abused the
prairies mightily already but their soils are so extensive and so deep that so far
we have continued to get away with it. The English wheat farmers were mostly
driven out of arable production by the onset of cheap prairie grains (from about
1875). British tables came to be supplied by relying on soils elsewhere.[20] Those
English farmers did well who could tip the balance of their farming operations
over to specialized dairying and meat-production for the ever-wealthier
British public, now thriving on its role as service-provider to the world
economy (making and running ships and railways, warehousing, selling insurance, providing short-term loans, etc.).

The railways (and new kinds of ships) did and still do move the prairie grains
to their extremely distant markets, but otherwise the role of the so-called

'industrial revolution' in all this has been greatly exaggerated and its effects seriously misconstrued. This is a matter of utmost significance for the socialist
vision propounded here. The level of industrial investment the world has actually experienced far exceeds the quantity needed for improving the standard of
living. The middle-class bias of the proponents of industry and their latter-day
spokespersons is mostly to blame for the travesty of logic involved in the usual
account of the British story. Until the twentieth century the middle class in
Britain was numerically insignificant and it has never had much political power,
because over the course of World War I Britain passed fairly painlessly (and
arguably pointlessly) from being an aristocratic polity to being a plutocracy.
Condemned from above and below, the British middle class has consequently
made a lot of self-righteous noise about its roles in history. It *did* play a large
role in commerce but that has been true throughout the last millennium, so
hardly counts as innovation. The middle class *can* also claim to have inaugurated
and overseen a revolution in industrial production techniques, but that this
constituted a world-historical 'achievement' is increasingly doubtful. The
benefit even for Britons has been overstated. In fact British prosperity was based
squarely on agriculture, finance, and commerce in hand-made goods until the
early nineteenth century, and on finance and commerce after the mid-nineteenth century. The brief period of growth in heavy industrial non-military
production in the middle of the nineteenth century was an absurd interlude
which the country as a whole could easily afford but hardly a reliable key to
the future. Employment in agriculture and domestic service outnumbered
employment in 'manufacturing' until well into the second half of the nineteenth century. During its last decades military industrial production became
very significant but that has more to do with improved standards of killing than
improved standards of living. The nineteenth century told us to identify modernity with fossil-fuel powered machinery, but the longer version of the English
story suggests that the division of labour is a better candidate, and that is very
good 'news' for a polluted planet bristling with arms.

    In order to explain what really occurred during the brief period when British
goods fabrication did undergo rapid technical change, it is thus necessary to
backtrack several centuries. Why did anything happen at all? Why there? The
eventual influence of the British pattern was ludicrously large, and that is why
its fabular significance has to be carefully assessed. Britain's heavily eroded island
geography had always made transportation costs unusually small as a proportion
of the commercial value of goods. Over the last half-millennium this allowed the
emergence of a complex of unusually highly integrated 'home' markets centred
on London, which dwarfed other towns as no other world-historical city did in
its own 'hinterland'. This caused steady growth in rural manufacturing (in the
etymologically original and coherent sense of hand-made goods). The division
of labour cut deeply, but for a long time neither people nor the land suffered
from that. Quite the contrary. The English peculiarity of cheap food in spite of
population growth led to unprecedented generalized prosperity, as a host of local

consumer markets also began to integrate.[21] Under the watchful eyes of the value-obsessed merchant-class capitalist social relations ramified through the manufacturing sectors and this created an enormous incentive to save labour as soon as effective non-muscle-powered machinery started to appear. Without cheap food a political revolution would doubtless have occurred, but non-muscle-powered machinery played no role in keeping food cheap.

In fact such machinery played no significant transformative role in British agricultural production levels until during World War II. Although harvesting can be mechanized (and was so by the late nineteenth century) it remains very difficult to get machinery as such to have any very significant effect on the amount of produce there to be harvested, which is what really matters. In the case of textiles, however, the situation was quite otherwise and the British middle classes showed real ingenuity at devising machines to throw their manu-facturing employees from one line of work to another. Saving labour in manufacturing by using the latest metal machinery led to a great new use of coal. This soon caused a new round of relative savings in transportation costs in the form of the railways, but these also catalyzed a round of centralization in the location of production facilities. This suited the owners of the plants but was otherwise senseless because it was so costly in social terms; few factory owners supplied housing in the new urban areas and most of what was supplied was wretched. In addition the countryside was de-industrialized in a matter of a few decades as the new pattern starved the formerly more or less equally remote villages both of markets and inputs. Rural women in particular were thrown out of non-domestic employment and were lucky to get jobs as servants in the towns. Unsurprisingly there was also a round of emigration from Britain on a scale not seen since the seventeenth-century religious and civil wars.

But the key overall effect of fossil-fuel-powered machinery was to weaken the bargaining position of unskilled labour. Thus was born the famous 'residuum' of chronically under-employed late Victorian and Edwardian poor who were only delivered from poverty by the break with fiscal orthodoxy and other financial innovations required by World War I. The heavy industry sector did bring new levels of wealth both to its owners and to their 'aristocracy of labour' under arms race conditions (more or less continuous from the mid-1880s), but such heavy industrial prosperity had very little to do with the general high levels of wealth in Britain except inasmuch as it supplied iron ships for world commerce and caused clusters of local multiplier effects in towns such as Newcastle. For it was the commercial and financial prosperity of late nine-teenth-century Britain that prevented its poor from starving. While City firms supplied fancy services to the world economy, the poor blackened their shoes and polished their brass. For most British people the much-touted industrial revolution thus had little effect other than causing a few bouts of inadvertent and pointless misery. Their one great overriding fear was anything that might cause food prices to increase. Thanks to the ploughing of the North American prairies the likelihood of that fell steadily during the last quarter of the nineteenth century. For the first time in British history the prices of labour and of food were disconnected. The British countryside experienced de-agricultural-ization and its caretakers stopped paying close attention to it, from duke down through tenant farmer to farmhand.[22] The new irrelevance of non-prairie land and the cheapness of fossil-fuel powered transportation caused and facilitated urban sprawl which further increased the centralization of production facilities and thus locked ever more people into a pattern of dependence on the long-distance transport of goods.

This we recognize as the general predicament of people all over the world now. This is the path down which Britain led the way – which is easy to see once the story of its 'industrial revolution' is reduced to its proper proportions, and the all-important wider context of agricultural change is recognized. Equipped with this more coherent and more materialist historical narrative it is then possible to challenge more effectively the grand *non sequiturs* of socialist thought that have done so much to mar this last appalling century.

CONCLUSIONS?

In the light of this re-analysis of the wider meaning of British modernity let us review the basic condition of current humanity in relation to the rest of nature. The problems can be marshalled under three heads:

1. Almost all humans currently depend on fossil fuel (and thereby also metal) for the transport of their food, but in many places they also need fossil fuel for heating shelters.
2. In many extensive areas no one is caring for complex patterns of vegeta-tion on the land, and many places have been denuded of vegetation to no good purpose.
3. In many places there seems to be nothing for most people to do.

Even if cheap, weather-indifferent transport were endlessly sustainable, we would have good reason to do something about points 2 and 3. But if we connect them to solve each other then we can also begin to lessen the dangers implied in point 1.

What is required is a social form for a new division of labour that will allow people who have no capital to care for land and sustainably derive from it prod-ucts that they can exchange with each other, and with wealthier people, until disparities in income and work-load begin to become more reasonable.

What is not needed in order to initiate socialist construction is a violent upheaval in property relations. This is partly because starting beneficial spirals of sustainable production from the land does not require large amounts of capital. It is not necessary to assemble in one place at great expense large quan-tities of special materials, fuels and equipment. Access to land, however, *is* required, but the time is in some ways as ripe as it has ever been since the adop-tion of agriculture several millennia ago. So long as the prairies keep world food prices low land prices and rents will also remain at historically low levels, and so it ought therefore to be possible for even poor people in many countries to get access to land and begin to do things with it, such as planting much-needed long-lived species of trees. The poor do not need to own the land they work and so no confiscation need be threatened by them or on their behalf. Since trees take time to grow and since the currently favourable situation may not last, we must not waste time in formal discussions of absolute ownership. As in medieval times, usufruct rights are the only ones technically needed to sustain production. So long as land is not subject to repeated changes in ownership a long-term perspective on its use is generally forthcoming. So for the moment the most radical policy we need recommend anywhere is that current owners be allowed to keep their land, but should forfeit the right to sell it and should be obliged to rent it out on long leases. After all, is it worth owning, or not? (Outraged newly permanent owners could instead ask themselves, is it worth destroying, or not?) Of course, where no one sees a problem, nothing can be done. But assuming there is a general recognition of the need to do something there are many places in the world where substantial starts could be made.

What is most specifically needed is a system for lubricating the new division of labour on the land that will not permit the continuous siphoning off of the benefits. Special currency systems already exist that can be set up on as large or small a local scale as may suit, and that effectively isolate the means-of-exchange function of money from all other possible functions, most notably the store-of-wealth function.[23] Such systems are virtually costless to set up and to operate; so, given access to land that cannot be alienated, the world's poor could then join in creating sustainable local circuits of goods exchange without the constant interference of distant wealthy people. Precisely because the currency in these systems can easily be set up so that it can nowise be used as capital it would actually be beneficial if local wealthy people started to participate. As people refined their techniques there could eventually emerge a set of circuits of production that need not compete with the conventional circuits run by merchant interests on behalf of industry and finance. On the contrary, the increasing success of 'locally made' circuits could gradually make the conventional ones less and less relevant. At first only a few goods might circulate in these local circuits but gradually some 'import substitution' could be undertaken at little capital cost and the special currencies could gradually become the principal media of exchange. Social change thus lubricated could therefore be truly transformative. If we could get the world's poor up to eighteenth-century British levels of prosperity, based likewise on replacing and/or renewing nature's capital, that would be a relative utopia indeed. The rest of the socialist project could then finally have a secure future socially. It already would have built itself a secure future environmentally.

For the key non-social advantage of this way of grounding utopia is that it builds in from the beginning a caretaking attitude to the environment. Vegetation alone can preserve soils and thus 'anchor' the atmospheric vessels of the water-cycle on which all life depends. Since people without capital have to enlist the help of the essential dynamism of vegetation, they will thus relearn how to distinguish the profligate from the sustainable use of land. If we can get the merchant point of view out of the sphere of production then socialism will be able to replace capitalism and also save the planet for future generations.

How does the idea developed here compare with other socialist models? Without embroiling ourselves in historico-semantic considerations we could perhaps all agree that socialism must mean that no one goes without food, medicines and surgery, and depending on geography, a varying sufficiency of clothing, shelter and fuel. Moreover, under socialism it is explicitly everyone's responsibility to see to it that no one is left out. Beyond such basics it's not so clear that what people have or do is everyone's business. Indeed so long as no one is using someone else as a means to some end, the only absolute justification for public concern about a person's activities can be their deleterious environmental implications, since those ultimately affect everyone.

The proposal advocated above is at least as likely to meet these criteria as any mainstream approach. The core strategy of traditional socialism over the last century was to deliver to everyone not only the basics but much more besides, and to achieve this by controlling the allocation of investible wealth. As is notorious, the idea of socially-directed control of investment flows is for the moment ruled out by the financial sector, so that the old models are hardly more feasible than mine. However, if any control of investment were offered to socialist-leaning governments I would hope they would make allocation first for dealing with basics, and second for setting up a system for the supply to persons and communities of a set of standardized, multi-purpose industrially produced commodities, such as nails, screws, rods, piping, metal tools, etc. For these are the basic ingredients for the small-scale production of personally-crafted consumption goods whose raw materials would ideally be overwhelmingly organic in provenance (indeed just the kinds of goods the rich usually prefer). The distinction I have in mind can be captured by suggesting that there should be socially-controlled production of 'quantitative' commodities and personally crafted fashioning of 'qualitative' goods.[24]

This brings up the question of scale. We need to consider an approach to socialist institution-building that allows for variations of scale depending on the purpose. For instance ecological considerations suggest that agriculture ought to be organized at the level of the bioregion, however defined. There is no need to dogmatize about this. It's something to figure out on an empirical basis whenever historians cannot uncover reliable past arrangements. Waste dispersal patterns might be our best guide, in which case presumably drainage systems would be the right size for human community reconstruction, but perhaps some finer mapping of tree species distribution patterns might be more appropriate. Special currencies for circulating the products of agriculture in these areas could then be developed. People living in such areas would of course share the use of a wider-level currency for the circulation of quantitative goods. Given the extent of urbanization today and the acute dependence of city-dwellers on external supplies of almost everything they use there would have to be some 'twinning' of rural with urban areas. The point is to envisage none of the boundaries or links as fixed. They ought to be flexibly adjusted as the state of affairs dictates, or allows. This is most emphatically not a counsel of all-embracing autarchy. On the contrary, it explicitly recognizes that different activities should be done on different scales. It is perhaps analogous to a pattern that informs the rest of nature. The rocky substrate of the Earth moves very slowly, waters move much faster and air circulates even more rapidly. But living creatures have an absolute need for all three material categories.

How does the idea developed here compare with other proffered solutions to the problem of the environment? It's hardly as though no other schemes for reform are under way, even though the pace so far has clearly not been impressive. For example, United Nations discussions about limiting emissions may well continue and in many countries they are clearly seen as worth the time of a great many highly trained people. But what would such limits really mean? In order not to lock ourselves casually into some arbitrary reduction we would have to look behind the total emissions data, examine the great variety of activities that generate them and then begin to assess which among such activities are useful and how we could substitute for the others. How much of the emissions are due merely to high levels of urbanization? How much are due to inexcusable waste and/or obscene luxury? How much are due to absurdly complex commerce? How much are due to the all too aptly named 'communication systems' that proliferate today as though there was nothing more important to think about? If we continue to acquiesce in a purely top-down approach these questions will eventually have to be examined critically anyway. Suppose, for example, we discovered that we absolutely need to burn a great deal of petroleum-type products just to keep this many people alive at all. We would then have found out that we are heading not just for probable global climate change problems but also probably for different and more old-fashioned problems of scarcity.

We of course do not yet know but it seems to me most likely that the future will resemble the past – but not the last century and a quarter so much as the previous millennium. Only by recovering and further refining long-past agricultures and silvicultures and aquacultures and gradually lowering our own population levels can we eventually become *certain* that we could someday return to the levels of casual abundance and low work-loads described by Marshall Sahlins in his seminal essay, 'The Original Affluent Society'.[25] Of course entirely new means for living other than the ones discussed above *may* soon appear out of nowhere, but it is absurd to take that idea as a basis for action. My insistence in grounding the material basis of future life in activities analogous to organic farming practices derives from a 'worst-case as best-case' logic. If we find we cannot live well by such means then we will know we are in deep long-term trouble as a species. But surely an approach such as I outline, in which ordinary people would themselves make what they thought they could out of local materials, would be more likely to generate a sustainable pattern overall than some top-down re-accounting of material life derived from remote calculations. I like to hope that the environmental problem could even convert some people to my kind of socialism, a type which I am happy to say would be more easily recognized by the likes of Robert Owen than by either Stalin or the Fabians.

NOTES

I would like to thank Tom Sekine, Rob Albritton, Harriet Friedmann and Colin Leys for encouraging my non-historical writing over the course of many years. Jeanette Neeson and Don Akenson were only ever asked to tolerate it but the latter has frequently gone out of his way to be helpful. Work done under the far-seeing and wide-ranging guidance of Abe Rotstein eventually made the approach outlined here much more coherent and grounded almost all of its optimism, inasmuch as it led to the opportunity to interview Michael Linton of Vancouver Island.

1.   It is especially appropriate in the present journal, given its name, to invoke here William Cobbett, whose severe criticism of social reality three centuries after More wrote *Utopia* included specific reference to the continuing consequences of Henry VIII's violently privatizing reign. Because industrial capitalism had not yet manifested its full tendencies at the time Cobbett wrote up his *Rural Rides*, he was able to suppose that the only real enemies of decency were unusually greedy people. His critique thus seems more political than sociological. From the point of view developed later in this paper, however, it is deeply ironic that Cobbett is today reviled more for being agrarian than for being utopian. In fact his thinking is profoundly relevant to contemporary socialists. Those in doubt must reread at least his account of the state of affairs in the Valley of the Avon (entries for 28th–30th August, 1826), which includes an inspirational, proto-feminist attack on Malthus. What so outraged Cobbett was that he knew as a matter of practical fact that the ordinary people of England were perfectly capable of living well from the land if only the gentry would stop disrupting rural affairs by insisting on fighting Jacobinism while refusing to pay for the war in specie. As Cobbett saw it, the financial consequences of reaction played a major role in so twisting commerce that machinery could become an obnoxious benefit, capable, for example, of throwing women out of gainful employment in places where alternatives were scanty.

2.   The rest of this essay consists of a way of unpacking this argument. In my book, *The Centrality of Agriculture: Between Humankind and the Rest of Nature* (Montréal & Kingston: McGill-Queen's University Press, 1996), I employed a different sequence of argumentation to make the same basic points. Much more detailed support for several of them can be found there. The present formulation may seem somewhat different in emphasis and that is partly because of the way the issues loomed during my most recent and somewhat differently focused writing process. See also soon my *Passing Our Time on Earth: A Conceptual Primer on Environment and History* (Montréal & Kingston: McGill-Queen's University Press, forthcoming). I thank that press for allowing me to reproduce the substance of many arguments here.

3.   Many of the imperial activities of companies of merchant adventurers certainly caused ecological (not to mention social) havoc in many places outside the European metropoles, but to say that the emergence of socially systematic capitalism absolutely depended on them is grossly to underestimate the distinctiveness of capitalism as a social system In any case imperial depredation as such goes back as far as agriculture, as shown by countless ancient empires all over the world. It is also worth noting that the total area of the globe affected by the plantation complex almost certainly remained under 10% of total cultivated area at all times.

4.   On the connection with trees see Oliver Rackham, *The History of the Countryside* (London: Dent, 1986) as well as J. Russell Smith, *Tree Crops: A Permanent Agriculture* (New York: Harcourt Brace, 1929).

5.   The globalization of environmental problems, if it turns out to be a real phenomenon (as it may well), is a recent innovation, and global solutions to global problems are unlikely to be developed unless and until we have some form of world government backed by a world-wide rule of law. Global solutions to the environmental problem may be possible but they will certainly be harder to implement and less reliable than multitudinous local ones. For abundant examples of local devastation in the past, see Vernon Carter and Tom Dale, *Topsoil and Civilization* (Norman: University of Oklahoma Press, 1974). See also Edward Hyams' analytically sharper 1952 warning, *Soil and Civilization* (reprinted, London: John Murray, 1976).

6.   On ecological essentials concerning life on our planet see, preferably in this order, the following: A. I. Oparin, *The Origins of Life* (1938), James Lovelock, *Gaia* (Oxford: Oxford University Press, 1979), and Mark and Diana MacMenamin, *Hypersea* (New York: Columbia University Press, 1994). A still useful supplement would be Marston Bates, *The Forest and the Sea* (New York: Vintage, 1960).

7.   The idea that we could probably feed even the world's current huge population of human beings by using only historical (ie., purely organic) means is obviously hypothetical and therefore contentious but, contingently, it still remains defensible. For an inkling of the considerations involved see the following sources on Asian achievements: F. H. King, *Farmers of Forty Centuries* (1911) and Clifford Geertz, *Agricultural Involution* (Berkeley: University of California Press, 1964). For the historical European potential, since somewhat squandered, see Eric Kerridge's book on England, *The Agricultural Revolution* (London: Allen & Unwin, 1967) and the commentary by F. M. L. Thompson, 'The Second Agricultural Revolution', *Economic History Review* 21 (1968): 62–77. On the very recent past see the account of how life could be lived in places like the Dordogne Valley in Philip Oyler, *The Generous Earth* (Harmondsworth: Penguin, 1961). On future possibilities seen modestly enough consult Kenneth Mellanby, *Can Britain Feed Itself?* (London: Merlin, 1975), but also consider the almost visionary approach exemplified in different ways in both Masanobu Fukuoka, *The One-Straw Revolution: An Introduction to Natural Farming* (Emmaus, Pennsylvania: Rodale, 1978) and Wes Jackson, *New Roots for Agriculture* (Lincoln: University of Nebraska Press, 1985). The latter tackles the crucial case of the prairies head on. Their absolute importance in this century was incontrovertibly demonstrated, however unintentionally, in Avner Offer, *The First World War: An Agrarian Interpretation* (Oxford: Oxford University Press, 1989).

8.   Those who are ignorant of the fire history of our planet typically are excessively

worried about this. As Stephen Pyne has made clear in book after book in his world historical series, *Cycle of Fire*, fire in forests and grasslands was generally normal until our species started to make massive efforts to eradicate it. The fundamental problem of human control of fire is not that we started to set fires but that we started to stop them, but it could not matter much until we also tried permanent deforestation. Back when the world was much more forested than it is now there must have been a great deal of combustion occurring at any given moment. It is probable that current total combustion rates are unprecedentedly large but it is unlikely that they are vastly larger than those common several millennia ago. It is the coincidence of high current combustion levels with the fact of continued deforestation that is alarming. When the world used to burn itself routinely, forests regrew by default, as it were, and so at any given time much carbon was stored in tree trunks. In temperate lands most tree species automatically regrow unless actively eradicated. On what trees want to do it is essential to read Oliver Rackham (note 4 above).

9.   Given the usual connotations of the term 'industry' and its cognates, 'industrial agriculture' ought to be an oxymoron. But currently a number of giant firms are making a massive fresh attempt to reduce the ecological complexity of farming to a minimum. On recent twists of this spiral see R. C. Lewontin's superbly clear if rather American-centred analysis, 'The Maturing of Capitalist Agriculture: Farmer as Proletarian', *Monthly Review* 50 (July/August 1998): 72–84.

10. See notes 4 and 7 above.

11. With respect to the need for all this labour, two points must be made. First, the world is full of people, vast numbers underemployed. Second, socialists must shed the absurd prejudice that outdoor work is demeaning. The world has been in chronic agricultural depression almost continuously since the 1870s and that is why so many people had to leave the countryside. Rents, profits and wages all fell catastrophically, and landscapes everywhere lost their caretakers. For complex reasons having nothing to do with production, food has generally come to be cheaper in urban areas. The world-wide exodus from the countryside that has occurred means only that the victims did not want to be hungry or even poor, not that working with plants and animals is inherently unpleasant. Unfortunately, most socialists have made the invalid inference and supposed that henceforth only the urban-industrial way of life is compatible with human dignity. The aristocracy of modern England, the most comfortable social grouping yet seen, could have told them that a seasonally balanced approach is the best one, part urban high-cultural, part bucolic. It is entirely telling that Edward David's *Sozialismus und Landwirtschaft*, the only thorough challenge from the left to the urban-industrial dogma, remains untranslated into English almost a century later. The first people to face the dogma head on, the peasants of the Bolshevik-controlled Russian Empire, clearly perceived its unattractiveness. See A. V. Chayanov's 1920 essay, 'The Journey of My Brother Alexis to the Land of Peasant Utopia', reprinted in translation in *Journal of Peasant Studies* 4 (1976). Peter Chapman's 'Parable of Erg' which opens his masterpiece, *Fuel's Paradise* (Harmondsworth: Penguin, 1975) shows how little we have advanced since Chayanov considered these matters. Nicholas Georgescu-Roegen helped us understand more about why all this matters in a number of articles. For an introduction see his 'Myths About Energy and Matter', *Growth and Change* (1979): 16–32.

12. G. F. Sprague, 'Agriculture in China', *Science* 188 (9 May, 1975): 549–55.

13. Robert Wolfe's *Farm Wars* (New York: St Martin's, 1998) details the most recent round of international hand-wringing about the ongoing and embarrassing failure to square contemporary capitalist ideology with agricultural reality.

14. It is remarkable that we had to wait until 1996 to have a competent general history of the Russian Revolution written by someone with expert knowledge of the sector in which four-fifths of the affected population actually lived Given his academic training Orlando Figes could not have failed to redress a gross imbalance in his *A People's Tragedy: The Russian Revolution 1891–1924* (London: Pimlico, 1997), but happily he did a far more than competent job overall.

15. For an attempt to make sense of some of the generally contradictory scholarly literature on this era see my article 'On Rapid Industrialization and Collectivization: An Essay in Historiographic Retrieval and Criticism', *Studies in Political Economy* 21 (1986): 137–55.

16. For an excellent general account see Donald Worster, *Dustbowl* (Oxford: Oxford University Press, 1979).

17. For a devastating comparison of the USA. and the USSR, equally embarrassing to ideologues on both sides of the Cold War, see Roy and Betty Laird, *Soviet Communism and Agrarian Revolution* (Harmondsworth: Penguin, 1970).

18. Smith explains that the only way to raise more grain is to apply more labour and that any attempt to favour agriculture that does not recognize that technical fact is absolutely bound to fail. The point is located in Book 4 near the end of Chapter 5 'Of Bounties', in the third paragraph prior to the section on herring busses. Ironically enough (given that he could not have predicted the prairies phenomenon) it is actually the basis of his influential bias in favour of free trade.

19. The idea that it could be starved of capital could only occur to someone who supposes that agricultural and industrial production activities are essentially similar, a notion completely inconsistent with distinctions between agriculture, manufacturing and commerce that Smith and many of his contemporaries had made with great care For Smith the relevant distinctions are emphatically not merely social but rather are grounded in technical facts about the material world. The key point appears with crystalline clarity in Book 2, about four pages into Chapter 5 'Of the different Employments of Capital'. That we have long since systematically de-improved much farmland and now farm with increasing indifference to land quality (as we increasingly rely on off-farm fertility inputs), shows that we have done much to try to make Smith's distinctions no longer relevant, but the damage done is not all permanent. We human beings could re-enlist nature's help. It seems unlikely that Smith could have conceived that we would ever spurn it.

20. British per capita reliance on soils actually increased because prairie farming consistently gave (and gives) lower yields per acre than mid-nineteenth century English high farming. If short-stalked varieties of wheat had been bred earlier than this century then the contrast would have been even more favourable to nineteenth-century England. This key innovation (achieved by means of classical plant-breeding experiments), which prevents high fertilization of plants from inviting mechanical stalk failure due to wind or hail, is necessarily of benefit to 'organic' and chemicalized agricultures alike.

21. In his 'Agricultural Origins of Industry', *Past & Present* 40 (1968): 58–71, E. L.

Jones makes it clear that patterns almost as beneficial obtained for long in many other parts of Europe as well, and it is not much of a stretch to include parts of China and India within this socio-analytic ambit.

22. E. J. T. Collins, 'Agriculture and Conservation in England: An Historical Overview, 1880–1939', *Journal of the Royal Agricultural Society of England* 146 (1985): 38–46.

23. The possibility of wealth becoming capital depends on that function For more on money and socialism see Sections iii and iv of Chapter 4 of my *The Centrality of Agriculture*. The recent piece by Finn Bowring 'L.E.T.S.: an Eco-Socialist Alternative', *New Left Review* 232 (November–December 1998): 91–111, rather misses the importance of analytic distinctions among what Karl Polanyi's student Walter Neale called 'moneyish' roles in his lapidary *Monies in Societies* (San Francisco: Chandler & Sharp, 1976).

24. Such a distinction and a few other of the notions all too sketchily developed here were first suggested to me by T. Sekine. See his 'Socialism as a Living Idea' in *Socialist Dilemmas: East and West* which he edited with H. Flakierski (Armonk, N.Y.: M. E. Sharpe, 1990).

25. Reprinted, after the original French publication, in his *Stone Age Economics* (New York: Aldine, 1972).

DEMOCRATIZE OR PERISH: HEALTH SCIENCES AS A PATH FOR SOCIAL CHANGE

Julian Tudor Hart

SINCE THE 1970s we have entered an era of paradox. Not since the 1930s has there been so wide a consensus that capitalism is fundamentally flawed, in its apparently uncontrollable pursuit of profit, regardless of human needs. Yet never has there been such universal despair of any feasible alternative. We don't need more books to prove the moral and cultural bankruptcy of capitalism, its obscene contrasts between human and market priorities, or the growing instability and mutual violence of a society forcing everyone to act only for themselves. We need a credible alternative.

Before 1917, a variety of alternative projects seemed credible because they had never been tried. October 1917 opened a real, material, fighting alternative to mutual annihilation in the trenches, with prospects so dazzling that selective blindness came easily. Though it was soon clear we could not have what we liked, either in the revolutionary East or the reforming West, we learned to like what we had as the price for any action at all. The 1917 revolution, and others following its model, led to an abyss. They were paths out of feudal autocracy and colonialism, but they were not paths to socialism as a way of organizing a more advanced society, including and surpassing all the real achievements of capitalism. So we are rightly cautious of all other alternatives so far on offer, particularly if they seem in any way to resemble revolutionary socialism. Having lost material hope for the future, millions of desperate people now turn to past superstitions as their only apparent alternatives to the inhuman world of the market.

Marx and Engels believed that each stage in evolving society creates its own gravediggers. More relevantly to our predicament, they believed that the builders of each new society were developed by the old, workers who were necessarily in conflict with it – because their new mode of production required new social relations, new divisions of labour, of power, and of property – but who were also essential to its continued development. They saw labourers, stripped of all productive property other than their own labour power, as the revolutionary class. Evolving capitalist production would simplify social divisions, until a diminishing number of owners of the means of production would face a growing majority of workers, whose interests required collective ownership and control, and who were able to understand production motivated by human needs rather than profit and expanded capital.

All this seems easily recognisable today – easier than at any time since 1848. At the heart of modern capitalism lies production of knowledge. Its ultimate products remain commodities, produced not because they are needed but because they are profitable, but its immediate and most important products are all different kinds of new knowledge. Trade in labour power as manual labour, even as highly skilled use of machines, is now being displaced by trade in intellectual skills – above all, by the capacity to learn. This has huge implications for the nature of production, and the social relations required by production.

In this essay, focusing on the production of health care, I hope to show that this new kind of production can't operate efficiently without creating new social relationships – and therefore new kinds of people – ultimately inimical to capitalist society, yet essential to its continued expansion. These new people will be a new and much more powerful army of gravediggers for the old society, but more importantly, they will be more imaginative and better informed builders of a new society. They will show that there *is* a feasible alternative, working better in every way than the old. They will bring huge reinforcements to an old labour movement which has not in fact disappeared, adding immense new power – the advent of truly scientific socialists, able to deal confidently with the world as it actually is, without recourse to romance.

A PRACTICAL EXAMPLE

How good medicine – genuinely scientific medicine – points firmly in the direction of a new kind of socialist society is exemplified in a new project now being developed in Wales. The south Wales valleys hold a quarter of the Welsh population, about seven hundred thousand people. Adding Swansea and Port Talbot, which resemble the valleys in their dependence on mostly collapsed heavy industry and were part of the coalfield at its peak of production before World War I, the population approaches a million. Its social problems closely resemble those throughout the world, wherever industrial commodity production is already exhausted, manual skills are no longer needed, and entire communities have ceased to be profitable for the owners of capital.

The south Wales valleys contain more poverty, hopelessness, and ill health than any other area in England or Wales of like size, the consequences of economic deconstruction and decline. For the past fifty years, it has been increasingly hard to recruit family doctors (General Practitioners, or GPs) to deal with these health problems, and their work has appeared increasingly futile, mainly because the causes of ill health are growing faster than either actual or even any possible medical remedies, since social conditions are undermining young people's will to live. Many GPs are therefore looking forward to early retirement and they will be replaced either by colleagues who can't find work anywhere else, or not at all. Even to maintain the barely adequate service the valleys now have, this impending crisis in recruitment must somehow be solved during the next decade. This will not be possible if central responsibility for primary care remains with GPs working as self-employed small businessmen, as they still are.

To respond to this a ten-year plan has been developed by the Socialist Health Association, *Going For Gold*, based on the valleys' history, culture, labour, and potential advantages for investment. It depends on four integrated themes: health care, education, research and employment.

Initial and continuing health care will be provided through a salaried primary medical and nursing service. Private ownership and administration by general practitioners as independently contracted small businessmen will be gradually and voluntarily phased out. It will be replaced by team care, with important roles for nurse-practitioners as well as for doctors. Teams will work from health centres, which will also offer dental and pharmaceutical services. They will build their work around anticipatory care of long-term health problems, intervening at an earlier stage in cascading misfortune than hitherto, reducing presently escalating demands for crisis and emergency care.

Education will be developed at two levels. First, mature adults with personal experience of chronic illness (for example, diabetes, epilepsy, or tobacco-related disorders) will be recruited locally to provide a range of specialized continuing anticipatory care and advice of a non-technical kind within primary care teams, as Chronic Problem Advisers (CPAs). After a brief introductory course, their higher professional training will depend on continued in-service learning and team development, based on extramural departments of the universities of Glamorgan and Swansea. Second, primary and secondary schools will develop local programmes to base science in the national curriculum on local health and health care data, aiming to shift popular perception of health sciences and health care to biological rather than engineering models, and raise learning to levels required for skilled biotechnical employment.

As for research, the third arm of the plan, the Rhondda Fach in south Wales was, as it happens, the birthplace of epidemiological research in the post-war world. This research extended the study of human health, health problems and health care beyond laboratories and hospitals, into real populations as they actually live and work. Important preconditions for this were the birth of the NHS itself, and the social attitudes and expectations associated with it, plus active support and co-operation from the then very powerful community network of the National Union of Mineworkers. Salaried primary care teams, supported by modern information technology, if combined with renewed social solidarity of the sort which gave birth to the NHS and gave trades unionism such deep roots in the valleys, offer exceptional potential for mass participation in research. As is shown below, this is needed to make health care more effective, efficient, and relevant to public health, and to advance fundamental biomedical knowledge, creating new weapons to promote health, and prevent or treat disease. Participation in research also has immense learning potential, both for those who organize it, and those who become research subjects.

In terms of employment, community participation in research, and rising standards of education producing potential skilled workers in biotechnology, could be integrated in a Valleys Health Sciences Industrial Park, attracting inward investment by pharmaceutical and other biotechnical industries. Together with greatly expanded, labour-intensive NHS primary care, this could make work in health care, health sciences, and health-related products a new staple employment comparable in scale with coal, steel, tinplate and other heavy industries in the past.

The valley communities developed collective bargaining to agree the terms on which they made their labour available to extract coal.[1] The valley communities today could develop collective bargaining to agree terms on which they would participate in creating and using new biotechnical knowledge. Only after collective agreement could researchers recruit individual participants. Payments for participation (other than refunding of expenses) would go to participating communities rather than individuals, by transfers from biomedical companies to schools, health and social services, or to other agreed community agencies. The chief gain and incentive for communities would be skilled, diverse, stable employment, retaining young people with higher education rather than exporting them, and eventually reversing population outflow.

This approach could restore hope, reverse depopulation, and end economic and social dereliction and dependency. Such social changes would have more powerful effects on health than any improvements in the quality and quantity of NHS care, necessary and important though these are. It is not an easy solution, but what solutions are? The plan, developed over two years, is already backed by three rival universities (academics will know how hard that is to achieve), by Welsh Assembly health minister Jane Hutt, by senior civil servants at the Welsh Office, and by health service unions UNISON, MSF and the BMA. It has an office, an executive team, and pilot sites to be set up in 1999. Most importantly, key figures among established local GPs endorse this plan as a broad framework within which primary care should develop.

Of course it is impossible to tell whether this strategy will succeed in these particular circumstances, though they are in many ways favourable. But I am fairly sure something very like it will succeed sooner or later, somewhere in the more exhausted parts of the industrialized world, and my reasons for thinking this go to the heart of the issues raised by Marx's and Engels' analysis. These reasons can best be explained by first looking briefly at the British National Health Service as it was originally conceived.

THE NATIONAL HEALTH SERVICE AS AUTHORITARIAN SOCIALISM

The NHS was launched in 1948, in my first year of clinical studies. It nationalized virtually the entire health care industry, then generally understood as having two main functions: cure (episodic repairs) for the relatively few problems that seemed curable, and care (continuing support) for the large majority of problems that seemed either self-limiting, or incurable. Prevention was seen as a subordinate activity, already separated from both caring and curing. Despite much unifying rhetoric and occasional steps toward unified practice, this separate view of prevention still persists.

The NHS almost entirely took over the production of what had hitherto been an extremely popular traded commodity, personal health care, previously supplied by doctors as self-employed entrepreneurs. It made an important and valued service available to everyone free. The main reason this zero-priced commodity did not generate infinite demand (contrary to educated expectation and later received wisdom) was that most people intuitively understood that medical care worked better as a social gift than as a traded commodity. Like its antecedents in workers' mutual aid societies, well people paid taxes throughout their lives to help sick people, for a service they hoped never to need themselves. Once people had experience of prepaid care, free at time of need, the concept of care as a human right rather than a commodity, and of a medical profession with a duty to provide continuing care rather than the episodic sale of body repairs, became rooted in British popular culture.

For thirty years, from 1948 to 1979, medical care virtually ceased to be regarded as a commodity, either by the public or by professionals. Though some private practice persisted for hospital specialists, particularly for surgeons, and this had important effects on the number of consultants, on consultant culture, and on NHS efficiency,[2] private medicine lost its moral authority, particularly in the medical schools. When Margaret Thatcher imposed market concepts on the NHS after 1979, she found her 'reforms' opposed by all organized health professionals, by doctors as much as by other health workers. This was a complete reversal of the situation in 1948. Doctors had learned, through personal experience, that they had more scope, greater security and more job satisfaction as public servants serving human needs than as private salesmen of medical care.

The NHS applied the principle 'from all according to their abilities, to all according to their needs', without cash transactions or profit. Contrary to all received economic wisdom, this produced a service costing several times less than marketed care in USA, though of roughly equivalent average clinical standard,[3] at least until the 1980s.[4] It presented an extremely popular, relatively cost-effective service compared with marketed health care systems.

However, though the face of the NHS was seldom inhuman, it was generally authoritarian. Most doctors were as ignorant of the real constraints of most people's daily lives as most patients were of the nature of clinical decisions. Apart from an important element of central planning to rationalize the geographical distribution of resources, for its first thirty years the NHS was run by doctors, virtually without lay control. They believed they ran the service primarily in the interests of patients rather than themselves, but in this respect they proved neither better nor worse than other professionals, all of whom shared the squire's traditional concern for, but ignorance of, his tenants. The resources of the NHS were in the personal gift of its doctors, in conditions of permanent scarcity of resources (depending as they did on a redistributive income tax which the right wing was determined to undo).

The right also understood that many patients could be induced to prefer being valued as customers to being objects of increasingly threadbare medical charity. From 1979 to 1997 the socialist principles of the NHS came under sustained assault from Conservative governments determined to remould every aspect of British society in the image of competitive small enterprise, while government itself concentrated power at the centre like a large corporation. The NHS, with its roots in popular culture and in a slowly democratizing new professional culture, was the largest and most stubborn obstacle to this remoulding process; but huge inroads were made into it, with immense damage to staff morale and traditions of public service, a rapid and extremely costly rise in litigation, and relentlessly rising demand, as patients were officially encouraged to expect more while resources were simultaneously reduced.

RELATIONS OF PRODUCTION IN HEALTH CARE

But these trends were and are in contradiction with a growing realisation among health practitioners that truly science-based medicine points in a quite different direction; and in spite of the pressures to 'marketize' the NHS there has also been continued growth in the idea of participative democracy in health care, with patients and professionals developing new roles as co-producers of health rather than as opposed consumers and providers of health care.[5] The aim is not to maximize profits but to increase public health — healthier births, healthier lives, and healthier deaths. To achieve this, democratic social relations are fundamental, for reasons that need to be made clear.

The first key elements in processes of clinical production are decisions about whether patients' problems really call for health care, and if so, what interventions are most likely to assist their solution. Clinical interventions themselves are essentially subordinate to these decisions. If a patient has problems which can't be solved by taking out her appendix, gall bladder or uterus, then however well these procedures may be performed, they will reduce efficiency (however it is measured), besides causing occasional operative deaths. Yet the relation between scientific knowledge and clinical practice is still extremely variable. Rates for these common surgical procedures (and for their occasional complications) show huge variability between countries, within countries, and even between localities with similar age distributions and social structures, and little relation to the statistical prevalence of the conditions for which the procedures are appropriate.[6] For tonsillectomy, for example, we still have no good controlled evidence that it is effective, though it is still the commonest surgical procedure in childhood. At best, the evidence suggests it may on average prevent about two moderate or severe episodes of sore throat in the two years following the operation.[7]

NHS doctors are moving toward evidence-based decisions, and doing so faster than their colleagues in marketed systems. There, surgical intervention rates are grossly inflated because the pursuit of profit rewards credulity and penalizes scepticism. Children in fee-driven US practice are eight times more likely to have a tonsillectomy than children in the fees-free NHS, while a study of coronary bypass surgery in USA showed that 22% of grafted patients had no symptoms of coronary disease, and had evidently been persuaded to undergo surgery on questionable evidence.[8] At the same time, poor people who needed surgery weren't getting it.[9]

But even without such perverse incentives clinicians in the NHS do still commonly fail to consider the full range of evidence needed for optimal decisions. Hasty decisions to intervene are still made when surgery is irrelevant to patients' real problems,[10] and poor people are still under-referred for interventions they need.[11] A similar wide variation is found in most diagnostic and treatment decisions. Public attention tends to concentrate on the quality of interventions, rather than on the quality of the preceding decisions, first on whether to intervene at all, and secondly on which intervention to choose. As the main scope for efficiency gains lies in making practice evidence-based and rational, this issue is central to the development of an affordable health service.[12]

WHAT COUNTS AS CLINICAL EVIDENCE IN SCIENTIFIC HEALTH CARE?

The quality of clinical decisions depends on the range and quality of evidence used to make them. This evidence is conventionally seen as coming from accumulated professional knowledge. Experienced doctors are said to use about two million pieces of information in reaching their decisions. The doubling time of the biomedical knowledge base is currently about nineteen years, so it increases about fourfold in a professional lifetime.[13] Simply to keep up with advances in general internal medicine, a doctor would need to read 19 articles each day, 365 days a year. But self-reported time spent in such reading averages well under one hour weekly for British medical specialists, or two hours for medical teachers. Actual times are probably less, and less still for GPs.[14] This gap has led to the centralized collection, analysis, evaluation and eventually (still unsystematic) distribution of new information from all over the world,[15] in a generally laudable movement toward 'evidence-based practice'.

Evidence-based practice is, then, necessary and long overdue, but what kinds of evidence should it include? Health professionals and patients have different perceptions of what seems most useful for clinical decisions and what patients want is seldom exactly what clinicians think they need.[16] But the main determinant of successful output from consultations is agreement between doctors and patients about the main problems presented. Improved teaching and resourcing can raise agreement between doctors and patients on the nature of the main problems to roughly 80% in teaching centres, but for most patients little has changed and agreement is much lower elsewhere.[17] In the USA in the late 1970s, Barbara Starfield found doctors and patients agreed on this in only about half of all visits.[18] Another study found that in consultations for bodily complaints, doctors and patients agreed on the nature of main problems in 75% of cases, but for those mainly concerning the mind, agreement fell to 6%.[19] Beckman found that doctors allowed patients an average of eighteen seconds to tell their story before interrupting and diverting them to doctor-preferred topics.[20] In Canada, McWhinney found 54% of patients' complaints and 45% of their concerns were not being elicited.[21]

The consequences can be stark. An audit of records for elderly London nursing home residents showed no medical information in 40%, no social information in 70%, and no nursing information in 30%.[22] And over one-third of them were found definitely to need home or residential care rather than nursing home care. They had been put in the wrong place, at an estimated lifetime added cost per misplaced resident of £42,250. 82% of these residents had been sent into long-term care from acute hospitals, so these decisions had been taken by health professionals.[23]

In general, all professionals are educated to see themselves as guardians of society, floodgate-keepers against potentially infinite demand on finite resources, whether in the NHS or any other social services. In reality, the opposite is more often true. Another study found only a quarter of residents in private nursing homes had been given any choice over where they went, and institutional care of any kind is in fact a last resort for the immense majority of people with a family member in need of care. The 'floodgates' idea is based on ignorance of the sociology of family relationships and, particularly, of reciprocity between generations. It insults millions of caring relatives.[24] It is another example of what happens when professionals take decisions, applying only their own narrow range of evidence and an unchallenged set of social assumptions, while ignoring evidence from patients and their families.

For health professionals and patients to relate to each other as co-producers rather than as providers and consumers, decisions must draw from both sources of evidence. If experienced health professionals have specific local knowledge not included in the general knowledge base, we need this too. Evidence-based practice must become an exercise in participative democracy, with evidence from patients valued equally with evidence from health professionals, and evidence from local experience valued equally with evidence from the academic knowledge base.[25] A shift in this direction has continued at an accelerating pace throughout my lifetime, though progress always seems painfully slow. In the early '80s even doctors who prided themselves on their patient-centred consultations were found to be ignoring patients' own ideas about their problems.[26] Since then there has been solid progress, even though the time constraints and bad habits formed by under-resourced and narrowly conceived care make this difficult.[27] But at least the currently dominant concept of good practice now places patients, and the evidence they bring, at the same level as health professionals.[28]

Among health policy-makers, the currently prevailing doctrine works against this. Economists and policy consultants demand that health professionals abandon their traditional responsibility as advocates for their patients and become instead agents of 'value-for-money' management and rationers of dwindling public services.[29] But very few people who are actually responsible for patient care will follow this suicidal policy. If patients lose confidence that their personal health advisers think and act in their personal interest, professionals will lose the immense gains in public standing and self-esteem they have made since 1948. They will lose their credibility as advisers *against* costly interventions that are likely to be futile or damaging, as well as their credibility as determined advocates on patients' behalf when they do need care, however costly. If public confidence in such independent judgements were lost, clinical decisions would face the full force of consumerism, with catastrophic consequences for an affordable NHS. Doctors would be mistrusted, litigation would escalate, patients would feel they must constantly try to 'get' as much health care as they could. The total cost of health care would rise while the health gain per pound spent would fall, just as it has in the USA.

Instead, the general direction clinical medicine must take involves the development of patients and their informal carers as co-producers of health rather than consumers of care. Respect for their evidence must come to be seen as no less necessary to accurate clinical decisions than the collective experience of medicine in the scientific literature, or the personal experience of clinicians. The speed of advance may be doubtful, because it depends on active struggle and argument, but of the aim we need have no doubts at all: scientific medicine must democratize or perish.

THE DEMOCRATIC BASIS OF CLINICAL RESEARCH

What is true for clinical relationships is equally true for research. Less than half of all treatments now in common use have ever been evaluated with the rigour that randomized controlled trials alone can make possible.[30] For all these treatments, the balance between health gain and collateral damage remains unknown. We should not assume this balance is positive, merely because we wish it so. Take hormone replacement therapy (HRT), for example. Despite billions of prescriptions, millions of tons of promotional newsprint, huge profits and reckless endorsement by numerous ageproof celebrities, HRT still rests on optimistic assumptions, not controlled evidence. There's room for some nasty shocks. The Medical Research Council (MRC) in Britain plans to recruit 34,000 women internationally for a randomized trial measuring the effects of HRT on coronary heart disease, stroke, fractures, breast cancer, Alzheimer's disease and autoimmune disease, as well as control of menopausal symptoms.[31]

This fundamental method in medical research is largely due to the work of the pioneering epidemiologist Archie Cochrane who, working initially in south Wales in the 1950s, was the first to recognize the importance and feasibility of studying virtually whole populations, rather than the compliant but unrepresentative subsets most readily available. He drew on wartime experience of operations research,[32] applying methods of experimental science to common-place diagnostic and treatment decisions and interventions. His crusade to base medical practice on evidence from randomized controlled trials met stiff resistance for about thirty years, but eventually the idea was rapidly assimilated into established wisdom. Now, trials for important treatments may require hundreds of thousands of participants observed over many years: by 1996 the British Medical Research Council's General Practice Research Framework included 6,490,000 people, 11% of the whole UK population.[33]

In 1961, after acquiring some elementary research skills while apprenticed to Cochrane, I returned to practice in Glyncorrwg, a coal-mining village not far from the Rhondda Fach where Cochrane's studies began in 1949.[34] In this small unit, serving about two thousand people, our doctor/nurse team developed a new style of work combining reactive care (traditional response to patient's presented complaints) with proactive care (active, systematic search for health needs). This entailed moving from a sole concern with episodes of sickness to a longer-term view of continuing health and illness. Improved clinical decisions depended on accumulating information in the form of life stories in what were then exceptionally comprehensive records, so that a wider range and better quality of evidence was available. On this basis we developed a system of *anticipatory care*, intervening at a much earlier stage in the cumulative and accelerating cascades of misfortune that lead to gross symptomatic disease.

This system, combining public health ideas of prevention with clinical medicine, was effective and efficient. With a small team giving patients roughly twice as much consultation time as the average general practice, and using much better records, age-standardized death rates were reduced over twenty-five years by roughly 28% in Glyncorrwg, compared with a neighbouring community with high quality but traditional care.[35] The data base created and maintained for anticipatory care of this registered, enumerated and defined population also provided the basic requirements for high quality epidemiological research. From 1968, first alone and later assisted by the MRC, the Glyncorrwg Unit produced a stream of publications in the major medical journals.[36]

Medical knowledge at the close of the twentieth century depends on many different levels of enquiry, not only in laboratories or hospital wards, but also where people live, work, and lead their lives. Effective methods of treatment rarely begin from unequivocal breakthroughs. In the early stages of innovation, significant differences between the outcomes of new and old treatments are usually marginal. For example, when I began work in 1952, childhood leukaemia was always fatal within a few months. By the late 1950s, new methods of treatment were prolonging life beyond a year in about 80% of cases, but after this brief reprieve they all died. Today, over 80% of children with leukaemia are cured permanently. Development of effective treatment depended on a long series of double-blind, randomized controlled trials. Where we had no good evidence on which to base a choice between an established treatment and a new treatment, we asked parents and children to help us find that evidence, by participating in trials in which patients were allocated randomly to one of the treatments in question. Results were not biased by the hopes and expectations of either doctors or patients, because neither of them knew till the end of the trial to which group each patient belonged.

The results of such trials are produced not only by researchers in basic sciences or innovative clinical specialists who formulate research questions, but also by patients who participate. Though their participation is clearly essential, it has hitherto been regarded as essentially passive, in the same way as patients were perceived as passive consumers in diagnosis and treatment. This is not so.

AN 'IMPOSSIBLE' TRIAL

The mostly unappreciated creative potential of trial participants is easier to see if we consider a case from my own experience, the MRC Thrombosis Prevention Trial (TPT) of low-dose warfarin and aspirin.[37] This entailed first, identifying men aged 45–64 in the top 20% of risk for coronary thrombosis. Then we asked them to accept randomization either to warfarin (rat poison) or a placebo, and blood sampling from their veins every three months for the next twelve years. When we began, there was a small but unknown risk of provoking bleeding. Experience showed this hardly ever happened at the doses we used, but that's hindsight. So great were the demands we made on trial participants that when we, and one other practice in England, first undertook the pilot studies for this project (later extended to over a hundred practices throughout the UK), the main question we had to answer was not how to organize it, but whether any such trial was feasible. In fact 82% of men in our target age group agreed to screening for categorization of risk, and 87% of those identified in the top 20% of risk had entered and stayed in the randomized treatment phase 18 months later. The overall UK response rate for screening was lower at 66%, and 52% of men in that top 20% of risk entered the randomized treatment phase. The trial ended in 1997, after 40,000 man-years of experience.

What did all this achieve? Treatment reduced all coronary heart attacks by about one-third (35%), and death rates for all causes by 17%. Strokes increased slightly, but treatment prevented about six heart attacks for each additional stroke. As in most scientific research, the new knowledge gained was complex, and harder to apply in practice than newspapers and television reporters wanted, but useful knowledge was gained which will improve patient care when fully applied.

Why did our participants and their communities take part in all these trials and research studies? Why should women agree to take part in HRT trials for a treatment already in widespread use? Why should mature men, knowing they were at high coronary risk, spend twelve years randomized either to rat poison or a placebo (neither they nor their doctors knowing which) and being bled every three months? These are serious questions. If we want rational and effective treatment, trials are essential on a mass scale. On what basis can we expect people to take part in them?

According to philosophizers of the Third Way, better education and rising consumption are associated with reduced social solidarity. As things get better, people get worse, de-solidaritized into a middle class defined by an upper class it envies and a lower class it fears. Though this common belief probably contains some truth, the historical process is far more complex. Education makes people more critical. Today more than ever before, people want full explanations before signing consent forms. Though the average quality of explanations by researchers of the risks and potential benefits of trials has probably always been better than explanations by surgeons and physicians of the risks and potential benefits of routine treatments, all have remained within the same set of cultural assumptions, in which doctors know best, and patients contribute only their bodies to the health care production process. For continued advance, we need not just formal assent, but the active use of their minds.

The high response rates obtained in the Rhondda Fach, and later in other apparently uncritically co-operative populations, tend to be seen as impossible to achieve in more sophisticated populations today. If this is true, the much larger trials we need will either not be performed at all, will have to make do with much lower response rates, will use unusual populations unable to refuse participation, or will have to start paying participants. This last solution entails large additional costs, erodes other motives for participation, may distort results by introducing new sources for potential bias, and is a one-way road from which it would be hard to return.

A wish to contribute to knowledge, and thus to help others in the future, is a powerful motive for participation in research, but this is not the only reason Cochrane achieved such high response rates in the Rhondda Fach, or the even higher rates we got in the Afan Valley. To be sustainable, population-based research of this kind requires a base in state-of-the-art routine medical and nursing care, and state-of-the-art clinical records. All epidemiological studies relate a numerator of events, strictly defined by specified criteria, to a denominator of population at risk, accurately defined and continually corrected. This means that trial participants generally get better care from better organized and more self-critical health professionals, making more use of the academic evidence base, and more open to evidence from patients and caring families. Whether randomized to a new treatment or to an old treatment or placebo, people who take part in trials consistently have better health outcomes and lower death rates than those who refuse.[38] Participants will participate in their own interest, if these requirements for research are met. If they are not, the research itself must be suspect.

These material considerations do not conflict with commitment to the cause of medical science and a better future for the human race. The conflict between altruism and self-interest which liberal employers learned from their life experience was generally absent from the life experience of industrial workers. For them, the need for solidarity was a fact of life, painfully learned through generations of experience; that though some who try to rise on the backs of others succeed, most fail. Solidarity has a material basis. If participation in research seems likely to result in material gain, in either money or health or a combination of both, this benefits both participants today, and their future descendants. For class-conscious workers, solidarity and altruism are interchangeable terms.

CONCLUSION

In sum, then: the brains of patients and of research participants are in fact a huge medical resource immediately available and capable of infinite expansion, to improve care and extend knowledge. The economists' parrot cry of infinite demands pressing on finite resources is in many ways the reverse of the truth. Of course, this resource is not an already developed fact, but an agenda. To make social progress, there's nowhere else to go, though it will be no easier than any other worthwhile task.

And this is the key idea behind the south Wales Valleys project, and why this project can and should be seen as the sort of first step towards a socialist future we need to explore. Co-production of health by patients and health professionals in a commodity-free health economy has potential counterparts wherever popular culture sees a difference between production of commodities and production of value. We have already got beyond the limits of consumerism for most fields of production. We can already see the destructive effects of profit motivation for education at all levels, for all kinds of cultural production, for food production, and even for an increasing proportion of useful material objects. A very similar analysis can (and should) be applied to education, as has been applied here to health and health care.

My guess is that health care is likely to lead the field, because of the way it has traditionally been seen in our culture (more than most others)[39] as a field in which business may be tolerated, but will never be loved. The NHS, as originally conceived (but increasingly democratized) provides a model for what we can do now, from where we are, with the people we have, maximizing our allies, dividing and isolating our relatively few irreconcilable enemies, and basing our strategy not on the commanding heights of the economy (which are not, and perhaps never were open to us, whatever our voting majority), but on the commanding depths of our culture.

Labour Prime Minister Tony Blair is not a profound thinker, but he expresses well the assumptions underlying all current received wisdom, especially the supposed decline of a working class imbued with a culture of solidarity, and its replacement by 'an expanding middle class' which will include millions of people who traditionally saw themselves as working class, but whose ambitions are far broader than their parents' and grandparents'.[40] Blair's conception of these ambitions is bound up with conventional notions of individual success and responsibility in a competitive market economy. Yet despite the effort put first by Margaret Thatcher, then by New Labour, into destroying the pride still felt by most people in their membership of the working class, survey research in 1997 showed that 61% of people in Britain still thought of themselves as working class, and this had hardly changed since 1979.[41] Moreover, 81% actually thought there was still a class struggle in Britain in the mid-1990s.[42] The fact that this is a massive increase over the 56% who thought there was class struggle in Britain in 1961 is perhaps not so surprising considering the class struggle from above that has been waged by the ruling classes in recent decades. Bitter experience – usually the best teacher – seems to have made people more politically literate. Yet if there is now to be a revival of class struggle from below, building on the rich tradition of solidarity in working class culture, it will have increasingly to be less about gravedigging and more about building on our knowledge so as to develop a truly democratic socialism. This is what the south Wales 'Going for Gold' project in health care is really about.

NOTES

I thank the following for patient advice and criticism of this or earlier drafts: Ray Catalano, Pat Devine, Martin Eve, Sheila Ryan Johansson, Ben Hart, Innes Herdan, Colin Leys, George Davey Smith, Tomi Spenser, Graham Watt, Dorothy Wedderburn, and Steinar Westin. They are not responsible for the final product.

1.   The creative nature of colliery labour underground, particularly before machines began to replace human labour in the 1930s, is generally underestimated. Simply to survive underground demanded imagination and understanding, so that there could be no such thing as unskilled mining labour on a large scale. The extraordinary variety and unpredictability of conditions in the south Wales coalfield made mining an essentially creative activity.
2.   J. Yates, *Private eye, heart and hip: surgical consultants, the National Health Service and private medicine*. London: Churchill Livingstone, 1995.
3.   P. Parker, 'A free market in health care', *Lancet*, i, 1988, pp. 1210–4.
4.   For insured citizens, marketed health care may now provide a wider range of 'cures' than the NHS, though much less continuing care. The Clinton reforms have greatly strengthened the insurance industry, and weakened professional ownership and control of medical trade. The insurance industry finds rich well people more profitable than poor sick people. Over 43 million people in USA, one sixth of the population, now have no health insurance. According to the *American Journal of Public Health* this number is rising by 100,000 a month.
5.   J. T. Hart, 'Two paths for medical practice', *Lancet*, 340, 1992, pp. 772–5.
6.   K. McPherson, 'International differences in medical care practices', in OECD Social

Policy Studies No. 7 *Health care systems in transition*. Paris: OECD, 1990, pp. 17–28; F. G. R. Fowkes, 'Overtreatment in surgery: discussion paper', *Journal of the Royal Society of Medicine*, 78, 1985, pp. 469–73; T. Bates, 'Avoiding inappropriate surgery: discussion paper', *Journal of the Royal Society of Medicine*, 83, 1990, pp. 176–8.

7. T. Marshall, 'A review of tonsillectomy for recurrent throat infection', *British Journal of General Practice*, 48, 1998, pp. 1331–5.

8. M. C. Petch, 'Investigation of coronary artery disease', *Journal of the Royal College of Physicians of London*, 20, 1986, pp. 21–4.

9. R. L. Dickman and S. Bukowski, 'Epidemiology and ethics of coronary artery bypass surgery in an Eastern county', *Journal of Family Practice*, 14, 1982, pp. 233–9.

10. A Coulter, J. Kelland, A. Long, et al., 'The management of menorrhagia', *Effective Health Care*, 1(9), 1994, pp. 1–16.

11. N. Payne and C. Saul, 'Variations in use of cardiology services in a health authority: comparison of coronary artery revascularization rates with prevalence of angina and coronary mortality', *British Medical Journal*, 314, 1997, pp. 257–61; N. Chaturvedi and Y. Ben-Shlomo, 'From the surgery to the surgeon: does deprivation influence consultation and operation rates?', *British Journal of General Practice*, 45, 1995, pp. 127–31.

12. L. Quam, 'Improving clinical effectiveness in the NHS: an alternative to the White Paper', *British Medical Journal*, 299, 1989, pp. 448–50.

13. R. Smith, 'What clinical information do doctors need?', *British Medical Journal*, 313, 1996, pp. 1062–8.

14. D. L. Sackett, W.M.C. Rosenberg, J.A.M. Gray, et al., 'Evidence based medicine: what it is and what it isn't', *British Medical Journal*, 312, 1996, pp. 71–2.

15. C. Silagy and T. Lancaster, 'The Cochrane collaboration in primary care', *Family Practice*, 10, 1993, pp. 364–5; T. A. Sheldon and A. Faulkner, 'Vetting new technologies', *British Medical Journal*, 313, 1996, p. 508.

16. J. Townsend, F. Taylor, Z. Clapp and M. McKinnon, 'Patients and GPs need to understand each other's perceptions of a consultation', *British Medical Journal*, 314, 1997, pp. 373–4.

17. S. Williams, J. Weinman, J. Dale and S. Newman, 'Patient expectations: what do primary care patients want from the GP and how far does meeting expectations affect patient satisfaction?', *Family Practice*, 12, 1995, pp. 193–201.

18. B. Starfield, C. Wray, K. Hess, et al., 'The influence of patient–practitioner agreement on outcome of care', *American Journal of Public Health*, 71, 1981, pp. 127–31.

19. R. C. Burack and R. R. Carpenter, 'The predictive value of the presenting complaint', *Journal of Family Practice*, 16, 1983, pp. 749–54.

20. H. B. Beckman and R. M. Frankel, 'The effect of physician behavior on the collection of data', *Annals of Internal Medicine*, 101, 1984, pp. 692–6.

21. M. A. Stewart, I. R. McWhinney and C. W. Buck, 'The doctor/patient relationship and its effect upon outcome', *Journal of the Royal College of General Practitioners*, 29, 1979, pp. 77–82.

22. M. Bennet, E. Smith and P. H. Millard, *The right person? The right place? The right time? An audit of the appropriateness of nursing home placements post Community Care Act*. London: Department of Geriatric Medicine, St. George's Hospital Medical School, 1995.

23. E. Dickinson, 'Long term care of older people', *British Medical Journal*, 312, 1996, pp. 862–3.

24. J. Bradshaw, *Financing private care for the elderly*. York: University of York Department of Social Policy & Social Work, 1988.

25. J. T. Hart, 'Society for Social Medicine Cochrane Lecture 1997: What evidence do we need for Evidence-Based Medicine?', *Journal of Epidemiology & Community Medicine*, 51, 1997, pp. 623–9.

26. D. Tuckett, M. Boulton, C. Olson and A. Williams, *Meetings between experts: an approach to sharing ideas in medical consultations*. London: Tavistock Publications, 1985.

27. J. T. Hart, 'Innovative consultation time as a common European currency', *European Journal of General Practice*, 1, 1995, pp. 34–7.

28. I. Heath, *The mystery of general practice*. John Fry Trust Fellowship 1995. London: Nuffield Provincial Hospitals Trust, 1995.

29. D. J. Hunter, *Desperately seeking solutions: Rationing Health Care*. Addison Wesley Longman, 1998.

30. R. Smith, 'Where is the wisdom…? The poverty of medical evidence', *British Medical Journal*, 303, 1991, pp. 798–9.

31. H. C. Wiles and T. W. Meade, 'Hormone replacement therapy in general practice: a survey of doctors in the MRC's General Practice Research Framework', *British Medical Journal*, 302, 1991, pp. 1317–20.

32. S. Proctor, 'Is this the end of research as we know it?', *British Medical Journal*, 315, 1997, p. 388.

33. *GPRF Newsletter*, issue 3, July 1996, p. 2.

34. A. L. Cochrane, J. G. Cox and T. F. Jarman, 'Pulmonary tuberculosis in the Rhondda Fach', *British Medical Journal*, ii, 1952, pp. 843–53.

35. J. T. Hart, C. Thomas, B. Gibbons, C. Edwards, M. Hart, J. Jones, M. Jones and P. Walton, 'Twenty-five years of audited screening in a socially deprived community', *British Medical Journal*, 302, 1991, pp. 1509–13.

36. J. T. Hart and G. Davey Smith, 'Response rates in south Wales 1950–1996: changing requirements for mass participation in human research', in I. Chalmers, A. Maynard, eds., *Non Random Reflections on Health Services Research: on the 25th Anniversary of Archie Cochrane's Effectiveness & Efficiency*. London: BMJ Publishing Group, 1997.

37. T. Meade and the Medical Research Council's General Practice Research Framework, 'Thrombosis Prevention Trial: randomized trial of low-intensity oral anticoagulation with warfarin and low-dose aspirin in the primary prevention of ischaemic heart disease in men at increased risk', *Lancet*, 351, 1998, pp. 233–41.

38. J. T. Hart and P. Dieppe, 'Caring effects', *Lancet*, 347, 1996, pp. 1606–8; Hypertension Detection & Follow-up Program Co-operative group, 'Five-year findings of the HDFP. I. Reduction in mortality of persons with high blood pressure, including mild hypertension', *Journal of the American Medical Association*, 242, 1979, pp. 2562–71 and 'Five-year findings of the HDFP. II. Mortality by race, sex and age', *Journal of the American Medical Association*, 242, 1979, pp. 2572–7; J. T. Hart, *Going for Gold: a new approach to primary medical care in the South Wales Valleys*. Third revision. Welsh Institute for Health & Social Care, University of Glamorgan, 1999.

39. R Jowell, S. Witherspoon and L. Brook, *British social attitudes: special international report*. Aldershot: SCPR & Gower Publishing, 1989.

40. *Financial Times*, January 15, 1999.

41. *Guardian*, January 15, 1999.

42. M. White, 'UK still engaged in class struggle', *Guardian*, August 23, 1996.

THE DYSTOPIA OF OUR TIMES: GENETIC TECHNOLOGY AND OTHER AFFLICTIONS

Varda Burstyn

HEALTH IS THE MOST basic measure of human well-being. As such, it is the first constituent condition of any conceivable utopia. Socialists have always understood the basic truth about health which epidemiology, medical economics, sociology and biostatistics arrived at only in the last twenty years, namely that the most important determinants of health are not medical (doctors and hospitals, though these are important, especially in urban cultures) but social: economic adequacy and security, adequate shelter and nutrition, healthy living and working environments and strong families and communities. It is the combination of these factors that best predicts whether any individual will choose a healthy 'life-style', and have the means whereby to pursue it. Every individual is located in a larger social ecology of health which affects those at the top as well as the bottom. The evidence unambiguously shows that above a certain level of per capita GDP what is crucial for the health of a population is not more income per head but the degree of equality in the distribution of income and wealth.[1] Cuba's high performance on health measure in comparison with the United States is one graphic example of this. So is the fact, identified in 1998 by the World Health Organization, that due to increases in 'poverty, unemployment, homelessness, excessive drinking, and smoking' and health reforms that are too reliant on 'market forces' – i.e., neo-liberalism – Europe's overall health is deteriorating for the first time in fifty years.[2] From this perspective, income equalization – and all the measures needed to bring it about, including full employment, education and social supports to women (the main paid and unpaid health providers in all societies) – is the public health metapolicy par excellence.

The economic determinants of health are old news to many socialists. But there is far less awareness about the damage that has been done by capitalist industry to the biosphere that sustains us, and, by extension, to our own health; and even less clarity about the solutions socialists should propose to arrest and reverse this damage. Today, on top of the toxic pollution caused by the old manufacturing, petrochemical and nuclear technologies, the computer and genetics technological revolutions are fuelling new waves of industrialization, with a whole new set of risks and hazards. Far from bringing about a utopia of leisure and well-being, as promised by their proponents, the technologies of production deployed in the last fifty years of industrialization have qualitatively breached the biosphere in which we humans live, and put us all at enormous risk.

Yesterday's production technologies are leaving behind harmful physical facts such as radioactivity, persistent organic pollutants and greenhouse gases that, even more than national debts to the World Bank and IMF, hang like a dead weight on the utopian possibilities of the future. Now, when we intervene into the mechanisms of life itself, as we have begun to do with industrial biotech-nologies, the potential to disrupt ecosystems grows to even greater levels, and becomes self-perpetuating. Already, thanks to the technologies of the late indus-trial age, the planet is witnessing a holocaust of natural extinctions. While species were dying at the rate of about one per decade in the early stages of industrial-ization, today they are dying at the rate of three per hour.[3] But the extent to which bio-diversity — literally the web of life — is suffering is only officially 'discovered' when crises prompt governments to investigate. To take just one recent example, it is becoming increasingly clear that phytoplankton — the basis of the ocean food chain — seed cloud formations, and hence are also involved in maintaining protection for the planet from ultraviolet rays and in mitigating global warming by absorbing carbon dioxide. These functions have been drawn to the public's attention by scientists because we have noticed huge die-offs of phytoplankton all over the world, and, among the remaining populations, the ascendance of a phytoplankton species that absorbs carbon dioxide poorly.[4] Enormous amounts of toxic pollution, industrial fishing techniques (such as drag nets) and global warming have disrupted vast tracts of ocean ecosystems. Directly and indirectly, the technological processes implicated in the extinction of plant and animal species are sickening and killing human beings as well.

This essay will concentrate on discussing, in turn, three areas of health — the emergence of new diseases, the harms of persistent organic pollutants, and the threats of biotechnology and genetic engineering — that are linked to ecology and technology. The health crises that will be entailed by the developments I trace in these areas will indelibly mark the first decades of the next century, and are already sounding harsh dystopic warnings around the world. I shall go on to argue that these developments must challenge socialists to find the political means of effecting new forms for international co-ordination and co-operation to recover control over the mobility and concentration of capital and the production technologies it employs; and of directing economic development according to the health criteria of human and environmental well-being at the community and sectoral levels where industrial production takes place.

NEW DISEASES

Because of their faith in the heroic powers of science, from the 1950s to the 1980s most people in the middle-class industrial North had a pretty complacent attitude toward disease, and a fundamentally laissez-faire attitude to medical and pharmacological science and industries. Drugs had appeared to vanquish the hideous plagues of the past. Tuberculosis and polio were defeated. In the South, malaria, dysentery, sleeping sickness and other ailments and fevers continued to plague millions, but in the North it was assumed that these too would eventually improve with modernization (industry plus doctors). Disconcertingly, though, cancer, heart disease, diabetes, lung diseases, allergies, neurological diseases and auto-immune disorders grew year by year. At first they were called the 'diseases of affluence'. By the 1980s and 1990s, they were being explained in increasingly genetic terms, as billions were poured into genetic science and human biotechnologies.

In the South, however, particularly in regions which failed to thrive in the post-colonial era, major disease disasters were unfolding as whole ecosystems and cultures were uprooted and degraded by the forces and technologies of neo-colonial resource extraction and processing. Thanks to the disruption and mixing of ecosystems that has resulted from these technologies, in addition to the disease-inducing effects of pauperization, populations in the South had to face new biological diseases, as well as battle old ones.[5] Displaced organisms, once living in relative harmony with their hosts in an environment in which they had co-evolved with other organisms, became virulent disease agents in their new environments.[6] Yellow fever, for example, can exist in a given area in Africa for decades without afflicting humans, because the mosquito that carries it feeds exclusively on jungle monkeys and marmosets. But take away the forest environment and the marmosets, and the mosquito can change its feeding habits overnight and start a human epidemic. This is what happened in Nigeria and Kenya in 1987, 1988, 1990 and 1993.[7]

The HIV virus that causes AIDS is also a traveller that began life in a different host and ecological niche. In February 1999 scientists definitively identified the human immunodeficiency virus as a descendent of a simian virus that lives in harmony with its chimpanzee host in Africa — a host now on the list of highly endangered species. Researchers speculate that at some point, perhaps in the 1960s, people of tribes that hunted the chimp contracted the virus through bites or ingestion, and passed it on to other humans. The displaced virus mutated (reassorted genes), turned virulent, and, through the human vector, spread outward across the globe.[8] HIV is a relatively slow killer. Much faster killers are also on the rise in the North, and are also part of the ecosystem disruption and mixing story. It is well known that the highly infectious and deadly Ebola virus, a haemorraghic fever, was brought from a Philippine rain forest to Reston,

Virginia, not far from Washington, DC, by green monkeys slated for medical experimentation; its outbreak was contained only with enormous effort, cost and risk.[9] And Ebola is only one of many super-lethal haemorraghic fevers: Hanta, Marburg and Lhasa viruses are also on the rise, as Laurie Garrett has shown in cataloguing and analysing the spread of the numerous viruses, bacteria, and parasites that have already attained, or are capable of attaining, mass lethality globally; Ebola is only one of many super-lethal haemorraghic fevers she discusses.[10]

Old killer bacteria such as tuberculosis and bubonic plague are back as well. Western medicine relied on antibiotics to bring many of the bacterial killers of the past under control in the post-Second World War period. This also amounted to a programme of selective breeding for stronger, more competitive bacterial micro-organisms, more resistant to our drugs. Streptococcus now brings necrotizing fasciitis (the 'flesh eating disease') as well as strep throat, and legionnaire's disease lurks in poorly ventilated ducts of office buildings, schools and hospitals. Virulent, resistant tuberculosis bacilli now thumb their cilia at sophisticated drugs in prisons, in poor neighbourhoods, on first nations reservations in North America, and throughout Africa, Russia and Asia, wherever poverty, overcrowding, and poor nutrition create ideal conditions for transmission.[11] Bubonic plague is on the horizon again with a large growth in the world population of rats due to massive urbanization and global warming. There are now antibiotic-resistant strains of plague in existence.[12] Less spectacularly, millions suffer from chronic resistant bacterial infections.

With global warming new territories are opened up for new micro-organisms – whether viral, bacterial, fungal or protozoan. In 1997, a woman in Toronto contracted malaria from a mosquito bite she received in her back yard.[13] She had not been out of Canada for ten years, and malaria is officially unknown in Canada. Nevertheless, increased international trade likely brought a malaria-bearing tiger mosquito from Asia, which survived in Canada and then infected her. As temperatures rise with global warming, we and our environments in the North become a more congenial home to new hosts and parasites alike. As well, in the wake of climate-linked natural disasters that compromise our sanitation, warmth and nutrition – for example the central North American ice storm of 1998 or Hurricane Mitch – we become tempting targets for microbes looking for a weak host. In fact, global warming is a health catastrophe, and must be understood as such.[14]

Behind the new virulence of many diseases, new and old, lie unregulated industrial technologies. New variant Creutzfeld-Jacob disease (nvCJD), for example, is on the rise in the North, and appears to be the result of humans indirectly ingesting the brains of animals with pathological prions in them. (Prions have no DNA, survive in autoclaves of 800 degrees, and, embedded in living tissue, have no known treatment; they cause a disintegration of the brain, and death.)[15] By feeding ground-up offal contaminated with sheep spongiform encephalopathy (scrapie) to beef cattle – that is, by turning cattle into carnivores (and in some cases, cannibals) in an effort to grow them faster – farmers passed on the sheep spongiform encephalopathy to cows, and, hypothetically, to the pigs, sheep and even chickens who were also given such feed, as well as to some of the humans who ate their meat. The kind of feed used by British farmers has been used throughout the agri-industrialized world. nvCJD can have a very long incubation period, so we do not know yet whether or not there will be a world-wide epidemic. But the possibility exists, and was noted with concern by medical experts meeting under the aegis of the World Health Organization in Geneva in February, 1998.[16]

POLLUTION'S THREATS TO HUMAN WELL-BEING

In addition to these threats to health from infectious diseases, the North has already begun to register the long-term consequences of petrochemical-based industrialization – the effects on human health of persistent organic pollutants (POPs). 'From 1940 to 1982, production of synthetic chemicals increased roughly 350 times, and billions of pounds of man-made chemicals poured into the environment ... In 1994, one hundred thousand synthetic chemicals were on the market, and a thousand new chemicals were being introduced per year.'[17] We are speaking here of industrial chemicals such as polychlorinated biphenyls (PCBs) and hexachlorobenzene, by-products such as dioxins and furans, heavy metals such as cadmium, mercury and lead, and a host of pesticides such as aldrin, chlordane, DDT and endrin, among others. The nuclear industry has brought us electricity, but also radioactivity. Heavy industry and petrochemical production have delivered the miracles of plastics and temporary pest control, but also persistent organic pollutants and heavy metals. These toxic substances are now present in our air, water, soil, food, household products and work environments.[18]

POPs are heavily present in all areas of past or present industrialization around the Earth, and dispersed by weather and bioaccumulation throughout the biosphere. Bald eagles on the Florida coast are affected by continental plumes of wind bringing poisons from the industrial heartland, and by the high concentrations of POPs they ingest when they eat fish which live in pesticide-laced waters. POPs migrate: from pacifiers to babies, as Canadians recently learned from a Greenpeace-initiated 'toxic toys' campaign, and from the centre of the planet to the poles, there to grow in ever larger concentrations in the tissues of fish, birds, and mammals that humans consume as food: the concentrations of toxic substances in Innuit women's breast milk are even higher than those of many women in the Great Lakes (which are famous for the very heavy chemical burden they carry on the North American continent).[19] Even after some of the worst culprits identified early on (e.g. DDT) have been removed from the market, and considerable environmental clean-ups have been achieved, organic pollutants from pesticides, plastics and other chemical-dependent industries have persisted in the environment, and today they are seriously eroding fertility, intelligence, and health. While almost all existing public health standards set for the levels of such pollutants have been based on concern with cancer, it has been convincingly demonstrated that the gravest damage done by persistent organic pollutants is related not to this disease, though this is also important, but to the disruption of the endocrine system, and the key functions that depend upon it – above all, in the fragile developmental progression of the foetus and new-born child.[20]

Some chemicals – especially, but not only, those from pesticides – act as pseudo-estrogens, overloading and distorting women's estrogen levels and introducing estrogen-like substances into men's bodies. These chemicals affect the development of the reproductive tract in foetuses. Other chemicals act as androgen blockers, and also bear on sexual development, especially in males. The estrogen and androgen disrupters are creating sterile, hermaphroditic and deformed animals, with impaired parenting behaviour.[21] In humans, they are lowering sperm count in men – down by 2.1 per cent a year for the last twenty-five years in Europe, and 1.5 per cent in North America, and still falling.[22] At this rate, they will produce a crisis in human reproduction in these regions within the next decade. As well, the neurological damage created by POPs thyroid disruption has been directly linked to serious learning, stress and attention disorders among children.[23] The scientific evidence of the harmful effects of these chemicals has finally begun to receive official attention: in 1998 the United Nations organized a conference in Montréal to devise a treaty to ban the twelve worst offenders ('the dirty dozen').

Endocrine disruption is a profoundly environmental and technological health problem – a problem knowing no borders and affecting everyone, the ultimate result of the petrochemical age. There is no way to address this problem without making fundamental changes in industrial and agricultural processes and technologies – in their development and their adoption – and undertaking large public health campaigns and environmental cleanups to address them. But while many communities attempt to seek such initiatives, neo-liberal provincial, state, and national governments loosen their vigilance on corporate polluters. Popular initiatives are often too little, too late relative to the toxicity and carnage capacity of capitalist- and state-directed industrial enterprises. In fact, instead of funding scientists to rapidly explore the full extent and meaning of POPs pollution, and propose solutions, funds flow to the destructive industries that are creating the problems. And this includes, more and more, investments in agricultural, animal, and human biotechnologies that apply environmentally unconscious industrial methods to the realm of life itself.

REPRODUCTIVE AND GENETIC ENGINEERING

The biotechnology sector comprises, on the one hand, thousands of small start-up 'brains trusts' with names like Amgen, Organogenesis, Genzyme, and Calgene, and on the other, a group of transnationals, such as Du Pont, Novartis, Upjohn, Monsanto, Eli Lilly, Rohm and Haas, and Dow Chemical. In the US alone, 1,300 biotech companies do nearly $3 billion business annually, and provide work for more than 100,000 employees.[24] But the TNCs control huge sectors of the agrochemical (81 per cent), life science (37 per cent), pharmaceutical (47 per cent), veterinary pharmaceutical (43 per cent) and food and beverage sectors.[25] These new 'life industries' are based on the proposition that they can develop biomachines – custom-designed, genetically engineered organisms – to solve challenges as diverse as ocean oil spillage and cold sensitivity in vegetables. Funded by governments, universities, and above all, corporations, scientists have been developing genetically modified viruses, bacteria, fungi, plants, and laboratory and agricultural animals in agricultural, medical, and military research. Many of these organisms are transgenic – that is, they are new creations involving the insertion of genes from one species (for example, a flounder, a firefly, a human) into another species (for example, a tomato, a tobacco plant, a pig), in order to enhance a particular quality (for example, cold resistance, genetic marking for patenting purposes, transgenic organs for human transplantation).

The risks involved are extraordinary on all counts, for in these biotechnologies we are creating new forms of non-evolved life, capable of self-replication once released to propagate in our ecosystem. Because of the many dangers of such biotechnologies, environmentalists, progressive agriculturists, consumers and public health advocates have all participated in extended campaigns to refuse government approval for many of the initiatives of the biotech sector in agriculture: the patenting of life forms, the pirating of genes, the transgeneticization of species, the creation of sterile seeds ('terminator genes'), and the genetic modification of foods.

US-based Monsanto Corporation is one major player in these technologies globally that has recently become embattled in several places. Polls in North America and Europe show that substantial majorities of their populations do not wish to eat or buy genetically-modified foods. This reaction, embodied in consumer and citizen mobilizations, constitutes a major threat to agricultural biotechnologies. In addition, in December 1998, the Canadian government rejected Monsanto's bovine growth hormone for approval in Canada. This rejection was a rare victory in the struggle to control the proliferation of biotechnologies in Canada, the result of a protracted battle waged by concerned NGOs from many different sectors, and the outright revolt of a group of federal Health Protection Branch scientists at being told to suppress their negative findings with respect to bovine health. In January 1999, the British government imposed a fine on Monsanto for allowing its genetically-engineered plants to spread beyond the experimental area and contaminate general agricultural land. The British and Canadian setbacks for Monsanto notwithstanding, agricultural biotechnology is far ahead of its opponents. In 1996 'more than three-quarters of Alabama's cotton crop was genetically engineered to kill insects. In 1997, farmers planted genetically-engineered soya on more than 8 million acres, and genetically-engineered corn on more than 3.5 million acres in the United States'.[26] We already live in an environment with extensive genetic pollution.[27] We cannot predict the effects on present and future ecosystems of every release. But our experience with other great industrial technologies, and with biotechnology to date, makes it virtually certain that there will be enormous problems and costs caused by agricultural biotechnology. Meanwhile, efforts by NGOs to ensure that countries have the power to resist such technologies are being fiercely resisted on the international level by the US government and the TNCs, who frame all such objections as new obstacles to free trade and the flow of capital.

The prospect of *fabricating human beings,* made possible by combining reproductive with genetic technologies, promises even greater financial returns. Funded by the transnationals and governments, scientists are hard at work on a variety of technologies that will make up the package necessary to manufacture human beings and their parts. The multi-government funded Genome Project is yielding insights into human genetic make-up on a weekly basis, and industrialists are looking for ways to apply this knowledge profitably. Craig Venter, the scientist who runs The Institute for Genomic Research (TIGR) in Rockville Maryland, has said he will sequence the whole genome in three years with the aid of private capital and a computer to be completed late in 1999 that he claims will surpass in power even that of the US Defense Department's computer built to simulate nuclear war.[28]

Information being gleaned from such macro research is being sold to enable the creation of micro procedures for many purposes, actual and experimental. Not all are equally problematic. Genetically-engineered drugs are already being used to treat cancer, heart disease, AIDS, diabetes, kidney and vascular disease, and new techniques for somatic gene therapy are being developed. (The leading pioneer in this field, William French Anderson, is on the board of Craig Venter's TIGR.) Leaving a host of problems in the patenting and marketing of human genetic technologies aside, somatic gene therapy has the potential to do the maximum good with the minimum of harm. Its effects are in theory not heritable, so do not saddle the future with the consequences of today's intervention.[29] Somatic therapy does no necessary physical harm to the 'donor' of therapeutic material, and benefits the recipient. Hence there may indeed be some value to a number of such forms of therapy. Motorola is developing technologies to produce chips on a single sliver of silicon that will integrate electronic and biological functions and render human DNA as bar codes. This technology and others which have been developed as a result of the genome project enable totalitarian controls and accelerate the creation of a eugenic society based on severe genetic discrimination.[30]

Such possibilities are posed even more acutely by the many planned applications of genetics to human germ line gene intervention – an intervention that will affect the sex cells of an embryo, and will be hereditary. Many technologies are being developed that will lead to or rely on human embryos as raw material. One crucial ability sought in human biotechnology is stem-cell propagation. Known as 'totipotent' cells, stem cells are produced in the early stages of embryo formation, and differentiate into the 210 different cell types required to construct human bodies. As such, they constitute unparalleled 'raw material' for human bio-fabrication, the ultimate bio-commodity gold-mine.[31] In late 1998, two teams of university and corporate-funded US scientists, working with 'surplus' embryos from in vitro fertilization clinics, announced that they had succeeded in propagating human embryo stem cells. Then a third team followed with the news that it had fused a human cell nucleus with an enucleated cow's egg, producing a transgenic human-cow tissue with many of the properties of stem cells. Another major technology – creating an artificial uterus – took a major leap forward thanks to Japanese scientist, Yoshinori Kuwabara, who sustained and birthed a goat foetus from an artificial uterus in 1997.[32] Cloning is yet another potential gold-mine technology, also embryo-dependent. First achieved with Dolly the sheep in 1997, its 'perfection' is moving rapidly along in animals and it is now being proposed by leading researchers and clinicians in human reproductive technologies as an alternative to human in vitro fertilization.[33]

All technologies have a price, and the price we will have to pay for the bioindustrialization of human life will be extremely high. This price includes the patenting of human stem cell lines, the creation and commodification of human embryos, foetuses, organs, and tissues, and gestational capacities, the growth of a market for these among the indigent,[34] the severing of genetic from sexual, gestational, and social parenthood, genetic discrimination and eugenic mentality, immense physical suffering for animals and humans, and potential catastrophes from mutational 'errors' that will inevitably occur as a result of crossing evolutionary species barriers.[35]

Some of the health risks of the new human biotechnologies are known, and they have been documented by physicians, scientists, and epidemiologists who specialize in risk assessment. Disease transmission via animal vectors in xeno-transplanation is just one of these. Laurie Garrett reported that the baboons used in the first of the 1992–93 Pittsburgh baboon transplant experiments were infected with 'SIV (the simian AIDS virus), CMV (the simian cytomegalovirus), EBV (the simian type of Epstein-Barr virus), and simian agent 8 (the baboon form of b [herpes cancer-causing] virus)'. Had the two patients survived the multiple infections they developed after transplantation, which they did not, they could have acted as vectors for all these simian viruses into the human population. The transplants were undertaken even though it was well known among transplant surgeons that patients usually die of secondary infections (from the transplanted tissue), not of organ rejection.[36] Yet pigs and primates are being developed for the harvesting of organs and tissues by corporations, scientists and clinicians, with the full support of governments and states.

As well, we cannot neglect the potentially devastating hazards now extant in biological labs, both commercial and military. Although the Soviet Union signed the international treaty banning biological warfare, it proceeded to establish a major industry that pursued just this end. Anthrax was a favourite disease for experimentation, and was grown by the ton in the laboratories of a state firm called MOD. In Sverdlovsk (now Ekaterinaburg) in 1977, an anthrax outbreak killed many people – estimates of 1,500 to 2,000 – when pathogens leaked from the plant.[37] It is feared that 'rogue states' and Mafia and terrorist organizations have access to these installations and will use their contents to advance their interests. Iraq has admitted to the UN that it produced 3,100 US gallons of one toxic germ, enough to kill the world's population several times over. The United States itself has a large Department of Defense programme and licensed the export of large quantities of toxic agents to Iraq during the Iraq–Iran war. In late 1998, the London *Sunday Times* reporters wrote that Israel was working on an 'ethno-bomb' – 'a biological weapon that would harm Arabs but not Jews'. Odious and bizarre as this seems – recalling the eugenics of Dr Mengele himself – 'the research mirrors biological studies conducted by South African scientists during the apartheid era and revealed in testimony before the truth and reconciliation commission'.[38] Lethal pathogens, developed as biocommodities by the pharmaceutical and medical industries, can be bought with no special qualifications on the open market. According to one newspaper report, there are '450 commercial germ collectors worldwide. More than 50 trade in anthrax; 34 sell the botulinum bacteria; 18 sell the plague'.[39] The development of these genetically-engineered lethal micro-organisms, which can never be fully safeguarded against release, is driven directly by profits, politics and states.

The most dangerous of the risks of existing directions in genetics are, however, literally unimaginable. This is because transgenic organisms have what are known as 'emergent properties' – properties that are new, unique, and unknowable consequences of recombining DNA. The health, environmental, and socio-political dangers of emergent properties are absent from the vast majority of mass media discourse on biotechnology, as they are from the corporate practice of genetic science. The green science paradigm – of diverse interdependent co-evolution – is entirely absent from corporate bio-commodification.

At present human reproductive and genetic technologies are rudimentary, risk-laden, and expensive. They are not yet credible answers to the problems of infertility, disability and disease that they purport to solve. Progressive health activists and officials can still argue that their costs and risks far outweigh their benefits; that instead of technologizing and geneticizing illness, public health policy should address the social and environmental determinants of health and fertility.[40] If we do not address these determinants, however, we may well bring these technologies rapidly into the main stream.[41] It is not difficult to foresee a day when fertility will decline to the point where many women and men will look to artificially-assisted reproduction, with its dangerous drugs and disability-prone multiple births, as the 'better way'; when the teratogenic properties of environmental toxins will motivate parents to submit their embryos to genetic screening and engineering, and masses of women to undergo *in vitro* fertilization, a day when the rich will clone headless genetic copies of themselves for tissue replacement, augmented by a trade in body parts, foetal tissue and embryonic cells provided by the poor.[42] Then the dystopic dynamics illustrated in

Margaret Atwood's *A Handmaid's Tale* will combine with those described by Aldous Huxley's *Brave New World* and William Gibson's cyberfuture *Neuromancer*.

THE POLITICAL VACUUM

The claims made for the therapeutic effects of genetic medicine are miraculous. Some of the claims for somatic gene therapy may be valid, and may indeed offer medical breakthroughs with benefits that clearly outweigh detriments. The positive effects of germ line intervention, on the other hand, are both unproved and highly dubious, especially when measured against their health, environmental, social and human rights risks. Moreover – and this is a key issue for socialists – less than ten per cent of disability at birth is genetically linked. Social and environmental determinants are responsible for the rest – over ninety per cent. Yet genetic science is attracting huge proportions of public and private dollars while the science and practice of preventive medicine and public health initiatives – which could address a much larger proportion of such disability – go begging.

The abundant ethical, evolutionary, health, environmental, animal rights and human rights objections to reproductive and genetic engineering have brought about a general call for moratoria on many of the key directions in biotechnology, and for a public process for the evaluation of their trade-offs. This call is being ignored by corporations and governments alike. As a result, corporations are being allowed to make crucial species decisions for humanity. With respect to human biotechnology, despite many government-sponsored commissions in many industrial countries, and some effort at legislation and regulation by a few (e.g., the UK, France and Germany), there have been no coherent national and international policy or structures to deal with an industry whose division of labour is fully internationalized.

As writers such Richard Sclove and Daniel Coleman point out, until very recently political theory foresaw no need to complement the market mechanism for making technological choices with any type of political oversight.[43] The historical lack of well-established and appropriate institutions for such oversight, and the recent curtailment of public funding for scientific research and technological evaluation in the neo-liberal era, has left production technologies to be driven entirely by profit and political imperatives (careerism, nationalism, war). To deal with the resulting health crises we now need to develop instruments of governance and new models of economic development capable of ensuring that production technologies in heavy industry, resource extraction, infrastructure construction, energy production, agriculture, biotechnology, and communications are greened in ways that enhance, not worsen, the other social determinants of health.

This will be a tremendous challenge because while the short-term drive for profits has been central in creating an environmentally unconscious growth of production industries, nation states also have a huge investment in them. In most countries the state has been heavily involved in developing vast economies of destructive industrial technologies, either in partnership with capital or on its own. The United Nations has estimated that 'in the early 1990s the state subsidized environmentally damaging industrial activities – energy, water, roads, agriculture – worldwide to the tune of at least \$710 billion every year'.[44] Many governments have actively pursued the development of major harmful industries as key strategies for national economic development, with no thought to their impacts on health. Tire plants, pesticide factories, nuclear power stations, hydro dams – all have been subsidized by governments, as have been both 'start-up' and transnational firms in biotechnology. The contested, long-standing refusal of the Canadian federal government to enact regulatory legislation on biotechnology, for example, can be read in light of the fact that Canada has more biotechnology firms per capita than any other jurisdiction in the world.[45] Government complicity in harmful production technologies has also been increased in the 1980s and 1990s as many governments worked to dismantle the public institutions charged with regulating the environmental impacts of heavy industry, agriculture, and the medical and pharmaceutical industries. This policy was of a piece with the larger attempt to downsize public services, and hence remove 'barriers to capital'. Finally, acting directly in the interests of the owning class, governments have sought to privatize many of the previously state-owned corporations that undertook industrial development in infrastructure and energy production, and the environmental and labour standards to which they held.

POLITICS FOR A HEALTHY FUTURE

If capitalist industrialization has 'depoliticized' technology – placed it in the realm of individual and private initiative, to be supported as an unalloyed good by states – production must now be repoliticized if the problems discussed in this essay are to be solved. Politics which work toward good health must contest the deployment of current technologies and find ways to create and employ alternative, health-enhancing technologies and systems of knowledge in the here and now. Many of these are already in hand. From organic agriculture, to wind and solar power, to sewage filtration plants that produce flowers, vegetables and drinking water as their end products, to new techniques of organic agriculture, to refrigerators that do no harm to the ozone layer, to hydrogen powered automobiles that produce water emissions – *homo fabricans* has already proved capable of developing the technical means of correcting our worst environmental abuses. Indeed, this is one of the brightest parts of the overall picture. The problems lie in the lack of political will and resources to further develop and deploy these technologies, and most governments' continuing support for nuclear, petrochemical and bio-technologies. By the uncritical facilitation of corporate agendas in many countries, the majority of public revenues still flow primarily to industries with the biggest investments in harmful technologies.

A health-driven politics of technological control must therefore include a plan for the reconstitution of a vital public sector in science and technology, through non-corporate-aligned universities and clinical and field researchers linked to producers; and it must propose structures and policies that subject technological decisions to socio-political oversight.[46] It must bring about the reorientation of the majority of public funds for research and programmes that address the environmental and social determinants of health; and support technologies best suited to maximizing these. Many examples exist of people and projects that would be supported by such politics – green scientists, sustainable production technologies, organic agriculture, communities that advance green plans for their industries and utilities, workers who develop conversion projects (from 'brown' to 'green' industries), and an impressive sector of public-interest NGOs in many social justice, health and environmental fields.[47]

But in most countries there are still no political parties that group all these forces together, and present programmes that embody a politics of public health, social egalitarianism, technological democracy, and green economic strategies. Environmentalists in social democratic parties have been trying to 'green' their parties since the late 1960s. But ultimately the commitment of existing social democratic parties to present forms of industrialization means that no such transformation has taken or will take place. Where green parties exist in Europe, they group together important activists, and in some cases field winning candidates in elections, but they – like most NGOs – often stop well short of a systematic critique of capitalism in relation to the environmental crisis. And in most jurisdictions, such parties are absent entirely, or have undeveloped connections to labour and other social movements, and gain little in the way of mass recognition or electoral support. New political parties are needed.

Such parties need to think through what kind of polities a healthy (just and environmentally sustainable) society needs. If we begin with an ecological appreciation of our existence, we need polities whose boundaries and jurisdictions are based primarily on their physical environments – their bio-regions – of which governments need to be the guardians. Equally such polities would politicize technological production issues as issues of health. To evolve such polities, we need new political forms at two levels, as well as reform in existing states. We need much closer international collaboration between states to address the mobility of capital and its international divisions of labour, and the global nature of environmental issues. Hence we need to demand accountability from existing politicians and public institutions in international as well as national arenas, and we need to suggest vehicles and processes for this accountability. We should be demanding measures such as proportional representation, recall, and the equalization of election spending at all electoral levels in order to advance a serious health agenda. And we should be proposing the creation of, and/or the reform of, government bodies charged with technological oversight. But second, we also need much stronger local polities that can wrest economic decisions from national elites, permit the exercise of direct democratic control over the technologies involved in daily life, and have the capacity to proactively pursue pro-social public and environmental policies at the local level. This means we must aim to build new mechanisms of participatory and direct democracy in industry and in local communities, where technology is constructed and operated.

The implication of this conclusion is that socialists must participate in planning and organizing for sustainable technologies of production in ways that integrate social and environmental goals. If capital is permitted to redesign industrial production on its own – the major oil and automotive corporations have purchased all the major patents on solar and clean-automobile technologies – workers will pay a terrible price. Remote economic elites and bureaucracies make poor decisions for those who carry out their decisions. Only people answerable to the communities and municipalities of which they are members and who live most directly with the consequences of the technologies they employ can make and implement adequate decisions regarding environmental sustainability and production technologies. The importance of direct democracy in communities and in sites of production is a theme developed in thoughtful and useful ways by authors such as Richard Sclove, Daniel Coleman and Wolfgang Sachs.[48] It is not possible to do this theme justice within a few concluding paragraphs. But let me give one glimpse, in the crucial realm of energy production, of the ways in which economic production and political organization could and should work together.

In the production of electric power, bureaucratic elites and capitalists have favoured huge hydro-electric dams, large coal- and oil-burning generating plants and nuclear power. The damaging effects of these technologies are now well known. Local communities (as well as the global biosphere) are better off with, and, if given a choice, are more likely to choose, solar, wind, and small-scale hydro power. They are also much more likely to derive direct economic benefits from the activities needed to construct and maintain such technologies. It thus makes sense to place the political power to organize energy production on the municipal and neighbourhood level, in non-profit (public) enterprises, linked to a regional (provincial, state, national) grid. Each community, or group of communities, determines its energy needs and production goals, according to its bio-regional and human characteristics and needs, and adopts appropriate technologies accordingly. Each community controls its energy production, contributes surplus energy to a larger grid, and draws on the grid as necessary. Each community creates jobs in the production, installation, administration and maintenance of the energy technologies. The role of national or regional government is to help fund the creation of this system, develop and fund transitional strategies to retrain and relocate workers in light of the changes involved, ensure the adoption of compatible criteria throughout the system, maintain, monitor and regulate the energy grid, and promote energy conservation and environmental protection. First nuclear plants, then dirty fossil fuel generation plants are decommissioned and attendant threats to the environment and human health are progressively diminished. And the global economies –

military as well as industrial – for nuclear and climate-changing energy production technologies shrink.[49]

CONCLUSION

Respected scientists such as evolutionary biologist Paul Ewald have demonstrated in the laboratory that the virulence of an infective agent is directly related to the ease of transmission between, and the multiplicity of, its available hosts.[50] Like Arno Karlen[51] and others, Ewald posits that organisms who live in balance with their hosts in a given ecosystem will become virulent only when the number of hosts available to them radically changes and expands. Limit the vectors for transmission – unsafe sex for AIDS, for example, or faeces in the water for cholera – and the organism will mutate to a condition in which it co-exists with, rather than wipes out, its host. Ewald posits that in Japan, where transmission rates are low due to widespread condom use and high health status, less virulent strains of HIV will evolve. The paradigm-shifting import of this new germ theory for medicine itself is that, in concert, proper social, environmental and medical policies really can prevent disease by limiting its vectors. Ewald's findings provide the basis for optimism about our ability to find strategies that will defuse many of the 'new plagues' I wrote about earlier. But expect major resistance to this view within science and the medical industries, because it potentially shifts social emphasis and dollars away from attempting the near-impossible, but highly profitable, task of managing these diseases medically and pharmacologically, and from genetic research, toward systems of knowledge, services, and forms of social and environmental prevention that are far more effective, if somewhat less commodifiable.[52]

Socialists have well understood the importance of defending the pro-social functions of the nation state, those that can permit us to address the socio-economic vectors of disease. Socialists have also understood the need for international organization and collaboration to deal with the forces of globalization that so strongly shape local jurisdictions. What we must now acknowledge is that to achieve good health for humanity, we must address ecological realities and find the means to exert technological control in our lives today. And this task is dependent on a much greater degree of democratic organization on a local level than now exists in most jurisdictions. Participatory democracy in economic development decisions and in public health is not a panacea for the looming threat to human survival on the planet. But it is an indispensable component of the solution – and probably the only basis upon which will rise the level of national and international co-operation needed to address production technology issues globally. An educated and real democracy seems the only possible general alternative to market forces.

The task of thinking through a practicable alternative paradigm of economic development – one that is truly red and green – is urgent, because humanity must bring the age of nuclear energy, fossil fuels and poisonous synthetics to an end sooner rather than later; the facts admit of no other conclusion. This necessitates the conversion of vast aspects of production from toxic to non-toxic technologies. Some experts estimate that chlorinated synthetic chemicals and the products made from them alone constitute as much as 45 percent of the world's GNP.[53] (This investment lies behind capital's resistance to meaningful government and state action needed to address the enormous health hazards of POPs.) A key task for socialists is to develop awareness of these realities, to help in creating local, regional, sectoral, national, and international social-justice strategies for green economic development, and to help make these central in the preoccupations of the labour movement.[54] This too will be an uphill task, for if appropriate technologies are deployed by communities and industries as they move toward a lower-consumption, lower-resource extraction economy, many of the industries in which unions have grown must change, shrink, and in some cases disappear – nuclear energy, for one. This threatens the unions in their present form, and constitutes a major challenge to the labour leadership: either to defend the institutions and industries, however problematic, in which they have been based, or to provide leadership in moving to better ones. If a clear 'eco-justice' programme for an alternative economy were being advanced by political parties, a programme into which the unions could have input, the second option could become a real one.

While there are many different political views and consciousnesses in the industrialized countries, there are also some commonalities: a profound disillusionment with the structures and institutions of liberal democracy, a profound sense that something is very wrong with the environment and a profound confusion about what to do. Participating in the effort to formulate radical systemic alternatives will pay off in broad support for socialists. Greens are increasingly joining socialists in demanding the reorganization of work and the redistribution of wealth: the cancellation of national debts in the South, the recasting of international trade agreements, international controls on capital, the shortening of the work week, and radical electoral reform.[55] And socialists are increasingly coming to understand the importance of environmentalism, and the politics of science and technology. Both movements meet at the point where human health is threatened. Politicizing health may well be one of the most unifying ways that socialists and greens can collaborate in forging a new political project – one that can take us to a truly 'post-industrial' age.

NOTES

1.   Robert Evans, Morris Barer and Theodore Marmor, *Why Are Some People Healthy and Others Not? The Determinants of the Health of the Population*, New York, Aldine de Gruyter, 1994, pp. 6–7.
2.   Adrea Mach, *The British Medical Journal*, September 19, 1998, p. 317/767.
3.   Jeremy Rifkin, *The Biotech Century: Harnessing the Gene and Remaking the World*, New York, Tarcher/Putnam, 1998, pp. 8, 109–110.
4.   'Extinctions caused by human activity risk more than just the loss of species: they may threaten the biosphere's ability to capture energy through photosynthesis,

cycle nutrients and resist the vagaries of climate', Bob Holmes, 'Life Support', *New Scientist*, August 15, 1998, p. 30.

5.   See *America's Vital Interest in Global Health*, Institute of Medicine, United States National Academy of Sciences, Washington DC, June 21, 1997, on links between global trade and travel and diseases discussed in this section

6.   See Arno Karlen, *Man and Microbes: Disease and Plagues in History and Modern Times*, New York, Touchstone, 1995. See also Judith Hooper, 'A new germ theory', *Atlantic Monthly*, February 1999, pp. 41–55.

7.   Laurie Garrett, *The Coming Plague: Newly Emergent Diseases in a World Out of Balance*, New York, Penguin, 1994, pp. 575–6.

8.   David Fox, 'UN announces significant increases in HIV/AIDS', Reuters/*Infobeat*, November 18, 1997. The UN estimates that 30 million people worldwide are infected with AIDS. On patterns of diffusion, see Hooper, p. 49 and Garrett, pp. 334–361.

9.   Richard Preston, *The Hot Zone*, New York, Anchor, 1994

10.   L. Garett, *The Coming Plague*, 1994, various chapters. In March, 1999, *New Scientist* reported: 'A mystery virus is complicating attempts by the Malaysian authorities to control an outbreak of encephalitis near pig farms which has already claimed 55 lives. There were 145 suspected cases, 42 of which had been confirmed as Japanese encephalitis. But a second, unrelated virus has cropped up in the spinal fluid from 5 patients. A team at the university of Malaya in Kuala Lumpur says that the unknown virus resembles the "Hendra" virus, first isolated near Brisbane, Australia, in 1994. It killed 15 horses and 2 out of the 3 people it infected.' 'Double Trouble', *New Scientist*, March 27, 1999.

11.   See 'New TB "Hot Zones" Threaten Epidemic', *The Globe and Mail*, Toronto, October 23, 1997, p. A1 (re Joint Report of the WHO, the US Centers for Disease Control, and the International Union against Tuberculosis and Lung Disease). For a summary report on tuberculosis epidemics in countries of the former Soviet Union, see 'World's next epidemic: Resistant tuberculosis', *The Gazette*, Montréal, March 18, 1999, World Section.

12.   See Gene Emery, 'Bubonic plague grows resistant to antibiotics-study', April 9, 1997, and 'Bubonic plague squirrels found in California', *Science Wire*, November 6, 1998.

13.   Trevor Hancock, 'Mosquito-born diseases will rise', *The Globe and Mail*, Toronto, November 4, 1997, p. A19.

14.   'Insurance companies have paid out $918 billion in losses from weather-related natural disasters in the 1990s so far, close to four times the weather-related claims handed out during the entire decade of the 1980s . . . The rising insurance claims of the last decade have coincided with rises in global temperatures: six of the ten warmest years on record have occurred since 1990.', *World Watch Institute*, Washington DC, March 30, 1999.

15.   Richard Rhodes: *Deadly Feasts: Tracking the Secrets of a Terrifying New Plague*, New York, Simon and Schuster, 1997.

16.   'WHO experts say "mad cow" epidemic possible', *Marketwatch Live Internet News*, February 12, 1998. 'In last three months of 1998, there were nine confirmed new cases in the United Kingdom. In the previous three years there had been no more than five new cases in a quarter.' From *The Lancet* (vol. 353, 979) as reported in *New Scientist*, March 27, 1999, p. 5.

17. See Theo Colborn, Dianne Dumanoski, and John Peterson Myers, *Our Stolen Future: Are We Threatening Our Fertility, Intelligence and Survival? A Scientific Detective Story*, Dutton, New York, 1996, pp. 137–139.

18. See 'Hazardous chemicals a top priority for global environment', UNEP press release, Geneva, April 1998, and *Le plastique de PVC et le dereglement hormonal*, Greenpeace, Montréal, 1997. For studies reporting that 'much of the precipitation in Europe contains such high levels of dissolved pesticides that it would be illegal to supply it as drinking water', and for links between pesticides and rising cancer rates see Fred Pearce and Debora Mackenzie, 'It's raining pesticides', *New Scientist*, April 3, 1999.

19. See T. Colborn, et al., *Our Stolen Future*, 1996, pp. 101–109.

20. T. Colborn, et al., *Our Stolen Future*, 1996. See also Lois Marie Gibbs, *Dying from Dioxin: A Citizen's Guide to Reclaiming our Health and Rebuilding Democracy*, Montréal, Black Rose Books, 1997.

21. For a discussion of sperm damage, see T. Colborn, et al., *Our Stolen Future*, 1996, pp. 68–86. The evidence of deformations due to endocrine disruption in other animals continue to accumulate. There have been many reports of deformed and hermaphroditic fish and frogs in the great lakes region and it was recently reported that 'female mollusks in a Lisbon lagoon are developing male characteristics apparently caused by pollution.', *The Gazette*, Montréal, January 16, 1999, p. J8. Note also 'low sperm count increases risk of testicular cancer', a report on a recent Danish study that links the two, *EXN Science Wire*, February 28, 1999.

22. See Maggie Fox, 'Report confirms fears – men are losing their sperm', Reuters/Infobeat, November 24, 1997

23. T. Colborn, et al., *Our Stolen Future*, 1994, pp. 186–194. See also 'Canadian study ties birth defect to solvents', Michael Conlon, *Reuters/Yahoo News*, March 24, 1999. Some experts have begun to suggest that despite its other benefits, women in heavily industrialized regions, or in regions where POPs are deposited, should forego breast-feeding for the developmental health of their children.

24. J. Rifkin, p. 15. See also 'Seed industry: Who owns whom?', RAFI Communique, July/August 1998, Rural Advancement Foundation International, Winnipeg.

25. J. Rifkin, *The Biotech Century*, 1998, p. 68.

26. Ibid., p. 18.

27. See Naomi Perrian, 'Strange new world: Genetically-engineered foods usher in an era of biological pollution', *Greenpeace Magazine*, Spring, 1999. See also Martha Crouch, 'How the terminator terminates: An explanation for the non-scientist of a remarkable patent for killing second generation seeds of crop plants', Edmonds, WA, *The Edmonds Institute*, 1998.

28. See Nicholas Wade, 'Scientists' plan: Map all DNA within 3 years', *The New York Times*, May 10, 1998. For information about Venter and TIGR, including its corporate partners, go to www.tigr.org

29. Although some researchers have raised the possibility that gene therapy could affect the sex cells of recipients, and thus cause transgenerational consequences Nell Boyce, 'Fertile is fine', *New Scientist*, March 20, 1999, p. 22.

30. 'Where no chip has gone before', Jonathan Knight, *New Scientist*, March 20 , 1990, p. 15. On the same page: 'Human bar codes'. 'Third Wave Technologies of Madison, Wisconsin, has developed a genetic screening method, called

Cleavage Fragment Length Polymorphism, that represents DNA samples as bar code patterns . . . claims their technique is faster than 80 per cent of conventional screening technologies . . . Comparing codes will allow researchers to quickly spot genetic mutations and will help in the treatment of hereditary disease.'

31. See Louise Vandelac, 'l'Embryo-économie du vivant … Ou du numéraire aux embryons surnuméraires', *Le Magasin Des Enfants*, Jacques Testart (ed.), Paris, Gallimard, Folio Actuel, 1994, pp. 161–193.

32. Peter Hadfield, 'Japanese pioneers raise kid in rubber womb', *New Scientist*, April 25, 1992; 'Here's looking at you, kid', *New Scientist*, July 26, 1997.

33. See Gina Kolata on Princeton molecular biologist Lee Silver G. Kolata, *Clone: The Road to Dolly and the Path Ahead*, New York, William Morrow, 1998, pp. 241–2. In agriculture, cloning is seen as an important way to reproduce transgenic animals such as sheep and pigs for farming and xenotransplantation. Hence cloning and transgeneticization are tied together. For an explanation of this, see Ian Wilmut, 'Cloning for medicine', *Scientific American*, December 1998, pp. 58–63. For some serious risks involved in cloning plus transgeneticization in mammals, see Philip Cohen, 'The great divide', *New Scientist*, December 12, 1998, p. 16.

34. See Mona Eltahawy, 'Egypt holds inquiry on sale of body parts', *Guardian Weekly*, March 28, 1999, p. 5.

35. While a very important theme in science fiction, and a major force in biotechnology, the term mutation is strangely absent from public discourse about biotechnology. Québecois sociologist Louise Vandelac has recently drawn attention to the need to assess and address the question of the mutation of life in research and in public policy. Louise Vandelac with Marie-Helen Bacon, 'Will We Be Taught Ethics by Our Clones? The Mutations of the Living: From Endocrine Disrupters to Genetics', *Ethical Problems in Obstetrics and Gynaecology*, Claude Sureau and Françoise Shenfield, eds., Baillières's Clinical Obstetrics and Gynaecology, London and New York, International Practice and Research, forthcoming 1999.

36. Laurie Garrett, *The Coming Plague*, 1994, pp. 573–5.

37. See 'Genetics and "Germ Warfare",' *The Gene Letter*, vol. 2, no. 2, March 1998, and Richard Preston, 'The Bioweaponeers', *The New Yorker*, March 9, 1998, pp. 52–65.

38. See Uzi Mahnaimi and Marie Colvin, 'Israel reported developing "ethno bomb",' *The Gazette*, Montréal, November 15, 1998, p. A11. It is difficult to believe that such a project could succeed, given the overlapping genetic heritage of many Israeli Jews of Arab extraction and Palestinians. Nevertheless, the report cites 'Israeli scientists' as making this claim while also naming South African and American military experts.

39. U. Mahnaimi and M. Colvin, 'For sale: Deadly germs. Cheap', *The Gazette*, Montréal, November 22, 1998, World Section.

40. See V. Burstyn, 'Making Babies', *Canadian Forum*, March 1992, pp. 12–17; 'Making Perfect Babies', *Canadian Forum*, April 1992, pp. 13–19, anthologized in Patricia Elliott, ed., *Rethinking the Future*, Saskatoon, Fifth House Publishers, 1993; and 'Breeding Discontent', *Saturday Night*, June 1992, pp. 15–17, 62–67, anthologized in Gwynne Basen, Abby Lipman, Margrit Eichler, *Misconceptions: The Social Construction of Choice and the Reproductive and Genetic Technologies*, Hull, QC, Voyageur Publishing, 1993.

41. L. Vandelac, 'Will we be taught ethics by our clones: The mutations of the living, from endocrine disrupters to genetics', *Ethical Problems in Obstetrics and Gynaecology*, 1998.

42. See 'British lab creates frog embryo without head', *Toronto Star*, October 13, 1997, p. A22.

43. See Richard E. Sclove, *Democracy and Technology*, New York, Guilford, 1995, and Daniel A. Coleman, *Ecopolitics: Building a Green Society*, New Brunswick (NJ), Rutgers University Press, 1994.

44. David Ransom, 'Red and green: Ecosocialism comes of age', *New Internationalist*, November, 1998, p. 9.

45. *Impacts du genie genetique sur agriculture*, Union des Productuers Agricole [de Québec], August, 1998, p. 11.

46. For a discussion of how economic incentives drive science, see Martha Crouch, 'The very structure of scientific research mitigates against developing products to help the environment, the poor, and the hungry', *Journal of Agricultural and Environmental Ethics*, 1991, and M. Crouch, 'Debating the responsibilities of plant scientists in the decade of the environment', *The Plant Cell*, Journal of the American Society of Plant Physiologists, April, 1990, pp. 275–277.

47. For some discussions of the potential of the non-profit, public interest sector of non-governmental organizations to play a large role in the reconstitution of civil society and politics, see Ulrich Beck, *Democracy without Enemies*, Polity Press, Cambridge, UK, 1998, and Jeremy Rifkin, *The End of Work: The Decline of the Global Labor Force and the Dawn of the Post-Market Era*, New York, Putnam, 1995

48. R. E. Sclove, *Democracy and Technology*, 1995, and D. A. Coleman, *Ecopolitics: Building a Green Society*, 1994, and Wolfgang Sachs, *Greening the North*, Zed, London, 1998.

49. For a larger discussion of the issues and models for green and red energy production, see D. A. Coleman, *Ecopolitics: Building a Green Society*, 1994, pp. 182–200. For an assessment of the disastrous consequences of deregulation of energy in the United States, see Harvey Wasserman, 'The Last Energy War', *The Nation*, March 16, 1998, pp. 11–15.

50. Ewald also points to chronic microbial infections as causes of diseases long thought to be degenerative, not infective, in nature (eg., heart disease, cancer, multiple sclerosis). See also Hooper, note 6 above.

51. See A. Karlen, *Man and Microbes: Disease and Plagues in History and Modern Times*, 1995.

52. For an example of these issues at work, see Michael Day, 'The hype about herpes', *New Scientist*, October 12, 1998, pp. 24–5.

53. T Colborn, et. al., *Our Stolen Future*, 1994, p. 245.

54. Two thematic issues of the *New Internationalist*, no 284, October 1996 ('Sun, wind, water, earth, air . . . The energy revolution') and no. 307, November 1998 ('Red and Green: eco-socialism comes of age') provide multiple examples of issues and developments in progressive technological organizing globally.

55. See W. Sachs, *Greening the North*, 1998, and Anders Hayden, 'The price of time', *New Internationalist*, November 1998, p. 17.

My thanks to environmentalist and geographer David S. Fenton for his invaluable assistance in researching and writing this article.

WARRIOR NIGHTMARES: AMERICAN REACTIONARY POPULISM AT THE MILLENNIUM

CARL BOGGS

THE DAWNING OF a new millennium, beset with global crisis and local upheavals, seems in many ways to harken back to the inter-war years when classical fascism first appeared as a powerful force across Europe. A resurgence of right-wing populist groups and ideologies in many countries over the past decade has rekindled political and scholarly interest in the fascist tradition.[1] Could the spread of right-wing tendencies, with their appeals to people who are marginalized or feel threatened by change, signal the replay of yet another cycle of ultra-authoritarian politics? The recent proliferation of explosive civil wars around the world, many of them rooted in bloody ethnic, regional, and religious strife, brings to this question an added salience.[2]

In the United States, a new reactionary populism, fuelled by intensifying social polarization, job insecurity, urban decay, fear of change, and simply alienation from politics-as-usual, has taken shape in forms of rebellion – militias, cults, fundamentalist groups, skinheads, some urban gangs – which in their xenophobic, nativist, authoritarian, and militaristic dimensions are (sometimes intentionally) reminiscent of fascism. Yet there are a number of critical differences. The movements led by Mussolini, Hitler and Franco always focused their attention on the realm of state power (Mussolini once stated: 'Everything for the state, nothing against the state, no one outside the state.'), and this stands in stark contrast to the insular, turf-oriented and localist anti-politics of modern reactionary populist groups in the United States. What is most characteristic of these groups is in fact the lack of any coherent, future-directed ideology that could give political shape to their anti-statist beliefs and irrational fantasies.

Their outlook embellishes an ethos of retreat, not an aggressive plan to transform the order of things, to create new social and authority relations, to build an entirely new state. In this sense, their ideology is quite remote from the more developed ideologies of classical European fascism on the road to political power. This is not to say they don't occupy an important place on the American stage at the millennium. But it is crucial to register these distinctions if we are to understand what they represent.

FROM CULTS TO MILITIAS

The widespread appearance of right-wing populism in the U.S. stems from the activism not only of free marketers, anti-tax partisans and libertarians but also of a bizarre variety of cults, sects, militias, and enclave groups which have taken off since the 1970s, often galvanized by the familiar 'angry white male' caught up in a backlash against social movements and disruptive change. Many see themselves as engaged in an all-out war against an evil and oppressive federal government that taxes and regulates American citizens against their will. Others see the national state apparatus as an agency or repository of international conspiracies, frequently involving the United Nations or other global organizations. Inevitably, violent confrontations between these groups and the state have occurred – the FBI assault at Ruby Ridge, the Waco stand-off and conflagration at the Branch Davidian compound, the Oklahoma City bombing, the holdout of the Montana Freemen, and the Amtrak train derailment in Arizona among others. In most of these episodes the very legitimacy of the U.S. government was being called into question. In hundreds of other lesser confrontations, generally in the west and midwest, federal agents and employees have been victims of threats, intimidation, and verbal attack. A Gallop Poll taken in May 1995 revealed that no less than 39 percent of Americans believe the federal government is 'an enemy of human rights'. In the first ten days following the Oklahoma City events, dozens of federal agencies received a total of 140 bomb threats. Twice (in 1994 and 1995) violent and angry citizens took employees hostage, in San Francisco and Puerto Rico, to protest shoddy treatment at the hands of the government. Public officials at all levels have often been the target of name-calling, threats, and harassment. Such expressions of public outrage can hardly be dismissed as the irrational response of marginals and crazies, though clearly this element does enter the picture; far more common is the visceral lashing-out of ordinary people who feel powerless and think, often quite rightly, that most government officials and politicians are totally indifferent to their needs and demands, or corrupt and untrustworthy, or simply incompetent.

The impact of cults and sects – dramatized by the collective suicide of 38 Heaven's Gate cult members in San Diego early in 1997 – is far deeper than the relatively small number of their adherents would suggest. While the exact number of members and supporters is not known, estimates run to no more than a few hundred thousand. Recent U.S. history is pervaded with the brief and often turbulent legacies of cult-like groups on both the left and right:

Weather Underground in the early 1970s, the Symbionese Liberation Army, the Peoples' Temple and Jonestown, the Moonies of Reverend Sun Yung Moon, the Hare Krishna sects, the Rejneesh Colony in Oregon, and various communes associated with the Guru Maharaj Ji, to name some of the most visible. What these cults and sects have in common is an intensely millenarian vision of the future, a strong attachment to charismatic leaders, and a manifest contempt for politics.

Often overlooked is the fact that popular belief in prophesies and mystical ideals, as well as a fascination with conspiracy theories, has a long tradition in American culture. Such millenarianism appeals to the widespread populist conviction that life entails a perpetual struggle against hated outside enemies, and that there can be no escape from the miseries of everyday life through either conventional religion or normal politics. Given this outlook, a presumably corrupt public sphere can never be the arena for genuine human self-activity or emancipation (however defined). Insecure about the future and cut off from the past, people responding to an atmosphere of change and crisis may be available to highly-seductive messages about promises of an entirely new life, especially where those messages are conveyed by strong, articulate leaders who offer the true path to empowerment.[3]

The search for an idyllic separate kingdom, made up of a community of believers standing firm against an oppressive world, motivated David Koresh and the Branch Davidians in their quest for religious transcendence. Their ideas had roots in the Millerite Christian movement founded by William Miller in the 1830s and inspired by Old Testament prophecies about the coming apocalypse. The Millerites were able to build a congregation of close to 100,000 followers dedicated to a renunciation of material possessions; members spent much of their time praying on hilltops, waiting for the second coming of Christ. This cult gave birth to the Seventh Day Adventists, who later produced a split-off group called the Davidians, out of which the Branch Davidians were formed under the stewardship of Ben Roden. Following Roden's death in 1978 his widow Lois formed the Mount Carmel Commune and entered into a relationship with Vernon Howell, who soon changed his name to David Koresh and then proclaimed himself the new Messiah, using his charisma to take over the organization in the early 1980s.[4] Taken to quoting long biblical verses, Koresh placed himself above any earthly criticism, talking incessantly about the future liberation and how it was destined to come about. He envisioned a strictly religious process confined to the Davidian faithful. Eventually the group came to embrace a series of wild prophecies, most of them linked to the idea of inevitable and perpetual conflict with a corrupt and hated outside world. Within this general scenario the Davidians established a specific target of fear and hatred: the U.S. government.

The Davidian siege outlook was based on a manichean and paranoid view of social reality that lent itself to a form of militarism which soon gripped the membership (totalling only a few hundred by 1990). By the early 1990s the

Davidians had amassed a huge stockpile of weapons at their compound in Waco, Texas, including a large assortment of grenades and automatic rifles. Following a series of FBI investigations into cult activities came a number of confrontations, both violent and non-violent, eventually leading to a 51-day stand-off in 1993 that ended when federal authorities moved in force against the compound. The resulting inferno cost the lives of 84 members (including Koresh), who apparently preferred total annihilation to surrender. To the very end, the rebels remained implacably hostile to the federal government, rejecting any compromise with its agents and refusing to extend legitimacy to it during negotiations. Yet beyond this fierce anti-government stance, the Davidians never articulated a coherent view of either their goals or a strategy for building a movement.

The Davidian cult thus bore striking resemblance to comparable religious and quasi-religious groups analysed by Eric Hobsbawm in *Primitive Rebels*.[5] One case study explored by Hobsbawm was the millenarian cult founded in Italy by David Lazzaretti in 1875, which appealed to hundreds of poor, marginalized, and uneducated people lured by images of quasi-religious salvation. Like Koresh, Lazzaretti set himself up as an earthly messiah whose mission was to perform miracles in order to end human suffering. Many peasants, especially in Southern Italy, were convinced by the power of a message that could challenge the hegemony of both the Catholic Church and the much-despised political system. But while Lazzaretti inspired an ethos of resistance by encouraging peasants to refuse their tax obligations, he offered neither a specific program nor a method for carrying out even minimal social reforms; the 'ideology' consisted of little more than unwavering belief in imminent miracles, a search for divine intervention. In 1878 Lazzaretti and most of his followers were killed fighting the *carabinieri,* choosing – as the Davidians did later – violent death over capitulation.[6]

The search for apocalyptic solutions likewise motivated the Heaven's Gate Commune near San Diego, 38 members of which decided to commit collective suicide in May 1997 in the belief that leaving Earth for spaceship travel behind the Hale-Bopp comet would take them to the 'next level'. Their millenarian ideology amounted to the most extreme and total escape from politics – indeed from society itself. What is most interesting about the Heaven's Gate phenomenon is how its members, followers of Marshall Applegate, incorporated a variety of mainstream beliefs and commitments while carrying them to apocalyptic extremes: science fiction, obsession with computers and high-tech, new-age mysticism, and conspiracy theories linked to UFOs and alien beings. In this respect Heaven's Gate can be seen as a quintessential end-of-the-century millenarian cult which, hardly by accident, was located in one of the most affluent San Diego suburbs (Rancho Santa Fe) and attracted members (overwhelmingly white and middle-class) who had worked in the high-tech sector. Their sense of alienation and powerlessness, their paranoid feelings of being under siege, could be overcome only through the ultimate apocalyptic act: departure from a mundane and corrupt earthly existence.

In contrast to the Davidians and the Heaven's Gate devotees, for whom apocalyptic belief was everything, the skinheads – bands of right-wing or neo-Nazi youth with an estimated 3,000 members across 31 states in the early 1990s – are more closely linked to elements of urban gang culture. Like the millenarian cults, however, the skinheads have attracted members largely from the poor, marginalized, and uneducated sectors, including above all young males who have yet to establish strong roots in work and family. While generally not overtly ideological, the skinheads often adopted the rhetoric of a racist, sexist, xenophobia subculture bent on reproducing the division between initiates and outsiders, between the (usually homogeneous) youth groups and various stereotyped 'others'. In many cases they took on the symbolic paraphernalia of historical fascism, adorning themselves with swastikas, German Eagle medals, and tattoos, listening to German marching music, and so forth. In most instances, however, skinhead groups expressed little interest in political ideology or in changing the world. As with most gangs, there was a strong attachment to turf and a swaggering, macho cult of violence that could easily be directed against scapegoats: rival gangs, feared or despised ethnic groups, other 'enemies'.[7] At a time when few good jobs and careers seemed available to poor youth, when the family had deteriorated as a source of cohesion and identity, and when politics was viewed as a boring, meaningless exercise, skinheads came to epitomize the alienation and nihilistic outlook of urban youth in general. Much like cults and sects, youth-based gangs of this sort can furnish solidarity where it is otherwise absent. But it is an emphatically *anti-political* solidarity that views any kind of routine institutional life (especially involving government) with total contempt: there is no vision of grass-roots politics. Even with all their Nazi symbols and culture of rebellion, therefore, skinheads have come to embrace an ethos of cynicism and nihilism that self-consciously refuses the duties and challenges of citizenship, that debunks the idea of winning (or influencing) political power, that looks with deep scepticism upon anything resembling official discourse.

Such retreat from the public sphere is, in a territorial sense, even more pronounced among the growing ranks of 'survivalists' than among cults, sects, and skinheads. Survivalists generally seek refuge in the wilderness, forming tightly-knit, isolated groups intent on preserving self-sufficient and (in most cases) traditional lifestyles. Unlike the millenarian cults, they have no single-minded religious or utopian mission; unlike the skinheads, their escape from society takes them into more insular rural enclaves; and unlike both, they adhere to relatively coherent beliefs. At the same time, survivalists typically appeal to the same constituency of marginalized, poorly-educated, lower-class white males. More significantly, they view politics with much the same degree of hostility: once again, while many participants may reject *in toto* the existing social order, the leaders seem to have little interest in framing alternative visions or strategies, even along fascistic lines.

The term 'survivalist' was first coined by Kurt Saxon in the early 1960s – a reference to purportedly superior beings who, bonded together in the remote wilderness, were prepared to endure some cataclysmic event such as nuclear war. Initially they were mainly consumed with the idea of self-protection from hostile intrusions: urban elites, cops, the United Nations, minorities, Communist aggression. Over time, as the survivalist ranks grew to tens of thousands, organizational and ideological coherence followed. Their elan was boosted by the influence of certain racist, neo-Nazi texts such as William Pierce's *The Turner Diaries*. Eventually the survivalist rebirth gave rise to such dispersed groups as the Aryan Nations, The Order, the Posse Comitatus, and numerous militias, which together claimed as many as 60,000 members scattered around the country.[8] Inspired by the Civil War Posse Comitatus Act, which prohibited federal troops from intervening in local disputes, the Posse formations refused to obey any government higher than the county level; all other jurisdictions were scorned as corrupt and implicated in a conspiratorial world governing body. The Posse groups of the 1990s include tax resisters, home schoolers, religious fundamentalists, gun enthusiasts and others who see their life as a perpetual struggle against an implacably corrupt and hostile world. Some leaders and activists predict an imminent race war that could threaten the survival of the white population. Within this ideological subculture many groups have taken on the veneer of a military structure, replete with uniforms, chains of command, large arms caches, shooting ranges, and the entire lingo of an army outfit.

As with other kindred groups, survivalists face the challenge of retaining their organizational dynamism over time. As participants age and mature, there is always a question of how long even the most strongly-dedicated activists can remain in such an isolated, paranoid, and hostile atmosphere rife with conspiratorial tales (at times survivalists have seemed ready to believe in virtually any outlandish scenario – indeed the more far-fetched, often the more credible). Moreover, without any presence as a genuine social movement or hope of achieving specific goals, members are hard put to point to actual or even potential worldly successes. In these circumstances insular groups will frequently turn more and more inward; in the process they may wind up fighting among themselves, splitting off, even disintegrating, as a result of ever-mounting levels of frustration. Destructive patterns of this sort have become one of the modern legacies of primitive rebellion – witness the fate of Weather Underground, the Symbionese Liberation Army, the Rajneesh Commune, Peoples' Temple, and more recently the Heaven's Gate cult. As the disillusioned survivalist founder Saxon remarked about these groups in the late 1980s: 'Leave them to their own devices and they'll wipe each other out.'[9] Even in the absence of such an implosion, however, it would seem that these groups are condemned to political irrelevance owing, at least in part, to their militantly isolationist stance.

Among all extreme right-wing groups operating on the fringes of the political system, by far the largest, most dispersed, most well-known, and probably most ominous have been the militias. By 1996, militias had an estimated membership of 250,000 with a sprawling base of support totalling between three and five million people across at least 30 states. Theirs is a thriving (and growing) nativist, anti-urban subculture which also views government and politicians of all stripes as objects of ridicule. In fact the paramilitary organizations have evolved in such a way during the 1990s as to incorporate the main thrust of these other tendencies, including much of their *modus operandi* and espoused aims, but with a clearer focus on the idea of armed mobilization. It seems clear from the evidence to date that the militias attract typically poor, working-class, rural or semi-rural Christian white males, with little or no college education, who are the most amenable to the whole panoply of racist, xenophobic, militarist, and conspiratorial messages.

What its members like to call the patriot movement gained its biggest notoriety at the time of the Oklahoma City federal building bombing in April 1995, but the militia presence goes back much further – probably as far back as the emergence of survivalists and kindred groups in the early 1960s. The movement is generally formed through networks of small, relatively autonomous, 'leaderless' cells that can move swiftly, flexibly, and secretly if necessary. They are inclined to stockpile weapons, dress in army fatigues, conduct periodic quasi-military 'manoeuvres' and hold 'intelligence-briefing' sessions, typically in remote rural areas. They come together under such banners as the 'Colorado Free Militias', the 'Florida State Militia', 'Christian Identity', the 'Militias of Montana', and the 'Viper Militia'. Significantly, support for the paramilitary movement actually *increased*, in some cases dramatically, in the period immediately after the Oklahoma City carnage – no doubt part of the macabre fascination with the intense media coverage of this and related events.

If the names and images of the U.S. militias convey a world-view thoroughly cut off from social reality, the groups nonetheless have an ideological rationale, however murky. They see the ordinary person (again mostly white and Christian) as politically disenfranchised, struggling for survival and identity under circumstances made more difficult by the actions and designs of a governmental behemoth. Crucial to that struggle is ownership of weapons that the federal government is viewed as illegitimately trying to deny law-abiding citizens. A popular refrain is: 'What will you do when they come for your guns?' Militia partisans are fond of apocalyptic scenarios – for example, the one where U.N. forces, assisted by the CIA, FBI, and perhaps the IRS, have mobilized to occupy the American heartland with the aim of delivering the country over to agents of a sinister (but never clearly-defined) 'New World Order'. Taking as their inspiration the Minutemen of the Revolutionary period, militia groups cherish a myth of rugged individualism and frontier heroism in which guns appear larger than life – symbol of a disappearing sense of historical mission.[10] Members harken back to a simpler, far more homogeneous world of rural harmony, religion, family values, and ethnic solidarity – a world in which outsiders, foreigners, and government agents are regarded as *personae non gratae*. Aside from books like *The Turner Diaries* a major conduit of propaganda for the militias has been the burgeoning ranks of extreme right-wing talk radio hosts like Chuck Harder in Michigan, who urge listeners to fight, violently if necessary, against the global demonic forces that are bent on disarming and enslaving American citizens.

A highly-celebrated case of patriot action was the protracted stand-off between the Freemen and federal agents in Jordan, Montana during the spring of 1996. Engaged in long-standing combat with the FBI and IRS, the Freemen – a group of less than 100 resisters led by Leroy Schusasinger – hoped to create their own republic (called Justus Township) replete with its own legal territory, constitution, currency, and armed units. Their overriding goal was local governance, but strictly within the framework of a white, patriarchal, rural, Christian order. For several years Freemen activists carried out a series of anti-government actions, often inundating local courts with bogus documents and claims, refusing to pay taxes, and making payments to creditors of up to 30 million dollars in counterfeit checks. They issued death threats to federal officials who, in the Freemen ideology, had no right to regulate, control, or tax individuals who, in any case, should not be required to pledge allegiance to the outlaw U.S. state. Federal arrest warrants were issued against several Freemen members in March 1996, leading to the prolonged encounter and culminating in the arrest of two leaders.

Another paramilitary group, the Phoenix-based Viper Militia, seemed to be preparing for an extended violent confrontation with the federal government – largely, as it turns out, without the knowledge of any local residents. In July 1996 agents from the Alcohol, Tobacco, and Firearms office, following a nine-month investigation, arrested twelve people involved in the Vipers and found an arsenal of machine guns, rifles, fifty-six boxes of ammunition, and hundreds of pounds of chemicals that could be used to manufacture bombs. Agents also found a videotape in which militia members gave detailed instructions for blowing up government buildings. Operating underground, the Vipers were a dispersed, loosely-organized network that was able to move about without attracting much public attention. Their nucleus was comprised of mostly ordinary working-class people, including housewives and a fairly large percentage of women. Relaxed gun-control laws in Arizona enabled the militias to go about normal daily activities, with members often dressed in fatigues with weapons visible . Their literature and videotapes showed that the Vipers apparently believed that 'urban warfare' and 'race wars' were imminent, and that it was the duty of citizens to mobilize for this, while militia partisans and spokespersons liked to represent themselves as simple folk just out for fun and games in the woods or the desert.

AN ANTI-POLITICAL CULT OF VIOLENCE

Like survivalists, skinheads, and some cults, the militias embrace a diffuse subculture – more an alternative way of life than an explicit ideology or political formation. As an expanding national presence, the militias carry forward – in quasi-militarized form – the familiar American idea of disenfranchised people fighting for identity, recognition, and local democratic control against a distant, impersonal, and bureaucratic government. The vast majority see themselves as bearers of a renewed citizenship that must be won by vigorous battle in the midst of a harsh and ever-threatening world. Their obsession with conspiracies, their fascination with mysterious schemes and plots, and their glorification of gun culture can easily draw them into the zone of domestic terrorism. The much-celebrated cult of violence, however, does not seem to detract from a populist image the militias have so patiently cultivated. Of course this is a reactionary form of populism, but its anti-government zeal does inspire a semblance of grassroots activism that shares some of the symbols and even aims of progressive populism. Indeed the militias' hostility to state power is deep, visceral, and generalized; it goes well beyond the targeting of specific office holders or legislators, or the familiar conservative assault on bureaucracy. Such grassroots sympathies are compromised, however, by their undeniably shadowy element: a sometimes virulent white racism, staunch social conservatism, an intensely parochial defence of turf, super-patriotism. More tellingly, their populist critique rarely extends to the power of multinational corporations; the struggle for local control is strangely directed against only the national state rather than big business, and against the civilian branches of the state, not the military. And like the other movements discussed above, the militias never mobilize popular support on the basis of some positive vision of the future – even a vaguely anarchistic one – but focus instead on people's fear of change, their insecurity about material and social dislocation, and a scapegoating of minorities, immigrants, and outsiders. The result is a kind of 'Rambo' syndrome – a macho defiance of elites, by any means necessary, along lines of the traditional American outlaw hero and the frontier ethos of rugged individualism.

The importance for the militias of a weapons subculture, of preparation for armed combat, of the image of everyday people locked in mortal struggle against a wicked federal bureaucracy, all involves carrying to extremes the worship of guns and violence, the attachment to rugged individualism, that is deeply embedded in post-war American culture. There are an estimated 220 million guns in civilian hands in the U.S., including several million automatic weapons, belonging to people who for the most part are able to roam freely across the rural and urban terrain. It is the hard-fought and well-financed lobbying campaigns of the National Rifle Association that have done so much to legitimate the gun culture. Add to this mix a mass media and popular culture saturated with images of violence, along with an increasingly Hobbesian civil society that feeds into a variety of angry and paranoid responses, and the resonance of messages predicting warfare involving ordinary citizens (as in Larry Pratt's widely-read *Armed People Victorious*) becomes more comprehensible.

As Bill Gibson observes in *Warrior Dreams*, guns and violence have become a powerful male obsession in the U.S. since the Vietnam war.[11] The weapons fetish has spread rapidly, across class and ethnic lines; more than three million assault rifles have been purchased in just the past two decades. Manifestations of male violence have been on the upswing since the 1960s, from street crime to domestic violence to serial murders. Films devoting macabre attention to mass killings – or just regular mayhem – like *Silence of the Lambs, Reservoir Dogs, Pulp Fiction*, and *Natural Born Killers*, have become the object of cult fascination. The immense popularity of televised coverage of the Persian Gulf War, much of it graphically depicting bloody carnage, is well known.[12] Reflecting upon this trend, Gibson points to the emergence of a 'new warrior hero' in American society that mirrors a shifting masculine ethos – one less focused on soldiers and cops, but rather advocating an everyday sort of warrior life that encourages ordinary people to take up arms, join quasi-military groups, and 'prepare for heroic battle against the enemies of society'.[13] So the modern male warrior, whether in the guise of the Freemen, patriot organizations, marauding bandits, gangs, or skinheads – or even a hermetic figure like the Unabomber – becomes the archetype of the renegade hero who in earlier days tamed the frontier, robbed trains and banks, or simply took the law into his own hands to fight Commies and other alien intruders.

The recurrent search for American male warrior identity goes back to the Minutemen, frontier settlers, and foreign adventures like Teddy Roosevelt's 'Roughriders', which attracted men looking to conquer the world, or at least hoping to defend their own territory, with a powerful sense of adventurism. It runs through the myths and rituals of the mafia and organized crime as well as urban street gangs. During the 1990s it has appealed far more to white men than to any other social category – to men who feel threatened by a heartless and encroaching urban world and who are attracted to ideas of racial superiority, sexism, male bonding, and the familiar ultra nationalism of fascist ideology. Writes Gibson: 'American men – lacking confidence in the government and the economy, troubled by changing relations between the sexes, uncertain of their identity or their future – began to dream, to fantasize about the powers and features of another kind of man who could retake and reorder the world.'[14]

The new paramilitary culture was shaped in part by a national mood of defeat and pessimism stemming from the aftermath of the Vietnam war. As Gibson points out, the Indochina debacle was a great blow to the collective American psyche, representing the end to a long U.S. tradition of military victories; it eclipsed the national doctrine of manifest destiny that had such deep roots in the imperial designs of American ruling elites going back to the early nineteenth century. U.S. military hegemony was challenged and smashed, at least in one geographical locale and for one historical moment. The result was a massive social-psychological disruption leading to a 'crisis of self-image' in the general culture but which seemed most disorienting for the military subculture. During a period of intense and rapid change, including the strong impact of feminism and erosion of long-established gender roles, a large number of men felt driven to recapture the patriarchal ethos of a simpler era. In this context many sought out images of violent power, which they found validated in the popular culture. But for such fantasies to make sense, to have credibility, they would have to be directed against purported enemies: Communists, foreign terrorists, drug dealers, illegal aliens, nebulous conspirators, even the U.S. government itself, which in fact was often seen as behind these other forces. In this fashion the national crisis intersected with a variety of identity crises (and perhaps economic hardships) that for good reasons seemed impervious to normal political initiative.

The most explicitly fascistic current in U.S. political culture is to be found among the angry right-wing extremists who form the backbone of rural groups like Aryan Nations, Christian Identity, The Order, and The Order-2, many of them based in Far West regions such as Idaho, Utah, Montana, and eastern Washington State. Richard Butler of the white supremacist organization Aryan Nations has set up an enclave of twenty acres behind barbed-wire fences in northern Idaho where members can meet, practice target-shooting, and generally vent their rage at a country that has sold out white people. Butler's goal: a 'ten percent solution' that would save one-tenth of the United States for a 'white homeland' while letting the rest of the country rot in its own corruption and decay. Funded in part by Silicon Valley high-tech money, Butler and his followers rejected the Klan and John Birch Society for being too 'liberal'; as of 1998 they had established close contacts with chapters in at least twelve states and with a variety of neo-Nazi groups worldwide. Referring to the bible as a 'book of separation', displaying photos of Hitler, and fascinated with both punk rock and German marching music, the Aryans envision a protracted 'war of freedom' – a 'war', however, that lacks any coherent political-strategic definition.

But even here the struggle is understood, for the moment at least, as essentially *cultural* – part of an historical battle to regain lost values and social structures (community, family, religion, etc.). Indeed, the anti-statist outlook of the militias and allied groupings is infused with such utter contempt for the public sphere – for any generalized mode of civic participation – that translation of their populist energy into movements for social change will be extremely difficult. This defect is compounded by their ethos of dispersion and secrecy, and by an intense commitment to localism, which is viewed as necessary to 'leaderless resistance'. Here the militia groups are doubly anti-political: they have an aversion to the whole realm of social governance and statecraft, and they reject the public arena *in principle* as a site of collective action. Dedicated and solidary as they may be, therefore, the militias, like the millenarian cults and the skinheads, are not, left to themselves, likely to amount to anything more than hotbeds of primitive rebellion: fragmented, local, insular, and lacking the capacity for political definition and expansion. They have little in the way of political language or methods that could give substance to their beliefs or connect their actions to social processes and historical possibilities. For the near future, at least, theirs is likely to be nothing more than a proto-fascist form of cathartic activity built around their own unique brand of anti-politics. While it is not impossible that such dispersed and inchoate groups will evolve into more established (and menacing) social movements or even political parties, in the foreseeable future their impact is most likely to be felt in a growing number of acts of terrorism.

Only recently, beginning in the 1990s, has ideologically-motivated violence become a fairly widespread *domestic* phenomenon in the U.S. This is an historically significant development, not only because of what it might portend for American politics but also because it reflects powerful trends at work in the society as a whole. Proto-fascist acts of violence directed at public targets may be less deviant or exceptional than is commonly believed; on the contrary, they are the work of mostly ordinary people taking a few very ordinary ideas (freedom, rugged individualism, patriotism, the right to bear arms) to fanatical excesses. As mentioned above, the cult of violence resonates throughout American society in the form of the gun lobby, images in the mass media, urban gang subcultures, astronomical rates of violent crime, and of course the war economy itself (which, though downsized, still devours more than $260 billion yearly).

In this social milieu the problem of right-wing terrorism cannot be dismissed as the isolated shenanigans of fringe crazies. Indeed local incidents of this kind of violence have been surprisingly common during the 1990s: according to the ATF there were no less than 2,400 bombings in the U.S. during 1993 alone, leading to 70 deaths and 1,375 injuries. Reportedly hundreds of other planned actions were intercepted by the FBI and police agencies. The heightened fascination with bombs and guns, including sophisticated assault weapons, is fuelled by mail-order companies that cater to paramilitary enthusiasts, not to mention Internet transmissions, short-wave radio, fax systems, and the omnipresent talk radio programs (some of them hosted by militia sympathizers). Aided by the Internet and alarmed about the coming of the new millennium, 'hate' groups around the country have multiplied rapidly in just the late 1990s. In 1998 observers from Klanwatch and the Militia Task Force documented an all-time high of 474 hate groups in the U.S. – an increase of 20 percent from 1996. Many activists who are biblical doomsayers, fascinated by violent rock lyrics, are drawn to domestic terrorism; they collect high-powered weapons, build bombs and chemical weapons from easy-to-obtain ingredients, and set up web-sites (163 all told as of early 1999) as intricate networks of communication. Their main target is an evil, tyrannical federal government. No longer confined to the South and Far West, such groups (they hardly constitute movements) now have the kind of nation-wide presence that enables them to avoid social and geographical isolation.

Right-wing terrorism thus goes deeper than the bombing of federal buildings and occasional acts of sabotage: there are the frequent assaults on women's health clinics, along with a tremendous increase in hate crimes directed against minorities and gays. And outside this quasi-fascist subculture there have also been recurrent Luddite efforts to smash the artefacts of modern technology – witness the Unabomber mail bombings to presumed agents of the industrial order during the 1980s and 1990s. Viewed in this context, terrorist episodes involving the World Trade Center, Oklahoma City, the Amtrak derailing, and the 1996 Olympics in Atlanta, to name only the most publicized, could be a prelude to mounting domestic insurgency that could spill beyond the boundaries of reactionary populism. The violent mood is nourished by a popular cynicism and frustration over the meaninglessness of normal politics – measured by the precipitous loss of efficacy that pervades any depoliticized society – and by the rapid spread of paranoid, conspiratorial beliefs often tied to some future apocalypse or fear of conquest by nebulous intruders from afar. Paranoid references to black helicopters, alien creatures, drug cartels, and secret military missions – all supposedly leading to a tyrannical New World Order – are best understood in this context. Such beliefs add up to a demonology which offers a substitute for the Communist 'evil empire'.

Of course the appearance of groups that place violence at the centre of their agenda has the effect of closing off public space for open dialogue and collective action by provoking a heightened degree of police and military vigilance and a curtailing of basic political freedoms – as in the case of Italy, where a once-thriving radical left was decimated by the end of the 1970s in the wake of the Aldo Moro abduction/murder by the Red Brigades. Random and widespread acts of violence generate fear and suspicion well beyond their points of origin, endowing the state security apparatus with more power, both institutionally and psychologically. Terrorist episodes can also spread the flames of racism and scapegoating that may already be deeply ingrained in the culture. Because of its generally capricious and murderous nature, civic violence feeds into a classical Hobbesian nightmare in which conflict spirals out of control, eviscerating political life as fear, cynicism, and hatred take hold of the public sphere. Given the complexity of modern society and the critical role played by the mass media and popular culture within it, severe political degeneration can result from just a few acts of terrorist violence – as the deadly work of the Red Brigades, Baader-Meinhof in Germany, and Supreme Truth in Japan has shown. The state becomes more authoritarian, while the other oppositional groups and movements are thrown on the defensive; democratic participation at the societal-wide level is readily blocked or crushed.

Terrorism is the inevitable result of anti–politics, a politics that refuses to aim at entering into the alliances that are necessary to occupy state power. Fascist movements and parties were once able to seize state power in Europe because large sectors of the power structure – aristocracy, Catholic Church, big business, the military – swung over to the fascist agenda at a decisive moment. Whatever the ideological affinity with earlier incarnations of fascism and neofascism, along with certain undeniable similarities in the historical context, in the U.S. today there are few signs of such a critical alignment. The cults, fundamentalists, and militias, for their part, generally want nothing to do with the elites, indeed nothing to do with politics. And the *squadrista* mentality of the armed groups is anathema to Wall Street, the Pentagon and the bulk of the political establishment not only because of their distaste for destabilizing domestic insurgency and terrorism, but also because the open xenophobia, racism, and fervent localism, which extends throughout the whole reactionary populist subculture, runs against the historical grain of economic globalization. The localized militarism and deep, often irrational anti-politics of the extreme right clashes with the globalizing priorities of the elites, who remain committed to economic rationalization and political order on a large scale.

The ruling elites are more likely to use the terrorism of the populist right as an occasion to repress opposition in general in the name of the state than enter into an explicit alliance with the anti-statist reactionary populist groups. The danger that reactionary populist groups pose for the left is not that they are about to turn into successful fascist parties. It is rather that they could have the effect of inducing a 'state of emergency' response from the state which will fail to discriminate (indeed may be only too ready not to try to discriminate) between right wing terrorism and legitimate left-wing political activity. In this way, even if the fate of reactionary populism is long-term political oblivion, the violence it spawns can nonetheless help to perpetuate a political climate in which progressive social change is stymied.

NOTES

1. See, for example, the recent work of Walter Laqueur, *Fascism: Past, Present, Future* (New York: Oxford University, 1997); Zeev Sternhell, *The Birth of Fascist Ideology* (Princeton, NJ.: Princeton University, 1994); and Roger Griffin, *The Nature of Fascism* (New York: Pinter, 1993).
2. Hans Magnus Enzensberger, *Civil Wars: from LA. to Bosnia* (New York: New Press, 1993).
3. See David H. Bennett, *The Party of Fear* (New York: University of North Carolina, 1995).
4. On the Koresh phenomenon within the Branch Davidians, see Marc Breault and Martin King, *Inside the Cult* (New York: Clarendon, 1993).
5. E. J. Hobsbawm, *Primitive Rebels* (New York: University Press, 1959), chs. 4–6.
6. Ibid., pp. 68–70.
7. William W. Zellner, *Countercultures* (New York: St. Martin's, 1995), ch. 1.
8. Ibid., p. 52.
9. Ibid., p. 67.
10. See Chip Berlet and Matthew N. Lyons, 'Militia Nation', *The Progressive* (June 1995).
11. James William Gibson, *Warrior Dreams* (New York: Hill and Wang, 1994).
12. Douglas Kellner, *The Persian Gulf TV War* (Boulder: Westview, 1992).
13. Gibson, *Warrior Dreams,* Introduction.
14. Ibid., p. 11.

MAKING SENSE OF NATO'S WAR ON YUGOSLAVIA

PETER GOWAN

ALTHOUGH EVERYBODY has had to work out where they stand on NATO's seventy-eight-day air war against Yugoslavia, they have had to do so in a context of scarce and selective information. In the English-speaking world there have been few books on the Kosovo background or on contemporary Serbian politics.[1] But no less important has been the absence of reliable information about the NATO side of the war. The diplomacy leading up to the war was, of course, shrouded in secrecy. The formal decision to launch the air war was, for example, taken by NATO's North Atlantic Council but we do not even know the decision rules which NATO now applies for taking military action outside the area of the NATO states.[2] The same secrecy applies to much of the conduct of the war and not least to its diplomatic side. Therefore in the case of this extremely important event for the future not only of the Balkans and of Europe but of the whole world, a wise policy would be one which recognizes that our initial judgements on the NATO air campaign should be subject to revision in the light of further research and of information released now that the war is over.

What is beyond doubt is that the launching of the NATO air war was the result of American diplomacy and in particular of the policy of the US Secretary of State, Madeleine Albright, supported by the National Security Council and President Clinton. Albright led a diplomatic campaign from the beginning of March 1998 on the issue of Kosovo, a campaign that culminated in the NATO action which began on 24th March 1999. The Clinton administration's Balkan experts seem to have been unenthusiastic about the Albright approach and so was the Pentagon. The Russian government, of course, but also most of the

European allies of the United States were, for most of this year-long campaign, in disagreement with the Albright approach. But in late January 1999 the British and French governments swung over to a policy of support for the Albright effort and this change of line in London and Paris was decisive in opening the way to the NATO attack on Yugoslavia. Neither the German nor the Italian governments, both of which had been prominent opponents of the Albright approach, felt able to stand out against the NATO action without the support of France. They therefore went along with the decision to launch the attack.

Thus to understand the background to the war we have to understand the character of the American State Department's aims. There are broadly speaking two approaches to this question. One approach begins with the proposition that the Clinton administration was reacting to events in the Western Balkans. This approach further suggests that the central pre-occupation of the US government in its reactive policy was the plight of the Kosovar Albanians. The war was launched as a humanitarian effort on their behalf.

This reading of the war does not, of course, exclude the possibility that wider political considerations played their part in US State Department thinking, but it suggests that these wider political benefits were perceived as spin-offs from the local humanitarian cause: the spin-offs could include new international moral authority for the US as a champion of human rights, the unification of NATO around a new approach to the use of force outside the NATO area on humanitarian military missions and, of course, domestic political benefits for President Clinton himself. On this reading, the hostility of the Russian government and the reluctance of West European governments could be read as a refusal to take human rights seriously, perhaps because of their continued attachment to traditional power politics based on state interest, narrowly conceived.

Some critics argue that US policy was governed by political objectives in the Balkans, but that these political objectives were traditional ones: to turn the Balkans into a strategic bridgehead for the US, providing it with military bases there, perhaps as staging posts en route to the Black and Caspian Seas or perhaps to shore up control over the Western shores of the Black Sea as part of US oil route security strategy; or in some interpretations, the US was interested in the valuable mineral resources of Kosovo itself. Yet these arguments seem weak. The US has ample staging posts to the Caspian through Turkey and it was already drawing Romania and Bulgaria into its security sphere. The Kosovar mineral deposits are surely not an adequate explanation, particularly since some of them are already Greek owned.

A more convincing alternative explanation of US policy in terms of local Balkan political objectives would be that Serbia under Milosevic and the Serbian Socialist Party was a local threat to US interests, particularly in Bosnia but perhaps more generally as an example of the possibility of resisting US-style free market capitalism. Yet despite the failure of the NATO's efforts at political integration in Bosnia, the Serbian government was not acting to disrupt that operation. There was no sign that Milosevic's influence was growing in other parts of the region, the Serbian economy was in a very bad state and the main regional threat to stability came from state collapse in Albania and growing Albanian nationalism in both Kosovo and Macedonia.

This absence of clearly discernible and strong US power politics objectives in the Western Balkans has played an important role in convincing some analysts that this NATO war really was about humanitarian issues in that region. There was no clear issue involving strategic resources (such as oil) or their transport routes. Nor was there a great strategic rivalry with a power like the Soviet Union of old. Of course, Russia had an involvement with Serbia and the NATO attack on Serbia was bound to enrage and humiliate the Russian state. But that inevitable effect was surely to be seen by NATO as a political cost of whatever goals the war had, rather than the very goal of the war. For once, therefore, so the argument runs, NATO really was taking human rights seriously in a particular locality, rather than imposing its strategic political interests upon a locality through aggressive war.

We will review the preparations for war and the war itself to explore this interpretation. We will then look at another way of understanding the NATO action, a way that has been largely absent from the public debates on the war and conclude with some thoughts on the possible consequences of the way the war ended.

I. PROBLEMS WITH THE MAINSTREAM VIEWS

1. The United Nations and Humanitarian Intervention

There is no serious dispute that from the standpoint of international law, the NATO attack on Yugoslavia was a legal violation of what have been cornerstones of the international order. The attack constituted a gross violation of Yugoslavia's sovereignty: it was an act of unprovoked aggression by a coalition of states against a sovereign state. It was thus a clear breach of the UN Charter and had no mandate whatever from the UN Security Council.

The decision to launch the war also involved gross and multiple violations of the new cornerstone agreement of 1997 between NATO and the Russian Federation, the so-called NATO–Russia Founding Act, designed to make NATO enlargement into Poland more acceptable to Russia by establishing certain restraints on NATO behaviour. Articles that were violated in that agreement include the following:

–   'NATO and Russia will observe in good faith their obligations under international law and international instruments, including the obligations of the United Nations Charter and the provisions of the Universal Declaration of Human Rights.'[3]

- 'NATO and Russia will co-operate to prevent any possibility of returning to a Europe of division and confrontation, or the isolation of any state.'
- 'This Act does not affect and cannot be regarded as affecting the primary responsibility of the UN Security Council for maintaining international peace and security.'
- Also the act commits both sides to 'refraining from the threat or use of force against each other as well as against any other state, its sovereignty, territorial integrity or political independence in any manner inconsistent with the United Nations Charter and with the Declaration of Principles Guiding Relations Between Participating States contained in the Helsinki Final Act.'

The US government and NATO said that the attack was nevertheless necessary because of a humanitarian disaster which was looming in Kosovo. In such circumstances, likened to the Rwandan genocide or to Nazi genocide during the second world war, NATO argued that the legal norms of the international order must be set aside. The implication of this is first that horrors of a quite exceptional kind had taken place or were about to take place in Kosovo; and second that neither the Russian nor the Chinese governments would have been prepared to respond adequately to these horrors by approving a UNSC resolution for intervention to stop them.

This NATO argument is not, of course, sustainable in a reactive sense: however awful the war between the KLA and the Serbian security forces in Kosovo had been during 1998 and early 1999, in international comparative terms it was a small-scale war. Deaths on both sides amounted to some 2,000 of which about half were Serbian. Deaths in nearby Turkey from the conflict involving the Kurds were about 30,000. Refugee figures were similarly far smaller in the case of Kosovo. Furthermore, the scale of the conflict had been reduced over the winter of 1998–99.[4]

But the basic justification for NATO's preparedness to violate international legal norms needs to be couched in pre-emptive terms, namely that if NATO had not acted, the Serbian government was preparing for a genocidal ethnic cleansing of Kosovo. Yet no evidence has been provided by NATO to demonstrate that the Serbian government had such a policy before the war started. It was therefore of great political importance for the US administration to be able to demonstrate during the war that Serbian government actions in Kosovo were genocidal and thus justified NATO's flouting of the UN.

And in weighing up the arguments, we should bear in mind that the United States government was already committed before the war to freeing NATO military operations from UN control and legality. It was a requirement of the Senate resolution ratifying NATO enlargement that NATO should not be constrained by UN authority and the US and Britain had already been openly flouting UN Security Council authority in their military actions against Iraq in 1998. Thus, if the humanitarian threat in Kosovo did justify NATO's undermining UN authority, it was certainly a happy coincidence that the US government happened to be inclined to undermine that authority in any case for quite other reasons.

The official explanation for and justification of the NATO war is, then, a quite specifically non-political one. It says that NATO was seeking to respond to the plight of the Kosovar Albanians and to save them from the murderous policies of the Serbian state. The strength of this argument lies in an unstated assumption, namely that a war against the Serbian state must be the other side of the coin of a war on behalf of its local enemy, the Kosovar Albanian population. NATO's war was unquestionably against the Serbian state. Therefore, it would appear that it was unquestionably on behalf of the Kosovar Albanians.

But this humanitarian standpoint then throws up the first set of contradictions: that between the supposed goal – protecting the Kosovo Albanians – and the means – a bombing campaign of a particular type which left the Serbian security forces free on the ground to do what they wished with the Kosovar Albanians.

When we look more closely at the way the war was actually launched this contradiction becomes very acute, indeed bizarre. The bombing campaign was launched on 24th March. But President Clinton announced on the 19th March that the bombing campaign would be launched and nothing now could block it. The US administration thus gave the Serbian government five days in which they could do as they pleased in Kosovo. And when the bombing started, it was organized so that the Serbian authorities could continue to have a completely free hand in Kosovo for more than a week. The air war's first phase was directed largely at targets outside the Kosovo theatre itself for a full week. At the same time, President Clinton ruled out a land war at the start of the campaign and this rejection was reiterated even more forcefully by Madeleine Albright on the third day of the war.

At the time when the war was launched, the Clinton administration legitimated this method of waging the war by claiming that President Milosevic actually wanted a deal along the lines of Rambouillet and the bombing campaign would enable him to sell Rambouillet to the Serbian electorate against the hard-line nationalists in Serbia. In other words, there was no threat from Serbia of atrocities, ethnic cleansing or genocide in the American administration's mind, so an air war was appropriate.

This notion that Milosevic himself accepted Rambouillet was, in reality, utterly false – pure spin. During the first week of the war Madeleine Albright argued that NATO had had to launch the war swiftly because they saw Serbian forces massing to enter Kosovo before 24th March. Serbian forces *were* massing there and indeed were pouring into Kosovo, but for the simple reason that they knew NATO was about to attack. And an important series of articles in the *Washington Post* at this time on the background to the war reveals that there was absolutely nothing improvised about its start. Indeed, the *Post* cites Clinton administration sources for its claim that over a full fourteen months the Clinton administration had been campaigning internationally to build a wide coalition for a war against Serbia on the Kosovo issue. These administration sources said the campaign was on the scale of the long US build-up to Desert Storm in 1990–1991. As an article by Barton Gellman published on the eve of the bombing campaign explains: 'Some critics have seen a lack of resolve in the successive warnings Washington has issued since [February 1998]. But what critics see as vacillation is described by policy makers in Washington as orchestration of international backing for military force, much as they said they accomplished in Iraq.'[5]

This is a very remarkable revelation and if true it casts the origins of the NATO war in a dramatically different light from the usual explanations which suggest the war came from a long and fruitless series of searches for negotiated solutions: a point to which we shall return. But the relevant point for the present discussion is the fact that the military-political planning of the air war was not in the slightest improvised. It was planned with meticulous care for over a year by thoroughly competent experts in the NSC. The *Washington Post* cited some of these experts as saying they spent a whole year in almost daily running of the tactics to be used in the war and the different variants of Serb and other responses to the different possible tactics. And these unnamed experts said that they foresaw very large floods of refugees being likely as the result of the air war tactics employed. Such experts could also obviously foresee that the air war would provoke intense warfare between Serbian security forces and suspected KLA activists in Kosovo. And all such wars produce atrocities, rapes, looting and burning: even highly trained solders can engage in wanton atrocities in war conditions. The tortures and other atrocities committed by NATO troops engaged in 'peacekeeping' in Somalia testify to that. All such developments could have been foreseen very easily by US war planners. And they could be foreseen regardless of the political orientation of the government in Belgrade. We also know that although Albright claimed that she expected the war to be over quickly the Pentagon foresaw and advised that it would be a long air war: the Serbian government would not surrender quickly.

In these circumstances, there is only one serious explanation for the tactics employed by the Clinton administration: these tactics did not put humanitarian considerations for the welfare of the Kosovar Albanians first. Such humanitarian considerations were put to one side and were put to one side with full deliberation and foresight.

So the question becomes: why this kind of air war? Why the disregard of the welfare of the Kosovar Albanians? Were there special reasons for this kind of air war? Is it conceivable that the planners could also foresee that TV pictures of the refugees and accounts of their harrowing ordeals as a result of the war could become a central means of sustaining public support for the continuation of the war? Only future documentary evidence will tell us if this was indeed the case.

2. The Political Programme of the War and the Kosovo National Question

One of the most remarkable aspects of the NATO war was that it was waged supposedly on behalf of the Kosovar Albanians against Serbia but *not on behalf of the Kosovar Albanians' political demands against Serbia*. On the contrary, NATO's stated political programme for Kosovo remained throughout more or less the same as the stated political programme for Kosovo of Slobodan Milosevic, for Kosovo to remain within Serbia but with very extensive internal autonomy. Neither of the two main rival leaderships amongst the Kosovar Albanian community – that of Ibrahim Rugova and that of the KLA – have supported that aim. Both have consistently demanded full independence for Kosovo. And the sufferings of the war have not resolved this core issue of the Kosovo national question. It has simply been postponed, to be the subject of future contestation, perhaps between NATO and elements within the Kosovar Albanian community.

This extraordinary mismatch between NATO's war enemy and allies on one side and NATO's war aims on the other, may be one explanation why the Clinton administration was so keen to keep war legitimation out of the political realm and within the purely humanitarian/moral realm. But it is surely the case that before we can come to an informed judgement about the war we need to make a prior analysis of the political conflict within Serbia, a conflict evidently to do with the national question.

The US administration's largely successful avoidance of a public debate centring on its programmatic stance on the Kosovo national question was allied to an at least implicit suggestion that there has not been a serious national problem in Serbia at all: instead there has been a Milosevic problem. Milosevic, in other words, has been the source of the conflict between Kosovar Albanians and Serbs.

While the other national conflicts that have engulfed the former Yugoslavia in the last decade have had their origins in the crisis of the Yugoslav state, the Kosovo problem has been different: it has its origin in the very inclusion of Kosovo in Yugoslavia and it was a problem when post-war Yugoslavia was not in crisis. Kosovo was a problem of Yugoslavia itself, or, put more historically, a problem left by the collapse of the Ottoman Empire in the Balkans. Kosovo was the birthplace of nineteenth-century Albanian nationalism, yet for political and military reasons it ended up in Serbian hands just before World War I.[6]

The inter-war Serbian monarchy sought to Serbianize Kosovo. Under German–Italian wartime occupation anti-Serbian Albanian forces took their revenge on the Serbian population and Kosovo itself was integrated into an Italian-controlled Albania. Kosovo Albanians formed an SS division to fight against the Communist-led partisans on behalf of the German Reich.

The new post-war Communist Yugoslavia lacked significant support in the Kosovar Albanian community and had to crush anti-Yugoslav resistance there when the new Yugoslavia was being created in 1945. Tito had a solution for Kosovo in a Balkan federation that would include Albania and Bulgaria. But this solution was aborted by the Tito–Stalin split. Kosovo remained, therefore, an autonomous province of Serbia. Despite the fact that it achieved substantial economic development within this framework, important segments of Kosovar Albanian society never accepted post-war Yugoslavia and always wanted out. During the 1950s and 1960s such separatist currents were harshly repressed.

After the fall of the strongly anti-separatist Rankovic in 1966, Kosovo Albanians were granted increasingly far-reaching political autonomy and polit-ical power within Yugoslavia. The 1974 constitution gave Kosovo far more extensive power within the Yugoslav federation than was enjoyed by other national minorities in Europe. The Albanian-led Kosovo Communist Party had, for example, veto rights within the Yugoslav federal executive. But still this extensive cultural and political autonomy and power did not bring an end to Kosovo Albanian separatism. By the start of the 1980s, Albanian separatist currents included not only anti-Communist trends on the right but also leftist trends among students and young intellectuals looking to Enver Hoxha's Albania as an egalitarian and national model. And there was significant and effective pres-sure from the Kosovar Albanians on the Serbian minority to leave Kosovo.

These problems came to a head in 1981, when widespread riots and distur-bances took place in Kosovo. The main demands of this protest movement were for Kosovo to achieve full Republican status within Yugoslavia. But the real significance of this demand lay not in the addition of new powers for Kosovo within the Yugoslav federation: the 1974 Constitution gave Kosovo all the effective policy autonomy enjoyed by full republics. The demand for republican status was seen both by the leaders of the protest movement and by the Yugoslav security forces as a demand for the right of Kosovo to secede from the federation. The Yugoslav authorities intervened to crush such separatist tendencies.

In the course of the riots in 1981, Serbs and Montenegrins in Kosovo were beaten, their homes and businesses burned, and their shops looted.[7] Also a mysterious fire was started at one of Serbia's most cherished religious shrines, the Pec Patriarchate in Kosovo, a complex of medieval churches and the histor-ical seat of the patriarch of the Serbian Orthodox Church.[8] Thousands of Serbs fled Kosovo following the violence. Pressure from Albanian nationalists on the Serbian minority in Kosovo continued during the 1980s. Some authors have tried to claim that the Serbian minority and Serb nationalists exaggerated or even fabricated claims of pressure and that the Serb emigration from Kosovo was largely an economic migration.[9] But Miranda Vickers and other authors have shown that this was not in fact the case. There was substantial pressure on the Serbian minority to leave. Vickers has concluded: 'many Serbs and Montenegrins who decided to leave Kosovo [in the 1980s] had experienced intimidation, pressure, violence, and other severe abuses of their human rights because of their ethnicity.'[10]

The Kosovo Serbs appealed to the Serbian Communist Party to protect them against harassment. The deputy leader of the Serbian League of

Communists, Milosevic, eventually pledged to ensure that the Serbian minority would be protected – a view subsequently presented in the West as a turn on Milosevic's part towards Serbian chauvinism. But in Serbia Milosevic's stance was viewed as that of a Communist finally ready to defend the national and civil rights of the Serbian minority in Kosovo.

In the late 1980s, this long-standing problem of Kosovar Albanian hostility to continued incorporation within Slav Yugoslavia became intertwined with the crisis of the Yugoslav state itself. This generalized crisis was marked by a number of overlapping features: a deep socio-economic crisis and a deep social conflict over whether Yugoslavia should go capitalist; strong separatist tendencies in Slovenia, later replicated in Croatia; and an attempt on the part of the Milosevic-led Serbian League of Communists to strengthen Serbia's political weight within the federation by abolishing the 1974 autonomy of Voivodina and Kosovo and to use this increased weight to hold the Yugoslav federation together in an alliance with the Yugoslav armed forces.

Under Milosevic's policy, Kosovo was to be allowed only the pre-1974 autonomy. Though this was, in legal terms, still extensive, the downgrading of Kosovo autonomy was viewed by the Kosovo Albanians as a denial of their national aspirations and led to a political confrontation between the Serbian government and all the main political forces in Kosovo. The Serbian government purged the provincial administration, installing Serbian officials, and also purged part of the management of the state industries to place them in Serbian hands. During the 1990s Kosovo was in a permanent state of emergency involving repression of militant separatist political activity. Repression was particularly severe in the smaller towns and in the countryside, especially after the KLA began its guerrilla campaign in 1996. There were, by the start of 1998, many cases reported of beatings by Serbian police, brutalities against prisoners and even the use of torture against KLA suspects.[11]

Although Kosovar Albanians retained their language rights in education and other areas, they were also required to pass exams in Serbo-Croatian. The University of Pristina was closed for a while and although independent Albanian newspapers were allowed, there were restrictions on the media. Kosovo Albanians retained their voting rights, but in the context of the denial of full 1974 autonomy for the province and the repression of various separatist groups, the Albanians responded through a boycott of Serbian state institutions and the organization of a parallel set of Albanian civil society and governance structures under the leadership of Ibrahim Rugova, a leadership overwhelmingly backed by the Kosovo population and demanding independence for Kosovo.[12]

The Kosovo problem was then, a long-term structural one centred on the question of independence and separation. The obvious solution to the problem lay in enabling the Kosovar Albanian community to merge with the Albanians of Albania and of Macedonia within a single political framework, the optimal one being a wider Balkan federation as the Yugoslav Communists had proposed in the 1940s. At the same time, the rights of the Serbian minority could have been guaranteed. Alternatively, some other mutually agreed solution involving a confederal relationship between Kosovo and Yugoslavia in the context of other changes in Yugoslavia itself could have been, in principle, possible.

But such co-operative solutions were not available in the late 1980s and the 1990s because of the crisis in, and break-up of, the Yugoslav state, and because of the political orientations of the Western powers towards Yugoslavia.

3. The US's Reactive, Mediating Posture and the Reality of its War Drive from the Start of 1998

Although the Clinton administration has systematically presented Slobodan Milosevic and the Serbian Socialist Party as genocidal ethnic cleansers and so on, they have been well aware of the fact that the Serbian Socialist Party could support an agreement involving radical internal autonomy for Kosovo. It is true that although a very large minority of Serbia's population had, by early 1990, swung over towards extreme ethnic nationalist politics such as those espoused by Seselj's Radical Party, this was not at all the position of Milosevic. Here indeed, was the convincing element in the mendacious NATO spin at the start of the war, that Milosevic actually wanted the bombing campaign to gain agreement to Rambouillet. The West European states knew very well that a negotiated settlement based on autonomy for Kosovo within Serbia was possible as far as the Serbian government was concerned.

Such a negotiated settlement had also been a possibility as far as Rugova was concerned. Although Ibrahim Rugova had always demanded independence for Kosovo, he was prepared to enter negotiations with the Serbian government in the spring of 1998 and in the late summer of 1998 he indicated that he was prepared to set aside his demand for independence for the sake of an end to the conflict. Rugova had been re-elected by the Kosovar Albanians as their leader by a huge majority in March 1998. On both sides, therefore, there was the basis at least in principle for a deal.

This potentiality was reinforced by the stance of the Russian government and that of most of the West European governments: they wanted a cease-fire between the KLA and the Serbian security forces, followed by a negotiated internal settlement.

During the NATO war itself, NATO leaders frequently said that they had tried everything short of war to get a negotiated settlement but all their efforts had been thwarted because of Milosevic. Yet the record of events suggests a different story. It was the US Secretary of State whose actions and words over fourteen months undermined the possibility of a negotiated settlement and led through Rambouillet into a NATO war which, according to the *Washington Post,* the Clinton administration had been working for since February 1998.

We cannot here survey all the evidence but some key turning points need to be borne in mind by anyone wishing to make an objective assessment of the causes of the NATO war.

A. The start of the campaign

At Christmas 1997, President Clinton warned that unless the Serbian government moved to solve the Kosovo crisis, the US would be prepared to intervene militarily. In January and February 1998, the KLA launched a major military effort within Kosovo against Serbian officials and also Serbian civilians. As Gary Dempsey explains: 'Pursuing a textbook strategy, the KLA carried out attacks on police and civilians aimed at provoking a government crackdown that would radicalize the ethnic Albanian population in Kosovo...'[13] In February 1998, the KLA targeted Serb houses in the villages of Kloina, Decani and Djakovica and a Serb refugee camp in Babaloc.[14]

There then followed a very curious incident. Madeleine Albright's Special Envoy in the Balkans, Robert Gelbard, flew into Pristina on 23rd February and held a press conference, in which, according to Robert Thomas, 'he praised Milosevic in lavish terms and described the UCK as a terrorist organization'.[15] The BBC correspondent in Yugoslavia quoted Gelbard as follows: ' "I know a terrorist when I see one and these men are terrorists," he said... At the time, the KLA was believed to number just several hundred armed men. Mr Gelbard's words were interpreted in the Yugoslav capital, Belgrade, as a green light for a security forces operation against the KLA and the special police conducted two raids in the Benitsa region in March.' Robert Thomas confirms this, saying that Milosevic interpreted 'Gelbard's gesture as a "green light" for a security crackdown in Kosovo'.[16]

A few days later, on 28th February 1998, the KLA killed four policemen in the Banitsar region and injured two more. On 5th March, Serbian security forces then launched a major counter-insurgency drive in Banitsar against the Jashari clan which was leading the KLA in that region and many members of the clan were killed. This news was reported on 6th March. The very next day, on 7th March 1998, in response to the Serbian security force operation in the Benitsar region of Kosovo, Madeleine Albright declared, 'We are not going to stand by and watch the Serbian authorities do in Kosovo what they can no longer get away with doing in Bosnia.'[17] Two days later she reserved the right for the US to take unilateral action against the Serbian government, saying, 'We know what we need to know to believe we are seeing ethnic cleansing all over again.'[18] This remained the US line right the way through from that first Serbian counter-insurgency drive against the KLA in Benitsar. Albright demanded war against Serbia. But the signal for the Serbian government to launch its counter-insurgency in Benistar also, intriguingly, came from Albright's own State Department.

B. Albright's strong support for the KLA and the undermining of Ibrahim Rugova

In the Spring of 1998 Richard Holbrooke arranged for negotiations to open between Ibrahim Rugova and the Serbian government. But within a month the US government was undermining Rugova's position by placing demands upon Serbia that indicated one unambiguous conclusion: the US government was seeking to strengthen the position of the KLA in the civil war in Kosovo.

The KLA was, of course, completely opposed to any negotiations with the Serbian government. By entering negotiations with that government Ibrahim Rugova was therefore taking a great political risk. He presumably took that risk on the assumption that the US government, which, in the form of Holbrooke, supported the negotiations, would help to strengthen his position. And that meant the Clinton administration distancing itself from the KLA. Yet the Clinton administration did the exact opposite.

US effective support for the KLA became blatant by June 1998, by which time NATO military planning for an attack on Yugoslavia was completed. In that month, White House spokesperson Mike McCurry asserted that Serbia 'must immediately withdraw security units involved in civilian repression, without linkage to … the stopping of terrorist activity.'[19] In parallel, Pentagon spokesperson Kenneth Bacon said: 'We don't think that there should be any linkage between an immediate withdrawal of forces by the Yugoslavs on the one hand, and stopping terrorist activities, on the other. There ought to be complete withdrawal of military forces so that negotiations can begin.' In other words, Washington was insisting that before any cease-fire or negotiations on a Kosovo peace settlement the Serbian authorities must withdraw all their forces from Kosovo, handing over the territory to the KLA's military forces despite the fact that the urban Albanian population of Kosovo was far more pro-Rugova than the KLA. Furthermore, while the Serbian forces were supposed to be withdrawing, KLA activity could continue, and indeed increase.

A similar pattern of Holbrooke moving in one direction, and the leadership of the administration moving in the opposite direction, occurred in October 1998. On 13th October Richard Holbrooke negotiated a cease-fire agreement with Yugoslav President Milosevic. The cease-fire would be monitored in Kosovo by OSCE observers. Milosevic agreed on the basis that the US administration would ensure that the KLA observed the cease-fire.

But the Clinton administration sabotaged the whole operation. The OSCE monitors did not enter Kosovo for a whole month after the agreement. During that time, the KLA did not respect the cease-fire, continued its operations and extended its reach in Kosovo. During the delay, the Clinton administration took control of the OSCE, placing William Walker, a key organizer of the Contra operation in Nicaragua and the blood-bath in El Salvador, in charge of the OSCE monitoring force. Some 2,000 trained monitors waiting in Bosnia to be sent into Kosovo were not drafted in and the US eventually put in ex-military personnel as monitors, people subsequently accused of acting as intelligence gatherers and operatives for NATO, very much along the lines of the US's perversion of UNSCOM's teams in Iraq – reporting on every item that could be relevant to a future NATO-KLA joint offensive.[20]

At the same time the European-Russian-UN line continued to seek an internal solution and to blame the KLA for the failure to achieve it. Thus, for example, at their General Affairs Council on 8th December 1998, Britain's Robin Cook and the other foreign ministers of the EU assessed the situation in Kosovo. The report of the meeting in the *Agence Europe Bulletin* of the following day stated: 'At the close of its debate on the situation in the Western Balkans, the General Affairs Council mainly expressed concern for the recent "intensification of military action" in Kosovo, noting that "increased activity by the KLA has prompted an increased presence of Serbian security forces in the region".' Thus, the EU saw the KLA as the driving force undermining the possibility of a cease-fire and a compromise solution. They were simply on a different line from Albright, and they continued to be right through January.[21]

C. Turning the Rambouillet negotiations into an ultimatum, while overthrowing the Rugova leadership

The idea of bringing the two sides together into face to face negotiations under international auspices came from the French government. The Clinton administration had been against such an idea, favouring a straight move towards bombing. But on this occasion, the differences were overcome in favour of the French getting their way on the *form* while the US would get its way on the *substance*. This was a turning point. The French and British switched over to the US position at a meeting of the contact group in London on 29th January 1999, exactly a week before the opening on 6th February of the Rambouillet 'negotiations'.[22] From that moment on the NATO attack on Yugoslavia was a virtual certainty. We can see why when we appreciate that the Rambouillet 'negotiations' were not negotiations at all: they were an ultimatum to the Serbian government which was drafted in such a way as to ensure that it would be rejected.

The Serbian government wanted face-to-face negotiations at Rambouillet with the Kosovo representatives. This the Americans absolutely refused, presumably with British and French support (since they were formally supposed to be in charge of the process). It is also fairly clear that there were some on the Kosovo side who were interested in discussing with the Serbian authorities. Why else would the Clinton administration have decided to overthrow the elected Rugova government of Kosovo and replace it with a KLA-led government, there and then at Rambouillet?

The Serbian side was then required to agree to the 'Agreement' without changing it, or face a NATO attack on Yugoslavia. If the Serbian government had signed the 'Agreement' the signature would have had no status in international law, since treaties signed under threat of aggression have no force in international law. But the Serbian authorities, probably wisely, did not have any confidence in their ability to rely upon international law, so they refused to sign.

Most people assume that the Serbian government refused to sign because the 'Agreement' would lead to the independence of Kosovo. The 'Agreement' did involve a *de facto* NATO Protectorate. (Not by the way a democratic entity;

the Chief of the Implementation Force could dictate on any aspect of policy he considered relevant to NATO – i.e., US – concerns.) Yet after the first round of Rambouillet it appeared that the Serbian government might accept the text with which it was presented.

Matters changed dramatically, however, at the start of the second phase of the Rambouillet process. The Serbian government representatives were confronted then with a new text, introduced by the US government: Annex B. The origins of this initiative and the mechanisms by which it occurred remain obscure. We do not know if the French government was in favour of the inclusion of the new annex. We do not know if the US arranged that the annex was the precondition for the KLA to approve the deal as a whole. But this text, which remained secret until the war was well under way, contained an exact repetition of the key sticking point of the Austro-Hungarian ulti-matum to Serbia which triggered the first world war: the demand that NATO forces could move freely across the whole territory of Yugoslavia and could do so with impunity.[23] This was a direct threat to the Serbian and Yugoslavian state. It is worth quoting these aspects of the Rambouillet text in some detail, bearing in mind the evidence from the *Washington Post* quoted earlier to the effect that the Clinton administration had indeed been campaigning for a war against Serbia by NATO for a full year.

– *NATO forces could move at will across the whole of Yugoslavia.* Thus, 'NATO personnel shall enjoy, together with their vehicles, vessels, aircraft, and equipment, free and unrestricted passage and unimpeded access throughout the FRY [Federal Republic of Yugoslavia] including associated airspace and territorial waters. This shall include, but not be limited to, the right of bivouac, manoeuvre, billet, and utilization of any areas or facilities as required for support, training, and operations.'

– *NATO would have the right to deploy in Kosovo whatever types of forces it wished:* 'NATO will establish and deploy a force (hereinafter KFOR) which may be composed of ground, air, and maritime units from NATO and non-NATO nations, operating under the authority and subject to the direction and the political control of the North Atlantic Council (NAC) through the NATO chain of command. The Parties agree to facilitate the deployment and operations of this force.' Thus, if the US wished to use Kosovo as a base for the invasion and occupation of the rest of Yugoslavia, it could do so.

– *NATO could also alter the infrastructure of Yugoslavia at will:* 'NATO may ... have need to make improvements or modifications to certain infrastruc-tures in the FRY, such as roads, bridges, tunnels, buildings, and utility systems.' It could thus move around investigating all Yugoslav infrastruc-tures with a view to destroying them later if it wished.

- *All Yugoslav public facilities including the mass media should be at NATO's disposal free of charge.* Thus the Yugoslav authorities 'shall provide, free of cost, such public facilities as NATO shall require.' The Yugoslav authorities 'shall, upon simple request, grant all telecommunications services, including broadcast services, needed for the Operation, as determined by NATO. This shall include the right to utilize such means and services as required to assure full ability to communicate ... free of cost. NATO is granted the use of airports, roads, rails, and ports without payment of fees, duties, dues, tolls, or charges occasioned by mere use.' The Yugoslav authorities must not merely tolerate this: they must facilitate it. 'The authorities in the FRY shall facilitate, on a priority basis and with all appropriate means, all movement of personnel, vehicles, vessels, aircraft, equipment, or supplies, through or in the airspace, ports, airports, or roads used. No charges may be assessed against NATO for air navigation, landing, or take-off of aircraft, whether government-owned or chartered. Similarly, no duties, dues, tolls or charges may be assessed against NATO ships, whether government-owned or chartered, for the mere entry and exit of ports.' The ultimatum also demonstrated that NATO was determined to intervene within the Serbian media. It demanded 'Free media, effectively accessible to registered political parties and candidates, and available to voters throughout Kosovo.' And it said that 'The IM [Implementation Mission] shall have its own broadcast frequencies for radio and television programming in Kosovo. The Federal Republic of Yugoslavia shall provide all necessary facilities...'

- *The US through NATO and the IMF/World Bank would dictate, not negotiate, the socio-economic programme in Kosovo* – which must be on free market principles – with the Yugoslav and Kosovo governments completely under the diktat of US policies. Thus, 'The economy of Kosovo shall function in accordance with free market principles.' And, 'There shall be no impediments to the free movement of persons, goods, services, and capital to and from Kosovo.' And again, 'Federal and other authorities shall within their respective powers and responsibilities ensure the free movement of persons, goods, services, and capital to Kosovo, including from international sources.' There must also be complete compliance with the IMF and World Bank. Thus, 'International assistance, with the exception of humanitarian aid, will be subject to full compliance with ... conditionalities defined in advance by the donors and the absorptive capacity of Kosovo.' The Yugoslav government must also agree to Western multinational companies being given the contracts for programmes in Serbia chosen by the international financial institutions. Thus, 'If expressly required by an international donor or lender, international contracts for reconstruction projects shall be concluded by the authorities of the Federal Republic of Yugoslavia.'

Rambouillet was thus an ultimatum for a war against Serbia and the terms of the ultimatum demonstrated that if the Serbian government accepted Rambouillet they would be vulnerable to a crushing attack in the future from NATO forces on Yugoslav soil.

It would be wrong to imagine that all the agencies within the Clinton administration and the American state supported the Albright policy of preparing the Western Balkans and the whole of Europe for an air war against Yugoslavia. There is a good deal of evidence that the administration's two leading Balkan specialists, Richard Holbrooke and Christopher Hill, were against Albright's approach. But it is equally true that Albright ran the diplomacy leading to war and Holbrooke and Hill, with their divergent styles, actually assisted the implementation of the policy through their effectively diversionary approaches at certain key moments.

And the evidence suggests both that a negotiated settlement of the national question could have been achieved and that the Clinton administration actively sought to undermine the conditions which made such a settlement possible. The administration undermined Rugova and gave active encouragement to the KLA campaign. Then it said that Rugova was too weak to strike a deal, then they engineered his replacement by a KLA-led interim government. Then they dictated an ultimatum to Serbia which was crafted to ensure rejection. And all the while the political programme of the US government on the cardinal political issue – the Kosovo national question – was most *opposed* to the programme of the KLA for a Greater Albania, and closest to that of Serbia. This war drive, whatever it was about, was absolutely not about safeguarding the welfare of the Albanians living in Kosovo in March 1999.

The more we examine the origins of this war the more we find ourselves in the midst of a very murky affair. At a gathering of intellectuals at the Marc-Bloc Foundation in Paris on 29th May 1999, Claude Lanzmann, the producer of *Shoah,* the documentary account of the Holocaust, spoke. He said that the NATO attack on Yugoslavia was a new Dreyfus Affair.[24] It was. But in this case the question is: what were the anti-Dreyfusards of Europe in 1999 up to? Why did they want this appalling war?

II. A THEORY OF A GEOPOLITICAL NATO WAR DIRECTED AT THE NATO ZONE ITSELF

An alternative take on the origins of the NATO war against Yugoslavia starts from the fact that the war did not derive from big power *reactions* to local events in the Balkans at all. Instead, this theory starts from the premise that the Clinton administration was seeking a war against Yugoslavia as a means for achieving political goals outside the Balkans altogether. The conflict between the Serbian state and the Kosovar Albanians was to be exploited as a means to achieve US strategic goals outside the Balkans on the international plane.

As we saw at the start of this essay there was one weakness in the argument that NATO had strategic political goals outside the Balkans for whose achievement a victory over Serbia would be valuable. The weakness was that nobody could identify any such credible NATO geopolitical goals. But this weakness only applies on one condition, namely that we treat NATO as basically a unitary actor, with common goals and interests. This is a deeply held assumption in public discourse within NATO-land. NATO is a 'we', the West, united in common values, etc. For decades during the Cold War we got used to the West acting as one in European politics. But we need to ask whether that unity carried over into the post-Soviet Europe of the 1990s. And if it did not, then a new set of questions, unexamined at the start of this essay, needs to be addressed. For example, did the Clinton administration have any conceivable political objectives in *Western Europe, within the NATO area itself,* whose achievement could be assisted through a successful war against Serbia? If so what were these objectives? What interests would Britain and France have had in doing their political somersault in late January 1999 to join the US in pulling the whole of NATO behind the air war? And why was an *air* war and, it seems, only an air war, so useful for the Clinton administration in this political context?

A glance at the history of European–American relations during the 1990s should demonstrate that on one European political question there was no agreement between the US and the French and German governments. That question has been an absolutely fundamental one. What should be the new political order in Europe after the Soviet Bloc and Soviet collapse? It is not usually addressed directly. Instead it is discussed intensively in languages of security or of military concepts and technicalities with headings and jargon such as a 'reform of NATO', a 'Two Pillar NATO or a Two Pillar Alliance', a 'European Security and Defence Identity', 'NATO out of area or out of business', 'separable but not separate' European military forces and the organization of 'Combined Joint Task Forces'. But behind this jargon has lain a fundamental political debate about the future power structure – in other words political structure of the European space. And it has not only been a debate.

This basic European political question arose because of the double-sided and paradoxical results of the Soviet collapse. On one side it made the United States overwhelmingly the most powerful power in resource terms, especially military resources. But simultaneously it destroyed the political structure through which US power resources could be converted into stable hegemony over Western Europe. That political structure had been Western Europe's security dependence on the US–Soviet relationship. The US–Soviet confrontation meant that the fate of Western Europe depended on decisions taken in Washington. This in turn ensured that the West European states, including the French, accepted US leadership on all fundamental European, and indeed world, questions. But without the US–Soviet confrontation this political structure collapsed. The institutions that expressed the structure – above all NATO – did not collapse. But NATO became an institution without a purpose. It was organized for defence against a military opponent which had disappeared. As such it was doomed to die, and with it could die the US's influence over the West European states' international orientation. The West European states would still, of course, respect America's overwhelming power resources. And there were also shared interests in managing world politics and economic affairs for mutual advantage. But the West European states could now hope to start doing their own thing, especially in the new field opening up east of the European Union.

During the 1990s, both the Bush administration and the Clinton administration have been working extremely energetically to build a new political structure ensuring the return of the United States to hegemonic leadership in Europe. We will not review all the steps in that campaign here.[25] But we will very briefly outline the central issue, the main elements in the US programme for restored hegemony, and the ways in which the tussle between the US and West European states was fought out.

1. The Central Political Issue

The central political issue can be briefly stated as follows: which Western power or coalition of Western powers could lead the other states of Europe in resolving important European political problems? Would it be France plus Germany through an increasingly integrated EU with its own defence and security authority and instruments as well as its economic statecraft? Or would it be the United States? These were the only two choices as far as the Western powers were concerned. Britain, for example, could not add its own positive variant: it could only act as a spoiler of the other two possible variants (and in practice acted as a spoiler mainly of the Franco–German variant but also, for a while in Bosnia, of the American variant).

This central political issue passed through several phases in the 1990s. At first the Franco–German variant seemed very strong, with the Maastricht Treaty involving EMU plus the Common Foreign and Security Policy. And Germany showed it had enough political weight to win recognition for Croatia, a major political issue of the day. Then the Franco–German variant weakened as the EU was unable to resolve the Bosnian conflict. The US programme strengthened as the US pushed ahead with the transformation of NATO into an entirely new organization, fitted, at least on paper, for ensuring US leadership and successfully insisting that there should be no separate European military policy authority or military command system outside NATO and US leadership. This phase included the US success in ending the Bosnia war and handling the Dayton agreement. Yet in the second half of the 1990s the revived US leadership of Europe was still not secure. The Franco–German EMU project forged ahead to the Euro's launch. This was likely to lead to a further deepening of the EU as a political bloc, perhaps even to a federal state with full, democratic will-formation and full political identity. And even within NATO, US leadership was not assured. The tussle with the French over the meaning of a so-called 'European Security and Defence Identity within NATO' was not yet resolved. The question of Russia's role in European affairs was not yet settled. Thus, though the West European states were going along with US leadership today, they still held in reserve instruments and potentialities for striking out autonomously. This was the situation in 1998 and early 1999 when the US was waging its diplomatic offensive for the NATO Kosovo war.

2. The US Programme for its Revived European Leadership

The key to the entire US programme was to transform the roles of NATO, to subordinate the West European states and multilateral institutions to NATO in the field of high politics and security, and to make NATO sovereign *vis-à-vis* the UN.

The transformation of NATO involved what Zbigniev Brzezinski calls the double enlargement: geographical enlargement into Poland and enlargement of NATO's military tasks from strategic defence to offensive strikes outside the NATO area. Both these changes are highly political.[26] NATO enlargement into Poland was simultaneously the exclusion of Russia from an institutionalized inclusion in Europe's high politics, since Russia was not to be allowed into NATO. But NATO's enlargement into Poland involved another crucial political element. On US insistence, NATO had to maintain the right to establish the bases of NATO powers (i.e., the US) and to position nuclear weapons in Poland. By insisting on this (while also insisting it had no current plans for actually doing either of these things) the US ensured that at any time it could create a state of emergency between Russia and Western and Central Europe simply by moving such weapons into Poland or by establishing a big US base there or by moving US forces up to the Polish border. This has the effect of giving the US control over the Russian-German and Russian-EU political relationship. A Russian-EU entente could jeopardize US leadership in Europe. Without a Russian-EU entente the West European powers could hardly risk a head to head stand-off with the United States. Such realities may sound brutal, but that is the way reality is with the kinds of states that lead the international system at the moment.

The second transformation of NATO involved giving it new missions to strike 'out of area' and providing it with the military forces for so doing. Only this change would ensure that NATO became once again a living military organization. The problem here, from the angle of the US government's political goal of establishing its European hegemony, was the following – to give NATO the kinds of strike missions that would require a central, leading military role *for American military assets*. Only if the West Europeans were dependent upon US military assets as they had been dependent on the US strategic arsenal during the Cold War would US military-political leadership of NATO be secure. The West Europeans would feel the need for military services that only the US could supply. Thus, the bigger and wider the 'out of area' mission statement the more assured was US military and therefore political dominance over NATO.

The third element in the US programme was to ensure that the European states and the EU, the WEU and the OSCE were all subordinated in the military policy and military command field to a US-led NATO. NATO had to have a monopoly of decision over the use of force in Europe, and the whole of Europe had to understand this.

The fourth element in the programme was to throw off the UN Security Council constraints on NATO decisions and actions. This was in one sense a logical corollary to the other elements in the programme but a vital one. If the US had untrammelled leadership within NATO but NATO was under UNSC authority, the French could challenge US leadership via the UNSC. If Russia was pushed out of institutionalized inclusion in European affairs but re-emerged at the centre of NATO's activities by exercising a veto over them in the UNSC, there would be no US-European hegemony.

3. The terrain on which the battle for US hegemony was fought out

To understand both the last decade of Yugoslav history and the battles over the new political structure of Europe, we have to understand the fact that the latter were in large part fought out within the former. Yugoslavia has been an absolutely central arena in which contending Western actors have sought to demonstrate to Europe and the world their capacity to lead Europe politically. And these contending actors have approached Yugoslav issues from this geopolitical angle. In particular, US behaviour in the Yugoslav theatre has been governed by its European strategic goal of blocking the emergence of Franco–German EU leadership and then of consolidating US leadership of European high politics.

In 1991 Hans Dietrich Genscher sought to demonstrate that Germany, not US military power, could settle a big difficult issue: the conflict between Yugoslavia and secessionist Croatia. Genscher triumphed on this in December 1991. As Lawrence Eagleberger, US Deputy Secretary of State for European affairs put it, Germany got ahead of the US on that issue.

But the Bush administration struck back by pushing the Bosnian government into a drive for an independent unitary Bosnia that the US administration knew, like all other informed observers, would lead to an atrocious war. At a meeting in Lisbon in March 1992 under the auspices of the EU the Bosnian Muslim government reached agreement with the Bosnian Croat and Bosnian Serb leaders to establish a confederal Bosnia based upon three ethnically based cantons. But as the *New York Times* later explained, the United States government persuaded Izetbegovic a week later to repudiate the agreement he had made 'and choose instead a sovereign Bosnia and Hercegovina under his presidency, saying that this was justified by the referendum on 1st March on independence. The problem with that referendum was that although the Bosnian Muslims and Croats overwhelmingly endorsed it, the Bosnian Serbs boycotted it, warning that was a prelude to civil war.'[27]

The resulting war was one that the EU tried to stop, but could not, because the Clinton administration did not wish the EU to be able to stop it and thus show its independent European leadership capacity. Paul Gebhard, Director for Policy Planning in the Pentagon, explains the position at this time. The West Europeans were trying to develop 'a European Security and Defence Identity in the WEU outside NATO. US criticism of European institutions, however, can only be credible if European policies are unsuccessful.'[28] As Gebhard explains, the key European goal in this effort was a Bosnian peace deal through the UN/EC Vance–Owen plan for Bosnia of 1993. He goes on: 'The EC claimed the lead in setting Western policy at the start of the Yugoslav crisis … The Europeans may have thought that Vance's participation as the US representative was sufficient to commit the US to whatever policy developed. By having a former Secretary of State on the team, they may have expected to bring the US into the negotiations without having to work with officials in Washington. This approach reflects a desire in European capitals for "Europe" to set the political agenda without official US participation on issues of European security.'

Gebhard goes on to describe the trip of Vance and Owen to Washington in February 1993 to try to persuade the US of their plan. 'Vance and Owen argued that the deal … was the best that could be crafted … Without its participation, the Clinton administration was not committed politically to the plan …' This is an understatement on Gebhard's part: the Clinton administration was committed politically *against* the plan because it was an independent EU plan. And by quietly undermining the plan it successfully undermined West European attempts at independent European leadership. As Gebhard explains, 'Because of the situation in Bosnia, the EC was unable to set the agenda for European security without the full participation of the United States … The political influence and military power of the US remain essential to security arrangements in Europe.' In short, US rhetoric was for a NATO military drive in defence of human rights against Serbia; but US policy on Bosnia was governed by the goal of demonstrating the ineffectiveness of the EU by sabotaging EU peace efforts. When that was done, the US Bosnian goal changed: to demonstrating with the US-led NATO offensive of 1995 that US leadership through NATO, and only that, could tackle Yugoslavia and thus lead Europe.

This framework for understanding the relationship between Yugoslav events and the intra-Western contest for European leadership then provides us with a new way of understanding the US campaign for the Kosovo war. It requires us to turn on its head the cognitive map used by the proponents of American humanitarian war. Thus, for example, instead of thinking that the US was ready to overthrow the authority of the UN Security Council for the sake of the Kosovar Albanians, we assume exactly the opposite: the US was wanting to overthrow that UN authority over NATO and used the Kosovo crisis as an instrument for doing so. Instead of imagining that the US was ready to shut Russia out of European politics for the sake of the Kosovar Albanians, we assume that the Clinton administration used the NATO attack on Yugoslavia precisely as an instrument for consolidating Russia's exclusion. And most crucially for understanding the absolute centrality of high-tech US air power as the central instrument of the seventy-eight-day air war, it was not a case of this US air power being an instrument used on behalf of the Kosovo Albanians; quite the reverse. The Kosovo Albanians' welfare interests were to be instrumentalized in order to demonstrate the efficacy of this unique US military asset to Europe and the world.

And last but not least, instead of assuming that the US firmly subordinated the West European states to its military and political leadership in order create a new dawn in the Western Balkans, it used a number of ingenious devices – especially the dilettantish vanity of messieurs Chirac and Jospin – to drag the West European states into a Balkan war that would consolidate US hegemony over them, turning the EU increasingly into a Euro–Atlantic sub-system.

III. THE ROLE OF FRANCE AND BRITAIN IN THE LAUNCH OF THE WAR AND THE ROLE OF GERMANY IN BRINGING IT TO AN END

The campaign for the Kosovo war was US-led from start to finish. But it would be very wrong to imagine that the US did it all on its own. Crucial to US goals was the fact that the war had to be a NATO war. That required one thing above everything else: French involvement. The Blair government, in this field, did not count: an Anglo–American operation opposed by a Franco–German led EU was a non-starter. But with France and Britain on board, Germany could not speak alone for Europe against an attack on Yugoslavia. The response from the American media would have been very straightforward, 'Germany opposes a war against genocide and ethnic cleansing. Given German history, nothing is more understandable.' Tony Blair's great contribution to the NATO war was to keep Hitler in high profile and thus keep Bonn in its place – for a while at least. But the French somersault in January 1999 needs explaining.

During the early 1990s, under President Mitterand, France had maintained its traditional Cold War posture of claiming European political leadership, if only Germany would break from the US and follow France. But this was an uncomfortable posture with a united Germany at the very centre (not to say the leadership) of European and transatlantic affairs. So President Chirac began to shift, first by waving French nuclear power through his Pacific nuclear tests. This was a mistake. So Chirac became interested in French reintegration into NATO as Europe's number one NATO power carving out a big new role for itself within the alliance (using the concept of the European security and defence identity). By 1997 this was beginning to reposition France between Germany and the United States, instead of being at one pole with Germany in the middle. Now France rather than Germany had the options. It could go with Germany (and Russia) on some issues, such as Iraq, against the Anglo-Americans. But it had a new range of options as well, to go with the British and the Americans in putting Germany 'in its place' (i.e. firmly under France). The US campaign for the Kosovo war offered France this option. Albright went further, and offered France the prestige craved by so many European leaders: a conference at Rambouillet, France, at the very heart of Europe's high politics.

But another background factor was the shift in the British government's posture on European defence. British governments throughout the 1990s had been resolutely hostile to the EU having any military role: all such matters had to be firmly under NATO. But once that principle had been won by the Americans, why not give the EU a military role as a subordinate arm of NATO? This thought gave the Blair government the basis for its turn. In the Autumn of 1998 it started supporting the idea of the EU having a military role, thus scrapping the notion that NATO's subordinate European instrument should be the WEU. The new Blair line enabled Britain to sound positive about a big EU 'field', the Common Foreign and Security field, and thus to claim a 'leadership' role for Britain in the EU.

This Blair turn, combined with the French turn towards a leading role in NATO laid the basis for the St Malo declaration of Blair and Chirac in December 1998, offering joint Anglo-French leadership in the military field for the EU. The first act of the new partnership was their gracious acceptance of the generous Albright offer that France and Britain might like joint chairmanship of Rambouillet. That did it. France and Britain were locked in to the Clinton administration's drive for war. The final touch was Annex B in the Rambouillet second round.

What is poorly understood is how the German government then brought the war to an end. Much of the intra-NATO politics during the war remains completely hidden from NATO electorates. But enough is known to make some rough outline of the main events along the following lines.

From very early on in the war the German government began its diplomacy to end it. As holders of the EU Presidency, Bonn produced a cease-fire and peace plan differing from the American terms. It hoped to line up the EU member states behind the plan. The Blair government leaked the plan to the media, saying it was just a discussion document. The aim was to get the German government to disown its own plan. Schroder refused to disown it. The question was whether Chirac would back Schroder. He refused, saying France had a different plan of its own (though it never surfaced). The German government then turned to Moscow and began intensive efforts to craft a German–Russian position for an end to the war which did not contradict the NATO position but did not endorse it either, and which brought the UN back into the picture. This time Bonn and Moscow used the G8 framework. And in the first week of May this tactic worked. The US officials at the G8 did not feel able to denounce the plan. But the tactic worked only for a day. Then the US air force hit the Chinese Embassy in Belgrade with five missiles. That sank German–Russian diplomacy for three more weeks of bombing. But when

Schroder flew to Peking he learned the full details of the American bombing of the embassy from the Chinese, and he decided to use those details.

Meanwhile, the German government was developing a new axis of its diplomacy: Bonn–Belgrade, via a secret Swedish intermediary. The Russian government was also involved. Thoroughly briefed by German state officials, this intermediary then thoroughly briefed Yugoslav President Milosevic on what was really going on within NATO. Through this channel a deal was struck secretly between Bonn and Serbia. The problem then was to make the deal stick and prevent another sabotage by Washington. First Schroder issued his threat. He demanded a public enquiry into the bombing of the Chinese embassy. This was a way of saying that he was ready to polarize NATO on that issue unless Washington backed the German peace deal. At the same time, Schroder assembled the heads of government of the European Union in Cologne for the EU Council meeting and simultaneously sent the Finnish president and Chernomyrdin off to Belgrade with the deal already agreed with Milosevic. When the two emissaries touched down again in Cologne they went straight to the EU Council and it proclaimed the triumph of peace. Only a plane crash could have stopped this tactic from working. The question then, was what Washington would do about this *fait accompli*. It carried on bombing for a while, then called it a day.

The terms for ending the war involved major concessions to the Yugoslav government: the repudiation of Annex B, the de-recognition of the KLA as the future governing force in Kosovo, the involvement of Russian forces in Kosovo, the return of the United Nations to centre stage. If these concessions had been offered in Rambouillet, there would have been no war. But the US government also gained its most vital minimum goal for being able to claim victory: a *de facto* NATO protectorate in Kosovo.

CONCLUSION

The end of the war leaves all the central issues at stake at the start unresolved and indeed exacerbated. The Kosovo national question is unresolved. Albania remains a shattered state and society. Macedonia is a state under enormous strain. Montenegro's future status is now a bitterly contested issue. Tensions between Greece and Turkey are running higher than ever. New domestic cleavages are opening in Bulgaria and Romania, both of whose economies are in parlous states, made much worse by the war. And in the midst of the region, Serbia is in a deep economic, social and political crisis, which the Americans and British are attempting to sharpen in an effort to engineer the overthrow and destruction of its main elected political parties. Beyond the region, the Russian state is now plunged into a new and deep antagonism towards the West as all the worst fears of opponents of NATO enlargement have been proved right. And the struggle between the United States and Russia for ascendancy in Ukraine is in full-swing. Europe is again dividing deeply. The division is economic, social, political and cultural. The field in which that division is likely to be most intense is in the Balkans.

At present the NATO powers are the military overlords in the Balkans. They are running a series of more and less formal protectorates in the region. These protectorates have a colonial character in that they are an attempt to use military-political domination over local populations with the aim of constructing client local political leaderships who are prepared to do NATO's bidding. Financial and other economic inducements and threats, media manipulation, direct administrative and political manipulation and the ultimate sanction of armed force will be applied to achieve NATO's goals. Such instruments will not in fact bring lasting peace and stability in the Balkans. Such a lasting peace will require a new political settlement which overcomes the fragmentation of the region into statelets which are, in the main, non-viable as independent entities.

But the system of NATO protectorates does transform political relationships within the NATO zone itself. The priorities of, and resources for, EU policy towards Eastern Europe have been radically shifted into the Balkans. The fate of the EU is now directly tied to the future situation in the Balkans. But the management of the Balkan area will be under US command since the US controls the NATO command structure. Unless the EU states were to transform themselves into a qualitatively different kind of unified political force, the result of the Kosovo war is, in this field, to place the Eastern policy of the EU more firmly than ever under US leadership. By achieving a NATO protectorate in Kosovo the US has achieved this geopolitical prize. And since Russia's relations with the West will now be focused more strongly than before on developments in the Balkans, Washington will be able to manage EU–Russian relations more strongly than ever.

The consequences of these results for Europe are potentially extremely serious. After this war, Europe is dangerously destabilized. There is an urgent need for discussions on a new European security project that will reunite the continent for economic, social and political development, a project that will replace Europe under NATO hegemony with an alternative, norm-based collective security structure. Such a project would also require a search for a new, inclusive political settlement in the Western Balkans, one that overcomes the region's political fragmentation in new confederal arrangements which offer lasting solutions to the national problems of the Albanians and the Serbs as well as the other peoples of the region. The starting point for rebuilding trust across the continent should be a determination in Western Europe to expose the truth about this dirty war, this European Dreyfus Affair, in order to assure people throughout Europe that such geopolitical power plays will never be allowed to happen again.

NOTES

1.   But on Serbian politics see: Robert Thomas, *Serbia Under Milosevic* (Hurst, 1999) pp. 405–406. On Kosovo see Miranda Vickers, *Between Serb and Albanian: A History of Kosovo* (Columbia University Press, 1998). By far the best general account of the Yugoslav crisis and disintegration is Susan Woodward, *The Balkan Tragedy* (Brookings, 1995). Also important is Catherine Samary, *Yugoslavia Dismembered* (Monthly Review Press, New York, 1995).

2.   At a press conference on 8th October 1998, Madeleine Albright indicated that NATO had adopted new procedures for such decisions, rather than the previous NATO procedure of the so-called non-voting 'consensus' but she did not indicate what these new procedures were. This is a significant omission for citizens of NATO countries wishing to know the way in which their NATO member state may be drawn into any future NATO war.

3.   Fergus Carr, 'NATO and the Russian Federation in the new Europe', in Czech Atlantic Commission (Prague): NATO Summit, 1997, and 'Further Enhancement of European Security' (Cesky Krumlov, 22nd–26th October 1997). Subsequent quotations from the Act are drawn from this source.

4.   The Clinton Administration attempted to claim that a mass execution of non-combatant civilians had taken place in Racak in January 1999. But there is very strong evidence from Western journalists on the scene and from subsequent forensic investigations to suggest that the Racak corpses were those of KLA fighters and the event was stage managed by William Walker to bounce the European states into war. For reports indicating a staged outrage see 'Les Morts de Racak: ont-ils vraiment massacre froidement?', *Le Monde*, 21st January 1999, p. 2, and 'Kosovo: zones d'omdre sur un massacre', *Le Figaro*, 20th January 1999, p. 3. A detailed analysis of the incident is to be found in the important article by Diana Johnstone, 'The Racak Incident', published in German in K. Bitterman and T. Deichmann (eds.): Wie Dr J. Fischer Lernte, die Bombe zu Lieben. Die Grünen, die SPD, Die NATO und der Krieg auf dem Balkan (Tiamat, Berlin, June 1999).

5.   Barton Gellman, 'Allies See No Credible Alternative', *Washington Post,* 23rd March 1999, p. A12.

6.   Serbia gained control of Kosovo in the 1912 Balkan war and this control was recognized in the 1913 Treaty of London.

7.   Miranda Vickers, *Between Serb and Albanian: A History of Kosovo* (Columbia University Press, 1998), p197.

8.   Ibid.

9.   This view is put forward in Branka Magas, *The Destruction of Yugoslavia* (Verso, 1992).

10.   Vickers, op cit., p. 220.

11.   Both Human Rights Watch and Amnesty International have provided extensive documentation of such allegations

12.   Thus, the Albanian leaders refused to end the boycott of Pristina University until the Serbian authorities allowed degrees to contain the title, 'Republic of Kosovo', a demand which the Serbian authorities would not accept.

13.   Gary T. Dempsey, 'Washington's Kosovo Policy: Consequences and Contradictions', *Policy Analysis,* No. 321, 8th October 1998.

14.   Ibid.

15.   Robert Thomas, *Serbia Under Milosevic* (Hurst, 1999) pp. 405–406. Thomas's

book, the best English account of contemporary Serbian politics, is resolutely hostile to Milosevic.

16. Ibid., p. 406. See also James Pettifer, 'We have been here before', *The World Today,* April 1998.

17. Steven Erlanger, 'Albright Warns Serbs on Kosovo Violence', *New York Times,* 8th March, 1998, p. A6.

18. Anne Swardson, 'West, Russia Agree on Sanctions for Belgrade', *Washington Post,* 10th March, 1998, p. A13.

19. Gary T. Dempsey, 'Washington's Kosovo Policy: Consequences and Contradictions', *Policy Analysis,* no. 321, 8th October 1998.

20. On Walker's background and his role in the OSCE mission, see the important article by Diana Johnstone, 'The Racak Incident', op. cit.

21. Once the war was under way, various West European leaders like Robin Cook tried to explain their complete reversal of their 1998 policy on the Kosovo problem by claiming that the behaviour of the Serbian security forces during the winter of 1998 forced them to reconsider their whole approach and opt for a war against a sovereign state without even UN authority But the evidence of Cook's own statements and of those of the EU General Affairs Council of EU foreign ministers indicates that this is simply a falsehood.

22. Daniel Vernet, 'Sursaut Européen au Kosovo', *Le Monde,* 5th February, 1999, p. 1.

23. Claude Lanzmann, 'La Nouvelle affaire Dreyfus', *Le Figaro,* 31st May 1999.

24. But see for further analysis Peter Gowan, 'The Twisted Road to Kosovo', *Labour Focus on Eastern Europe,* 62/1999 and Peter Gowan, *The Global Gamble* (Verso, 1999).

25. Brzezinski, working through Clinton national security adviser Anthony Lake, was the intellectual architect of this Clinton administration strategy of 'double enlargement' Brzezinski formulates the goal as being 'to perpetuate the prevailing geopolitical pluralism on the map of Eurasia' and engage in 'maneuver and manipulation in order to prevent the emergence of a hostile coalition that could eventually seek to challenge America's primacy' (Z. Brzezinski, *The Grand Chessboard* (Basic Books, New York, 1997). Madeleine Albright is a long-standing member of the Brzezinski school of geopolitics. On the strategic debate within the Clinton administration see Gilbert Achcar, 'Raspoutine joue aux échecs, ou comment le monde bascula dans une Nouvelle Guerre Froide' (to be published in English by Verso, London, Autumn 1999).

26. *The New York Times,* 17th June 1993.

27. Paul R. S. Gebhard, *The United States and European Security*, Adelphi Paper 286 (International Institute for Strategic Studies, London, February 1994). Subsequent quotations of Gebhard are taken from this same source.

28. An important US goal in this area has been to ensure its effective leverage over EU policy on the future direction of the Euro. On these goals see Marc Grossman, Assistant Secretary of State for European Affairs, 'Remarks on the Euro–Atlantic Partnership', Centre for Strategic and International Studies, Washington, DC, 10th February 1999 (USIA, Euro-Atlantic Partnership, 2/10/99). See also the important speech by Deputy Secretary of State Strobe Talbott, 'Remarks to the German Society for Foreign Policy', 4th February 1999 (USIA, Euro-Atlantic Partnership, 2/4/99). For general background analysis of these issues, see Peter Gowan, *The Global Gamble* (Verso, 1999).

1990–1999
A Decade of the *Socialist Register*

1999 GLOBAL CAPITALISM VERSUS DEMOCRACY

Hugo Radice, Taking Globalization Seriously
Ursula Huws, Material World: The Myth of the Weightless Economy
Konstantinos Tsoukalas, Globalization and the Executive Committee:
   The Contemporary Capitalist State
Wally Seccombe, Contradictions of Shareholder Capitalism
David Coates, Labour Power and International Competitiveness
Birgit Mahnkopf, The German Model Under the Pressure of Globalization
Mitchell Bernard, East Asia's Tumbling Dominoes: Financial Crises and
   the Myth of the Regional Model
Atilio Boron, State Decay and Democratic Decadence in Latin America
Haroldo Dilla, Comrades and Investors: The Uncertain Transition in Cuba
Adam Tickell, Unstable Futures: Controlling and Creating Risks in
   International Money
Joachim Hirsch, Globalization, Class and the Question of Democracy
Boris Kagarlitsky, The Challenge for the Left: Reclaiming the State
Colin Leys, The Public Sphere and the Media: Market Supremacy versus
   Democracy
Sheila Rowbotham, The Tale that Never Ends

1998 THE COMMUNIST MANIFESTO NOW

Sheila Rowbotham, Dear Dr. Marx: A Letter from a Socialist Feminist
Colin Leys & Leo Panitch, The Political Legacy of the Manifesto
David Harvey, The Geography of the Manifesto
Sam Gindin, Socialism with Sober Senses: Developing Workers' Capacities
Sheila Cohen & Kim Moody, Unions, Strikes and Class Consciousness
   Today
Peter Gowan, Passages of the Russian and Eastern European Left
Bernard Moss, Marx and the Permanent Revolution in France
John Bellamy Foster, The Communist Manifesto and the Environment
Peter Osborne, The Communist Manifesto as Historical and Cultural
   Form
Paul Thomas, Marx's Manifesto, Derrida's Apparition
Rob Beamish, The Making of the Manifesto
Marx and Engels, The Communist Manifesto

1997 RUTHLESS CRITICISM OF ALL THAT EXISTS

1996 ARE THERE ALTERNATIVES?

1993 REAL PROBLEMS. FALSE SOLUTIONS

David Harvey, The Nature of Environment: Dialectics of Social and Environmental Change

Christopher Norris, Old Themes for New Times: Basildon Revisited

Marsha A. Hewitt, The Regressive Implications of Post-Modernism

Lynne Segal, Anti-Pornography Feminism

John Griffith, The Rights Stuff

Michael Löwy, Why Nationalism?

John S. Saul, Rethinking the Frelimo State

K. S. Karol, After Perestroika

Stephen Hellman, The Left and the Decomposition of the Party System in Italy

Rudolf Meidner, Why Did the Swedish Model Fail?

Saul Landau, Borders: The New Berlin Walls

Daniel Singer, In Defence of Utopia

1992 NEW WORLD ORDER?

Leo Panitch & Ralph Miliband, The New World Order and the Socialist Agenda

Robert W. Cox, Global *Perestroika*

Harry Magdoff, Globalization – To What End?

Andrew Glyn & Bob Sutcliffe, Global but Leaderless? The New Capitalist Order

Immanuel Wallerstein, The Collapse of Liberalism

Reg Whitaker, Security and Intelligence in the Post-Cold War World

Michael T. Klare, US Military Policy in the Post-Cold War Era

John Palmer, Europe in a Multi-Polar World

Stephen Gill, The Emerging World Order and European Change

Makoto Itoh, Japan in a New World Order

Basil Davidson, Africa: The Politics of Failure

Avishai Ehrlich, The Gulf War and the New World Order

Roger Burbach, The Transformation of the US–Latin American System

Joel Kovel, Post-Communist Anti-Communism: America's New Ideological Frontiers

Scott Forsyth, Hollywood's War on the World: The New World Order as Movie

1991 COMMUNIST REGIMES. THE AFTERMATH

John Saville, The Communist Experience: A Personal Appraisal
Leo Panitch & Sam Gindin, Perestroika and the Proletariat
Justin Schwartz, A Future for Socialism in the USSR?
David Mandel, The Struggle for Power in the Soviet Economy
Patrick Flaherty, Perestroika and the Neo-Liberal Project
Robert Cox, 'Real Socialism' in Historical Perspective
Ernest Mandel, The Roots of the Present Crisis in the Soviet Economy
Daniel Singer, Privilegentsia, Property and Power
Alexander Buzgalin & Andrei Kalganov, For a Socialist Rebirth: A
    Soviet View
Tadeusz Kowalik, Marketization and Privatization: the Polish Case
Peter Bihari, Reflections on Hungary's Social Revolution
Carlos Vilas, Nicaragua: A Revolution that Fell from Grace of the People
Susan Woodward, Soviet Rehearsal in Russia? Contradictions of the
    Socialist Liberal Strategy
Michael Lebowitz, The Socialist Fetter: A Cautionary Tale
Ralph Miliband, What Comes After Communist Regimes?

1990 THE SOCIALIST REGISTER

Norman Geras, Seven Types of Obloquy: Travesties of Marxism
John Saville, *Marxism Today*: An Anatomy
Ellen Meiksins Wood, The Uses and Abuses of 'Civil Society'
Terry Eagleton, Defending the Free World
Frederic Jameson, Post-modernism and the Market
Bryan D. Palmer, Marxism and the Writing of Social History in the 1980s
Paul Cammack, Statism, New Institutionalism, and Marxism
Linda Gordon, The Welfare State: Towards a Socialist-Feminist
    Perspective
George Ross, Intellectuals against the Left: The Case of France
Eleanor MacDonald, Derrida and the Politics of Interpretation
Amy Bartholomew, Should A Marxist Believe in Marx on Rights?
John Bellamy Foster, Liberal Practicality and the US Left
Stephen Gill, Intellectuals and Transnational Capital
Arthur MacEwan, Why We Are Still Socialists and Marxists After All This
Richard Levins, Reflections on the Future of Socialism
Ralph Miliband, Counter-Hegemonic Struggles

**Consult our web site at <www.yorku.ca/org/socreg/>
for further back volumes**

OTHER TITLES FROM
MERLIN PRESS

———

Edited by Walter Kemsley

MARTIN EVE REMEMBERED

Martin Eve was one of the most remarkable socialist publishers of the twentieth century. This is a tribute by family, friends, colleagues, and authors, which highlights his many achievements. The book features a biographical sketch written by Martin Eve himself, which tells the story of the development of Merlin Press, the publishing house which he created and managed for over forty years.

108pp   0 85036 485 X   pbk   £5.95

István Mészáros

BEYOND CAPITAL

Towards a Theory of Transition

"With theoretical sophistication, a wealth of information and lively polemical passages, *Beyond Capital* is a carefully coherent construction enabling us to discover new horizons." Daniel Singer, *The Nation*.

1020pp   0 85036 432 9   pbk   £14.95
0 85036 454 X   hbk   £45

By the same author:

MARX'S THEORY OF ALIENATION

Awarded the Isaac Deutscher Memorial Prize.
"In the hands of a creative thinker, conviction and passion can give wings to the freedom struggle. Meszaros' book is a 'winger' - one of the most far-reaching books on the subject of Marx's theory of alienation since Lukács' seminal *Geschichte und Klassenbewusstsein*." *The Review of Metaphysics*.

356pp   *8th impression*   0 85036 191 5   pbk   £9.95

Edited by Susan Weissman

THE IDEAS OF VICTOR SERGE

A Life as a Work of Art

'Victor Serge devoted his life and his brilliant pen to the revolution which for him knew no frontiers. An anarchist turned Bolshevik, he was unorthodox by nature, often a heretic but never a renegade. This important collective study of the still insufficiently known revolutionary figure is not only a restitution of our past. It is also a significant contribution to our urgent search for a radically different society.'

Daniel Singer, European correspondent of *The Nation*, author of *The Road To Gdansk*.

"Victor Serge is one of the great political and moral heroes of the 20th century. He is akin to George Orwell in the way he combined a wide-ranging passion for justice with great literary skill and with an unrelenting refusal to adhere to any orthodoxy, great or small. But to imagine his life and work you must imagine an Orwell who spent seven years in prison, who saw most of his comrades shot, and who survived and recorded the terrible years in which the Russian Revolution turned in upon itself and transformed the Soviet Union into a killing ground. Serge has long been far too little known in the United States, but this admirable book goes a long way towards honouring this man with the thoughtful critical attention he deserves. It is a joy to find that his example has affected many other people's lives as much as it has affected my own."

Adam Hochschild, co-founder and publisher of *Mother Jones*, and the author, among other books, of *The Unquiet Ghosts: Russians Remember Stalin*.

In association with *Critique*

258pp   0850364833   pbk   £12

Edited by Owen Ashton,
Robert Fyson & Stephen Roberts

THE CHARTIST LEGACY

This volume comprises eleven essays written by leading scholars of the
Chartist Movement. The essays are prefaced by an introduction by Asa Briggs,
who previously edited a similar collection, *Chartist Studies* (1959). With contributions from political, social and literary historians based in Britain, Australia
and the United States, this is truly a multi-disciplinary and wide-ranging
collection. It makes clear the priorities and interests of scholars working on
Chartism at the end of the twentieth century, and points the way ahead for
future research.

The editors have spent many years researching and writing about Chartism,
recently producing *The Chartists' Movement. A New Annotated Bibliography*
(1995).

*Asa Briggs *Introduction* *Miles Taylor *The Prehistory of the Six Points c. 1760-
1837* *Joan Hugman *'A Small Drop of Ink': Tyneside Chartism & the Northern
Liberator* *Owen Ashton *Orators and Oratory in the Chartist Movement 1840-
47* *Robert Fyson *The Transported Chartist: The Case of William Ellis 1842-47*
*Stephen Roberts *Feargus O'Connor in the House of Commons 1846-52* *Paul
Pickering *Feargus O'Connor and Ireland 1849-50* *Jamie Bronstein *Chartism
and Its Relationship With the United States* *Tim Randall *Chartist Poetry and
Song* *Kelly Mays *Reading Chartist Autobiographies* *Antony Taylor
Commemoration, Memorialisation and Political Memory in Post-Chartist
Radicalism: The 1885 Halifax Chartist Reunion.*

0 85036 484 1   pbk   £12.95
0 85036 486 8   hbk   £25.00

Stephen Roberts and Dorothy Thompson

IMAGES OF CHARTISM

Many books have told the story of Chartism and no doubt others will celebrate the sesquicentenary of its climactic year. For the first time, this book draws together a pictorial record. Formal photographs exist of some of the leaders after 1848, but for the rest we rely on contemporary engravings. Many of these are hostile, including lampoons, but some are clearly sympathetic and show graphically the serious, determined and popular character of the Chartist movement.

Over seventy pictures are reproduced, many of them from Dorothy Thompson's private collection, the rest found in libraries and archives from all over the country. All the pictures are explained and put into context, making this an essential addition to any Chartist library.

112pp   085036 475 2   pbk   £12.95

Sukomal Sen

WORKING CLASS OF INDIA

History of Emergence and Movement 1830-1990

The revolutionary significance of the Indian Working class as a new social force and the great dynamism of its development have hardly ever been evaluated in hitherto published social and political history of India. The present work is a distinguished and erudite contribution in this direction and caters for a long-felt need.

Distributed by Merlin Press for K. P. Bagchi and Company, Calcutta

817074 189 0   pbk   £12.95

Books by E. P. Thompson

BEYOND THE FRONTIER

The Politics of a Failed Mission in Bulgaria 1944

"Admirers of E. P. Thompson's earnest prose will find in this moving and disturbing book everything they could have hoped for." *New Statesman*

110pp   0 85036 461 2   pbk   £8.95

THE POVERTY OF THEORY

"There can be no doubt that *The Poverty of Theory* is an essay that will have lasting impact. It will resonate throughout discussions of history, Marxist theory and socialist politics." *Media, Culture and Society*

303pp   *4th impression*   0 85036 446 9   pbk   £8.95

THE ROMANTICS

England in a Revolutionary Age

Foreword by Dorothy Thompson
Wordsworth and Coleridge dominate these essays, with associates like the radical poet and lecturer, John Thelwall, and influences such as Godwin and Rousseau.

242pp   0 85036 474 4   pbk   £12.95

WILLIAM MORRIS

Romantic to Revolutionary

"Two impressive figures, William Morris as subject and E. P. Thompson as author, are conjoined in this immense historical study, and both of them have gained in interest since the first edition of the book was published."
New York Times Book Review

825pp/illus   *Revised edition*
0 85036 205 9   pbk   £12.95   0 85036 204 0   hbk   £20

Books by Georg Lukacs

THE HISTORICAL NOVEL

Translated by Hannah and Stanley Mitchell

"One of the permanent classics of criticism."
Raymond Williams, *The Listener*

364pp   0 85036 378 0   pbk   £9.95

STUDIES IN EUROPEAN REALISM

Translated by Edith Bone

A sociological survey of the Writings of Balzac, Stendhal, Zola, Tolstoy, Gorki
and others. These essays celebrate the humanist tradition of European
literature.

278pp   *3rd impression*   0 85036 211 3   pbk   £8.95

HISTORY AND CLASS CONSCIOUSNESS

Studies in Marxist Dialectics

Translated by Rodney Livingstone

"It is one of the indispensable works of the twentieth century."
Raymond Williams, *Guardian*

404pp   *4th impression*
0 85036 197 4   pbk   £9.95
0 85036 129 X   hbk   £16.95

TO ORDER FURTHER COPIES OF *Socialist Register* **OR OTHER MERLIN PRESS BOOKS, CONTACT:**

in **Australia**: Eleanor Brash, PO Box 586, Artamon, NSW 2064
ebe@enternet.com.au

in **Canada**: Fernwood Publishing, PO Box 9409, Station A, Halifax, Nova Scotia, B3K 5S3
fernwood@istar.ca

in **India**: K. P. Bagchi, 286 B.B. Ganguly Street, Calcutta, 700 012
kpbagchi@hotmail.com

in **South Africa**: Phambili Agencies, PO Box 28680, Kensington, 2101

in **Europe**: Global Book Marketing, 38 King Street, London, WC2E 8JT
ea28@dial.pipex.com

in the **USA**: Monthly Review Press, 122 West 27th Street, New York, NY 10001
mreview@igc.org

Paul & Co, PO Box 442, Concord, MA 01742
paulinc@tiac.net